THE PURE THEORY OF CAPITAL

THE
PURE THEORY
OF
CAPITAL

BY

FRIEDRICH A. HAYEK

THE UNIVERSITY OF CHICAGO PRESS
CHICAGO · ILLINOIS

THE UNIVERSITY OF CHICAGO PRESS, CHICAGO 60637
THE UNIVERSITY OF CHICAGO PRESS, LTD., LONDON

Published 1941. Midway Reprint 1975
Printed in the United States of America

International Standard Book Number: 0-226-32081-2

PREFACE

THIS highly abstract study of a problem of pure economic theory has grovn out of the concern with one of the most practical and pressing questions which economists have to face, the problem of the causes of industrial fluctuations. The attempt to elaborate a chain of reasoning which seems to throw important light on this question had made it painfully clear to me that some of the theoretical tools with which we are at present equipped are quite inadequate for the task. The nature of the contribution to the explanation of industrial fluctuation which I had attempted involved an extensive use of concepts and theorems which fall within the province of the theory of capital and interest. This is, of course, a field which almost above all others has been the centre of theoretical interest since the beginning of our science. The reason why, in spite of this, the results of past work on these problems proved unsatisfactory tools in the analysis of more complicated phenomena seems to be, as I try to explain in the introductory chapters, that in the past these phenomena have been studied for a different purpose and on assumptions which deprive them of most of their significance in a different context.

In this state of affairs it seemed imperative, before going on with a further elaboration of the explanation of industrial fluctuations, to turn back to the revision of the fundamentals and to work out a theory of capitalist production which would prove adequate for the analysis of dynamic changes. It was with great reluctance that I convinced myself of this necessity, and I have much sympathy with the prevailing attitude which shows an increasing impatience with all attempts at further refinement of the abstract groundwork and which is anxious to

v

proceed with the more concrete work on the processes which we observe in the real world. Yet I have become definitely convinced that nothing holds up real progress so much as this very impatience which disregards the necessity of first getting the foundations clearly laid out.

My reluctance to undertake this work would have been even greater if from the beginning I had been aware of the magnitude of the task that awaited me. As at first contemplated, this study was intended as little more than a systematic exposition of what I imagined to be a fairly complete body of doctrine which, in the course of years, had evolved from the foundations laid by Jevons, Böhm-Bawerk, and Wicksell. I had little idea that this task of systematisation would uncover serious gaps in the reasoning which had yet to be bridged, and that some of the simplifications employed by the earlier writers had such far-reaching consequences as to make their conceptual tools almost useless in the analysis of more complicated situations. The most important of these inappropriate simplifications, of the dangers of which I became aware at a comparatively early stage, was the attempt to introduce the time factor into the theory of capital in the form of one single relevant time interval — the "average period of production". But it gradually became clear that this supposed simplification evaded so many essential problems that the attempt to replace it by a more adequate treatment of the time factor raised a host of new questions which had never been really considered and to which answers had to be found.

It was inevitable that in a first approach to an analysis of the dynamic problems in this field I should have used whatever tools were available, and I must not complain of the manifold misunderstandings which the use of these imperfect instruments caused and of the objections to which it has given rise. And it would be idle to pretend that I was myself always aware of all the limitations and dangers of what I then still regarded as legitimate simplifications. But while I still believe in the fundamental correctness of the general approach which I then followed, it would be inexcusable if at this stage I neglected to attempt to remedy the all too evident defects of the older theoretical tools.

It might be objected that whatever revision of pure theory may be necessary should be done in connection with the work on the concrete phenomena, where all its results could immediately be tested for their usefulness ; and that all that has been said here does not justify the publication of a volume of this size confined entirely to pure theory. I hope that the reader, before he has proceeded very far in this book, will realise that the difficulty and complexity of the problems involved make a systematic treatment of these questions by themselves very necessary. The fact is that as soon as we remove the more important of the simplifications traditionally employed in this field by economists, we face new problems of a type which in other parts of economics have been solved long ago by patient analysis, while in the field of the theory of capital this task still awaits fulfilment. In other departments of economics there may be much justification for the impatience often shown for any further refinements so long as we have not successfully made use of the more abstract work already done. But it is precisely further analysis which the theory of capital requires.

I fear, however, that the reader will find the actual shortcomings of this book not so much in its limitation to the more abstract problems but rather in the fact that even within these limits it leaves some problems of real importance unsolved. In particular I am painfully conscious that the discussion of the important problem of the effects of changes in the supply of capital on the relative prices of various factors of production in the later sections of Part III is not fully adequate and would require considerable elaboration to make it anything like exhaustive. It would undoubtedly be highly desirable, granted that we must retrace our steps and go once again over the whole field of the pure theory of capital, that this should be done once and for all. I can make no pretence to have succeeded in doing this. It will no doubt require a good deal of further discussion before this part of general theory is in an entirely satisfactory state. I can only plead that I have grappled honestly and patiently with what even now appears to me by far the most difficult part of economic theory, and that the present book with all its shortcomings is the outcome of work over a period so prolonged that I doubt whether further effort on my part would be repaid by the results. Perhaps there is even something to be said at this stage in favour of an exposition which confines itself to the central problems without pursuing into all its ramifications and detail the consequences of the solution offered.

In addition to these limitations, to which I had voluntarily resigned myself, the circumstances of the time have now enforced a further curtailment of the original plan of the book. The final draft was in an advanced state of completion when the war broke out, and it became clear that, if I could hope to publish the book at all, I must not delay too long nor make it unduly large. The result of this is that Part IV has become rather more condensed and sketchy than I had intended and that several further appendices had to be sacrificed in which I had hoped to deal with controversial points which in recent years have been the subject of extensive discussion. The same fate has also befallen a mathematical appendix in which I had at one time hoped to restate the central theoretical propositions in algebraic form. But I am not sure that its abandonment is to be regarded as a loss. The mathematical form of expression is of assistance where it helps us to deal with a greater number of variables than can conveniently be dealt with in ordinary language. But the power of the mathematical tools —

and most certainly of those which I could command—also has its limits. And the problems with which we have to deal here are so complex that I soon found that, in order to make them amenable to exact mathematical treatment and at the same time to keep this treatment on a plane where I could even attempt it, I had to introduce much more drastic simplifications than seemed compatible with the object.

So far as was practicable I have tried to keep the body of the book free from controversy. This has not always been easy, since in the years during which the volume has been in preparation its subject has once again become the centre of extensive discussions in the learned journals. But although the book is to some extent intended as an answer to many objections raised against the approach I have employed in my earlier work on industrial fluctuations, and although I hope in the course of the systematic exposition to touch on most of the important points made by way of criticism, I have generally found it inadvisable to interrupt the main argument by explicit references to particular views. Even where the more famous doctrines and disputes of the past are concerned, I have considered them in greater detail only where this seemed to shed further light on a point under discussion. Apart from this, an attempt to trace the development of particular doctrines has been made only in a few instances in the appendices. Attractive as the task of writing a history of doctrines in this field would be, it cannot be combined with a systematic exposition without obscuring the main outline of the positive solution. In so far as the more recent contributions are concerned, I have listed those which have come to my knowledge in the bibliography at the end of the volume. Absence of further reference to any particular work must not be taken to mean that I have not profited from it in one way or another.

It only remains for me to acknowledge my numerous

obligations to those who otherwise than through their published work have helped me in the development of the ideas here outlined or in the actual preparation of the book. I should like to place first the debt of gratitude to the untiring questions of a host of students at the London School of Economics whose curiosity and critical acumen were not easily satisfied and some of whom have since made their own contribution to the complex of problems discussed here. I particularly want to mention in this connection, since their work is still mostly unpublished, Dr. Victor Edelberg, Dr. Helen Makower, and Dr. G. L. Shackle, from whose dissertations on closely related subjects I have derived much instruction. Several friends, including Dr. F. Benham, Professor G. Haberler, Professor F. Machlup, and Professor L. C. Robbins, have read one or more drafts and helped me with their advice, and it is largely due to them if the book approaches intelligibility. Finally, Dr. V. C. Lutz has given me much patient help in what was to be the final revision of the manuscript for publication ; but as the text has since undergone a good deal of further change, Dr. Lutz no more than any other of my friends bears any responsibility for the blunders or blemishes which the reader no doubt will detect.

F. A. HAYEK

THE LONDON SCHOOL OF ECONOMICS
AND POLITICAL SCIENCE
June, 1940

CONTENTS

xi

PART III
CAPITALISTIC PRODUCTION IN A COMPETITIVE COMMUNITY

PART IV
THE RATE OF INTEREST IN A MONEY ECONOMY

ANALYTICAL TABLE OF CONTENTS

In most cases, however, durability is aimed at because it gives additional services for a less than proportional increase in costs.

Effects of variations in durability on the amounts of services obtained at different periods.

Changes in the quantity of durable goods used.

This will usually involve a change towards more or less labour-saving (" automatic ") type of equipment.

CHAPTER VII

The relation between the stock of capital and current investment.

Under perfectly stationary conditions the stock of non-permanent resources would be identical with the stock of produced means of production.

Most capital problems arise only outside the limits of a stationary state.

Under dynamic conditions the relevant fact is only that resources are non-permanent, and not that they have been produced.

The traditional capital concept is a remnant of the cost of production theory of value.

The double aspect of the capital problem.

The significance of the " augmentability " of resources.

The sense in which the constituents of the stock of capital can be said to have a common quality.

The concept of capital as a fund.

PART II
INVESTMENT IN A SIMPLE ECONOMY

CHAPTER VIII

The plan of this part of the investigation.

Simplifying assumptions.

The stock of capital at any moment represents definite contributions to the income expected at different future dates.

Diagrammatic representation of the two portions of the output stream.

The curve describing the time distribution of the returns from current input.

The use of curves in this and later connections involves the abstract concept of a time rate of flow.

The output curve.

Interpretation as a cumulative frequency distribution.

The same situation represented by a simple frequency curve.

CHAPTER XIII

PART III

CAPITALISTIC PRODUCTION IN A COMPETITIVE COMMUNITY

CHAPTER XXI

PART IV

THE RATE OF INTEREST IN A MONEY ECONOMY

CHAPTER XXVI

Analytical Table of Contents xxxi

PAGE

Effects of changes in relative liquidity of different types
of assets —
— similar to effects of changes in quantity of money.
It is often difficult to decide whether a particular change
is better treated as a change in the liquidity of an asset or
as a change in the quantity of money.

PART I
INTRODUCTORY

CHAPTER I

THE SCOPE OF THE INQUIRY

THE subject of this study is indicated in the title by the heading under which it is conventionally treated. It gives, however, no indication of the approach which we shall adopt. The contents of the following pages would perhaps have been more appropriately described as an Introduction to the Dynamics of Capitalistic Production, provided the emphasis were laid on the word Introduction, and provided that it were clearly understood that it deals only with a part of the wider subject to which it is merely a preliminary. The whole of the present discussion is essentially preparatory to a more comprehensive and more realistic study of the phenomena of capitalistic production, and it stops deliberately short of some of the most important problems that fall within that wider context.

The central aim of this study is to make a systematic survey of the interrelations between the different parts of the material structure of the process of production, and the way in which it will adapt itself to changing conditions. In so far as these complex problems have been explicitly discussed in the past they have been treated as part of the theory of capital and interest. Here they will be treated from a somewhat different viewpoint. Our main concern will be to discuss in general terms what type of equipment it will be most profitable to create under various conditions, and how the equipment existing at any moment will be used, rather than to explain the factors which determined the value of a given stock of productive equipment and of the income that will be derived from it. As will appear presently, there are in this field a number of fairly

Aims and limitations of the investigation

important and difficult problems which fall into what is usually regarded as the sphere of equilibrium analysis, but which have not yet received adequate attention. By far the greater part of the present investigation will be confined to that part of the subject which belongs to equilibrium analysis proper. A full treatment of the economic process as it proceeds in time, and of the monetary problems that are connected with this process, is outside the compass of this book. The discussion in justification of the distinction that is involved here, and of the methodological issues underlying it, will be reserved for the two following chapters. All that I wish to explain at this point is why the task of merely putting those elements of the theory of capital which are commonly treated as belonging to general equilibrium analysis into a form in which they will prove useful for the analysis of the monetary phenomena of the real world, is important enough to merit a separate study.

It may at first be somewhat disconcerting to be told that the theory of a subject which has been so widely and so vigorously discussed right from the beginning of **Why these problems discussed here were neglected in the past** economic science as the theory of capital, should need almost complete recasting as soon as we try to use its results in the analysis of the more complex phenomena of the real world. But there are very good reasons why the theory of capital in the form in which it now exists has proved less useful than we should wish for the purposes for which we now need it. The fact is that the problems of capital as here understood, that is, the problems arising out of the dependence of production on the availability of " capital " in certain forms and quantities, have hardly ever been studied for their own sake and importance. And, as we shall see, the theory of *stationary* equilibrium, within which they were treated, did not really offer any opportunity for their explicit discussion. Such analysis as they have received has been almost entirely subordinate to

The Scope of the Inquiry

another problem. the problem of explaining interest. And the treatment of the theory of capital as an adjunct to the theory of interest has had somewhat unfortunate effects on its development. This for two reasons.

Firstly, it was carried only just so far as seemed necessary for the main purpose of explaining interest, and this explanation aimed at illustrating a general principle by the simplest imaginable cases rather than at providing an adequate account of the interrelationships under more complex conditions.

Secondly, and this is even more important, the attempts to explain interest, by analogy with wages and rent, as the price of the services of some definitely given "factor" of production,[1] has nearly always led to a tendency to regard capital as a homogeneous substance the "quantity" of which could be regarded as a "datum", and which, once it had been properly defined, could be substituted, for purposes of economic analysis, for the fuller description of the concrete elements of which it consisted. It was inevitable in these circumstances that different authors should have singled out different aspects of the same phenomenon as the relevant ones, and the consequences of this were those unending discussions about the "nature" of capital which are among the least edifying chapters of economic science.

There were of course praiseworthy exceptions, the most notable of which are to be found in the works of Jevons, Böhm-Bawerk, and Wicksell, who did at least begin with the analysis of the process of production and the rôle of capital in it, instead of with a concept of capital defined as some quasi-homogeneous magnitude. But even these authors and their followers used this analysis only in order

Attempts in the right direction were stultified by the treatment of capital as a single factor

[1] Cf. Armstrong, **1936**, p. 3 : ". . . the treatment of capital . . . as a factor of production on a par with land and labour has led to many erroneous conclusions ". (The full titles of the publications referred to in this manner will be found in the Bibliography at the end of this volume.)

to arrive ultimately at some single definition which, for the purposes of further analysis, lumped together as one quasi-homogeneous mass all or most of the different items of man-made wealth ; and this definition was then used in the place of the fuller description from which they had started.

As we shall see, it is more than doubtful whether the discussion of " capital " in terms of some single magnitude, however defined, was fortunate even for its immediate purpose, *i.e.* the explanation of interest. And there can be no doubt that for the understanding of the dynamic processes it was disastrous.

The proper starting point is a full description of the component parts of the capital structure

The problems that are raised by any attempt to analyse the dynamics of production are mainly problems connected with the inter-relationships between the different parts of the elaborate structure of productive equipment which man has built to serve his needs. But all the essential differences between these parts were obscured by the general endeavour to subsume them under one comprehensive definition of the stock of capital. The fact that this stock of capital is not an amorphous mass but possesses a definite structure, that it is organised in a definite way, and that its composition of essentially different items is much more important than its aggregate " quantity ", was systematically disregarded. Nor did it help much further when it was occasionally emphasised that capital was an " integrated organic conception ",[1] so long as such hints were not followed up by a careful analysis of the way in which the different parts were made to fit together.

This concentration on a particular capital concept to the neglect of all the multitudinous meanings which attach to the word capital in everyday speech has a further disadvantage. It is not only that the term capital in any of its " real " senses does not refer to a homogeneous substance. There is the further difficulty

[1] Knight, **1935a**, p. 83.

that even if we describe physically all the items of which the real structure of production is composed we have not described all the factors which will dictate their mode of utilisation. The various meanings of the term capital in everyday speech are an unconscious tribute to the complexity of the problem, and it has been unfortunate

Concentration on single capital concepts also caused neglect of important aspects of the problem

that the majority of authors seem to have assumed that somewhere or other there was some single substance corresponding to the singleness of the term which had discharged so many functions.

In fact there are at least two kinds of relevant magnitudes or rather proportions which must be taken into account if we want to understand the working of the price mechanism in this field; neither of them is a simple " quantity ", and neither of them stands in a unique relationship to

The two relevant quantitative relationships

the rate of interest except through its relation to the other. The first is the dimensions of the real structure of productive equipment, describing how it is organised for, or capable of, yielding various quantities of final output at different dates. The second is the proportional demands, or the relative prices, which are expected to rule for these different quantities of output at different dates. The first of these two quantitative relationships describes the proportions between the existing quantities of concrete resources in terms of their relative costs, while the second describes the relative demand for the two kinds of resources. But only together do these two sets of quantitative relationships or proportions determine what is usually regarded as the supply of capital in value terms.

The treatment of the capital problem in terms of the demand for and supply of one single magnitude is only possible on the assumption that the proportions just described stand in a certain equilibrium relationship to one another. On this assumption the result of a given supply of concrete capital goods meeting an exactly corresponding demand for them could be represented as a single-value magnitude, a quantity of capital in

These differences have been disregarded because they disappear in stationary equilibrium

the abstract which could be set against a marginal productivity schedule for capital as such ; and in this sense there would be a unique correlation between " the " quantity of capital and the rate of interest. As a first explanation of the rate of interest, the consideration of such an imaginary state of ultimate equilibrium may have certain advantages. There can be little doubt that the traditional theories of interest do little more than describe the conditions of such a long-term stationary equilibrium. Since this concept of long-term equilibrium assumes that the quantities of the individual resources measured in terms of costs are in perfect correspondence with their respective values, the description of capital in terms of an aggregate of value is sufficient. Even for the purposes of what is sometimes called " comparative statics ", that is the comparison of alternative states of stationary equilibrium, it is still possible to assume that the two magnitudes move in step with each other from one position of equilibrium to another, so that it never becomes necessary to distinguish between them.

The problem takes on a different complexion, however, as soon as we ask how a state of stationary equilibrium can ever be brought about, or what will be the reaction of a given system to an unforeseen change.

For dynamic analysis the two concepts must, however, be carefully distinguished

It is then no longer possible to treat the different aspects of capital as one, and it becomes evident that the " quantity of capital " as a value magnitude is not a datum,[1] but only a result, of the equilibrating process. With the

---

[1] Cf. Wicksell, *Lectures on Political Economy*, vol. i, p. 202 : " But it would clearly be meaningless — if not altogether inconceivable — to maintain that the amount of capital is already fixed before equilibrium between production and consumption has been achieved ".

disappearance of stationary equilibrium, capital splits into two different entities whose movements have to be traced separately and whose interaction becomes the real problem. There is no longer one supply of a single factor, capital, which can be compared with the productivity schedule of capital in the abstract : and the terms demand and supply, as referring to magnitudes which affect the rate of interest, take on a new meaning. It is the existing real structure of productive equipment (which in long-term equilibrium is said to represent the supply) which now determines the demand for capital; and to describe what constitutes the supply, writers have usually been compelled to introduce such vague and usually undefined terms as " free " or " disposable " capital. Even those writers who at earlier stages of their exposition have most emphatically decided in favour of only one of the meanings of the term capital, and that a " real " capital concept, later find it necessary either to use the word " capital " in another sense, or to introduce some new term for something which in ordinary language is also called capital. The consequent ambiguity of the term capital has been the source of unending confusion, and the suggestion has often been made [1] (and in one or two instances even put into practice [2]), that the term should be banned entirely from scientific usage. But much as there may be to be said in favour of this procedure, it seems on the whole preferable to use the expression as a technical term for one of the magnitudes in question, without, however, ignoring the other magnitudes which are sometimes denoted by this term. As will be more fully explained below (Chapter IV), we shall use the term capital as a name for the total stock of the non-permanent factors of production.

We cannot go into too many details at this stage.

---

[1] *E.g.* by Schumpeter, *Handwörterbuch der Staatswissenschaften*, 4. Aufl., vol. 5, p. 582.

[2] *E.g.* by Cannan, *Elementary Political Economy* (1888).

But it may be helpful to add a few words, by way of illustration, about the reasons for the general failure seriously to take account of the essentially non-homogeneous nature of the different capital items, and about the consequences of this failure. Two ideas in particular have had a very harmful effect on the whole theory of capital. The first is the idea that particular capital items represented a definite value independently of the use that could be made of them, a value which was apparently thought to be determined by the amounts " invested " in these items. This idea is a remnant of the old cost-of-production theories of value whose influence has lingered longer in the theory of capital than perhaps anywhere else in economic theory.[1] The second is the conception that additions to the stock of capital always mean additions of new items similar to those already in existence, or that an increase of capital normally takes the form of a simple multiplication of the instruments used before, and that consequently every addition is complete in itself and independent of what existed previously. This treatment of capital as if it consisted of a single sort of instrument or a collection of certain kinds of instruments in fixed proportions — a treatment which has won favour from the fact that it has sometimes been used explicitly as a supposed simplification — is perhaps more than anything else responsible for the idea that capital may be regarded as a simple, physically determined quantity, and that the rate of interest may be explained as a simple (decreasing) function of this quantity. It would of course follow from these assumptions that the rate of interest must steadily and continuously fall in the course of economic progress since every addition to the stock of capital would tend to

Some causes and consequences of the treatment of real capital as a homogeneous quantity

[1] Cf. Knight, **1935c**, p. 45: " Historically, this notion goes back to the classical theory of capital as the product of labour, hence is an indirect consequence of that fountainhead of error, the labour theory of value."

lower it ; and the familiar fact that the rate of interest fluctuates widely over comparatively short periods would appear to be without any foundation in the real facts and would therefore have to be ascribed entirely to the influence of monetary factors.

The organisation of the structure of real resources corresponding to any expected aggregate value of the existing stock of capital will of course depend on the kind of productive technique that is possible with that amount of capital. And the assertion that under equilibrium con- *This leads to an over-simplified theory of derived demand* ditions a different structural organisation will be associated with a different value of the stock of capital means that changes in the supply of capital will bring about changes in the productive technique. The widely held idea that capital consists of (or is) a definite collection of instruments combined in fixed proportions, and the corollary of this idea, that there is at any one time only one practicable productive technique (which is supposed to be determined either by the state of technological knowledge or by the already existing durable instruments) leads to another fallacy. This fallacy, which may be conveniently described as the " theory of derived demand ", has played an important rôle in recent discussions of trade cycle problems.

The error inherent in this view is of course not the mere assertion that the demand for productive equipment is derived from the expected demand for consumers' goods, which is quite correct, but the idea that the amount of productive equipment which is required in order to satisfy an additional demand for consumers' goods is uniquely determined by the " existing state of technique ". If the productive technique to be employed were fixed by extra-economic factors, and particularly if it were assumed to be independent of the rate of interest, then a given change in the demand for consumers' goods would indeed automatically be transmitted at a given rate to the earlier stages of production, and be transformed there into a demand for a uniquely determined quantity of equipment. This is a conclusion uniformly arrived at by authors who are able to think of an increase of capital only in terms of a simple duplication of equipment of the type already in existence,[1] and who completely disregard the changes in productive technique connected with the transition from less to more " capitalistic " methods of production and vice versa. This view has become widely known in the discussion of trade cycle problems as the " acceleration principle of derived demand ". It derives a certain specious plausibility from the fact that under certain monetary conditions things may for a time work in accordance with it.[2] But, as we shall see, the fact that monetary influences may sometimes temporarily obscure, or even reverse, the more permanent influences of the underlying real factors, is one of the main reasons why it is essential to make a systematic study of the significance of these real factors.

A last instance may be mentioned of the unfortunate effects which these simplified ideas on capital have exerted on the analysis of dynamic phenomena such as The concept of net industrial fluctuations. I refer to the crude Investment distinction which is commonly made between current production and new investment, or between the reproduction of the existing stock of capital and additions to that stock, and the even cruder distinction between the gross production of capital goods and the production of consumers' goods. Here too the idea that the growth of capital takes place in such a form that new items of a

---

[1] Although a great deal of the current discussion of trade cycle problems is to some extent affected by this idea, there is probably no other book by a reputable economist where it is used so crudely as in H. G. Moulton's *Formation of Capital* (Washington, 1935), a book which is also, apart from this particular point, a veritable treasure-box of most of the current fallacies connected with capital.

[2] See Part IV below, and Hayek, **1939,** where the significance of the " acceleration principle of derived demand " is discussed in some detail.

similar nature to those previously in existence are added to an otherwise unchanged stock, has been responsible for a good deal of confusion in contemporary discussion. The same applies to the cognate idea that for purposes of analysis the whole capital problem can be adequately dealt with by dividing industries into two groups, those producing consumers' goods and those producing investment goods. But the problems involved here are obviously too complex to allow more than a mere mention at this stage. They are to some extent connected with the distinction between long and short periods, and the various concepts of equilibrium, which will be discussed in the next chapter.

CHAPTER II

EQUILIBRIUM ANALYSIS AND THE CAPITAL PROBLEM

IT was suggested in the first chapter that most of the shortcomings of the theory of capital in its present form are due to the fact that it has in effect only been studied under the assumptions of a stationary state, where most of the interesting and important capital problems are absent. This is so largely because the characteristic problems of capital theory are problems of the interdependence of different industries and consequently only arise in connection with a theory of *general* equilibrium, and because most of the current systems of economic theory (particularly the most influential, that of Marshall) do not really consider any state of general equilibrium which is not at the same time stationary. The so-called short-term equilibria, if this concept is to have any meaning, must necessarily be conceived as *partial* equilibria.[1] And the long-period equilibrium, which alone is a general equilibrium, is (as Marshall himself has pointed out) identical with " the supposition of a stationary state of industry ".[2]

The construction of a stationary state is unsuitable for discussion of capital problems

[1] The reason for this will become clear as we proceed. Here it need only be pointed out that the method of short-term equilibrium essentially consists in disregarding all these consequences of a given change whose significance, for the problem immediately under consideration, is of the second order of smalls. This means that we deliberately neglect consequences because they do not affect the parts of the system with which we are mainly concerned — a procedure which is clearly inadmissible when we are interested in the equilibrium of the system as a whole.

[2] Cf. A. Marshall, *Principles of Economics*, 7th ed., p. 379 note : " But in fact a theoretically long period must give time enough to enable not only the factors of production of the commodity to be adjusted to demand, but also the factors of production of those factors of production to be adjusted, and so on ; and this, when carried to its logical consequences, will be found to involve the supposition of a

An effective discussion of the problems of capital theory must, however, move precisely in that neglected field which deals with general equilibria that are *not* at the same time stationary states. It must proceed by way of a theory of *general* equilibrium because it deals with the interrelationships

General equilibria which are not stationary

between groups of industries, and in particular with those effects of changes in one industry on another which are deliberately neglected when we study the particular short-period equilibrium of a special industry or group of industries. And it must *not* be confined to the stationary state, because here *ex definitione* most of the problems with which the theory of capital must be concerned have disappeared.[1] The main problems are to explain what types of instruments will be produced under given conditions, and what will be the consequences of producing particular instruments. And these problems will of course be non-existent if we assume from the beginning that the same stock of instruments will be constantly reproduced. The impossibility of treating the problems of capital adequately within the framework of a stationary equilibrium becomes, of course, even more obvious as soon as we include, as we must, the problems relating to what are usually described as " saving " and (new) " investment ", since these are activities which imply by

---

stationary state of industry in which the requirements of a future age can be anticipated an indefinite time beforehand. . . . Relatively short and long periods go generally on similar lines. In both use is made of that paramount device, the partial or total isolation for special study of some set of relations." See also *ibid.* p. 367, where the stationary state is described as a state in which " the same amount of things per head of the population will have been produced in the same ways by the same classes of people for many generations together ; and therefore this supply of the appliances for production will have had full time to be adjusted to the steady demand."

[1] Cf. W. E. Armstrong, **1936,** p. 1 : " All that is significant and vital in the concept of Waiting (as the equivalent of Capital) belongs to the economics of the developing community, and cannot without violent wrenching of ideas outside their proper context be transferred to the study of Stationary States ".

definition that the persons undertaking them want to alter their future position, and consequently will do in the future something different from what they are doing in the present.

Perhaps the irrelevance of the stationary equilibrium construction for the treatment of capital problems comes out most clearly when we remember that this fictitious state could not conceivably be brought about at any given moment in society as it exists, but could be reached only after the lapse of a very long time.[1] The equipment which is given at any moment is always the inheritance from a past in which future developments have been foreseen only very imperfectly. And, as we shall see, it is precisely the existence of this equipment and its effect in determining what we can and what we cannot do for a very long time ahead, which constitutes the datum that creates the peculiar problem of capital. A theory which starts out by assuming that adjustments have proceeded to the point where no further changes are required

Stationary equilibrium without reference to what happens in the process of reaching it

---

[1] Stationary equilibrium presupposes the existence of equilibrium relations between the existing *things*, that is, it assumes that the existing goods are of exactly the same kind as those which under existing conditions it will be profitable to reproduce. It is not an equilibrium determined by the types of goods which happen to exist, but an equilibrium which has found expression in the past production of particular types and quantities of goods. For this reason it is without significance for the explanation of what happens prior to the time when all goods that are not permanent have been replaced by such goods as it will be advantageous to reproduce indefinitely in identical forms and quantities. It is supposed to be determined solely by the permanent resources and the vague concept of a given supply of free capital, and to be independent of the particular forms in which capital actually exists. The equilibrium in which we are interested here is not an equilibrium that is already embodied in the things, but an equilibrium between the different activities of creating new goods, as determined by the goods which happen to exist at the outset. This concept is in fact no less realistic than that of a stationary equilibrium : since in order to arrive at a stationary equilibrium it would be necessary to pass through a phase in which the changes required to bring about a stationary state were still going on but their results were correctly foreseen.

is without relevance to our problems. What we need is a theory which helps us to explain the interrelations between the *actions* of different members of the community during the period (which is the only period of practical importance) *before* the material structure of productive equipment has been brought to a state which will make an unchanging, self-repeating process possible.

This extension of the technique of equilibrium analysis which we propose to use here is still somewhat unfamiliar. It may therefore be useful, before we proceed to develop it further, to throw some added light on to the difference between the two concepts of equilibrium involved, by a short discussion of a closely related ambiguity in the use of the concept of dynamics in economics. This concept has indeed two altogether different meanings according as it is used in contrast to the concept of a stationary state or in contrast to the wider concept of equilibrium. When it is used in contrast to equilibrium analysis in general, it refers to an explanation of the economic process as it proceeds in time, an explanation in terms of causation which must necessarily be treated as a chain of historical sequences. What we find here is not mutual interdependence between all phenomena but a unilateral dependence of the succeeding event on the preceding one. This kind of causal explanation of the process in time is of course the ultimate goal of all economic analysis, and equilibrium analysis is significant only in so far as it is preparatory to this main task. But between the concept of a stationary state and the problems of dynamics in this sense, there is an intermediate field through which we have to pass in order to go from one to the other. The term dynamics is sometimes also applied to this intermediate field, but here it refers to phenomena which still come within the scope of equilibrium analysis in the wider sense. All that the use of the term dynamics means here is that

The ambiguity of the concept of "dynamics"

we do not postulate the existence of a stationary state ; but it says nothing about the method which we use.[1]

Now as I have tried to show elsewhere,[2] the general idea of equilibrium, of which the stationary state is merely a particular instance, refers to a certain type **Non-stationary equi-** of relationship between the plans of **libria defined** different members of a society. It refers, that is, to the case where these plans are fully adjusted to one another, so that it is possible for all of them to be carried out because the plans of any one member are based on the expectation of such actions on the part of the other members as are contained in the plans which those others are making at the same time. This is clearly the case where people know exactly what is going to happen for the reason that the same operations have been repeated time after time over a very long period. But the concept as such can also be applied to situations which are not stationary and where the same correspondence between plans prevails, not because people just continue to do what they have been doing in the past, but because they correctly foresee what changes will occur in the actions of others. This sort of fictitious state of equilibrium which (irrespective of whether there is any reason to believe that it will actually come about) can be *conceived* to comprise any sort of planned change, is indis-

---

[1] It is at least questionable whether the introduction of the terms statics and dynamics into economics (by J. S. Mill following A. Comte's similar division of sociology) which is responsible for this confusion was beneficial. It seems to me that the only relevant distinction is between two methods, that of logical analysis of the different plans existing at one moment ("equilibrium analysis") and that of causal analysis of a process in time. For this distinction the terms statics and dynamics seem altogether inappropriate, and it would probably be better if they were to disappear entirely from economics.

[2] In an article on " Economics and Knowledge ", *Economica*, N.S., vol. iv, no. 13 (February 1937), and, in a rather unsatisfactory form, much earlier, in an article on " Das intertemporale Gleichgewichtssystem der Preise und die Bewegungen des Geldwertes "; *Weltwirtschaftliches Archiv*, vol. 28 (1928).

pensable if we want to apply the technique of equilibrium
analysis at all to phenomena which are *ex definitione*
absent in a stationary state. It is in this sphere alone
that we can usefully discuss equilibrium relations extending over time, and in which consequently the pure
theory of capital mainly falls, and the latter might almost
be said to be identical with the whole of this intermediate
field between the theory of the stationary state and
economic dynamics proper. Yet this field has never been
systematically explored.

It must be admitted, however, that there is partial
justification for this in the fact that there is no reason to
believe that any general equilibrium could ever be fully
realised except after all changes in data
had ceased (that is as a stationary state
was reached), and that in consequence there
is no obvious need for the explanation of the
economic process as it proceeds in time to make use of
such a hypothetical construction. It may be thought that
this is more than we require or can expect from the equilibrium method : and that all we need do is to explain how
temporary equilibria are formed on particular markets.
This would involve explaining how, once the more mobile
elements have been adjusted, a temporary state of rest is
arrived at which will last until the slower changes in the
more permanent part of the productive equipment are
effected. We would then describe the conditions that will
prevail when all these changes have been completed (that
is the hypothetical state which would ultimately be reached
where all the data would remain unchanged). After all,
decisions about what and how to produce are being made
and revised periodically at fairly short intervals, and it may
seem that period analysis which makes use of the concept of
partial short-term equilibrium at each stage takes account
of this essential fact and will come as near a realistic
explanation of events as we can reasonably hope for from
this type of approach.

Why the concept of a temporary partial equilibrium is inade-quate for our pur-pose

There arises serious doubt, however, whether the concept of short-period equilibrium, if applied to an economic system as a whole,[1] has any definite meaning. The question is whether there is any such interval of comparative rest between the moment when the more mobile factors have been adjusted and the time when the more rigid elements of the structure can be effectively adjusted.[2] This presupposes that with respect to the time it takes to adapt them to new circumstances, the existing means of production can be divided into two distinct groups. It assumes that the times it takes to alter different items of the stock of existing resources by using them up and producing new ones (which will depend on the durability of the individual resources and the time it takes to produce them) are not dispersed over a fairly continuous range but are definitely clustered about two most frequent points with a more or less empty interval between them. It seems highly doubtful whether this assumption is in any way justified by the facts, and for this investigation at any rate I prefer to adopt what seems to me the more plausible assumption that these periods are spread fairly continuously and without any

----

[1] *I.e.* as distinct from a particular industry in which special conditions make it possible to mark off a particular period as being short compared with another.

[2] Without some such assumption the use of the term equilibrium has no justification whatsoever. It becomes a completely empty concept, saying no more than that at *any* moment some factors have had time to adjust themselves and others have not had time, and this would be true of any position. The distinction between short- and long-period equilibrium does of course make sense where, as in all the examples used by Marshall, it is applied to a particular industry, because in many cases the changes inside that industry will take place in two stages separated by an interval of time. But to make the later of these changes (*i.e.* the changes in the durable equipment) possible, changes must be going on during the interval in some other industry. And while we may be justified in disregarding these changes elsewhere so long as we are only concerned with the situation in the first industry, this becomes clearly illegitimate when we speak about the system as a whole. The use of the concept of a *general* short-term equilibrium in recent monetary analysis seems to me highly questionable.

marked break (though not necessarily evenly) over the whole range of periods in question.[1]

Yet, quite apart from this particular point, it is apparent that this use of the equilibrium concept fails to take advantage of some of the most valuable aids that are to be derived from this powerful intellectual tool. So long as the pretence is kept up that the idea of equilibrium must refer to something which we can observe in the real world, or which at least can be shown

To make full use of the equilibrium concept we must abandon the pretence that it refers to something real

to arise spontaneously under certain conditions, there is probably no other way of dealing with these problems. But I am inclined to believe that these attempts to give the equilibrium concept a realistic interpretation (the legitimacy of which remains in any case somewhat doubtful) have deprived us of an at least equally important use, which the concept will serve if we frankly recognise its purely fictitious character. It has often been emphasised that the concept of a state of equilibrium is independent of any possibility of showing how such a state will ever come about. The reason why this assertion has had so little effect on the use which is actually made of the equilibrium concept is probably that those who made it did not properly show how such a fictitious construction could help to explain real events. In fact when it came to any concrete use of the concept, either it was defined as timeless,[2]

---

[1] The distinction between the "short" and the "long" period equilibrium is the most general case of a distinction which arises in several interconnected fields. The distinctions between "prime" and "supplementary" cost, between "circulating" and "fixed" capital, and between "current" production and (gross) "investment", all belong to the same category and raise the same difficulties. They ought all to be treated, and will be so treated here, as limiting cases of a continuous range of variations, and not as representative of a particularly characteristic or most frequent type. No attempt will be made here to draw any arbitrary line of division in place of a frank recognition that these forms of the phenomena in question shade imperceptibly into each other.

[2] In which case, as I have tried to show in the article already referred to, it is meaningless.

or else resort was had to the stationary state.

In the sphere of capital theory, as we have seen, the construction of a stationary state is particularly useless because the main problem, that of investment, arises

Intertemporal equilibrium and capital analysis just because people intend to do in the future something different from what they are doing in the present. The investment itself they may intend continuously to repeat as the instruments created need replacement. But the results of investment, whether they be direct services for consumption or (as in the majority of cases) an aid to further production, will necessarily alter the things that need to be done and can be done in the future. To postulate a self-repeating stationary state is to abstract from the very phenomena that we want to study. Nevertheless there is a very significant sense in which the concept of equilibrium can be of great use if it is made to include plans for action varying at successive moments of time. The essential problem remains that of whether the plans of different individuals will tally and will accordingly all stand a chance of being successful, or whether the present situation carries the seed of inevitable disappointment to some, which will make it necessary for them to change their plans. We must not lose sight of the reason why we are interested in the analysis of a particular economic system at a given moment of time : our purpose is to be able to proceed from a diagnosis of the existing state of affairs to a prognosis of what is likely to happen in the future. Now, if we want to predict at all, it must be on the basis of the plans which entrepreneurs are likely to make in the light of their present knowledge, and of an analysis of the factors which in the course of time will determine whether they will be able to carry out these plans or whether they will have to alter them. It seems natural to begin by constructing, as an intellectual tool, a fictitious state under which these plans are in complete correspondence without, however, asking whether this state will ever, or can ever, come about. For it is only by contrast with this imaginary state, which serves as a kind of foil, that we are able to predict what will happen if entrepreneurs attempt to carry out any given set of plans. The description of the equilibrium position in this sense is at the same time a description of the mutual interdependence of the decisions of different entrepreneurs.

The direction in which an entrepreneur will have to revise his plans will depend on the direction in which events prove to differ from his expectations. The statement of the conditions under which individual plans will be compatible is therefore implicitly a statement of what will happen if they are not compatible.[1]

It will be seen that this extension of the equilibrium concept provides the bridge from equilibrium analysis to the explanation in terms of causal sequences, since it is designed to elucidate the factors which will compel entrepreneurs to change their plans and to help us to understand the way in which their plans will have to be changed.

Relation to causal analysis and to the ex ante and ex post view of a given situation

In fact this use of the equilibrium concept is not fundamentally different from the comparison between the prospective and retrospective (or *ex ante* and *ex post*) views of a particular situation, as used by the younger Swedish economists,[2] since the *ex post* situation can be derived from the *ex ante* only by reference to the degree of correspondence or non-correspondence between individual intentions. The state of equilibrium as here understood is a state of complete compatibility of *ex ante* plans, where in consequence (unless changes occur in the external data about which economic theory cannot say anything

---

[1] This is strictly true only if we are thinking of a single deviation of a particular element in a situation which is otherwise in equilibrium, that is on the assumption that all other expectations are confirmed. If more than one element turns out to be different from what was expected, the relation is no longer so simple.

[2] Cf. G. Myrdal, *Monetary Equilibrium* (London, 1939), p. 46.

in any case) the *ex post* situation is identical with the
ex ante. It serves as a kind of standard case by reference
to which we are able to judge what to expect in any
concrete situation.

The significance of these abstract considerations will
be clearer if we illustrate them by reference to the problems of investment. The problems of capital or of
Application to prob-   investment, as here defined, are problems
lems of investment   connected with the activity of making
provision in the present for the more or less distant
future. The relevant future with which we are concerned is, however, somewhat more extensive than
the periods for which the individual consciously invests
at a particular date. His plans at any moment will be
based on the expectations of a certain future state of the
market which will allow him to dispose of his products
at a certain price ; and beyond this his interest will not
extend. But the objective " state of the market " on
which he counts is largely the result of the present
decisions of other people. In order that he may succeed
in disposing of his products as he expected, it will be
necessary for others to have made preparations which
will enable them to use just those products at the prices
at which he expected to sell them. In other words, the
state of the market at the time for which he plans will
largely depend on what others have decided at the same
time as he made his plans. This is so not only, or even
mainly, because the incomes which these other people
will have to spend will depend on what they have produced, but also because what instruments and materials
they will need will depend on what plans for production
they have embarked upon. This means that although
every individual will be guided only by (more or less well-
founded) expectations of particular prices, he will actually
be performing part of a larger process of the rest of
which he knows little ; and his success or failure will
depend on whether what he does fits in with the other

parts of that larger process which are undertaken or contemplated at the same time by other people. What he performs will in the majority of cases be no more than a single step in a long chain of successive operations. His action may be removed from ultimate consumption by many stages, and its success will be dependent at each stage, not so much on the final demand as on the presence or absence of complementary instruments in proportionate quantities, and on there being people willing to use them in subsequent stages of production. All these successive operations have to be viewed as parts of one integral process, each of them having chances of success only by reason of its position in the whole.

In any system with extensive division of labour (particularly where it is of the "vertical" type and many successive operations by different entrepreneurs are dependent chainwise upon one another) every decision to produce one thing rather than another will be dependent for its success on other things being produced in appropriate quantities. Thus we have definite quantitative relationships between the required output of different kinds of goods, which (owing to the technological character of the process) will usually be of a more rigid character in the case of producers' goods than in the case of consumers' goods. Almost any quantitative combination of different kinds of consumers' goods will be capable of use in some way or other. But the limits within which the proportions between the quantities of the different kinds of producers' goods may vary are much narrower. There are definite proportionalities, quantitative relations, between the different parts of the structure of production, which must be preserved if some of these parts are not to become completely useless.

It is clearly possible to study the quantitative relations between the different parts of the real structure of pro-

duction that will result from current plans, independently
of the question of the forces which will secure, or fail
to secure, the actual bringing about of such a correspondence.   In any given situation there will be one (and

The correspondence
between production
plans analysed by
treating them as parts
of a single plan

in most instances only one) way in which
the plans of the various entrepreneurs can
be made to harmonise with one another
and with the preferences of the consumers.
The use of the equilibrium method here then means constructing an imaginary state in which the plans of the
different people (entrepreneurs and consumers generally)
are so adjusted to one another that each individual will
be able to sell or buy exactly those quantities of commodities which he has been planning to sell or buy.   What
will exist will of course still be only the separate plans of
different individuals which are connected only by the fact
that the quantities of goods which are expected to pass
at different dates out of and into the possession of the
various individuals exactly match.   Any particular person
need know neither who will take his products nor who
will provide him with what he expects to get — he will
only have expectations about what the anonymous [1]
group called the market will provide and take ;   nor need
he know much about the way in which the goods which
pass into his hands have been produced, or about the
way in which the goods he has produced will be used.
Nevertheless coincident expectations about the quantities
and qualities of goods which will pass from one person's
possession into another's will in effect co-ordinate all
these different plans into one single plan, although this
" plan " will not exist in any one mind.   It can only be
constructed, and it is in fact often convenient to adopt
the practice, which has been followed by many economists,
of proceeding for a time on the assumption that the actions
of the different individuals are directed by somebody in

[1] Cf. F. Machlup, " Why Bother with Methodology ? " *Economica*,
N.S., vol. iii, no. 9 (February 1936), pp. 43 *et seq.*

accordance with a single plan.[1] In the nature of the case this fictitious assumption can be only provisional, and must later be abandoned in favour of the assumption of separate but perfectly matched plans of the different individuals—that is : of competitive equilibrium in the sense outlined above.

It is inevitable that opinion will be divided about the usefulness of such an admittedly fictitious construction as the concept of equilibrium here employed. And there is no way of demonstrating its usefulness other than by applying it to a particular problem. It is, however, important that no misunderstanding should arise about the justification that is claimed for it. Its justification is not that it allows us to explain why real conditions should ever in any degree approximate towards a state of equilibrium, but that observation shows that they do to some extent [2]

Relation of this state of equilibrium to reality

---

[1] This device was used most systematically by F. Wieser, first in his *Natural Value* and later in his *Social Economics*, where he prefixed his theory of the social economy with an elaborate theory of what he called a " simple economy ", *i.e.* a centrally directed economy. More recently Professor Pigou (in his *Economics of Stationary States*, 1935) has once again made use of Robinson Crusoe for the same purpose. It is interesting to note that Marshall, when he comes to discuss investment, finds it also convenient first to discuss it " by watching the action of a person who neither buys what he wants nor sells what he makes, but works on his own behalf " (*Principles*, 7th ed. Book V, chap. iv/1).

[2] It should be remembered that nearly the whole of economic science is based on the empirical observation that prices " tend " to correspond to costs of production, and that it was this observation which led to the construction of a hypothetical state in which this " tendency " was fully realised. A good deal of confusion has been caused in this connection by the vagueness of the term tendency. A given phenomenon may tend to (approximate towards) a certain magnitude if in a great number of cases it may be expected to be fairly near that magnitude, even if there is no reason to expect that it will ever actually reach it, however long the time allowed for the adjustment. In this sense " tendency " does not mean, as it is usually understood to mean, a movement towards a certain magnitude but merely the probability that the variable under consideration will be near this magnitude. The ideal state in which all the variables would be at the magnitude to which they tend to approximate in this sense is a state which one could not expect ever to be reached.

so approximate, and that the functioning of the existing economic system will depend on the degree to which it approaches such a condition. The explanation of why things ever should, and under what conditions and to what extent they ever can, be expected to approximate to it, requires a different technique, that of the causal explanation of events proceeding in time. But the fact that it is probably impossible to formulate any conditions under which such a state would ever be fully realised does not destroy its value as an intellectual tool. On the contrary it seems to be a weakness of the traditional use of the concept of equilibrium that it has been confined to cases where some specious " reality " could be claimed for it. In order to derive full advantage from this technique we must abandon every pretence that it possesses reality, in the sense that we can state the conditions under which a particular state of equilibrium would come about. Its function is simply to serve as a guide to the analysis of concrete situations, showing what their relations would be under " ideal " conditions, and so helping us to discover causes of impending changes not yet contemplated by any of the individuals concerned.

CHAPTER III

THE SIGNIFICANCE OF ANALYSIS IN REAL TERMS

THE analysis of the relations between the production plans of different entrepreneurs must necessarily proceed in what is known as " real terms ". If we assume — as we must if we are to investigate the compatibility of the different plans — that the entrepreneurs make definite and detailed plans for fairly long periods, there is indeed little room for money in the picture at all, except as " mere counters " which stand for definite quantities of particular commodities. In fact, so long as we assume entrepreneurs to decide every detail in advance in the certain expectation that they will be able to adhere to all their plans, the need for holding money almost vanishes. For in the actual world money is largely held because the *decision* as to when to buy or to pay for something is deliberately postponed ; and this is contrary to our assumptions. But even to the extent to which money would still be held under these conditions (because of the discontinuity of transactions and the cost or inconvenience of investing it for the short periods until it was needed) it would cease to play a significant rôle. For money would enter into the plans, not in the quasi-independent character of command over things in general (that is as something which confers on its holders the chance of taking advantage of unforeseen opportunities), but only as a transitory item representing the definite quantities of commodities for the purchase of which the particular amounts of money are held.

The existence of such a condition in which all that would be relevant to the plans made by the public would

Equilibrium analysis is analysis in real terms

be the concrete quantities of goods which they expected
to get in exchange for money, but not the quantities
of money itself, is often silently assumed, usually illegitimately. On our assumptions such a con-
dition would actually exist. We should
therefore gain nothing if we were to introduce quantities of money as separate magnitudes into this type of analysis in place
of the quantities of commodities for which the money
would stand. Such a procedure would merely entail a very
considerable and unnecessary complication of the argument. Particular money prices stand in a determinate
relationship to quantities of goods which will be produced
or sold at these prices only on the assumption that all other
prices are given. In principle any particular money price
for a commodity may correspond to the production or sale
of any quantity of that commodity, according as the prices
of other commodities vary. There are no such definite
relationships between prices in money terms and quantity
of goods, as there are between the real ratios of exchange
and such quantities. The introduction of money at this
stage would therefore merely have the effect of introducing
an additional variable which is irrelevant for our purpose
and would make it more difficult to see the relationships,
between quantities of commodities and real ratios of
exchange, in which we are here interested.

Economists have often felt the need for some such
analysis in real terms, and in fact a considerable part of
classical economics, explicitly or implicitly, makes use of
this idea. Its exact meaning and significance have,
however, scarcely ever been made clear. Recently the
concept of " neutral money " [1] has been widely used in
this connection. While this has at least the advantage of

The introduction of
money into equilib-
rium analysis would
cause unnecessary
and irrelevant com-
plications

---

[1] The present author must plead guilty of some responsibility for
the popularity of this concept and even for the incautious way in which
attempts have occasionally been made to use it as a practical ideal of
monetary policy. But while for this second purpose it is clearly not
of much help, it still appears to me as a useful concept to describe a

drawing attention to the existence of a problem, it is in itself, of course, nothing more than a new name for an old problem and does not provide us with a solution. It makes it clear that we cannot, as has often been done, treat money as non-existent so long as its value remains stable, and that it is erroneous to assume that if its value remains stable it exerts no influence on the formation of prices. Neither do the special constructions which certain economists have used to meet this difficulty really solve the problem. The best known of these is Walras' "numéraire". According to definition the "numéraire", which may be any of the commodities, serves merely as a unit of account ; but it is not actually used as a medium of exchange and consequently there will be no additional demand for it to hold it as money. All that the introduction of this concept does is to solve the difficulty of the mathematical economist in expressing all the different ratios of exchange in one common unit. It contributes nothing to the explanation of how the triangular and multi-angular exchange transactions, which are necessary to bring about equilibrium, can be effected without the use of one or more media of exchange which are demanded and held merely for the purpose of exchanging them against other commodities.

Defects of traditional attempts to " abstract from money "

The crux of the matter is that where analysis aims directly at a causal explanation of the economic process as it proceeds in time, the use of the conception of a money-less exchange economy is misplaced. It is self-contradictory to discuss a process which admittedly could not take place without money, and at the same time to assume that money is absent or has no effect. In the case of our ideal position of equilibrium, which we construct as a guide to

Real term analysis is legitimate only within equilibrium construction

real theoretical problem : the conditions under which it would be conceivable that in a monetary economy prices would behave as they are supposed to behave in equilibrium analysis.

interpretation, and in which all parts are assumed to be perfectly matched, the case is different. Here analysis in real terms is not only in place, but is almost essential. Since at each point money is in the strictest sense only an intermediary between definite quantities of certain goods, all the essential relations in this system are relations between goods (rates of substitution between certain quantities of goods determined by the total quantities of these goods). Or, in other words, it will be true of this system — what has sometimes been asserted to be true in the real world — that the total supply of goods and the total demand for goods must be identical. (This so-called " Law of Markets " of J. B. Say is indeed one of the first formulations of the modern concept of equilibrium.)

It would, however, be a mistake to believe that, since these relationships will exist only in a purely fictitious state of equilibrium, it is mere waste of time to work **Analysis in real terms** it out. The fact that in the real world **not useless** relations between money prices, and not real ratios of exchange, directly determine human action, does not make these real ratios uninteresting. Relations between money prices in themselves tell us little, unless we know what prices are appropriate to the existing real structure of productive equipment, or what price relationships are required to enable people to go on with the plans they have made. Nor is it sufficient, as is sometimes supposed, to know whether the prices of finished products exceed or fall short of a given money cost of production as represented by the prices of a particular combination of productive resources. Whether this or some other combination of resources will be used in the manufacture of the product will itself depend on prices. The costs of production of a particular good do not therefore move in exact conformity with prices of any particular collection of resources, but are also affected by changes in the technique of production made profitable by changes in the relative prices of the different resources.

In the real world production is so obviously dependent in the first instance on concrete money prices that the suggestion that it " ultimately " depends on some real relationships which lie behind these money Usual argument in defence of real term analysis unsatisfactory prices, is undoubtedly, as the whole history of economics shows, in sharp contrast with the conclusions that are first suggested by experience. It is therefore necessary to justify our procedure somewhat more fully than by merely repeating the mostly metaphorical phrases which are commonly used in its defence. That there are " underlying real forces which tend to reassert themselves, although they may be temporarily hidden by the monetary surface ", or that the real relationships which " ultimately " determine the relations between prices show a certain resiliency and are more permanent than the temporary distortion caused by money, or that the real determinants are more fundamental or basic in the sense that they will be restored when the monetary disturbances have disappeared, is all approximately true ; but it hardly proves or explains the significance of these real factors.

It is undeniably true that in the absence of continuous progressive monetary changes, and with given tastes and a given distribution of incomes, the relations between the prices of different commodities will be Instability and self-reversing character of monetary changes uniquely determined by the quantities of these goods in existence. But this is not the whole story, because these quantities can themselves be changed by monetary influences. The decisive fact, however, is that the effect on prices of these changes in quantities brought about by monetary influences will be in exactly the opposite direction from the direct effect on prices of these same monetary changes. We may suppose, for instance, that, at the point where a net addition to the total money stream makes its first impact on the commodity markets, there will result an increase first of the prices and then the output of the commodities affected.

The effect of this increase in output will be that, as soon as the additions to the money stream cease, the prices of these commodities will fall relatively to the prices of all other commodities and will reach a lower level than prevailed before the monetary change. Monetary changes have this effect in common with all merely temporary changes which are not recognised as such. But they have it in a particularly high degree. This is so not only because by their very nature they cannot continue indefinitely, but more especially because a change in the volume of the money stream which takes place at one point of the economic system works round and is bound to cause further changes in all other prices. Monetary changes are therefore in a peculiar sense self-reversing and the position created by them is inherently unstable. For sooner or later any deviation from the equilibrium position — as determined by the real quantities — will cause a swing of the pendulum in the opposite direction.[1]

Unfortunately the significance of these real factors cannot be fully demonstrated without a systematic analysis of the operation of the monetary factors which we propose largely to disregard in this study. But an illustration may be given by referring briefly to the main problem in connection with which this question is continually cropping up. This problem relates to the possible differences between the prospective profitability of a given investment according to whether the investor has to use real resources which he owns or borrows, or whether he can obtain those resources by borrowing *money* for the purpose. There can be no doubt that under certain circumstances the possibility of borrowing money will make investments profitable which would never appear attractive if the investors could only use such resources as they owned or could borrow *in natura*. The reason

An Illustration of the different effects of real and monetary changes

---

[1] Cf. in this connection the discussion in my *Monetary Nationalism and International Stability*, pp. 31 *et seq.*

for this, now very familiar, is that the amounts of money offered on the loan market are capable of changing quite independently of the supply of real resources available for investment purposes.[1]

In point of fact, monetary changes facilitate investments and cause resources to be put to uses which are not in accordance with a state of equilibrium between the demand for and the supply of real resources. This does not, of course, mean to say that monetary factors may not change the composition of the real quantities in existence. On the contrary. By affecting the uses to which the available resources are put, they will inevitably bring about a change in the real structure of production. But the point is that this new, changed, material structure of production will require for its maintenance a new set of price-relationships, namely those which the initial monetary change temporarily created or led people to expect, but which this monetary change cannot perpetuate. Most additions to, or deductions from, the money stream will not stay where they have first appeared ; they have the inherent tendency to reverse[2] the changes in price-relationships which they have caused. But the significance of the further changes in relative prices which will be brought about by the monetary change will have to be judged in relation to the price structure appropriate to the changed organisation of production.

[1] Much confusion has been caused in this connection by the assumption sometimes made that there could be a real capital market without money on which there would be some determinate *in natura* rate of interest. In fact there would not and could not be one rate of interest without money, and the effect of the limitation placed on the possible amount of waiting by the scarcity of the stock of non-permanent resources would make itself felt exclusively via the changes in relative prices of the different kinds of commodities.

[2] Of course this does not mean that the position which would have existed without the monetary disturbance will — or even can — ever be fully restored. The losses and redistributions of incomes caused by the misdirection of production will naturally have a permanent effect — but an effect in a direction opposite to the impact effect of the monetary change.

We cannot judge the effect of any change in money prices without a knowledge of the system of prices which is appropriate to the existing structure of production.

Certain conditions of stability can be stated in real terms and in real terms only

There is thus a task which is logically prior to the study of the monetary mechanism : the task of analysing the principle on which particular systems of quantities of goods and particular systems of prices (or real ratios of exchange) are co-ordinated. This is what the so-called analysis in real terms attempts. Like equilibrium analysis in general its aim is not to give a direct explanation of any real phenomena, but to analyse in isolation a set of relationships which are relevant for the explanation of actual events. In other words : there are conditions of stability of the economic system which not only can be described more simply if we neglect the monetary factor, but which, although they can be changed by monetary influences, exist independently of them. These conditions are at any moment determined by the technical structure of the material equipment in existence and by the tastes of the people.

In the particular case we have to study the amount of abstraction involved in disregarding money is especially great. We are setting out to investigate problems of capital

Analysis in real terms involves abstraction from lending and borrowing of money

and at the same time the possibility of lending and borrowing money. Now this is of course a phenomenon with which the problems of capital and interest are so closely connected in real life that it may appear futile to talk about capital at all without taking money-lending into account. But that this appears so only goes to show that in our minds the terms capital and interest are so closely connected with monetary phenomena that it would perhaps have been better if they had never been used by economists in connection with the real phenomena which, though somehow connected with the monetary phenomena, would exist even in a money-less capitalist society. It has, however, become so firmly

established a usage to apply the same terms to the underlying real phenomena as were first applied to their
monetary manifestations that it would be difficult, at
this stage, to introduce new terms for them.

In one respect, indeed, this tradition has recently been
seriously challenged. In his last work [1] Mr. Keynes has
placed very strong emphasis on the desirability of con-
fining the term " rate of interest " to the
rate at which money can be borrowed.
And quite apart from the fact that his
use of the term would be more in conformity with its
meaning in ordinary life, there can be no doubt that
it is only in this form that interest appears as a price
actually quoted in the market and directly entering into
the calculations of entrepreneurs. The real or commodity
rates of interest, which have played such a prominent
rôle in traditional economic theory, are in comparison
merely secondary or constructed magnitudes which,
besides, vary according to the commodity in terms of
which we compute them. These considerations probably
make it advisable, in all investigations dealing with
monetary phenomena, to restrict the term interest, as
Mr. Keynes suggests, to the money rate, and to introduce
some other term for the " real rates ". This objection,
however, does not apply, or at least not as strongly,
so long as we confine ourselves to the real aspects of the
problem. Here the danger of confusion does not arise,
and it has seemed on the whole expedient to use the term
interest here in the sense in which it has become customary
to use it in pure economics, that is as referring to real
percentage rates of return.

In what sense and to what extent it is justified under
the assumptions made here to speak of one uniform rate
of return can be shown only as the investigation proceeds.
But in order that the term *rate of interest* which we propose to use in this connection should not mislead, it is

Use of the term " rate of interest " in this study

[1] Cf. Keynes, **1936.**

necessary at this stage to explain at least a little more fully what will be designated by this term. It has already been mentioned that the rate of interest in these conditions is not a price of any particular thing. It is an element in the relations between the various prices of different commodities, a ratio between the prices of the factors of production and the expected prices of their products, which stands in a certain relationship to the time interval between the purchase of the factors and the sale of the product. The problem of the rate of interest in the sense in which it will be discussed in this book is therefore the problem why there is such a difference between the prices of the factors and the prices of the products and what determines the size of this difference. It would perhaps be more correct if we referred to this difference between cost and prices as profits rather than interest. But as it has become customary — particularly since Böhm-Bawerk, to whom this particular statement of the problem of interest is due — to refer to this difference in equilibrium analysis as the rate of interest, and as the term rate of profit is now generally reserved for such " abnormal " differences as will arise only under dynamic conditions, it will probably cause less confusion if in equilibrium analysis we retain this established although somewhat unfortunate term.

That these differences between costs and prices which pervade — and are expressed in — the whole system of relative prices will in equilibrium stand in a definite relationship to each other which can be expressed, in some sense, as a uniform time rate is, strictly speaking, a fact which should not be assumed at the beginning of this investigation but forms one of its results. But as in this respect we are only going over ground which has often been covered in a similar manner, there can be no harm in anticipating this result, with which every reader will be familiar, and in occasionally speaking of a rate of interest in this sense before we have shown why there should be a tendency to adjust all the various price differences to a common standard.

If this methodological discussion is not to grow to disproportionate length, we must leave it with this rather cursory discussion of the relation between analysis in real terms and analysis in monetary terms. *Limitations of analysis in real terms* A more systematic and exhaustive treatment would be impossible without explicit consideration of the rôle money does actually play ; and this is just what we want to avoid here. What has been said is merely an attempt to indicate certain consequences which follow from the treatment of the problem of capital as part of general equilibrium analysis.

There is only one more point which should be stressed in conclusion of this discussion. The fact that almost this entire volume is devoted to the equilibrium or " real " aspects of our problem must not be taken to mean that we attach excessive importance to these aspects. The idea is rather to emphasise the width of the gulf which separates this exercise in economic logic from any attempt directly to explain the processes of the real world. It would have been easy enough to expand this exposition with occasional disquisitions about the significance of the considerations advanced here in a scheme of causal explanation of the real economic process. The author has on the whole tried to resist this temptation as far as possible and to keep strictly within the limits explained in this and the preceding chapter. The application of the results of equilibrium analysis to the real world means a transition to an altogether different plane of argument and requires a very careful re-statement of the assumptions on which it proceeds. It is impossible to do this by occasional remarks without running the risk of illegitimately turning analytic propositions into assertions about causation. It seems much better frankly to recognise the limits of what can be achieved with the method here employed, and to reserve the task of applying the results to causal explanation for separate investigation. Some suggestions concerning the treatment of these further problems which will arise in a money economy will be found in Part IV of the present study.

CHAPTER IV

THE RELATION OF THIS STUDY TO THE CURRENT
THEORIES OF CAPITAL

As already remarked above, the explanation of interest
will not be the sole or central purpose of the present study,
as was the case with most of the similar investigations in
the past. The explanation of interest will   The " productivity "
be an incidental though necessary result   theories of Interest
                                             most helpful for our
of an attempt to analyse the forces which   purpose
determine the use made of the productive resources. Our
main task is not to explain a particular form of income,
or the price of a particular factor of production, but to
display the connection between the supply of the various
kinds of productive resources, the demand for real income
at different dates, and the technique of production that
will be chosen. Most of the analytical tools which we
shall have to use were, however, created in the past in
the search for the explanation of interest. And it is
natural that the theories of interest which have contributed most to the elucidation of the problems which
we are going to study should be those which stressed the
" productivity of capital " and were in consequence based
on an analysis of the material structure of production.

What follows is in some respects no more than an
attempt towards a systematic development and elaboration of the fundamental ideas underlying the theory of
interest of W. S. Jevons, E. v. Böhm-   The founders of
Bawerk, and Knut Wicksell. If, in the   modern productivity
                                         analysis
course of its reformulation, parts of their
theory are changed beyond recognition, this does not
alter the fact that their work contains, though perhaps in
a somewhat crude and excessively simplified form, nearly

41

all the basic ideas on which the following exposition builds. Jevons' work, although he was not given time to formulate it in a way in which it was readily intelligible, contained the essential elements of the more fully developed theory.[1] Böhm-Bawerk in many respects simply developed the ideas propounded by Jevons and made them intelligible to wider circles by elaborating them : but at the same time he gave the impetus to a movement away from what seems to me to be the more fruitful approach on Jevonian lines.[2] His effective, although I think mistaken, critique of the earlier productivity theories of interest had the effect of causing later development to centre increasingly round the " psychological " or " time-preference " element in his theory rather than the productivity element.

In the first instance Professor Irving Fisher, without in any way denying the importance of the productivity element, has, in a number of earlier works,[3] stressed the

---

[1] Apart from the relevant chapters of the *Theory of Political Economy* (1st ed. 1871, 4th ed. 1911, particularly chap. vii), his unfinished *Principles of Economics* (1905) and the additional chapter to this work, printed as Appendix II to the fourth edition of the *Theory*, should be consulted.

[2] Cf. *Kapital und Kapitalzins*, published in two parts (1886 and 1889) and translated under the titles *Capital and Interest* (1890) and *The Positive Theory of Capital* (1891), which is still by far the most elaborate and comprehensive discussion of the problems of capital. The third and fourth German editions contain a good deal of important additional material in the form of further elucidations, replies to criticisms, and discussions of later theories. This material has not so far been available in English, although a new complete translation by Mr. Hugh Gaitskell is in preparation. This additional material is particularly important for its treatment of durable goods, which were unduly neglected in the first edition available in English — a fact which has given rise to much misunderstanding of Böhm-Bawerk's doctrines among English-speaking economists. Some remarks on this subject will be found in Böhm-Bawerk's *Recent Literature on Interest* (1903). A number of smaller essays in German dealing with particular problems in this field were collected after Böhm-Bawerk's death by Professor F. X. Weiss under the title *Klein:·e Abhandlungen über Kapital und Zins* (1926).

[3] Particularly *The Nature of Capital and Income* (1906) and *The Rate of Interest* (1907), which in spite of the new exposition of the

psychological factor so much more than the productivity factor that he was at least understood to attach more importance to the former. More recently he has, however, given us, in the most systematic work on the subject which we possess, a formally unimpugnable exposition of the theory of interest.[1] It is a work with which every student of the subject must be familiar. The development of the time-preference approach

But because of a different distribution of emphasis, and in particular his concentration on interest rather than on the methods of production, Professor Fisher's work hardly touches on a good deal of what is treated as important in the present study.

The time-preference element has, however, been stressed much more exclusively by another author who has developed this side of the Böhm-Bawerkian analysis, namely Professor F. A. Fetter. His writings on the subject, which, apart from the relevant sections of his two textbooks,[2] include numerous articles in various periodicals, will be found very suggestive, and in spite of certain obvious differences, have a close affinity to some of the leading ideas of the investigation that follows. This is particularly true of the idea of the rate of interest as an element pervading the whole price structure.

In addition to this branch there is a second branch which also springs from the Jevons–Böhm-Bawerk stem. This is represented almost exclusively by K. Wicksell[3]

same set of problems which the author has given us since, will still be found useful for their more detailed treatment of particular problems.

[1] *The Theory of Interest* (1930).

[2] *Principles of Economics* (1907) and *Economic Principles* (1915).

[3] Wicksell first treated these problems *in extenso* in 1893 in his *Wert, Kapital und Rente* (now reprinted as no. 15 of the *Series of Reprints of Scarce Tracts in Economics and Political Science*, 1933). He later incorporated the main argument, with some improvements, in his *Vorlesungen* (vol. 1, 1913, and earlier in Swedish), now available in English under the title *Lectures on Political Economy* (vol. i, 1934). Certain important points are also contained in his *Finanztheoretische Untersuchungen* (1896) and *Geldzins und Güterpreise* (1898; English edition, *Interest and Prices*, 1936).

and his pupils (particularly Professor G. Akerman [1] and Professor E. Lindahl [2]), who, with the help of certain ideas derived from L. Walras,[3] have systematically de-

The development of the productivity approach

veloped the productivity approach. It is in the shape into which this type of theory has been fashioned by Wicksell that it provides the most useful basis for the present study. Wicksell has seen nearly all the important problems left open by Böhm-Bawerk ; and in fact, after one has oneself found the solution of a difficulty arising when one abandons Böhm-Bawerk's simplifications, one frequently finds it implied or even explicitly stated in some inconspicuous remark in Wicksell's work. It must, however, be admitted that Wicksell did not give an adequate answer to Böhm-Bawerk's objections to an explanation of interest which was based mainly on the marginal productivity principle, and it will be one of the tasks of the present investigation to show why the factors affecting the supply of new capital ought to be relegated to a secondary place, at least in an analysis which is not primarily concerned with the conditions of long-term stationary equilibrium.

Besides the three authors who were responsible for the main steps in the development of the marginal productivity analysis of interest, there are several others who should be mentioned as having helped to shape those

[1] G. Åkerman, *Realkapital und Kapitalzins*, 2 Parts (1923 and 1924).

[2] Most of Professor Lindahl's contributions are now available in English in a volume *Studies in the Theory of Money and Capital* (1939). See, however, also the Bibliography at the end of the present volume.

[3] *Éléments d'économie politique pure* (1847–77, 4th ed. 1900), section 5. Probably Walras deserves more than this mention in passing, although his direct influence in this field was not very considerable, and even Wicksell, who in most other respects had absorbed so much of Walras' teaching, fully comprehended his theory of interest only at a late stage. See his *Lectures*, vol. i, p. 226, particularly the footnote — which incidentally is also interesting for the distinction between what is now known as the *ex ante* and *ex post* rate of interest (or the anticipated and the actual rate of interest, as Wicksell calls them).

doctrines.   In the first place there are the ingenious predecessors of this school, H. von Thünen and, more especially, John Rae.[1] The latter's *New Principles on the Subject
of Political Economy* (1834)[2] contains some
acute analyses of points of detail still not
to be found elsewhere, and has had con-
siderable effect through its influence on J. S. Mill.   With
regard to more recent contributions this study owes much
to Professor F. W. Taussig's *Wages and Capital* (1897),[3]
especially for the more felicitous terminology which he
has introduced in certain connections.   Among the great
mass of other pre-war monographs Professor A. Landry's
L'Intérêt du capital (1904) deserves special mention.   And
finally, L. von Mises, although his published work deals
mainly with the more complex problems that only arise
beyond the point at which this study ends, has suggested
some of the angles from which the more abstract problem
is approached in this book.   For reasons already explained
in the preface, this general acknowledgement of the main
obligations will have to stand in place of more detailed
references throughout the text.   Particularly in the case
of Jevons, Böhm-Bawerk, and Wicksell, the constant
references which an adequate acknowledgement of the
real indebtedness would require have been omitted.   But
the same applies to most other authors, and the comparatively few references that are given are intended not

Predecessors and other
Important contribu-
tions

---

[1] Perhaps Ricardo should also be mentioned here, even if he could
scarcely have been aware of all the implications of his theory which Dr.
Victor Edelberg has so ingeniously worked out (**1933**).   There can be
no doubt, however, that Wicksell was to a large extent inspired by
Ricardo.

[2] Republished in a rearranged form with an Introduction by
Professor C. W. Mixter under the title *The Sociological Theory of
Capital* (1905).

[3] Reprinted as no. 13 of the *Series of Reprints of Scarce Tracts in
Economics and Political Science* (London, 1932).   Cf. also Professor
Taussig's articles : " Capital, Interest and Diminishing Returns ",
Quarterly Journal of Economics, vol. xxii/3 (1908), and " Outlines of
a Theory of Wages ", *American Economic Association Quarterly*, Third
Series, vol. xi, 1910.

so much as an acknowledgement of an obligation as an illustration, by similarity or contrast, of the point under discussion.[1]

The general line of thought which this investigation follows has of late often been described as the " Austrian " theory of capital. In view of the varied nationality of

The two current methods of approach to the capital problem

the founders of this theory, and in view of the fact that the men who are commonly regarded as the leaders of the " Austrian School " of economics are by no means in agreement on it,[2] it is questionable whether this designation is appropriate. But, in spite of Jevons and the other English and American adherents, it cannot be denied that these views have in recent times intruded into Anglo-American discussions as a sort of alien element. And perhaps it will assist the reader if an attempt is made to sketch the main points on which the approach followed here differs from the traditional Anglo-American treatment of the same problems, and particularly, it seems, from the views of those authors who were mainly influenced by the teachings of Alfred Marshall. This may be conveniently done by setting out the differences point for point in tabular form. In order to make them quite clear one may also be permitted to state the points that are emphasised by the two lines of thought in a rather trenchant and even exaggerated form. It is of course not claimed that the description of either of these approaches in its extreme form does justice to the real position. Indeed one of the tasks of the following pages will be to amalgamate the two lines of thought into a coherent whole. All that is claimed is that in the " Anglo-

---

[1] While references in the text to contemporary discussions of these problems have been kept to a minimum, a fairly full list of contributions in this field during the past ten or twenty years which have come to the knowledge of the author has been added as an appendix to this volume.

[2] Neither C. Menger nor F. von Wieser, nor — to mention only one name from the later generation — Professor Schumpeter accepted Böhm-Bawerk's views.

American " treatment the aspects stressed by the second or " Austrian " approach have in more recent times [1] been unduly neglected.

In the following list of propositions the first of each pair is intended to represent the traditional or " Anglo-American " point of view, while the second gives the contrasting " Austrian " view on the same problem :

1A. Stress is laid exclusively on the rôle of fixed capital as if capital consisted only of very durable goods.

1B. Stress is laid on the rôle of circulating capital which arises out of the duration of the process of production, because this brings out particularly clearly some of the characteristics of all capital.[2]

2A. The term capital goods is reserved to durable goods which are treated as needing replacement only discontinuously or periodically.[3]

2B. Non-permanence is regarded as the characteristic attribute of all capital goods, and the emphasis is accordingly laid on the need for continuous reproduction of all capital.[4]

---

[1] It may perhaps be mentioned here that the classical English economists since Ricardo, and particularly J. S. Mill (the latter probably partly under the influence of J. Rae), were in this sense much more " Austrian " than their successors.

[2] Cf. Wicksell, *Lectures*, vol. i, p. 186 : " Strictly speaking only short-period capital (in other words circulating capital) can be regarded as capital proper ".

[3] A consequence of this concept of capital which we cannot discuss here further is the concept of *gross investment* as referring to the aggregate production of durable goods, and the belief that this magnitude is of special significance. It is, of course, closely connected with the distinction between *the* short and *the* long period, which, as was shown before, has little meaning for the economic system as a whole.

[4] Cf. J. S. Mill, *Principles*, I/v/7, ed. Ashley, p. 74 : " Capital is kept in existence from age to age not by preservation but by perpetual reproduction ; every part of it is used and destroyed, but those who destroy it are employed meanwhile in producing more " ; and Wicksell, *Lectures*, vol. i, p. 203 : " The accumulation of capital is itself, even under stationary conditions, a necessary element in the problem of production and exchange ".

3A. The supply of capital goods is assumed to be given for the comparatively short run.

3B. It is assumed that the stock of capital goods is being constantly used up and reproduced.

4A. The relevant time factor which we need to consider in order to be able to understand the effect of changes in the rate of interest on the value of a particular capital good is assumed to be its individual durability.

4B. It is not the individual durability of a particular good but the time that will elapse before the final services to which it contributes will mature that is regarded as the decisive factor. That is, it is not the attributes of the individual good but its position in the whole time structure of production that is regarded as relevant.

5A. The technique employed in production is supposed to be unalterably determined by the given state of technological knowledge.

5B. Which of the many known technological methods of production will be employed is assumed to be determined by the supply of capital available at each moment.

6A. The need for more capital is assumed to arise mainly out of a *lateral* expansion of production, *i.e.* a mere duplication of equipment of the kind already in existence.

6B. Additional capital is assumed to be needed for making changes possible in the technique of production (*i.e.* in the way in which individual resources are used), and to lead to *longitudinal* changes in the structure of production.

7A. The change that will initiate additions to the stock of capital is sought in an increase in *absolute* demand, *i.e.* in the total money expenditure on consumers' goods.

7B. Changes in the stock of capital are supposed to be determined by changes in the *relative* demand for consumers' and producers' goods respectively.

8A. In order to make a lateral expansion of production appear possible, the existence

8B. In order to stress the changes in productive technique connected with an in-of unemployed resources of all kinds is postulated.

crease of capital, the existence of full employment is usually postulated.

9A. The demand for capital goods is assumed to vary in the same direction as the demand for consumers' goods but in an exaggerated degree.

9B. The demand for capital goods is assumed to vary in the opposite direction from the demand for consumers' goods.

And, finally :

10A. The analysis is carried out in monetary terms, and a change in demand is assumed to mean a corresponding change in the size of the total money stream.

10B. The analysis is carried out in " real " terms, and an increase in demand somewhere must therefore necessarily mean a corresponding decrease in demand somewhere else.

The last four propositions relate to problems which are already outside the pure theory of capital which forms the subject of this book : they belong more properly to the main theory of monetary problems to which the present study is merely preparatory. But their inclusion in the list may help the reader to see the practical significance of these different ways of approach.

CHAPTER V

THE NATURE OF THE CAPITAL PROBLEM [1]

IN the first stage of economic analysis it is usually assumed that all productive resources are given in an unalterable form. They are regarded as sources of services which will continue permanently to be available inde-

Elementary equilibrium analysis proceeds as if all productive resources were permanent

pendently of any deliberate action to provide them. This is nearly enough true of free [2] human labour (which is not deliberately created from economic considerations) and perhaps also of the so-called " indestructible powers of the soil ". And the shorter the period of time which we regard as relevant, the wider will be the circle of resources which, for that period, can be regarded as definitively given.

This procedure is convenient as a first approach, because it allows us to analyse a number of important relationships without the complications which arise as soon as we take account of the fact that many of the existing resources may be of only limited durability. It is one of the devices which enables us to treat the economic process as " stationary " and to disregard all changes which occur in time. It will be assumed here that this part of economic theory has been fully worked out.[3]

There can be no doubt that the picture obtained in this way corresponds very little with reality. If we look at the productive resources of any society at a given moment, we find that only a very small part of them (even apart from the human beings themselves) will con-

---

[1] An earlier version of this chapter has appeared in German as an article in the *Zeitschrift für Nationalökonomie,* 1937.

[2] " Free " as opposed to slave labour.

[3] This part of pure economic theory is sometimes referred to as the theory of *kapitallose Wirtschaft.*

tinue indefinitely to render useful services without any
deliberate provision for their upkeep or replacement;
they cannot therefore be regarded as "permanent" or
"self perpetuating".[1]   This is not only   Actually most pro-
true of practically all those bearers of use-   ductive resources are
ful services which have been created by   of limited durability
man in the past, and can rarely, if ever, be expected to
last indefinitely or to remain permanently useful.   It
applies [2] to all the capacities acquired by human beings
through education and training, and also to the greater
part of the natural resources. Some of the latter, such as
the fertility of the soil, can only be expected to endure
permanently if we take care to preserve them.   Others,
such as mineral deposits, are inevitably exhausted by
their use and cannot possibly render the same services for
ever.

This distinction between permanent and non-permanent (or "consumable" [3]) resources is of fundamental
importance for the approach to the capital problem that
will be followed in this study. It is not,   Permanent and non-
however, a distinction which is in all cases   permanent resources
unambiguous. The main point to be kept in mind is that
what matters is not permanency in any absolute sense,
but the opinion of the economic subject as to whether particular resources at his command will last throughout the

---

[1] Cf. Wicksell, *Lectures*, vol. i, p. 150.

[2] At least from a social point of view : the individual can hardly
use up his knowledge and training before he ceases to be interested in
its usefulness (except possibly by overwork). It comes to the same
thing when Professor Knight (**1936,** p. 641) makes the capital quality
of human capacities dependent on their " presenting any possibility of
deliberate over- or under-maintenance ".

[3] It is unfortunate that in English the term " consumable " refers
so definitely to final consumption that it can hardly be used, without
danger of misunderstanding, to include things used up in production.
If this were not the case it might be preferable to " non-permanent "
in this connection, and Walras (*Éléments*, édition définitive, 1926, p. 246)
uses " consommables " as one of the essential characteristics of the
" capitaux proprement dits ", although he adds that they must also
be " produits ".

period in which he is interested (be it his lifetime or a longer period), or whether they will be exhausted or used up earlier than this. In this sense his own person may be regarded as a permanent resource if he is not interested in what will happen after his death. It could of course be argued with some plausibility that, strictly speaking, all resources are non-permanent. But this would only mean that our distinction is merely a distinction of degree, and would by no means deprive it of its significance. What may be regarded as an even more fundamental basis for the distinction is the fact that the future services of some resources cannot be anticipated, as they will continue to give the same services in the future no matter how they are used in the present, while the present use of the services of other resources decreases the amount of such services which will be available in the future. This is not affected by the objection that no rigid line can be drawn between permanent and non-permanent resources. The underlying fact, and in a sense the most general aspect of the phenomenon under consideration, is the *irreversability of time* which puts the future services of certain resources beyond our reach in the present and so makes it impossible to anticipate their use, whereas the present services of those resources can as a rule be postponed.[1]

[1] An alternate concept which is probably better but clumsier than the concept of permanent resources is the concept of non-anticipatable returns, *i.e.* those final services which would still be available at any future date even if up to that date their consumption had been kept at the maximum level attainable at every moment without regard to the future. In order that a resource may be permanent in this sense it is not essential for it to be indestructible in a physical sense. All that is necessary is that it should be expected to be useful, not in consequence of being kept in that state at a sacrifice, but because no present advantage would arise from destroying its future usefulness.

It is evident that certain resources may have to be treated as permanent in this sense, because their expected future services cannot be sacrificed in order to increase satisfaction in an earlier period, but will have to be treated as non-permanent in the other sense because their services, once they become available, are non-recurrent. In cases

The non-permanent nature of all " wasting assets " creates a problem which is not dealt with in the theory of timeless production. These assets cannot be *directly* used to contribute to the output of the time when they have ceased to exist. In so far as their existence does help to maintain output permanently above the level at which it could be kept with the help of the permanent resources alone, it must do so in an indirect manner. If the fact that we have command over resources which remain useful only for a limited period of time did not help us to use the services of the permanent resources more effectively, it would be quite impossible to keep our income permanently above the level where it would stay if these non-permanent resources had never been available. We might stretch their use over a longer period of time, but ultimately we should inevitably exhaust them

The central problem how the existence of non-permanent resources increases the permanent income stream

like these the significance of what we have called the irreversability of time, *i.e.* the fact that we can postpone but not anticipate the use of certain resources, becomes particularly clear. The range of time during which any force of nature can be turned to useful purposes has, as it were, always a definite beginning but frequently no necessary end.

It should be clear from these considerations that it would be equally misleading to gloss over this distinction by treating all resources as non-permanent, as it is to treat all resources as permanent. It is the existence of differences between the resources in this respect, and not the existence of extreme types, that is relevant.

Whether there are no really permanent resources in this sense, as is sometimes suggested, is open to doubt. When we remember that the relevant fact is not indestructibility in a physical sense but the lack of any inducement to destroy, there can be little doubt that, apart from the human beings themselves, not only a number of forces such as water-power but also quite a considerable part of the productive power of the soil must be regarded as permanent. A great deal of land (pastures) retains its fertility, not because provision is made to keep it fertile, nor despite its being used for current needs, but just because it is being used each year in such a way as to give the greatest possible service in that year. If anyone wanted seriously to deny (as I understand Mr. Kaldor does) that there are such things as permanent resources, he would have to assert that it is conceivable that by raising the rate of consumption (or rate of output) to the highest level obtainable in the near future, the productive capacity of the more distant future could be reduced to zero.

and should then have to be content with what services
the permanent resources could render by themselves. It
is this problem of why the existence of a stock of *non-
permanent* resources enables us to maintain production
permanently at a higher level than would be possible without them, which is the peculiar problem connected with
what we call capital.[1]

The term *capital* itself, in so far as it is required to
describe a particular part of the productive resources,
will accordingly be used here to designate the aggregate

Capital as the aggre-
gate of all non-
permanent resources

of those non-permanent resources which can
be used only in this indirect manner to
contribute to the *permanent* maintenance
of the income at a particular level.[2] It should be specially

[1] Cf. F. von Wieser, *Natural Value* (1893), p. 124 : " On the other hand,
it is a matter for wonder to find that the perishable powers of the soil,
and all the movable means of production, raw materials, auxiliary
materials, implements, tools, machinery, buildings, and other productive apparatus and plant, which are consumed, quickly or slowly,
in the service of production, are sources of permanent returns, —
returns which are constantly renewed, although the first factors of
their production may have been long before used up. This brings us
face to face with one of the most important and difficult problems of
economic theory ; with the question, namely, how we are to explain
the fact that capital yields a net return." In a footnote to this passage
Wieser adds that " in what follows I understand by the term capital
the perishable or (with the extended meaning explained in the text)
the movable means of production ". A similar passage occurs in K.
Wicksell, *Wert, Kapital und Rente* (1893), p. 73 : " Dass nun aber die
verbrauchbaren Güter, d. h. Güter, die in einer begrenzten Reihe von
Verbrauchsakten ihren ganzen Nutzgehalt zu erschöpfen scheinen,
dennoch ' kapitalistisch ' angewandt werden können, so dass ihr ganzer
Wert dem Eigentümer aufbewahrt bleibt und sie ihm dennoch Ein-
kommen schaffen, diese scheinbar paradoxe Erscheinung, dieses per-
petuum mobile des Volkswirtschaftsmechanismus bildet, wie früher
gesagt, den eigentlichen Kern der Kapitaltheorie ".

[2] This definition of capital is far less revolutionary than may at
first appear. The first move in this direction was made by Ricardo
when he decided to include " permanent improvements " with the
" original and indestructible powers of the soil " because, " when once
made, the return obtained will ever after be wholly of the nature of
rent and will be subject to all the variations of rent ", differing in this
from the " perishable improvements " which " require to be constantly
renewed and therefore do not obtain for the landlord any permanent

noted, however, that the important point is not whether it is expedient to use the term capital for this purpose ; on this reasonable people may differ, although they will scarcely find it worth while to argue about it. The

addition to his rent " (*Principles*, chap. xviii ; *Works*, ed. McCulloch, p. 158, note) ; and when for similar reasons he excluded from rent proper " the compensation given for the mine or quarry " (*Principles*, chap. ii ; *Works*, p. 35). Cf. also J. S. Mill, *Principles of Political Economy*, ed. Ashley, Part I, chap. vi, p. 93 : " But as the capital . . . cannot be withdrawn, its productivity is thenceforth indissolubly blended with that arising from the original qualities of the soil, and the remuneration for the use of it thenceforth depends, not upon the laws which govern the returns to labour and capital, but on those which govern the recompense for natural agents ".

The definition adopted here is essentially the same as Wicksell's, and Wicksell in turn seems to be indebted to Wieser for it. Cf. Wicksell, *Wert, Kapital und Rente* (1892), pp. 72-73 : " Der wichtigste volkswirtschaftliche Unterschied zwischen dem Grund und Boden und den produzierten Sachgütern scheint nämlich darin zu liegen, dass ersterer seine Nutzleistungen nur successive in einer vorher bestimmten und *unveränderlichen* zeitlichen Reihenfolge, dafür aber auch in einer *unendlichen* Reihenfolge abgiebt, wogegen die produzierten Güter nur eine endliche Summe von Nutzleistungen, diese aber beinahe in beliebiger Reihenfolge abgeben können . . . ; man kann sagen, dass die Produktionswerkzeuge um so mehr einen kapitalistischen Charakter (im engeren Sinne) bewahren, als sie nach Belieben verwendet werden können, z. B. die Maschinen, welche in schnelleren oder langsameren Lauf versetzt werden oder auch still stehen können, dabei aber keine Abnützung erfahren. Andere Vorrichtungen im Gegenteil, z. B. gewisse Bodenmeliorationen, sind, einmal angestellt, so ganz und gar mit dem Grund und Boden verwachsen, dass sie den erwähnten Charakter verlieren, d. h. nunmehr eigentlich Rentengüter, nicht mehr Kapitalgüter im engeren Sinne sind " ; and on p. 79 of the same book : " Für die folgenden Untersuchungen scheint es mir jedoch am zweckmässigsten, die verschiedenen Kapitalien einfach *nach ihrer Dauerbarkeit* zu rangieren. Die eminent dauerbaren Güter, seien sie selbst Produkte oder, wie *der jungfräuliche Boden, reine Naturalgüter*, und mögen sie ihre Nutzleistungen spontan oder nur unter Zusetzung von menschlicher Arbeit abgeben, nenne ich im folgenden *Rentengüter*. Die *verbrauchbaren oder schnell abgenützten Produktions- oder Konsumtionsgüter*, solange letztere sich noch nicht in den Händen der Konsumenten befinden, nenne ich *Kapitalgüter oder Kapitalien im engeren Sinne*." (Italics not in the original.) See also *ibid.* pp. 93-94, and the same author's *Finanztheoretische Untersuchungen* (1896), pp. 28 *et seq.*, *Geldzins und Güterpreise*, pp. 117-118, and *Lectures*, vol. i, pp. 186-187 ; and the passage from Wieser's *Natural Value*, quoted in the previous footnote, to which Wicksell refers in this connection.

essential point is that the existence of this kind of resources creates an important and peculiar problem which is different from and, we believe, of much greater significance than the problem of the kind of time-discount which would exist even in a society where all resources are permanent. It is this problem to which the present study is mainly devoted and it is for this purpose that we find it most useful to employ the term capital in the sense indicated. And at a later stage we shall attempt to show that it was this problem which originally gave rise to the conception of capital in ordinary business usage.[1]

It is, however, not necessary that this definition should be interpreted and applied with too rigid adherence to the literal sense of the terms " permanent " and " non-permanent ". In fact, what in a particular situation will have to be regarded as capital will to some extent depend on the context in which we use the concept. Perhaps it would even be better to attempt a general definition of capital only in the negative form of saying that the only things which never will have to be regarded as capital are the really permanent resources in the strictest sense of the term. In the case of all resources which are not strictly permanent the decision whether we have to treat them as capital or not will depend on whether or not they can be used up (or used up more quickly) during the period of time relevant for the problem in question.[2] Certain kinds of goods, particularly those which are commonly referred to as circulating capital, can be used up even during very short periods and will therefore have to be treated as capital in practically all contexts (this is the reason why circulating capital shows the peculiar characteristics of capital in a particularly high degree, while with respect to others the problem of the gradual exhaustion and the

---

[1] See below, Chapter VII, p. 89.

[2] Cf. Wicksell, *Lectures*, vol. i, p. 186 : " If, therefore, our analysis is only applicable within a fairly short period, then, strictly speaking, only short-period capital (in other words, circulating capital) can be regarded as capital proper ".

CH. V *The Nature of the Capital Problem* 57

need for replacement will arise only when the period relevant to the problem in hand is much longer.)

The final justification of any particular definition of the term capital can of course come only from its use as a tool of analysis. At this stage we do not propose to dwell much longer on the definition; we want only specially to emphasise its comprehensive character. Included under this term are not only the man-made productive equipment in so far as it is not expected to remain useful for ever but also natural resources in so far as they are " wasting assets ", and all consumers' goods existing at the moment in so far as they are non-permanent sources of final income. But although this concept is related to the familiar concept of the " produced means of production ", it is not identical with it. It does not necessarily include all the produced means of production, since it is at least conceivable, although not very probable, that some of the produced means of production may be expected, once they have been created, to remain useful for ever; [1] and in this case they would not be capital in our definition of the term. [2]

> Relation of this to other capital concepts

---

[1] It may sound curious that we reckon, *e.g.*, houses as capital only if and in so far as they are non-permanent. There can of course be no doubt that we would be better off if houses, once they are built, lasted for ever, and the fact that they need replacement is clearly a disadvantage. Yet it is this fact, that we have to replace them by something if we want to keep our income stream at a given level, and that we can use the amortisation quotas earned on houses in the same way as the amortisation quotas earned on any other capital good to replace these capital goods by whatever form of new investment appears most advantageous at the moment, which gives all the capital goods a common attribute, that of being the source of the " fund " which makes current investment possible — and necessary.

[2] Cf. Wicksell, *Lectures*, vol. i, p. 186 : " Such improvements to the land often leave a permanent residual benefit. This happens, for example, in the case of major blasting operations to secure water in mountain regions, the building of roads, protective afforestation, etc. Thus new qualities which, once acquired, the land retains for all posterity, cannot be distinguished either physically or economically from the original powers of the soil ; in the future they are to be regarded not as capital, but as *land*. . . . It may be further pointed out that nearly all the long-term capital investments, nearly all

Nor is it identical with the wider concept which identifies capital with the total stock of wealth,[1] for it excludes the sources of really permanent services.[2]

so-called fixed capital (houses, buildings, durable machinery, etc.) are, economically speaking, on the border-line between capital in the strict sense, and land."

[1] This latter definition of the concept of capital, which has been given wide currency through the writings of Professor Irving Fisher (and has also been used by Walras, although he singles out the consumable and produced capital as " capitaux proprement dits "), has the advantage of great logical clearness and of avoiding any distinction based on mere differences of degree. Its disadvantage for our purposes, however, is not only that it uses the term capital for a magnitude for which there are other terms (particularly " wealth ") available and in general use, but, what is more important, that it severs all connection with the special problems which have given rise to the concept of capital and which, since they need close study, are most conveniently treated under that general heading. Where the definition of capital is entirely subservient to an explanation of interest, as has been the case with most of the traditional discussions, this definition may be usefully adopted. But where the peculiar problems arising out of production in time are the main subject of discussion, it would be a pity to have to invent a new term so long as the term capital is available for the purpose.

[2] It may be useful to summarise the relation between the various capital concepts and the categories of resources which they include, with the help of a schematic table :

Kinds of Resources	Permanent (Non-consumable)	Non-permanent (Consumable)
Non-producible (" original ")	a	b
Producible (" augmentable ")	c	d

Our definition includes the categories b and d, while the more familiar definition of capital as produced means of production (or as " augmentable resources " in the revised form in which Mr. Kaldor has recently revived this definition — see **1937,** p. 219) would include c and d. Professor Fisher's definition (and the wider capital concept used by Walras) would of course include all four groups, while Walras' narrower concept (the " capitaux proprement dits ") would include d only. We shall later see (see Chapter VII, p. 90, below) that while of the things which exist at any moment only those belonging to the groups b and d serve as capital, their existence enables us to " invest " by creating things belonging either to the group d or to the group c, the latter ceasing thereby, however, to be capital in our sense.

The first question to which we have to turn, then, is how the existence of a stock of non-permanent resources enables us to maintain our income at a raised level for an indefinite period. The answer to this question is especially significant because it also explains why a great part of those resources, namely those which are " produced means of production ", ever came into existence. The answer is of course that the non-permanent resources provide an income stream for a limited period ; and that in consequence we are in a position to postpone the return from some of the current services of the permanent resources without reducing our consumption below the level at which it can be permanently kept. We are thus able to take advantage of the celebrated productivity of the " round-about methods " of production [1] which have been the cause of so much misunderstanding. In other words, the existence of non-permanent resources makes it at the same time possible and necessary to " invest " some of the current productive services, that is to use them in such a way that they will not yield consumable services until a later date than they might otherwise have done, but will then yield a larger amount of such services than they would have done at the earlier date. It is only because of this that the provision of an additional amount of services for a limited period in the future puts us in a position to raise for all time the return which we may hope to obtain from the meagre supply of really permanent resources.

The temporary services of the non-permanent resources enable us to invest the services of the permanent resources and thereby to increase their return

[1] This was not, of course, a new discovery of Böhm-Bawerk's, although he invented the term " round-about methods of production " and brought out the rôle of time in production much more clearly than anyone before him. The essential point was understood fairly well by most of the classical writers and it was particularly well formulated by N. W. Senior in the third of his " Four Elementary Propositions of the Science of Political Economy ", viz. " That the powers of Labour, and the other instruments which produce wealth, may be indefinitely increased by using their Products as a means of further Production " (*Political Economy*, 1836, 8vo edition, p. 26).

But why should the more time-consuming methods of production yield a greater return ? Ever since the time when it was first put forward this proposition has been the source of unending confusion, and it has given rise to so many misunderstandings that, however much space one were prepared to give to the subject, it would scarcely be possible to deal with all of them. Nor is it certain that there is any single explanation that will necessarily fit all cases. There is, however, one general fact which makes it appear probable that it will always be possible to increase the amount of final services which can be obtained from given resources if more time is allowed to elapse between the time when the resources are applied and the time when their final product emerges. And this is of course all that is required.

The causes of the productivity of investment

This general fact is, briefly, that there will almost always exist potential but unused resources which could be made to yield a useful return, but only after some time and not immediately ; and that the exploitation of such resources will usually require that other resources, which could yield a return immediately or in the near future, have to be used in order to make these other resources yield any return at all. This simple fact fully suffices to explain why there will nearly always be possibilities of increasing the output obtained from the available resources by investing some of them for longer periods.

It has never been asserted that *every* investment for a longer period will necessarily yield a larger product, although the critics have sometimes attacked the theory on these grounds. All that is important is that, so long as there are possibilities of increasing the product by investing for a longer period, only such prolongations of investment periods will be chosen as will actually give a greater product. The rather obvious reasons for this we shall consider later.

Not all postponements of returns will cause them to increase

CH. V The Nature of the Capital Problem 61

The explanation of the greater productivity of some
time-consuming methods of production is closely connected with another question, namely : In what sense
can it be said that the services of the per- Scarce and free, used
manent resources are given in a definite and latent services of
quantity?   It is necessary to begin by resources
considering the meaning of this assumption in detail.   Of
all the potential sources of satisfaction of human needs
only comparatively few can be used directly.   There are
always an infinite number of natural forces which are
capable of being turned to some human use, and which
are in this sense potential or latent resources.   And of
those actually used only a part will be scarce, and will
therefore be counted as valuable assets on the use of which
the satisfaction of human needs depends.   What part of
the total of the potential resources will actually be used,
and what part will be scarce, will always depend on concrete circumstances and will vary with these circumstances.   When we speak here of a constant stream of
services from the permanent resources being available,
what we have in mind is always the totality of such
potential resources, irrespective of what part of them is
actually being used at any particular moment or what
part of them has become scarce.[1]   It is only in this
sense that they can be regarded as an extra-economic
" datum ".   What part of them will be used and
what part will be scarce and therefore have value,
will depend on human decisions which it is the task of
economists to explain.   In general, the reason why resources
which are capable of being turned to some useful purpose

---

[1] The fact that with changing circumstances the amount of the
services accruing from permanent resources that are scarce will vary
instead of remaining constant, creates a serious difficulty which it will
hardly be possible to take into account at all stages of the exposition
without making it unduly complicated.   During the earlier part of the
analysis, which is devoted to a mere description of the technological
interrelations, we shall in any case have to take it as a given fact that
only a certain part of the potential resources is scarce and must therefore be taken into account, the free resources being neglected.

are not actually so used is that they would have to be combined with other resources which are more urgently needed elsewhere. So long as these other, complementary, resources cannot be spared because the total quantity of them available is required for purposes where they will yield a greater return than they would yield in co-operation with the potential resource in question, this resource will remain unused, or latent, and will not become scarce.

This general phenomenon of complementarity between different productive resources becomes significant for our particular problem if the potential resources, which might be used to produce useful services, will not yield these services until some time after they have been combined with other resources which can be used to produce such services immediately. It is of course by no means *a priori* necessary that the product which will be obtained in this time-consuming way shall be greater than (*i.e.* that it will be preferable to) that which would have been obtained from the direct use of the complementary resources. All that we can say in general is that men will take the trouble to use the services of additional resources only if, as a result, the product not only becomes different but is also preferable to what it would otherwise have been.[1] But that it is technically possible does not mean that it will always be done. So long as the other resources, such as human labour, which are required to utilise the potential resources, but which can also be used for the satisfaction of immediate current wants, cannot be spared, these potential resources will remain unused. And so long as they remain unused we can hardly regard them as separate resources since they

Many potential resources remain unused because their exploitation would require the withdrawal of other resources from current use

---

[1] It is, perhaps, not unnecessary to-day to stress the fact that the goal of economic activity is not to use the greatest possible quantity of resources, but to produce the maximum of satisfaction, and that these two things are not identical.

naturally remain free goods. Even when it has become possible to divert some of the other resources from the service of current needs to utilise the latent resources, it will be some time before the latter grow scarce. And although the increased product will be due to the fact that use is now being made of resources which it was impossible to use previously, we need pay no attention to this fact so long as these additional resources are free and not " economic " or scarce factors.

From among the different latent resources some can be made to give a return after a short interval and some only after a long one. Under otherwise equal circumstances, those which yield a return The return from in-sooner will be taken up first.[1] But among vestment has to be the other circumstances which must be considered relatively to the loss of current equal in order for this to be true is the size satisfaction and the time we have to wait of the return which may be obtained by for the return applying to them a certain amount of resources withdrawn from use for current consumption. If in a particular instance the return obtainable from investing resources for a certain period is considerably greater than twice the return obtainable from investing the same resources for half that period, the longer investment will evidently be taken up first. But the detailed consideration of this question must be reserved for a later chapter.

For the moment another point is more important. At first what count as " investments " are only the services of those resources which might also have given an immediate return. So long as they are the only resources which can be used at all, or fully used, it is only their

---

[1] Suppose that there are two latent resources of which one can be made, by the application of labour, to yield a return after one year, and the other, with the same application, will yield a return of equal size only after two years. Then if we assume that both of these investments will be repeated continuously, the return obtained during any stated period will always be greater from the first resource than from the second.

investment which leads to a reduction of current output. But as, in consequence of these earlier investments, the formerly latent resources, with which the other resources are combined, become first effective and then gradually scarce, these too will begin to count, because some consumption will be dependent on the particular use to which they are put. If they are then combined with some other potential resources which will not yield a consumable product until still later, this will represent an additional postponement of consumption. This fact that, as investment proceeds, more and more of those natural forces which before were only potential resources are utilised and gradually drawn into the circle of scarce goods, and have in turn themselves to be counted as investments, is of great importance for the understanding of the whole process.[1]

As more current resources are invested some of the formerly latent resources will also grow scarce and begin to count as investments

We shall have to return to this question of the general function of capital in the process of production in the next chapter but one. But before we can do so it is necessary to consider somewhat more concretely the various forms in which time enters into the process of production. This will have to be the task of the next chapter.

[1] Cf. C. Menger, *Grundsätze der Volkswirtschaftslehre* (1st ed. 1871; reprinted London, 1934), pp. 129-130.

CHAPTER VI

THE DURATION OF THE PROCESS OF PRODUCTION AND THE
DURABILITY OF GOODS : SOME DEFINITIONS

WE must now begin to consider the process of investment in its more concrete manifestations. There are two main ways in which the productivity of investment shows itself, and although the distinction is not fundamental, it is well to keep them clearly apart. The difference is due to the fact that the investment of any group of services of the permanent resources can be combined into one single " process " of production in two ways. In the one case it is the *duration of the actual process of production* where the time factor enters, and in the other case it is the *durability of the product* (or of the non-permanent resources used in production). In the first case the essential point is that resources will have to be applied some time before, and frequently throughout a considerable period before, any consumable services are produced. In the second case the essential point is that it will not be worth while to make the investment unless it results in a stream of useful services that will continue to accrue for some time to come.

The " flow of services from the permanent resources " which becomes available during any given period of time (or, in the limiting case, at a moment of time) we shall henceforth describe, following a suggestion of Dr. Hawtrey's,[1] as the amount of *pure input* of that period (or

---

[1] Hawtrey, **1937**, p. 15 : " We may apply to the operation of the original factors of production in any interval of time the convenient term ' input '. When we treat capital as a factor of production, we shall call the operations of the original factors in conjunction with capital ' mixed input ', and if we want to distinguish input in the former sense from mixed input we shall call it ' pure input '." It will

65

moment). It should be specially noted, however, that the term input will not be confined to that part of the services of the permanent resources which is " invested " Definition of " In- put " and " output " in the ordinary sense of the word but will comprise all the pure input that is used at all, including that part which is used to produce current output. The term *investment* (or " an investment ") will correspondingly describe the act of applying a unit of input in any process of production. Since, as we shall see later, it is not only pure input in the strict sense of services of the permanent resources which can be invested for varying periods, but also the services of non-permanent resources, we shall also adopt Dr. Hawtrey's expression *mixed input* when we want to emphasise that the latter kind of input is also included.

The term *output* will be used to describe the stream of final services to the consumer.

The distinction mentioned in the opening paragraph of this chapter amounts to a difference in the way in which aggregates of input are connected with aggregates The " continuous in- put — point output " and the " point input — continuous out- put " cases of output. In the real world the two cases are of course never completely separate. But it is useful to construct ideal limiting cases which show their peculiarities in the purest form. The first case is best represented if we conceive of a continuous application of input through a period of time, leading to an output all of which matures at a moment of time at the end of the period. This has been described as the " *continuous input — point output* " case.[1] The second case is ideally represented if we imagine a durable good which is produced at a moment of time and be noticed that the definition of pure input used in the text, in conformity with the terminology used throughout this book, substitutes " permanent resources " for Dr. Hawtrey's " original factors ". The term " input " itself had been devised earlier, probably by Professor R. Frisch in connection with the distinction to which the next footnote refers.

[1] These terms were, I believe, first suggested by Professor Ragnar Frisch.

then renders services continuously over a period of time. This case has correspondingly been described as the "*point input — continuous output* " case. As we proceed we shall have to devote a good deal of attention to the relationships ideally described by those extreme cases.

Before going on to discuss the way in which the productivity of investment manifests itself in each of these two cases, we must mention another way of describing them which seems to bring out the relevant peculiarities even more clearly, and to have the further advantage of stating them in a way which is more in accordance with the concepts used in other branches of economic theory. The first case, where the actual process of production takes time, may be regarded as a case where the final services wanted at a particular moment of time give rise to a *joint demand* for factors to be applied at different moments of time. The second case, where it is a question of the durability of the good, may be regarded as a case where the investment made at a moment of time gives rise to a *joint supply* of services over a period of time.[1]

They are special cases of joint demand and joint supply

As has already been observed, it is almost impossible in real life to find cases where time elapses between the application of the factors and the enjoyment of the results in only one of these ways. It is only under comparatively primitive conditions that we can conceive of cases which will correspond perfectly to either of the two extreme types. If we could assume that fireworks were made without the use of any durable tools or machinery, the work of our hands over a period of time would lead to a display lasting little more than a moment ; and this would therefore correspond fairly closely to the " continuous input — point output " case. If on the other hand we cut a

Combination of the two aspects in the complete process of production

---

[1] Cf. Wicksell, *Lectures*, vol. i, p. 260 : " The annual uses [of a capital good] successively following one another constitute a kind of joint supply (to use Marshall's terminology) ".

straight branch from a tree and used it for years as a walking-stick, we should have a fairly good instance of the " point input — continuous output " case. But as a rule the two sets of relationships are so completely intertwined that it is extremely difficult to disentangle them. This means that in practice we shall almost always have to deal with cases of a stream of consumption services accruing at successive moments of time which are the joint product of a process which also involves a joint demand for factors applied at successive moments of time. But this only makes it so much the more necessary to try to isolate conceptually the way in which each of these two kinds of investment increases the output from given resources.

For purposes of theoretical analysis it is necessary to isolate the connection between individual units of input and individual units of output, and at the same time we have to recognise that in real life production is as a rule continuous. Experience has shown that it is sometimes difficult to keep the right balance between these two aspects. It is important always to remember that the continuity of the actual process of production is due not so much to the fact that the same sort of process is continuously being repeated as to the fact that most of the investments which form part of the continuous process are made with a view to obtaining a stream of returns over a period of time, and that almost all returns are due not to a particular investment but to a range of investments over a period of time.[1] It requires a high degree

---

[1] Even Professor Knight, who in general is so thoroughly unsympathetic towards the whole investment period analysis, appears to admit the necessity of distinguishing between the investment periods of various units of input — although on other occasions he appears to deny the possibility of such a distinction. This, at all events, is the only meaning I can make of the following passage from one of his more recent articles (**1936**, p. 447) : " Because the process of investment must be spread over time and because, in general, there is more or less disinvestment in connection with the yield of any particular capital good, it is necessary to recognise the separate periods of invest-

of abstraction to arrive at the idea of separate individual processes which consist of separate and clearly distinguishable [1] inputs and outputs and which will yield a continuous stream of output only if they are continually repeated in an unchanged manner. But it is only by means of such abstraction that it is possible to isolate the relevant relationships between the different parts of the continuous process.

The fact that a series of successive investments is usually combined in order to produce any kind of commodity, and that the same productive operation results in a stream of final services extending over a period of time, is the source of another serious difficulty when we come to consider the changes in investment periods involved in changes in technique. The fundamental fact with which we are concerned is the change in the periods for which particular units of input are invested, that is, in the interval between the application of a unit of input and the maturing of the quantity of output due to that input. This interval of time we shall describe as the *investment period* of that unit of input.

Investment periods and " periods of production " or the " length of the process "

If the variation in the technique of production used always either affected the investment period of only one unit of the input or else affected the investment periods of all units in the same direction, there would be no problem, and we should be able to speak of changes in *the* " period of production ", or *the* " length of the process as a whole ", as a short way of referring to changes in the investment periods of the various factors used. In fact, however, most of the changes in productive technique are likely to involve changes in the investment

ment, from zero to infinity, of each infinitesimal increment of capital invested in any source or capital good. Only in this way can different investments be made at the same rate and the maximum yield obtained on the whole capital, which is possible under the given economic conditions."

[1] That is, distinguishable on technological grounds.

periods of different units of input to a different degree
and perhaps in different directions. This raises all kinds
of difficulties which we shall have to consider later. In
particular it makes it impossible to use the terms " changes
in investment periods " and " changes in the length of the
process " or " changes in *the* period of production "
synonymously. It must indeed appear doubtful whether
the second and third of these concepts, which necessarily
refer to aggregates of investment periods, have any clear
meaning. It is rather unfortunate that the time aspect of
production should have been first introduced into theoretical analysis in this form, for it has led to much
unnecessary confusion. But since the use of the expression
" changes in the length of the process " is a convenient
way of describing the type of change in a whole process
where the changes in the investment periods are pre-
dominantly in one direction, there is probably something
to be said for retaining it, provided it is used cautiously,
until we are ready to give a fuller explanation of what is
meant by one process as a whole involving more waiting
than another.

It is necessary, however, to define somewhat more
exactly than has been done so far what is meant by *one
process of production*. In general the expression refers to
The meaning of a   the series of operations which lead up to
" single process "   the production of a particular kind of good.
But this still leaves some ambiguity of meaning. The
term process may be used to describe the whole series of
operations which lead up to the production of a definite
quantity of the product at a particular moment of time.
The work of a potter who makes a clay vessel under
primitive conditions, and bakes the clay on a fire made
for the occasion, would represent a single process in this
sense. The term may, however, also refer to the whole
chain of continuously repeated operations which lead to
a continuous output of pottery. If the term process is
used without a qualifying adjective it will here refer to

the first concept, and the " *continuous process* " will be described either as such or as a " *line of production* ". It will soon be seen that the concept of a process in the first sense involves a considerable amount of abstraction and in most instances does not refer to anything which can be clearly isolated in the real world.

The advantages of time-consuming processes of production are closely connected with the advantages of the division of labour. If the process which leads up to a certain final service to the consumer is broken up into a number of separate operations, it becomes possible to use

Investment and changes in the technique of production

certain capacities, materials, and tools which could not have been used if all the labour had to be applied in the way that would give the final result by the shortest possible route. But we must not be deceived here by a further ambiguity of the term " one process ", *i.e.* the reference to a particular *technique* of production which it occasionally implies. If the advantages of the division of labour consisted solely in the fact that the same series of operations as were previously performed by one man were divided between a number of men, and in consequence each of them became more efficient at his special task, the effect would probably be to shorten the duration of the process instead of lengthening it. But in many cases the division of the process which leads up to the satisfaction of any particular need will be a division among a greater number of co-operating factors, including some that before were not used at all. It will mean a change in the method of production, and in the materials, tools, and human capacities used. And the resulting product may be technically a very different one from what it was previously. If the needs which it serves, however, are the same, these needs will now be provided for by a different and longer process.[1] In fact the greater productivity of this longer process will frequently express

[1] Cf., however, F. X. Weiss, 1921.

itself in the circumstance that the new product serves the same ends more effectively, or perhaps serves other ends at the same time.

In all cases the greater output derived from the inputs which are now invested for longer periods will be due to their combination with forces which could not be put to any use during the shorter period. It may be that, as with natural processes of growth or fermentation, the natural forces will exercise their effect to the desired extent only if they are left to operate for a considerable period of time. Or the materials, tools, or accessories which it is advantageous to use may themselves be obtainable only as the result of a process which takes time. In short, the increase in output will always be due to a change in the method of production used, a technical improvement.

The term improvement, however, although it is quite appropriate and is frequently used in this connection, is yet another source of possible misunderstanding which should be guarded against from the out-

Only those more productive methods which are known but not used at any given moment will involve more waiting

set. The term has often been understood, when used in this connection, to refer to inventions or discoveries. The argument would then seem to imply that technical progress in this sense, the advancement of knowledge, tends necessarily to increase the duration of the productive process. Against this it has been rightly argued that the discovery of new, hitherto unknown, ways of producing a thing will be just as likely — or perhaps even more likely — to shorten the duration of the process as to lengthen it. The considerations advanced above — and it is important to remember this throughout the discussion -- have nothing to do with technological progress in this sense. On the contrary, they refer to changes under conditions where knowledge is stationary. All that is assumed is that at any moment there are known possible ways of using the available resources which would yield a greater return than those actually adopted, but would not yield this return until a later date, and for this reason are not actually used.

Among the wide range of possible methods of production known at any one time there will be some which will yield their product after shorter periods of time and some which will not yield it until after longer periods. From among each group of methods involving the same " amount of waiting " — if we may make provisional use of this vague term — the one that will be chosen will be the one which yields the greatest return from a given investment of factors. But so long as there is any limitation on the " amount of waiting " for which people are prepared, processes that take more time will evidently not be adopted unless they yield a greater return than those that take less time.

We must return now to the relation of these changes in productive technique to the division of labour. The important thing about the transition to processes which on the whole involve investments for longer periods is that it is always undertaken in order to make use of additional forces of
Investment and the division of the process into stages

nature, and that in consequence it will as a rule involve a greater number of successive applications of distinct factors of production. Once this is understood it is easy to see how the transition to these processes will tend to give rise to the phenomenon which has been described as the *vertical* or *successive division* of labour as distinguished from the horizontal or simultaneous division of labour (*i.e.* the type of division which is due to the fact that people specialise in the production of different final products). The vertical or successive division of labour means that the process leading up to any one product is broken up into distinct " stages ", or, that is, into a number of separate operations which in the modern organisation of society will be performed by different firms. But although the number of these separate " stages " in any one line of production will often tend to increase with the lengthening of the process, we must not expect any strict proportionality between the time a process will take and the number of stages into which it will be divided.

In this sense, as the part of a complete process which is under the control of a particular firm, the concept of a " stage " of production is of little theoretical interest. The term, however, can be conveniently used for a grouping of the various kinds of capital goods according to their remoteness from ultimate consumption. In this sense it serves simply as a means of a further and very necessary subdivision beyond the usual rough division of goods into consumers' goods and capital goods. It has the advantage that it takes better account of the fact that we have to deal with a continuous range of various kinds of goods, and that wherever we draw the line between consumers' goods and capital goods by far the greater proportion of the goods existing at any moment will always fall into the latter category. Here the concept of stages and the distinction between earlier and later stages provides the distinction which will prove very necessary later on. When in the further course of this discussion the term *stage* is used, it will always be in this abstract sense and will not imply any reference to a division of the process between different firms or persons.[1]

It would be a mistake, however, to concentrate too much attention on this vertical division of labour. It would be quite wrong to suppose that the lengthening of the investment periods will always mean an increase in the number of separate operations which follow each other in linear succession. What is no less important is that, in the course of the lengthening of the process, the stream of operations leading up to a given product

---

[1] For a characteristic misunderstanding of the sense in which the concept of " stages of production " is used in theoretical analysis, cf. Ellis, 1935.

will as a rule be split up into many branches and sub-branches. And it may be that, long before the first move is made to produce the actual material from which the product is to be made, work is being taken in hand to provide some auxiliary material or tool which will be needed later to convert the raw material into the final product. At each stage of the process from the raw material to the finished product the main stream will be joined by tributaries which in some cases may already have run through a much longer course than the main stream itself. But all these activities, many of which may be carried on at the same time at different places, have to be regarded as part of the same process, and have to be taken into account when we talk about its length. The series of operations which are required in order to provide the fuel or lubricant, and the tools or machines which are needed for turning the raw material into the finished product, are just as much part of the process of production of the good as the operations performed on the raw material.

There is some difficulty about introducing tools, and still more machinery, into the picture at this stage, because they raise the problem of durability which still awaits discussion. This is in fact one of the main instances of the way in which the problems of the duration of the process of production and the durability of goods are so inextricably mixed up. Now, although tools are usually durable, they are not always so. The moulds needed in many kinds of casting processes, or the dynamite used for blasting, probably have to be regarded as tools although they can only be used once. They are examples of how extensive preparations, resulting in elaborate tools or auxiliary materials, may be necessary in order to make use of certain laws of nature in the transformation of any raw material into a useful form. The significance of the circumstance that tools and machines are as a rule durable

The complete process of production includes the provision of tools which are usually durable

will be discussed presently along with the general problem connected with the durability of goods.

Before we can pass on to this problem it is necessary to return for a moment to the difficulty of talking about changes in the length of the process of production. It will probably be fairly obvious by now that as the complete processes of production with which we have to deal become increasingly complex it becomes more and more difficult, and may in some cases be impossible, to say in any general way which of several alternative processes under consideration is as a whole the shortest or the longest. The total length of time which elapses between the very beginning of the process and the completion of the product may be shorter in one process than in another, and yet by far the greater part of the input used may be applied very early in the first process and very late in the second process. Which of these two processes is to be regarded as the longer ? It is impossible to answer this question at the present stage, and there is in fact no general answer to it. It is only mentioned at this point in order to warn the reader against any attempt to provide himself with an answer by introducing some concept of an " average period " of production. Such a concept, as we shall see, is not only unnecessary but is also highly misleading.

The concept of the period of investment, as applied to a process as a whole, has no indefinite meaning

For our present purposes we do not need to know whether a whole process as such is longer or shorter than another. The only points that are relevant here are, first, the periods for which units of input are invested, and, secondly, the fact that they will not be invested for longer periods unless the return due to them will be greater in consequence.[1] The reader will save himself a

The relevant time intervals are the periods for which the individual units of input are invested

---

[1] An exception to this rule, which may be disregarded at this stage, occurs when in the course of a thorough change in the technique of production employed which leads to an increase of the total output, the product due to particular kinds of input may possibly decrease.

good deal of trouble if he accustoms himself from the
start to the habit of regarding the periods for which
particular units of input are invested as the primary
factor and of regarding the length of the whole process
of production from which a particular product results
as only a secondary phenomenon.

The distinction between the periods for which we have
to wait for the product of a unit of input and the period
for which we have to wait for a unit of output will occupy
us yet a good deal. At this point, however, one particular misunderstanding of the theorem that round-
about processes of production are more productive may
be mentioned, as it is due to a confusion between these
two concepts. It has sometimes been argued that an increase of capital is more likely to shorten than to lengthen
the time during which we have to wait for the product.
And this is quite true when we speak of the time interval
which will elapse before a given quantity of output will
emerge. But this is quite compatible with a simultaneous
increase in the periods for which we have to wait for the
product of particular units of input. The use of elaborate
machinery may not only very much shorten the time it
takes to turn the raw material into a finished product but
even make the time between the moment when the first
input is invested in the machinery and the moment when
the first output emerges shorter than the period during
which we had before to wait for the product. Yet this
has been made possible only by investing some of the
input used in producing the machinery for a much longer
period than any had been invested before.[1]

This way of looking at the concept of the period of
investment also prevents us from falling into another
common error. It is frequently supposed that all in-

[1] Cf. A. A. Young, **1929,** p. 796 : " The use of capital saves time,
in the sense that a larger product can be had with a given amount of
labour. But it increases the average interval of time which elapses
before the products of a given day's labour reach their final form and
pass into the hands of consumers."

creases in the quantity of capital per head (at least when they do not involve changes in the quantities of durable goods) must mean that some commodities will now be produced by longer processes than before. But so long as the processes used in different industries are of different lengths, this is by no means a necessary consequence of a change in the investment periods of particular units of input. If input is transferred from industries using shorter processes to industries using longer processes, there will be no change in the length of the period of production in any industry, nor any change in the methods of production of any particular commodity, but merely an increase in the periods for which particular units of input are invested. The significance of these changes in the investment periods of particular units of input will, however, be exactly the same as it would be if they were the consequence of a change in the length of particular processes of production.

Investment periods of particular units of input may change without any change in the technique of production used in any particular industry

In referring to tools and machinery we have already had occasion to mention one of the most important groups of durable goods. These instances also show the sense in which the word *durable* is used in the present context. It may be not altogether unnecessary to point out that the word is not used here merely to indicate that a good will not soon perish, like meat or fruit, by the mere lapse of time.[1] It is used here to describe goods that are not destroyed in a moment by a single act of use but can be used repeatedly

The significance of the durability of goods

[1] The use of " durable " in the sense of merely storable is fairly widespread in the English literature on the subject (cf. for instance J. M. Keynes, 1936, p. 222) and is probably one of the reasons why the term " capital good " is so widely used by English writers to describe durable goods in the sense in which this term is used in the text. It seems, however, preferable, and more in conformity with the usage by the classical economists, to distinguish between perishable, non-perishable, durable, and permanent goods and to reserve the term capital goods as a description of all the first three types, that is all non-permanent goods.

or continuously over a period of time. Durability in the
first, more restricted sense may also give rise to investment,
as when it is possible to produce a commodity at a season
when it is cheapest to produce, and then to store it. But
this would not be durability of the kind with which we are
here concerned. Otherwise indistinguishable commodities
which are available at different times of the year (*e.g.* ice
in January and ice in July) must, for the purpose of economic analysis, be regarded as different commodities, and
storage (transformation in time) as part of one possible
technique of production. This case is therefore more
properly to be regarded as an instance where a longer
process of production gives a larger product.

Changes in the use made of durable goods may affect
the quantity of capital used in two different ways. Either
the quantity of durable goods used in a
given process may change, or the durability
of the goods may change. We shall first
consider the effect of changes in the durability of the
goods used.

The use of durable goods and the quantity of capital

Even within the category of durable goods in the
narrower sense in which the term is here used some further
distinction has to be made with regard to the way in
which the durability of a particular good
is determined. It is possible to conceive
of a durable good which will last for a predetermined
period of time irrespective of the amount of use to which
it is subjected. During that given period it may be used
more or less intensively and will accordingly give a greater
or smaller amount of services. But once it is made its
durability is finally determined, and we can speak of
variability in its durability only in so far as we have the
choice of producing otherwise similar goods of greater or
lesser durability. Most buildings probably belong to this
class. The other extreme will be represented by a good
which embodies a definite quantity of services which can
be used up at will either over a shorter or over a longer

Factors determining durability

interval of time. In this case the time the good will last
is determined not by the way in which it is made but by
the way in which it is used. The obvious example here is
machinery of most kinds, *e.g.* a motor-car. Neither of
these types of durable goods is ever likely to be encountered
in its pure form. In actual life we have to deal with
various combinations of the two elements, though it will
sometimes be useful to group them according as they
approach more closely to the one or the other of the
two extreme types.

More important, however, than this distinction is a
similar one which is connected with the reasons why
durable goods are used. It may happen that a particular
The reasons for using instrument *can* only be made in a form in
durable goods which it will last, and that the costs of
making it are such that it is only profitable to produce it
provided it will be used repeatedly or for a certain period
of time. *Or* it may be that although a particular instrument could be made so as to serve for a single time only,
its services are provided more cheaply if it is made in a
durable form.

The first case is the rule where an instrument does not
give off part of its substance or energy in the process of
being used, but serves merely " as a tool ". A hammer or a
Sometimes the strength derrick which would break while it was
required of an instru- being used would be no good at all, and
ment makes it inci-
dentally durable there are an almost infinite number of cases
where a tool, in order to be useful, has to be made so strong
that it will last — and in most cases remain useful — for a
considerable period of time. But once it is known to last,
it will be produced in such quantities, and the value of its
services will fall to such a level, that if each tool were used
only a single time it would not repay its cost : *i.e.* input
will deliberately be invested in order to obtain a stream
of services spread over a period of time. The question of
what share of the input invested in such a durable good
has to be regarded as invested for particular periods of time

presents difficulties with which we cannot attempt to deal until later. For the present all that we need to consider is the fact that in many instances advantage cannot be taken of the help that instruments will render unless input which will repay its costs only over a considerable period of time is actually applied before the results begin to mature.

But this case where a particular instrument can be made only of a certain durability or not at all is but one of a much wider group of cases where the use of durable equipment enables us to obtain a greater return from given quantities of input. The more frequent case is associated with the fact that as a rule the additional expenditure involved in making equipment more durable so that it will give a greater amount of service, is much less than proportional to this added service. Even if it were possible to build a house which would last only for a month but would serve its purpose properly during this time, it would hardly be worth while to do so because such a house would probably cost little less than one which lasts for years. And although there will generally be some additional expenditure involved in making a good more durable, this additional expenditure will usually be very much smaller than the expenditure that is required to obtain the same amount of service during the early life of the good.

In most cases, however, durability is aimed at because it gives additional services for a less than proportional increase in costs

The effect of this can be best seen if we assume for a moment that a fixed amount of input is set aside in a society for the provision of particular durable goods. This input may be used to produce these durable goods in their cheapest and least durable form. In this case a large number of the durable goods will soon be available, and for some time the total amount of services obtained from them will continue to increase. But fairly soon a maximum will be reached : as soon as the goods which

Effects of variations in durability on the amounts of services obtained at different periods

were produced first begin to wear out, all the available input will be needed for replacing them and no further increase in services will take place.

Compare this with the case where the input set aside for making durable goods is used to make fewer goods but more durable ones. At first the amount of services available will be smaller than in the first case. But since the durability of the individual good will increase more than in proportion to the increase in the expenditure on it, the total number of such goods which will have been created before the ones that were produced first begin to wear out (*i.e.* before it becomes necessary to devote the available resources to mere replacement purposes) will be greater than in the first case. The effect of using a given quantity of input for making more durable goods will thus be to provide a smaller quantity of services for some time at the beginning, but ultimately and permanently to provide a larger quantity.

As has already been suggested, what is called a transition to the use of " more durable goods " may mean two very different things, which, although the effect is very much the same for our purpose, must be clearly distinguished. First, it may mean a change towards the use of goods of greater durability ; that is, it may refer to the phenomenon we have just discussed. But although this is probably the case most commonly referred to under this heading, it is not the only case and probably not even the more important case. " More durable goods " may also mean that a greater quantity of goods of a given durability (or of durable goods in general) will be used, compared with the amount of pure input which is invested in circulating capital. In this way the amount of capital may be increased by the use of " more durable goods ", although every individual durable good used now may be actually less durable than was the case before, because the quantity of such durable goods used in proportion to the pure input

Changes in the quantity of durable goods used

employed has increased more than the durability of the individual durable goods has decreased.

In practice a change to the use of more goods of a given durability (as distinguished from a change to the use of goods which are more durable) will as a rule mean that a different, more expensive, and more labour-saving type of equipment will be used in a given process of production. Professor G. Åkerman, who has devoted a special study to this phenomenon, has proposed to de- This will usually in-
scribe this difference between different instruments of the same durability which are designed to co-operate with a proportionately larger or smaller amount of " labour " (pure input) as the degree of *automatism* of these different kinds of capital goods.[1]   They can also be described as more or less *labour-saving* types.   In certain contexts these terms are convenient and we shall occasionally use them.   But it is important to remember that the use of more " automatic " or more "labour-saving " machinery is only a special instance of a change towards the use of more durable instruments and that, whether a greater quantity of durable goods (in the sense of durable goods possessing a greater value and probably of a different kind) or durable goods of greater durability are being used, comes for our purposes to very much the same thing.   In both cases part of the total pure input used in the process of production will now be invested for longer periods. The only important difference is that in the first case input which has already been invested in durable goods will now (together with some additional quantities of pure input) be invested in still more durable goods, while in the second case input invested in durable goods is substituted for input invested in goods in process.   Nor should the question why it should become profitable to

The marginal note beside the paragraph reads: This will usually in-volve a change to-wards more or less labour-saving ("automatic") type of equipment

---

[1] See G. Åkerman, 1923, chap. iii/4 and chap. v/1, pp. 27, 39 *et seq.*, and 1924, p. 284 ; also Wicksell, *Lectures*, vol. i, appendix, and Lindahl, 1925, p. 81.

use a greater quantity of durable goods require any further explanation beyond that already given for why durable goods should be used at all. The fact is simply that of the various tools, etc., that can be used some will be more efficient than others ; that among the tools of equal costs and equal durability the most efficient will always be chosen ; that consequently the adoption of still more efficient instruments will require more capital because these more efficient instruments will be either more durable or more costly for some other reason ; and that, therefore, if capital is supplied more amply and cheaply, this will lead either to the use of tools of greater durability, or to the use of more costly tools of given durability, or both.[1]

[1] It is also possible that the increase in the supply of capital may bring about one of these effects to which an extent would more than offset the consequences of the other effect going in the opposite direction.

CHAPTER VII

CAPITAL AND THE "SUBSISTENCE FUND"[1]

WE must return now to the considerations from which we started in Chapter V. The significance of the various forms of the productivity of investment which we discussed in the last chapter is, as we have seen, that the existence of a stock of resources of limited durability enables us to keep income permanently above the level that could be secured by the direct use of current pure input. It does so by providing income during the time that we have to wait for the return of the input that is being currently invested. But it is important, even at this early stage of the exposition, that we should not unduly simplify the relationship between the stock of non-permanent resources and the possible range of investment periods. The very expressive term " subsistence fund " which has been used to describe this function of the stock of non-permanent resources is apt to be misleading in a number of ways. It is of course not a stock of actual means of subsistence, but only a stock of resources which can be turned into means of subsistence, *i.e.* into consumers' goods.[1] The

The relation between the stock of capital and current investment

[1] N. W. Senior was again the first person until comparatively recent times who saw this connection at all clearly. " Nor is it absolutely necessary ", he writes (*Political Economy*, 1836, pp. 78-79), " though if Adam Smith's words were taken literally, such a necessity might be inferred, that, before a man dedicates himself to a peculiar brand of production, a stock of goods should be stored up to supply him with his subsistence and materials and tools, till his own product has been completed and sold. That he must be kept supplied with these articles is true ; but they need not have been stored up before he first sets to work, they may have been produced while his work is in progress. . . . That fund must comprise in specie some of the things wanted. The painter must have his canvas, the weaver his loom, and materials, not enough, perhaps, to complete his web, but to commence it. As to

process of transforming these resources into consumers'
goods requires the co-operation of current input ; and the
amount of consumers' goods that they will yield and the
time when those consumers' goods will accrue, will depend
on the way in which the services of the permanent and
the non-permanent resources are combined. The latter,
therefore, do not represent a fixed quantity of consumers'
goods or a stream of them of fixed time shape. It is all a
question of which combination of the different resources
is most advantageous. The fact that it is the existence of
non-permanent resources which enables us to invest the
services of the permanent resources does not mean that
the fruits of the former will always be consumed at the
earliest date when they can be made available, and that
only the latter will be invested. Whenever a greater
output is to be expected from further postponing the
return from non-permanent resources, and in the meantime
using the services of the permanent resources, this arrangement will be the one to be adopted. It cannot be too
strongly emphasised that the services from non-permanent
resources, no less than those from permanent resources,
are objects of investment.

As has already been remarked, most non-permanent
resources owe their existence to the fact that they make
investment possible without a temporary reduction in the
income stream. All or nearly all the man-
made equipment is non-permanent, and
the greater part, although by no means all,
of the non-permanent resources existing
at any moment consists of man-made
equipment. This brings us back to the
relation of my definition of capital as the " stock of non-
permanent resources " to the traditional one of the
" produced means of production ".

Under perfectly
stationary conditions
the stock of non-
permanent resources
would be identical
with the stock of
produced means of
production

those commodities, however, which the workman subsequently requires,
it is enough if the fund on which he relies is a productive fund, keeping
pace with his wants, and virtually set apart to answer them."

Indeed these two definitions merely emphasise different aspects of the same process, which, as completely stationary conditions were approached, would tend to become identical.   As time goes on the non-permanent resources have to be replaced by deliberately produced equipment, and ultimately, if technological progress stopped, all non-permanent resources which were the gift of nature would be exhausted.   And there would of course be no additions to strictly permanent resources in a stationary state.   Consequently, under perfectly stationary conditions, where everything continually repeated itself in an unchanging way, the genetic definition of capital as the produced means of production would also define the non-permanent resources and the way in which they would be currently reproduced.

But the fact that a definition would be adequate under purely stationary conditions means less in the theory of capital than almost anywhere else in economics (with the exception of the theory of money).   The theory of capital is largely concerned with the significance of those wasting resources **Most capital problems arise only outside the limits of a stationary state** which, in Wicksell's words, " cannot, strictly speaking, be included in the scheme of a stationary economy ".[1] Thus it is only by an extreme and almost numbing effort of abstraction that the theory of capital can be made to satisfy the requirements of stationary analysis.   In actual life the existing stock of capital goods is always the result of an accidental historical process, consisting of a succession of unforeseen changes, and they will never be reproduced in exactly the same form.   They were only produced in this particular form because certain kinds of equipment happened to be available as the result of past history.

The essential characteristic of capital, and the one which affects the use of current input, is that it needs replacement and in consequence leads to investment.

[1] Cf. *Lectures,* vol. i, p. 151.

This in turn leads to the creation of new capital, but once this new capital exists the historical aspect becomes irrelevant. The important thing is not that the capital has been produced, but that it (or some equivalent) has to be reproduced. Under stationary conditions the two aspects will of course coincide. But under dynamic conditions this will not be so. If income is to be maintained permanently at the higher level which the wasting natural resources make possible, these resources will, as they are exhausted, have to be replaced by produced means of production.[1] And occasionally it may be found advantageous to replace non-permanent resources by some change of the surface of the earth, which, like a tunnel, may be expected to remain permanently useful.

Under dynamic conditions the relevant fact is only that resources are non-permanent, and not that they have been produced

The last case is particularly interesting because it points to a significant difference between the two definitions. On the classical definition the tunnel, and any other piece of man-made equipment that was regarded as permanent, would be counted as capital merely because of its historical origin. Actually, however, once it existed it would have none of those effects on the use of current input which are peculiar to the non-permanent resources. It would no longer represent a supply of capital which, if conditions changed, could be transformed into a more desirable shape. Nor would it (either from the social or from the private viewpoint) represent a reserve on which

[1] It may be pointed out here, although it does not strictly belong to our present subject, that a treatment of the problem of the conservation of exhaustible resources under the aspect of their representing part of the national capital, would at last put the somewhat confused discussion of these problems on a sounder basis. There is, of course, no reason why, *e.g.*, forests should be maintained at the particular size at which they happen to be at any given historical moment — although there may be other considerations that have to be taken into account than merely the direct profitability of the forests in question (effects on climate, soil erosion, aesthetic considerations, etc.). But it should always be kept in mind that any exhaustible resource represents just one item of the national capital which may be more useful in some other form into which it can be converted.

one could draw in order to obtain a temporary increase in current income. Although it would be a " produced means of production ", it would have none of the characteristics which create the special problems relating to " capital ".[1]

It should be observed at this point that the concept of capital arose out of the need for distinguishing the " substance " of an asset (which has to be replaced) from its yield : that is, for dividing gross returns between amortisation and interest. This is of itself sufficient reason for reserving the term for non-permanent assets. Where there is no " turnover " of stock, but only a permanent stream of services, no problems of capital arise.

But there is another, even more fundamental, reason why the definition of capital as the produced means of production should be definitely abandoned. And this is, that it is a remnant of the cost of production theories of value, of the old views which sought the explanation of the economic attributes of a thing in the forces embodied in it.[2] But, except as a source of knowledge, the actual history of a particular thing, *i.e.* the way in which it has acquired its qualities, is entirely irrelevant. It has nothing whatever to do with the decision as to how the thing shall be used henceforth. Bygones are bygones in the theory of capital no less than elsewhere in economics. And the use of concepts which see the significance of a good in past expenditure on it can only be misleading.

The traditional capital concept is a remnant of the cost of production theory of value

All this does not mean that the relation of capital to investment, and the creation of capital by investment, is not of the utmost importance. In fact it is so important that the greater part of what follows will consist of an attempt to clarify this relationship. What it does mean

---

[1] Cf. the passage from Wicksell, quoted above, p. 57, footnote.

[2] Cf. C. Menger, *Zur Theorie des Capitals*, *passim*, and the passage from Professor F. H. Knight's discussion of these problems already quoted (see above, p. 10, footnote).

is that the important thing is not the relation of existing capital to past investment, but its influence on current investment, its influence on the creation of the capital goods of the future. For all problems connected with the demand for capital, the possibility of producing new equipment is fundamental. And all the time concepts used in the theory of capital, particularly those of the various investment periods, refer to prospective periods, and are always "forward-looking" and never "backward-looking". But for determining what resources are functioning as capital at any given moment, the essential point is not that particular resources have been produced; it is that they are not permanent, but of limited durability, and therefore must be replaced by some new resources if the income stream is not to decline.

If in our definition of which of the present resources are to be considered as capital and which are not, we single out the non-permanent resources as capital, we The double aspect of must not overlook in doing so that in a the capital problem sense the capital problem is double-faced and that its two aspects make it necessary to recognise two categories of goods which are not necessarily identical. From the first point of view we are concerned with what it is that enables us to wait, and from the second point of view with what it is that enables us to draw advantage from this possibility of waiting. The investment which the waiting makes possible can of course take the form only of things which can be produced. And when we are thinking of the capital to be produced this can of course consist only of such things as can be produced. But what we mean when we say that the existence of particular present resources makes waiting possible is that these resources provide a temporary income stream during the period while we wait for some other income to mature. There is no other concrete meaning which we can attach to the vague but much used concept of the " amount of waiting " available than the amount of services available

in the near future as compared with those which will only
be available in the more distant future.   And there can
be no doubt that this is the sense in which the term
capital is used in everyday speech.   A person who in the
present year cannot lay hands upon a greater amount of
resources than will recurrently become available to him
in every successive year is not commonly regarded as
commanding any capital in addition to his income,
however large that income may be.   A big landowner,
for instance, may well be short of capital and, unless he
is able to " raise capital " on the security of his land, be
unable to make any investments to intensify the cultiva-
tion of his land.[1]   And a country may be very rich in
land and lack the capital, which may be supplied by
another country whose total wealth may be much smaller.
A person or a country, on the other hand, who in addition
to a secured (and non-anticipatable) stream of permanent
income commands an amount of resources which can be
used up in the near future, is generally held to own
capital.

It has recently been suggested [2] that instead of the
traditional concept of produced means of production or
of the concept of non-permanent resources used here, the
reproducible   or   augmentable   resources   The significance of
ought   to   be   considered   as   representing   the "augmentability"
" capital ".   But quite apart from the fact   of resources
that the criterion of augmentability is either exceedingly
vague or, if taken literally, would narrow down the range
of augmentable resources in such a way as to make the

---

[1] It is true that because of this possibility to borrow on the security
of land (or any other permanent resource) the distinction between
capital and land tends to become blurred and individuals more and
more tend to treat land as a part of their " capital ".   But the distinction between capital and land is surely not an invention of the economists and I find it difficult to believe that the efforts of a number of
modern economists (particularly Professor Fisher, Professor Fetter, and
Edwin Cannan) to expand the concept of capital so as to include all
wealth are to be recommended.

[2] N. Kaldor, 1937, p. 219.

concept useless for our purpose,[1] the point that is relevant
for our problem is not that certain existing resources *can*
be replaced by others which are in some technological
sense similar to them, but that they have to be replaced
by something, whether similar or not, if the income
stream is not to decline. A deposit of metal ore is no less
capital because it cannot be reproduced, and vice versa
the water-power of an existing stream would not become
capital in the relevant sense because of the possibility of
creating a new stream by collecting rain-water which is
now allowed to evaporate.

What determines the special common characteristics
of capital goods is not that they can be reproduced, but
how they can be used : namely, that they can be made to
yield all their services in the comparatively
near future. And it is this fact and no
other which in a sense makes them one common " fund " ; that they are capable of
producing income for the same period of time, the comparatively near future. Even very different consumers'
goods that are available at the same time are substitutes
to a much higher degree than even otherwise identical
goods which, however, are available at dates very distant
from each other. And so long as we can increase our income by investing, that is, postponing the date when some
resources will yield consumable services, everything which
can be used to give an income during the interval, and so

The sense in which the constituents of the stock of capital can be said to have a common quality

---

[1] **Mr.** Kaldor's definition of " producible " or " augmentable "
resources appears to be that they have perfect (or at least very close)
substitutes which it is economically possible (*i.e.* profitable) to produce.
If perfect substitutability (in the sense of the goods by which the
existing resources are replaced having an infinite elasticity of substitution
with the latter) were required, nothing except goods which it is profitable to reproduce in exactly identical form would have to be counted
as capital. But if only the existence of close substitutes is required,
where is one to draw the line ? On the other hand, if only resources
which it is economically possible to reproduce are to be counted as
capital, all obsolete machinery would cease to be capital as soon as
better machines became available ; while if the technological possi-

will enable us to make use of the opportunities of investment, possesses the common attribute of being a condition
of making investment possible. In other words, so long
as there is a special inducement to postpone the date when
some resources will yield their final services, the common
attribute of the things capable of rendering services in the
interval is a scarce " factor " on which certain additions
to our future income depend. But if the opportunities of
adding to output by investment should cease, although
part of our resources would still have the exclusive attribute of being capable of rendering services in the near
future, yet the existence of any particular unit of such
factors would cease to be a condition for the possibility
of investment and their common quality of being available
in the near future would cease to be scarce relatively to
demand.

The recognition that the constituents of the stock of
capital possess in this sense a common quality has often
led economists to speak of it as if it could be treated
as a homogeneous " fund ", an " amount The concept of cap-
of waiting ", or as a given quantity of ital as a fund
" capital disposal " or of " pure capital " in the abstract.
If these terms were used occasionally to express no more
than has been explained in the preceding paragraphs, little
objection would be raised against them. Unfortunately,
however, much more far-reaching assertions have been
made about the real existence of such a fund which I
cannot but regard as pure mysticism. The best known
representatives of this view are of course J. B. Clark and
Professor Gustav Cassel, and the views of the former
have recently been revived by no less an authority than
Professor F. H. Knight. In his opinion, the " basic issue "
which at present divides economists " is the old and
familiar one between two conceptions of capital. In one

bility of producing substitutes were to decide, even land could not be
excluded, since it is possible to grow practically any fruit in artificial
compounds (" tray farming ").

view it consists of 'things' of limited life which are periodically worn out and reproduced ; in the other it is a 'fund' which is maintained intact though the things in which it is invested may go and come to any extent. In the second view, which is of course the one advocated here,[1] the capital 'fund' may be thought of as either a value or a 'capacity' to produce a perpetual flow of income." [2] I am afraid, with all due respect to Professor Knight, I cannot take this view seriously because I cannot attach any meaning to this mystical " fund " and I shall not treat this view as a serious rival of the one here adopted. What I have to say about the former I have said in another place,[3] and here I shall not discuss it again beyond pointing out certain errors which are due to its influence.[4]

[1] *I.e.* by Professor Knight.
[2] F. H. Knight, **1935c,** p. 57.
[3] Hayek, **1936a.**
[4] See below, Chapters XXIII-XXV.

PART II

INVESTMENT IN A SIMPLE ECONOMY

CHAPTER VIII

THE OUTPUT FUNCTION AND THE INPUT FUNCTION

THE task of this part of our investigation will be to study the various possible relationships between the organisation of production and the size of the product with special regard to the productivity of "invest- The plan of this part ment ", that is, the use of different sorts of of the investigation time-consuming methods of production. The different ways in which time may enter between the application of resources and the maturing of the product are, however, so varied and are in real life usually combined in so many complicated and complex patterns, that before we can successfully investigate the influence of productivity considerations on the choice of a particular investment structure, it will be necessary to set out in some detail the different types of relationships that may occur.

This part of our way leads through a rather arid tract where the profit which we derive from our labour will for some time be difficult to see. And it is not surprising that nearly all of our predecessors, anxious to get on to what are the more interesting problems, were satisfied with a few simple generalisations about the " period of produc- tion ", and proceeded, without really analysing the nature and interrelationship of the various time-intervals involved, to consider their relation to the productivity of investment. We shall see later that this procedure almost inevitably leads to muddles and confusions which are very difficult to clear up at a later stage. In view of this experience we shall do well, before we approach the problem of the pro- ductivity of investment at all, patiently to explore all the types of relationships with which we shall have to deal.

The first three chapters of this Part will accordingly

be devoted entirely to describing the formal character of the various possible relationships between the stock of non-permanent resources existing at a moment of time, the stream of income expected from this stock, and the way in which the current input is being invested. These relationships will here be considered merely as technological facts which arise out of the circumstance that production takes time. Our task here will be essentially to provide a convenient way of describing the possible relationships in a manner which will assist in the later treatment of the economic problems involved. In the present chapter in particular we shall consider the various ways in which quantities of input and quantities of output may be related in isolation. In the following chapter we shall see how the technique evolved here helps us to describe a continuous process of production in all its aspects, and in Chapter X certain peculiarities connected with durable goods will be separately considered.

And not until the completion of this preliminary task shall we then be prepared to study the effect of the different productivity of different forms of investment on the choice of a particular investment structure. These relationships between the productivity of the different forms of investment, the particular investment structure that will be adopted under different conditions, the uniform rate of interest that will characterise a state of equilibrium, and the value of the capital goods in existence will occupy us for the greater portion of this part of the investigation. For a considerable part of the way (Chapters XI–XV) we shall try to concentrate on the effects of the productivity of investment on the investment structure by making special assumptions which will enable us more or less to disregard the psychological element of " time-preference " which forms of course an essential part of the complete picture. This element will be introduced in the last two chapters of this Part.

Throughout this part of the book we shall adhere to

a number of simplifying assumptions.   Until in Part III we
explicitly introduce the market, it will be assumed that we
have to deal with a closed economic system in which all
economic activity is directed by a single   Simplifying assump-
will and according to a coherent plan.   We   tions
shall deal, that is, either with the economy of an isolated
individual, or with that of a communist society where all
economic activity is directed by a dictator.

Until we get to the two final chapters of this Part, it
will further be assumed that the available resources are
to be used to produce an output stream of unvarying
size for an indefinite or perhaps infinite period.   We shall
not for the moment go into the question of the exact
meaning of a constant income stream.   For our present
purpose we shall simply assume that the output for which
the dictator plans consists at successive dates either of
constant quantities of one homogeneous commodity, or
at least of constant proportions of various commodities,
so that it can be measured in physical units.   During the
next few chapters we shall also disregard the considerations which will have to be taken into account in order
that the greatest possible output stream may be obtained.
All these economic or value problems will have to be
taken up systematically from Chapter XI onwards.   At
the moment we shall simply assume that one particular
plan has been decided upon for using the stock of resources
with which our society is provided.   Similarly we shall
for the time being assume that, within this production
plan, each separate unit of available input is expected to
make a definite and determinable contribution to the
output stream of the future.   How the magnitude of
these specific contributions is to be determined, that is,
on what principle particular parts of the future output
stream can be attributed to particular units of input, is
also a question which must wait for later discussion.[1]

---

[1] It will later be seen that, in the discussion of the economic problems
involved, we need not necessarily know the connection between all the

It is probable that the stock of non-permanent resources existing at any moment will embody a very considerable part of the output of the immediate future and a constantly diminishing proportion of the output of more and more distant future dates. Nearly all the output of the very next moment will already be in existence in the form of intermediate, semi-finished products or in the form of durable goods which will continue to render services for some time to come. The part of the output of the immediate future which is not yet in existence in some such form (that is, as what Professor Taussig has described as " inchoate wealth ") will be added in the interval by the use of some part of the input which is applied during that time.

The stock of capital at any moment represents definite contributions to the income expected at different future dates

As we look forward to more distant future dates, the part of the total final output which is already available in an inchoate form as non-permanent resources will become smaller and smaller, and the part which has yet to be provided for (by the application of input which does not become disposable until a later date) will become correspondingly larger and larger. The more distant the future date, the smaller will be the part of the output of that date which can be said to be already provided for. But although this share of future output will become very small when we look towards the very distant future, it is doubtful whether, within any period in which we are at all interested, it will vanish completely and whether some of the " non-permanent " resources will not cease to make contributions only at a date in which we are not really interested. But since we are using the concept of non-permanent not in an absolute sense but with reference

individual units of input and the corresponding units of output, or all the individual investment periods, but that it will prove sufficient if we know those affected by marginal changes. But for the present purpose of constructing an apparatus for the description of the technological relationships involved it will be convenient to retain the assumption stated in the text.

to the period for which the person in question plans, this problem need not trouble us further.

The position can be conveniently represented by a simple diagram. In Fig. 1 the horizontal or r-axis measures quantities of output and the vertical or t-axis time.[1]

The two parallel vertical lines Ot and RQ indicate the expected output stream, the distance between these two lines representing its constant size. The base line represents the present, and the two vertical lines may be conceived to extend indefinitely into the future. The area under the curve T_2R represents the part of the future output which is already provided for in the form of some kind of non-permanent resources. The curve itself has been drawn concave on the plausible assumption that the proportion of the output of increasingly distant future dates which is already provided for, will diminish at a decreasing rate.

Diagrammatic representation of the two portions of the output stream

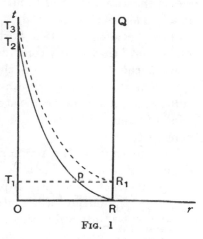

Fig. 1

Under stationary conditions we should find a similar situation at every subsequent moment. The part of the stock of non-permanent resources which had been consumed in the meantime would have been replaced by the application of current pure input during the interval. The dotted

The curve describing the time distribution of the returns from current input .

curve T_3R_1 gives the situation as it would appear after a short interval. The area T_1ORR_1 represents the amount

---

[1] For reason of convenience in the construction of some of the later more complicated diagrams for which this will have to serve as a basis, it has been found expedient to represent time not, as is the usual practice, along the abscissa, but along the ordinate.

that has been consumed during the interval OT'_1 and the area between the two curves T_2R and T_3R_1 shows the output which is expected to accrue in the future from the investment (in instruments and other non-permanent resources) of the input that became available during the interval OT_1.

For certain purposes it is useful, instead of referring to the contribution made by the input invested during some definite period of time, to refer to the marginal increment due to the application of input at a particular moment of time.[1] This can be shown in the diagram by making the interval between the two horizontal lines smaller and smaller until they finally coincide. In place of the interval between the two curves we then have the single curve T_2R. The slope of this curve at any point represents the addition to the future income stream (at the corresponding point of time) which is due to the pure input applied at moment O.

The concept of the product due to the input at a moment of time is of course an altogether unrealistic, purely abstract concept. Input can be applied, and

The use of curves in this and later connections involves the abstract concept of a time rate of flow

output will mature, only during a finite interval of time. But the concept of a rate of flow at a moment of time is a convenient mathematical device for expressing the volume of the flow independently of the assumption of a period of particular length. It helps us to isolate certain

[1] This use of the concept of the marginal increment may at first appear somewhat unfamiliar, but it is quite in conformity with the strict meaning of the term. We have to deal here with small variations in one quantity (the stream of output) relative to the change in another quantity (the stream of input). In the more familiar application of the concept of a marginal increment it is usually assumed that the quantity varies at a given moment of time, *i.e.* that instead of one quantity another slightly greater or smaller quantity is given at that moment. In the present case the independent variable (input) is a flow in time which varies not in width but in length. The marginal increment of output is consequently due, not to the fact that more input is being applied at any one moment, but to the fact that the stream of input is applied over a somewhat longer period.

aspects of continuous processes, and enables us to determine the size of the concrete magnitudes involved for any period of time we may choose. We shall repeatedly make use of such curves (and the corresponding functions), which refer only to time rates and not to actual quantities. So long as we keep in mind that they are only artificial devices intended to describe certain aspects of an essentially continuous process, the fact that they do not refer directly to something tangible need be no objection to their use.

The distribution in time of the product of a moment's input can thus be represented by a curve : the curve that bounds the area representing the part of the future income which is due to all the non-permanent resources already in existence   The output curve
at the given moment. The curve indicates, as we have seen, the marginal increment of this area due to the application of the moment's input. Its ordinates (the distances from the base) describe the full range of different periods for which we have to wait for the different units of the output which are due to a moment's input. And its slope shows the rate at which the product of that input matures at the corresponding dates.[1] In many respects this curve (which we shall call the *output curve* or the curve representing the *output function*) is one of the most fundamental magnitudes that are necessary for describing the capitalistic process of production.

The diagram we have been discussing was originally introduced, it will be remembered, not to show the output curve (*i.e.* the time distribution of the output due to a moment's input) but to show the time distribution of the product of the stock of non-permanent resources existing

---

[1] Strictly speaking, the rate at which output matures is measured by the inverse value of the slope : the rate becoming smaller as the slope becomes steeper (and therefore larger in algebraic terms) and approaching zero as the curve tends to become perpendicular (that is, as the slope becomes " infinite ").

at the given date.[1] The amount of the output due to a moment's pure input which will mature at each successive date is shown only indirectly by the slope of the curve. This is due to the fact that the curve shows the time distribution of this output in a cumulative fashion. Under stationary conditions, the total of all the units of output due to a moment's input must be equal to the total output maturing at a moment (that is, to the distance between the two vertical lines). And for any future moment the part of the line to the right of the curve in Fig. 1 (for instance PR_1 at the moment T_1) gives us the portion of this total which has already accrued, and the part of the line to the left (T_1P) gives us the portion which has still to accrue. The curve may therefore be regarded as a cumulative frequency curve (or ogive — cumulated downwards)[2] representing the part of the product of a given moment's input which remains invested beyond any particular date.

Interpretation as a cumulative frequency distribution

Although this manner of representation is in some ways more instructive, and will be used extensively in what follows, it will facilitate the understanding of the exact meaning of the output curve if we show the same time distribution of the product of a moment's input in a way which is more directly appropriate to this purpose, *i.e.* by a simple (non-cumulative) frequency curve. We now measure along the abscissa (Fig. 2), not the part of the input at O which has not yet matured, but the rate at which that output will mature at any moment (*i.e.* the magnitude represented by the negative slope of the output curve in Fig. 1). In this way we obtain a vertical strip which directly represents the shape of the output stream

The same situation represented by a simple frequency curve

---

[1] The quantity of product which is yielded by this stock at each successive moment is shown by the abscissa of the curve at the corresponding point.

[2] The student who experiences difficulties at this point is advised to refer to any textbook of statistics for a fuller explanation of the relation between a simple and a cumulative frequency curve.

due to a moment's input. It will be seen without difficulty
that this strip will be of rectangular shape if the output
function is linear and the output " curve " therefore a
straight line, that it will be of decreasing width upwards
if the output curve is concave, and that it will itself be
concave if the slope of the output curve decreases at a
decreasing rate. These three cases are represented by the
diagrams marked *a*, *b*, and *c* respectively, in Fig. 2. (The

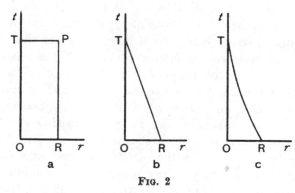

Fig. 2

relationship between the two sets of curves is the general
one between a simple frequency curve and the ogive, *i.e.*
the former represents the first derivative of the latter.)

It is advisable immediately to contrast the concepts
of the output curve or output function with another
closely related and no less important concept which is
easily confused with it. As has just been
explained, the output curve describes the
range of periods for which we have to *wait*
for the different units of output which are the
product of a moment's input. This is not

*The description of the
range of periods dur-
ing which we have to
wait for the different
units of output must
be supplemented —*

the same thing as the range of periods for which we have
to *wait for the products of different units of input of equal
size.*[1] The two curves representing these ranges of

---

[1] As in the case of output we shall have to assume for our present
purposes either that input is completely homogeneous or that, if it is
composed of services of different resources, these are always used in
constant proportions.

periods would be identical for any given process only if equal quantities of input always yielded equal quantities of output, no matter what the period for which these different units of input were invested. But this is evidently not the case. Although we have not yet systematically considered the productivity of investment or the source of interest, we know that they exist and we ought therefore to leave room for them in our diagrams. In general terms the significance of these factors for our present purpose is that units of input which are invested for longer periods will yield a larger product than those which are invested for shorter periods. There are, therefore, two ways of representing the range of waiting periods according as we use units of input or units of output as units of reference. The difference between the two ways of looking at the range of waiting periods is due to the fact that in the first case we take units of input (or factor units) and in the second case we take units of output (or commodity units) as our units of reference. If we speak in terms of units of output, the share of the total product for which we have to wait a comparatively long time will clearly be larger than the share of total input for whose product we have to wait an equally long time.

This distinction is a little difficult to grasp. But it is so important for what follows that it — by a description of the range of periods is necessary to be quite clear about it. for which we have to wait for the products Perhaps it will be easier if we re-state the of different units of difference by beginning with a definition input of the second of the two curves, the *input curve*, or the curve representing the *input function*.[1]

In order to draw this curve we require a system of co-ordinates in which the abscissa, instead of measuring quantities of output as in the former diagram, measures quantities of input (or such quantities of output as are

---

[1] This is the same function (and curve) which in an earlier publication (**1934b**) I have discussed under the name of " investment function " (or curve).

due to these quantities of input), and the ordinate as before measures time, the present being indicated by the zero point. The points on the curve (which may again be represented by Fig. 1) will then show the points of time at which the product of The construction of the input curve particular parts of the total input applied at zero hour will mature. The general principle of the arrangement is of course again that of a cumulative frequency curve. The abscissa indicates the quantities of input which are invested beyond any of the periods shown along the ordinate. The slope of the curve so obtained describes the rate at which the products of equal units of input mature at different points of time. The whole curve thus gives us a description of the complete range of periods for which the services of the different units of input are invested.

In the sense in which the term " invested " is used here all input is invested, although some of it (the part which is shown at the extreme right of the base of our figure) will be invested only for very short, and in the limiting case zero, periods. But All input applied is here described as being invested since it would be entirely arbitrary to fix some minimum interval which must elapse between the application of the input and the maturing of the product before we can speak of the input's being invested, and since in fact only a negligible part of the input can be consumed immediately it becomes available, it is on the whole more consistent to speak of all input as being invested. In any case the input curve must be understood to refer to *all* input used, whether it is being invested in the usual sense of the word or used in current production. If some part of the input actually serves consumption the moment it becomes available (as will be the case with some personal services), this will be shown by the input curve coinciding for some distance on the right with the base line. The same applies, *mutatis mutandis*, to the output curve.

The amount of input whose product will mature at any moment will not be proportional to the amount of output (due to that input) which will mature at the same

The difference be-
tween the output
curve and the input
curve

moment. The reason is that the size of the product will depend not only on the amount of the input but also on the time for which it has been invested. In order to obtain the value of the output due to a particular amount of input, compound interest for the period of investment has to be added to the value of that input. This means that the proportional share of aggregate product of a given input which will mature in the more distant future will be larger than the proportional share of the input which is invested for these longer periods. In terms of our curves this means that the input curve will be steeper at the top than the output curve, showing that towards the end of the range of investment periods the rate at which the product of given units of input matures will fall off more rapidly than the rate at which the output (measured in terms of its own) becomes available.

If we measure input as well as output in terms of value, we can show both curves on the same diagram. The expected total output at any date will consist partly of the value equivalent of the input whose product matures at that moment and partly of interest. If total output already provided for for each date is shown by the output curve TV_2, we can divide the output expected at each moment of time into these two parts and obtain thus a second curve, TV_1. The horizontal distance between this curve and the ordinate gives us for each moment of time the value of the input whose product matures at that moment, while the horizontal distance, at the same point, between the new curve and the output curve, gives us the additional value of the output due to interest accrued on the value of the input.

We have then in the same diagram two descriptions of the time distribution of the output due to a given input :

one in terms of the products of given units of input (in
factor terms) and the other in terms of units of output
(commodity terms). Of these two curves the second is of
course the output curve and the first the input curve.
The important point, however, is the difference between
the shapes of these two curves. The proportional addition
due to interest (compared with the value of the input on
which it accrues) will of course become larger and larger

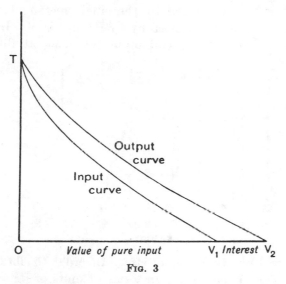

Fig. 3

as we go further into the future ; or, in terms of the diagram, the distance between the input curve and the output
curve, although it will become absolutely smaller as we
move upwards along the ordinate, will become relatively
larger compared with the abscissa of the input curve. This
means that towards the top of our diagram the curvature
of the input curve will become greater (or its steepness
will increase more rapidly than that of the output curve).
This expresses the fact that as we move further into the
future the rate at which products of given units of input
mature will decrease more rapidly than the rate at which
given units of output mature.

The difference between the two curves can perhaps be seen more clearly if we again use the non-cumulative form of representation.   Let us first assume that the invest-

The difference re-
stated in terms of non-
cumulative curves ment periods of different units of input are spread evenly over the whole range, so that the products of the given units of input will mature at a constant rate.   Measured in terms of the units of input to which it is due, the stream of output can then be represented by the single rectangular strip shown before and indicated by *ORPT* in Fig. 4.   But the products of equal units of input maturing at different

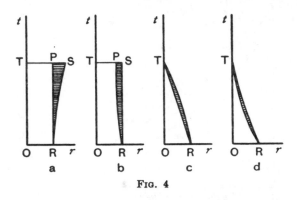

Fig. 4

dates will not be of equal size.   In order to obtain the magnitude of the output in terms of units of its own we shall have to add compound interest, at the ruling rate, for the time for which the different units of input have been invested.   Assuming the rate of interest to be given, we can depict this on the diagram by adding to the abscissa at each point a quantity corresponding to compound interest on the initial quantity of input invested for the periods shown along the ordinate.   The result is the compound interest curve *RS*, and the output stream corresponding to an even distribution of the investment periods of the different units of input will be of the shape indicated by *ORST*.   Instead of starting from a linear input curve and deriving the shape of the output stream from it, we might of course start from a constant output stream and deduct interest from it in order to derive the rate at which products of equal units of input will mature. Starting from a constant output stream this process of discounting gives us the distribution of input over the different investment periods which is indicated by the strip marked *ORPT* in Fig. 4 (*b*).   Figs. 4 (*c*) and 4 (*d*) illustrate the two other types of case which were considered before.

Later on we shall have to discuss the nature of the relationship between the input curve and the output curve, and their mutual interdependence. We shall then see that in certain cases, particularly where it is the duration of the process of production with which we have to deal, the input function is the fundamental magnitude from which we have to start, and the output curve can only be derived from it by construction. In other cases, particularly those of durable goods, the output function is the initial datum from which we have to start, and the input curve has to be constructed from it. In the former case (the " continuous input — point output " case) we know when particular units of input are invested and when the total product of a process matures. This means that we know how long we have to wait for the product of particular units of input invested. But as we do not always know what share of the product is due to each of these units of input, we may be unable to decide on technical grounds how long we have to wait for particular units of output. In the second case (the " point input — continuous output " case) we know when *all* the input has been invested in a particular process, and when the particular units of the product of that process mature, but we do not necessarily know how long we have to wait for the product of particular units of input. And in the real world, where " continuous input — continuous output " cases are the rule, the situation is, of course, still more complicated.

Both the input and the output curve are required for the discussion of the economic problems involved

We shall see that in a great many cases only one of the two magnitudes is directly given and that the other has to be derived by a process of discounting or accumulation. And it is only by such methods of convert-

Either may, however, serve as a basis for the schematic description of the continuous process of production

ing one into the other that we are able to arrive at a complete picture of the whole structure of investment in terms of either the input function or the output function. For the present, however, we shall neglect these difficulties and shall make use of only one of these two concepts for describing the process as a whole.

CHAPTER IX

THE CONTINUOUS PROCESS OF PRODUCTION

FOR a number of practical and historical reasons, we shall base our descriptions of the continuous process of production on the input function rather than the output function. It was in the form of an input function that the time dimension was first explicitly introduced into the theory of production by W. S. Jevons.[1] And it is probably the approach which is more easily comprehended. This very fact, however, is associated with certain pitfalls to which the use of the input function easily leads. It is essentially an approach to the problem of capital from a cost angle. Such an approach is even tolerably adequate only under strictly stationary conditions, and the dangers attaching to its use have already been pointed out. It does, however, help to elucidate a number of important relationships, and we shall use it here with the attached warning that it may prove misleading in certain connections if used incautiously. But so long as we confine ourselves to the consideration of stationary conditions we can disregard these difficulties.

The problems which we want to study with the help of this concept are first, the relationships that exist under stationary conditions between the stock of non-permanent resources (or, what in these conditions amounts to the same thing, the stock of " intermediate products ")

[1] Dr. Marschak, **1933,** has suggested that for this reason we should speak of the " Jevonian Investment Figure ". Although I have, on an earlier occasion, myself used the terms " investment function " and " investment curve " in this context, the terms " input function " and " input curve " now seem to me to be preferable by reason both of their brevity and of the analogy to the term " output function ".

113

9

and the range of periods for which current input is invested ; and secondly, the interconnections between the different ways in which the input function can be used to describe a continuous and stationary process of production.

Let us commence by considering the result of the continuous repetition of an investment for a given period in the simplest case imaginable : the " point input —

The result of continuously repeated investment in the simplest ("point input — point output") case

point output " case. We may assume that input is continuously applied to start some natural process of fermentation or growth which, without requiring any further application of labour, will yield a certain product after a given interval of time. We assume in other words that any quantity of input applied at a moment of time will result after a fixed interval in a definite product at another moment of time, and that input is applied, and consequently output matures, continuously at a constant rate.

This may be conveniently illustrated by a diagram (Fig. 5). If we measure time along the ordinate Ot and quantities of input and output (the latter of course in such units as are the product of a unit of input) along the abscissa Or, any constant rate of flow through time of input or output will be represented by a straight line of appropriate slope (*e.g.* OP). For any interval on the ordinate measuring time, say T_1T_2, the corresponding segment on the abscissa R_1R_2 will give us the quantity of input invested during that interval. If we assume that this input is invested for constant periods, say of the length OT_1, we can represent the resulting flow of output by a parallel sloping line T_1Q. The product of any input invested at any point of time and shown by the point on the line OP corresponding to the appropriate point on the time-axis, will be indicated by a point with the same abscissa (*i.e.* directly above the former) on the line T_1Q. Every process leading from a moment's investment to the product of the investment may then be represented by a vertical line connecting the two sloping lines. Since we assume that similar processes are started continuously at every moment of time, we have to conceive of the whole area between the two sloping lines as being completely filled by such vertical lines denoting individual processes. This means that every horizontal line drawn from any point corresponding to any moment of time (*e.g.* T_2) will

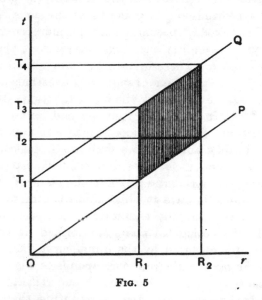

FIG. 5

cut those vertical lines at a series of points which will include every possible point from the beginning to the end of a single process.

Translating back from diagrammatic to real terms, this means that where a process is continuously repeated all the successive stages or phases through which each individual process passes will also coexist "Synchronised" pro-
at any moment of time. This conclusion duction
is important for the understanding of the subsequent analysis. Another way of formulating it is as follows : on the assumption of stationary conditions in which investment is carried on continuously, the complete

description of the historical process of production as it proceeds in time is also, and at the same time, a complete description of all the different stages of different indi-vidual processes which exist simultaneously at any one moment of time. Or, as the same thing has sometimes been expressed,[1] at any one moment of time we find all the phases through which the process of production passes " synchronised " or going on at the same time.

This relationship becomes slightly more complicated if, instead of assuming one single investment period, we consider a process where investments are spread over the continuous range of investment periods described by the input function. It is only in this form that we can obtain a really useful picture of the relations which exist in the real world. The diagram which we shall use in this connection has to be drawn in a three-dimensional system of co-ordinates. The horizontal r-axis in the plane of the paper again measures the rate at which input becomes available, while the t-axis, moving backwards into space, measures time. In the horizontal plane tOr formed by these two axes, the area enclosed by the input curve RQ_3 is shown shaded. So far the diagram corresponds to Fig. 1 above : the whole strip enclosed between Ot and RR_1R_2 . . . and moving backwards into time representing the expected stream of output. And the shaded portion of this strip shows that part of the stream of products which is already provided for by the " inchoate wealth " or " intermediate products " existing at zero hour.

Continuous Invest-
ment over a range
of periods

Everything in the base plane refers therefore to final products, present or future. In order to be able to show the stock of " intermediate products " (the transitory form which the input takes on its way to the final con-sumable product) in the same diagram, a third or s-axis is introduced. The quantities of such intermediate pro-

[1] This term is due to J. B. Clark, *The Distribution of Wealth* (1899), chap. xx.

ducts existing at any moment are ranged along this perpendicular axis according to the "stage" they have
reached in the process. Intermediate products which are
very near consumption or in a late stage Representation of the
(goods of a relatively low order) are stock of intermediate
products existing at a
shown near the base, while those belong- moment of time
ing to earlier stages are shown correspondingly higher up
in the triangular figure.

The connection between the individual items in this

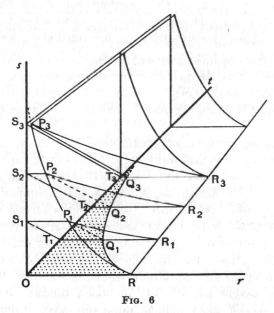

FIG. 6

stock of capital goods existing at zero hour and the
contribution to future income which they are expected to
yield is shown by the slanting planes which Representation of the
connect points on the perpendicular triangle process in time
with the corresponding points on the horizontal triangle.
At the base the two triangles coincide, expressing the fact
that the whole of the product to be consumed at the initial
moment must at this moment exist in finished form. If
we go a little higher up in the perpendicular triangle,

S_3OR, say to the goods in the earlier stage represented by the line S_1P_1, these will be goods which constitute part of the product expected at time T_1. Similarly the amount of intermediate products at the still earlier stage indicated by the line S_2P_2, represents part of the product that will mature at T_2. It will be noticed that in both cases — and in the cases of all the planes that can be visualised as coming between — the intermediate products already existing at the initial moment O represent only part of the total product of the moment for which they are destined, and a part which decreases as we go on to earlier stages. Thus the quantity of intermediate goods S_2P_2 represents only the small part T_2Q_2 of the product at T_2 ; and much the larger part, indicated by Q_2R_2, has yet to be created by the further application of input which will only become available in the interval between O and T_2. The rate at which this input will be applied can be read off from the curves P_1R_1 and P_2R_2.

When we reach still higher stages, *e.g.* that shown at the top of the diagram, we find that very little of the product of the relatively distant moment T_3 is in exist-
The range of invest-ence at the initial moment, and that nearly
ment periods may all of that product will have to be created
extend into the in-
definite future by the application of input in the interval between O and T_3. The diagram has, however, deliberately not been continued, as it conceivably might have been, to a point where all the future product has to be created by the application of input in the future. Under actual conditions we shall always find that however far we may look into the future, some small part of the product of that future moment will already be provided for by some part of the existing non-permanent equipment. This part will tend to become negligible as we go far into the future, but it will not disappear altogether within any time we can conveniently represent in the diagram. Account has been taken of this by leaving the diagram open at the top, so to speak, and by similarly

indicating that the shaded triangle in the base plane is bounded by a curve which approaches Ot asymptotically.

Special interest attaches to the topmost of the three slanting planes in the diagram — the not quite complete, curvilinear triangle, $S_3T_3R_3P_3$. As will easily be seen, it reproduces the input curve in an inverted form with the narrow part of the triangular figure which it bounds pointing towards us and the base pointing away from us. In this form the curve has a special significance. It describes the actual process of applying the input, the rate at which it will be applied from now onwards till the moment T_3 in order to produce the output of that moment. In other words, it describes the continuous input which leads to the output of the moment T_3.[1] Later on we shall sometimes make use of this inverted form of the input curve in discussing the case where we have to deal with a stock of goods in process which are the result of the actual duration of the process of production (as distinguished from the durability of the goods). For the present, however, it is only necessary to be aware of the relation of this aspect of the figure to the aspects that have already been discussed.

The whole solid body of the figure can obviously be conceived as being made up of an infinite number of planes, similar to the one that has just been described. Any one of the perpendicular planes thus represents a cross-section through an infinite number of these slanting curvilinear triangles each of which represents a single process. This means

The input curve in its inverted form

The meaning of the solid

---

[1] It was in this form that I first used the triangular figures in *Prices and Production*. But since in this inverted form the input function has sometimes been interpreted as " backward-looking ", it should perhaps be emphasised that even in this form it is " forward-looking " as it refers to all the investments that will have to be made from to-day onwards in order to obtain the product that will mature at some future date.

that each of the perpendicular triangles which represent
the stock of intermediate products existing at the moment
concerned is shown to consist of all the different stages
through which the different processes going on at that
moment are passing. In this respect the figure corresponds to the simpler diagram used previously (Fig. 5,
p. 115), except that we are now considering the case, not
of a single uniform investment period, but of a continuous
range of investment periods of different lengths. Since
we are considering stationary conditions we again have,
of course, identity between each of the various phases
through which the process passes in time and each of the
various "stages" represented by the stock of intermediate products existing at a moment of time.

In fact, the whole solid body represents all the phases
through which all the processes now under way, or to be
started at any time in the future, will pass. Any perpendicular cross-section of the solid, representing the stock
of intermediate products at the corresponding moment,
will be like every other in that it will consist of the same
combination of intermediate goods. But, no individual
good will be in the same position at two successive
moments. As time passes, *i.e.* as we move in the diagram
backwards into space, each good progresses downwards to
more advanced stages, its place being taken by other
goods which are simultaneously advancing in like manner
from still earlier stages. All these movements, all these
transformations, are of course effected by the continuous
application of current input, which is constantly becoming
available and being combined with the stock of intermediate goods in the different stages. The distribution
of the total flow of input at any one moment between the
different stages is shown by the vertical curve P_3R, the
continuous application of input in any one process by the
slanting curve P_3R_3, and the distribution in time of the
marginal additions to the product of the input applied at
the initial moment by the curve RQ_3.

There are thus *three fundamental aspects* [1] of the input function. In its original form it describes the time distribution of the output due to a moment's input ; it can also be used (as in the perpendicular triangles of our figure) to describe the stock of intermediate products existing at any *The three fundamental aspects of the input function* moment of time ; and finally it can be used in an inverted form (as in the slanting planes) to describe the process leading up to the product maturing at a moment of time. Under stationary conditions all these triangles would be exactly similar. They are all carved out, so to speak, from the more complete picture of the total process given by the solid figure, and it is only in relation to this that their significance can be fully understood. So long as we confine ourselves to stationary conditions it really does not matter which aspect we use, but it has been found convenient to treat the one shown in the base plane as the basic one, because of the use that will be made of it later. For certain purposes, however, the interpretation of the function in its inverted form, that is as a description of the historical process leading to the output of a particular moment, may be more instructive.

The foregoing exposition should have made clear what is meant when it is said that the picture given by any one of the inclined planes represents no more than an abstract description of the continuous process of real life. The " quantity " of product in which each process results, and which is *The relation between the time rates shown in the diagram and concrete quantities* indicated by the horizontal line in the base plane (*e.g.* T_3R_3), is really only a time rate at which the product matures at that moment, and not an actual quantity. It becomes an actual quantity only if we multiply it by time and so obtain, in place of a rate of flow at a moment of time, the amount produced during a period of time. In

[1] A fourth aspect in which the input function is represented in the diagram, namely by the surface P_3RR_3, will be discussed below, p. 195.

order to make our shadow-processes into something concrete we should therefore have to replace our merely two-dimensional planes by corresponding " slices " of some definite thickness. What period of time we take as the unit is, of course, entirely arbitrary, and the actual thickness of the " slice " will depend on this choice. In describing a stationary continuous process it is convenient to make the unit-period as short as possible and ultimately to go to the limit where this dimension disappears. But we must never forget that this method of isolating a particular aspect (the time rate of flow) is a mathematical device, a process of abstraction, and that the result assumes concrete meaning only when we reintroduce the dimension which we have disregarded.

The appearance of the input curve in its inverted form, in which it is particularly useful for depicting a single process in the narrower sense of that term, offers a welcome

The input function as a description of time-consuming processes

opportunity to add a few words on the meaning of this curve and the factors which determine its shape.[1] The more difficult question of how durable goods can be fitted into the general scheme will be reserved for the next chapter.

I begin with the question of the *shape* of the input curve. So long as we confine ourselves to considering the process of production of a particular commodity, there is

Its shape in a single branch-process of production

little reason for supposing that the curve is more likely to be concave, as I have drawn it, than either straight or convex. It seems just as probable that, in any one process, relatively more will be invested in the early stages than in the late stages, or that investment will proceed at a constant rate through-

---

[1] It is important to remember that the description of the process here runs in terms of physical quantities. In consequence we have either to assume that we have to deal with the production of only one commodity and that only one homogeneous factor is being used, or, if we want to apply the diagram to cases where more than one commodity and more than one factor are involved, we have to assume that the relative values are known and constant.

out, as that more will be invested in the later stages than in the earlier ones.

The question takes on a somewhat different complexion, however, when we remember that even the process leading up to a particular commodity is not usually linear, but will as a rule consist of many separate branches of different lengths which gradually join up together to form the main stream. In order to obtain the input function for the complete process, we must of course make a summation at each stage of all the input invested at the same moment (that is, in that same stage) in all the various branches of the process. Beginning with the one which starts earliest, we shall, as we progress to later stages, have to include more and more of these branch processes which have for a time been going on simultaneously but separately. Now, even if input is applied at a constant rate in each of these sub-processes, the aggregate effect must be that, as the number of such sub-processes which are going on simultaneously increases, the rate at which input is applied in the process as a whole will tend also to increase.

Its shape in the complete process of production of one commodity

This tendency for the input curve to be concave will be even more marked if we use the curve to describe the rate at which input is applied, not merely in a single process leading up to a particular product, but in all the different processes going on in the economic system. The total length of the processes in the different industries will of course vary widely. Some of them will be very long and will begin at a time when no other preparations are yet being made for the product of the time when they will finally mature. As we pass to the next stage of these processes, some other processes will be starting up, and so on as we get nearer to consumption. The total number of individual processes going on parallel will constantly increase as we proceed to later stages. And this will mean that, even if input is

Its shape for the system as a whole

applied at a constant rate in any one process, for the economic system as a whole the rate at which input is applied at the successive stages will constantly increase, *i.e.* the aggregate curve will be concave.

It is perhaps reasonable to assume that the amount of input which is applied to the stock of intermediate products in each stage will bear a constant proportion to the amount of those intermediate products (or, in more popular but more inexact terminology, that the proportion between capital and labour will be roughly the same in all stages). In this case the input curve will be some kind of exponential curve.

The second question is the meaning of the concept of "the rate at which input is invested" in the course of the process. The term is deliberately vague. It may cover two different things. It may refer to the value of the input which is invested at each point of the process, or it may refer to the physical quantities. If the input used is homogeneous and of one kind, the same curve will describe both. But the situation is different if, as will of course usually be the case, different kinds of input are used in the same process. In this case a single input curve cannot be drawn in physical terms at all ; and it can only be drawn in terms of value if we assume given relative values for the different kinds of input. The shape of this curve will depend on these relative values and will change with every change in them. It will cease to be a technological datum which describes the technical character of the process in physical terms. For this purpose we should have to start with separate input functions each of which describes the rate at which one particular factor is applied. These functions would all belong together and would have to be considered jointly in order to obtain a complete description of the particular type of process. Indeed it will be groups of input functions of this type which we shall have to use later in our discussion of the productivity of investment.

The units in terms of which input is measured

It is worth mentioning in conclusion that it is possible to modify the diagram used in this chapter so as to show certain consequences of changes either in the investment periods or in the amount of input that becomes available for investment. An increase in the investment periods would *Application of the diagram to the representation of changes* be shown by a gradual increase in the height of the figure, and an increase in population or any other increase in the amount of input would be shown by an increase in the width of its base. It would then be possible to trace with precision the effect of any such change on the stream of products, an effect which would only manifest itself after periods varying with the varying investment periods. But since all conclusions drawn from this construction would have to be based on a rather artificial assumption, namely, that only the investment periods of the input could be changed and that all the intermediate products were so completely specific that they could only be used as originally intended, it would be of very limited usefulness.

CHAPTER X

In the last chapter the emphasis was entirely on goods in process, that is, on the accumulation of capital due to the actual duration of the process of production. The importance of This must not be taken to mean that this durable goods form of capital accumulation is the more important one. On the contrary, there can be little doubt that under modern conditions the much more important rôle is played by durable goods. The reason for our procedure was merely that certain relationships can be shown more clearly and easily for the case of a time-consuming process where the input function has a simple and obvious meaning. In the ideal case of this sort (the " continuous input — point output " case) there is a definite moment when all the results of investment belonging to the process mature, and it is therefore possible to say at once for how long each additional unit of input is invested. The input function, describing the range of investment periods for the different units of input, lends itself particularly well to description by the three-dimensional figure which we have just used.

Turning now to durable goods, we shall again first consider " ideal " durable goods, that is, the " point input — continuous output " case. This means that we "Ideal" durable assume, firstly, that the time it takes to goods assumed make a durable good is so short that it can be disregarded, and, secondly, that the durable good, once it has been produced, will render direct services to the consumer without any further co-operation from current pure input. In other words, we disregard the

126

time it takes to make the durable good (and the time it may take for the products produced with the help of the durable good to reach the consumer) as well as the fact that further input may have to be applied to utilise the durable good once it exists.

As we have already seen, in the case of durable goods the input function which we have used in connection with goods in process is not directly known. Even in the case of an ideal durable good we shall be Limitations to use of able to state on technological grounds input function merely how long we have to wait for the various units of its services, but not how long we have to wait for the products of particular units of input invested. In other words, all that is initially given as a technological "datum" is the output function, the range of periods during which we have to wait for the different units of output. We have already seen (see pp. 111-112 above) that there is no constant or invariable connection between these two magnitudes, and that the one cannot be unequivocally converted into the other. It would no doubt be possible to make the output function the basis of the construction analogous to that used in the last chapter, but this would not avoid the real difficulty. For the moment it will be better to neglect the difficulty of attributing particular units of output (that is, of the services of the durable good) to definite quantities of input invested in the production of durable goods. We shall assume provisionally that this problem is solved. On this assumption, that is, provided we know how long the various units of input remain invested in the durable good, it is easy to show how durable goods can be fitted into the schematic representation of the complete process. It will be for later chapters to show how far this provisional assumption is justified.

In considering how far durable goods can be fitted into the schematic picture of the continuous process given in the last chapter we shall refer once more to the three-dimensional figure used there and ask what meaning we can attach to its various parts when they are interpreted to refer to a stock of durable goods.

There is no special difficulty about the interpretation of the curvilinear triangle in the base plane of our figure. It represents, in the already familiar manner, the flow Shape of the (con- of services (in terms of such units as are structed) input curve the product of units of input) which we may expect to accrue from the existing stock of durable goods. The only point which needs further explanation is why, in this case too, we should expect the input curve to be concave. If we had to deal only with one kind of durable good which gave a constant stream of services throughout its lifetime, we should expect the rate at which services from the existing stock of these goods would accrue to fall off at an approximately [1] constant rate as the existing goods successively wore out. If goods of all ages, from those which had only just been completed to those which were on the point of wearing out, existed simultaneously, as would be the case under stationary conditions, the number of goods (from the initial moment's stock) which were still in existence, and consequently the amount of services which they rendered, would decrease at a constant rate at every successive moment. The input curve would be a straight line.

There are, however, two reasons why in fact, and for the economic system as a whole, this is not likely to be the case. The first and less important reason is that most durable goods will yield, during their lifetime, not a constant stream of services but a decreasing one. In consequence, even if the number of goods surviving successive dates decreases at a constant rate, the amount of services rendered by them will fall off only at a decreasing rate. The second and more important reason, however, is that the different durable goods existing in an economic system will be of very different degrees of dur-

[1] *I.e.* neglecting interest.

ability. Thus even if within each group of durable goods of any one kind the individual items wear out at a constant rate, the aggregate effect must be that the total stock of durable goods of all kinds will be worn out only at a decreasing rate ; this is because parts of the total stock will wear out at a faster rate and others at a much slower rate than the average. The best way of showing this is to conceive of the streams of services accruing from the different groups of goods of given durability as being represented by separate triangles of different heights, and then to imagine that they are combined in a single figure. The broken line which we thus obtain in place of the hypotenuse of the combined triangular figure will tend to become a continuous curve as the number of different goods increases.

The question of continuity, to which we have referred a moment ago, raises a further problem. When we were dealing with goods in process, the assumption of complete continuity, although not entirely realistic, Discontinuity of re- was at least not so far from reality as to placement seem unreasonable. But in the case of durable goods the assumption of continuity would mean that, at every moment, one piece of every kind of durable good was completed and put into service to replace one which was just being worn out. Where we have to deal with goods of comparatively small durability and of which a considerable number are simultaneously in existence, this assumption may still not be too far from reality. But where goods of very great durability and of which comparatively few are in existence (*e.g.* railway engines or even bridges) are concerned, this assumption obviously becomes absurd. It is undeniable that for such goods production and replacement will inevitably be discontinuous, and that in consequence the composition of the stock of such goods in existence will undergo periodic changes. In practice the effect will be that, if the quantity of capital is to be maintained intact, at certain times

there will be a large number of goods of small durability
to be replaced and at other times a smaller number of
goods of greater durability. This means that the shape of
the input curve itself will undergo periodic changes. It
could also be shown, by a further slight modification of
our diagram, that it is possible for this to take place in a
way which will preserve a certain kind of continuity such
that the stock of durable goods as a whole will be replaced
and maintained constantly. But it would take too long
to go into these complications here. It must suffice to
point out their existence, and to proceed with the exposition on the assumption of that perfect continuity
which is implicit in the drawing of the diagram.

We turn now to the interpretation of the vertical planes
in the three-dimensional diagram (Fig. 6) applying to
durable goods. When they referred to goods in process,
The stock of durable these planes represented the stock of such
goods   goods existing at any moment of time,
and this interpretation still applies to durable goods. The
only difference relates to the concept of stages. The
goods in process could be regarded as advancing bodily
from stage to stage, so that at every successive moment
the same material units would have moved forward to
later stages. With durable goods the situation is that the
services which will mature at different dates are all embodied in the same material unit. Every such good has
thus to be regarded as consisting of units of future services which will mature at different dates and therefore
belong to different " stages ". Perhaps the situation can
again best be explained by having recourse to the non-
cumulative representation of the time distribution of the
services derived from the good. We may conceive of the
stream of services which a good is expected to render as
being represented by a vertical strip, of which the width
indicates the rate at which the services will accrue and
the length the period during which they will accrue. In
Fig. 7a the durability of the good is indicated by sub-

dividing the strip into sections corresponding to the number of unit-periods, say months or years, for which the good will last. In this way we can depict the whole collection of goods of different ages, but of the same kind, which exist at any one moment. Let us assume that the good of the type in question lasts for five unit-periods, and that during each such unit-period one such good is worn out and one is produced to replace it. Then at the beginning of each period we shall have the position shown in the diagram. We shall have one good which has just been completed and still represents five unit-periods of

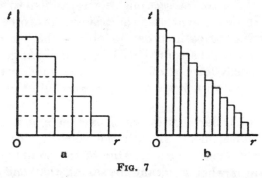

Fig. 7

service, one which has already served for one unit-period and represents only four unit-periods more, and so on until we come to the oldest good of the kind still in existence which represents services for only one more period.

It is evident that as the number of goods simultaneously in existence increases, and the intervals at which new ones are put into service become correspondingly smaller, the shape of the figure will tend to approach more and more closely to that of a simple triangle. As the number of goods approaches infinity and the share of the total services represented by a single good becomes infinitely small, the " stepped " line will tend to become a straight line. (We thus arrive back, of course, at the cumulative representation of the time distribution of services. For the amount of services which are still unexhausted in a good at a particular moment of its life will, under our assumptions, necessarily be equal to the total amount of services which are being rendered at that same moment by all the goods which still remain from among those which existed at the time the good in question was first put into service.)

The main difference between this triangle and the similar triangles which we used in connection with goods in process relates to the concept of stages. In the former

The concept of stages in the case of durable goods

case the different " stages ", which were obtained by dividing the triangle into horizontal sections, corresponded to different

goods. In the present case the triangle has to be divided into vertical strips in order to obtain the share of the output that will be contributed by individual goods, and all such goods (except of course those which are on the point of being worn out) will belong to a number of different stages.

The triangular figures which we have just obtained are, of course, identical with the vertical planes in the three-dimensional diagram. One of the points they help to explain is what is meant by saying that one and the same good may at any one time belong to several or even many stages.[1] We shall see that this is far from being a useless or artificial concept, and that it is really essential for the understanding of the factors affecting the prices of such goods. What we want to do now, however, is to show how the supply of services which accrues from these durable goods at any moment of time can be linked up with the investments which are necessary to produce these goods.

---

[1] Cf. A. Marshall, *Principles of Economics*, 1st ed., p. 109, note : " Of course, a good may belong to several orders at the same time. For instance, a railway train may be carrying people on a pleasure excursion, and so far it is a good of the first order ; if it happens to be carrying at the same time some tins of biscuits, some milling machinery and some machinery that is used for making milling machinery, it is at the same time a good of the second, third, and fourth order."

For this purpose we shall once more make use of the input function in its inverted form, *i.e.* as shown by the slanting planes in the three-dimensional diagram. The services rendered at any moment of time by the total stock of durable goods will be rendered partly by goods which are almost used up and which were produced a long time ago, partly by goods which have only just been completed and will consequently last for a long time to come, and partly by goods in all stages intermediate between these two extremes. If we represent the services which will accrue at any given moment from all the goods in existence by the horizontal line $T_3 R_3$ at the base of the slanting triangle $S_3 T_3 R_3 P_3$ in Fig. 5, then the curve $P_3 R_3$ (which takes the place of the hypotenuse of a straight-line triangle) will give us the dates at which the various investments have been made to which the respective fractions of the services of the durable goods in existence at T_3 are due.

We have already mentioned the *a priori* ground on which it appears probable that in the case of durable goods too this input curve is likely to be concave. It is exceedingly difficult to get much empirical evidence for its actual shape. But what-ever information we possess about the actual length of life of durable goods used in the present world tends to confirm this conclusion. The most complete figures of this kind which are available refer to the output of business capital goods in the United States in one year (1929).[1] From our point of view these figures suffer from the defect that they exclude durable consumers' goods and that of course the services rendered by the durable producers' goods may still be many stages removed from consumption. But as these data are based on depreciation rates (the assumed length of life is simply the reciprocal of depreciation rate), they correspond roughly to our input function (*i.e.* they show the part of

Distribution of expected useful life of durable goods

[1] Fabricant, 1938, p. 181.

the original investment which is assumed to be returned year by year). And since our purpose is merely to illustrate a general point, it may be worth while to construct from the available figures a hypothetical description of the stock of durable producers' goods that would be in existence at any moment if the annual production were repeated continuously year after year at the same rate at which

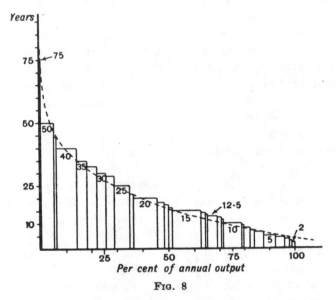

FIG. 8

such goods were produced in the year to which our figures refer. The result of this calculation, represented in the same way as in the schematic diagrams just used, is shown in the accompanying Fig. 8. The conspicuous irregularities are clearly due to a preference for round figures (10, 15, 20, 40 years) as a basis for depreciation. But even so it will be clear that the " input curve " for durable goods which we obtain if we smooth out the original data (as has been roughly done in the figure) is strongly concave.[1]

[1] Another point of general interest arising out of Dr. Fabricant's figures is that they show an essentially continuous distribution and no predominance of any particular figure for the expected length of life

The use of the inverted input form in this connection offers an opportunity to say a few words about a problem which we have so far neglected. Up to this point durable goods have been treated as if their produc- *The period of gesta-* tion did not take any time, *i.e.* they were *tion of durable goods* treated as clear instances of the ideal "point input — continuous output" case. This is of course even less true than the supposition that a time-consuming process of production will ever exactly correspond to the "continuous input — point output" case. It will always take time to make a durable good, and in consequence the investments to which the flow of services from the good is due will always extend over a certain period of time before the good actually begins to yield its services.

It was to illustrate this point that Jevons originally introduced his investment figure. He used a double

for durable goods in general. This is, of course, very much in conformity with our general attitude of stressing the essential continuity of the distribution of investment periods over a long range. And it flatly contradicts the assumption of the predominant frequency of a particular duration (especially ten years) which ever since Karl Marx has been made, on the slenderest evidence, the basis of generalisation, particularly in the theory of the trade cycle. A good instance of this is the statement by Professor Pigou that "there is reason to believe that many different sorts of machinery enjoy the same sort of length of life. Ten years seems to be not merely the average, but also the markedly predominant length. This at all events is the view of the Director of the British Census of Production." (*Industrial Fluctuations*, 2nd ed., 1929, pp. 229-230 ; see also *Economics of Welfare*, 4th ed., 1932, p. 38). When one turns, however, to the pages of the *Final Report on the First Census of Production of the United Kingdom* (1907) (London, 1922, pp. 35 and 36) to which Professor Pigou refers, his assertion is hardly borne out. All that the Director of the Census says is that " In determining the amount probably necessary for depreciation allowance on industrial capital, it may be remembered that it is commonly held by cautious manufacturers that provision should be made in business accounts for the renewal of buildings [*sic*] and plants in ten years " and " The consideration that part of the capital does not require renewal in so short a period as ten years may be set off, not only against the fact that more speedy renewal is required in other cases, but also against the fact that the provision which is the subject of the present estimate is required to cover current repairs as well as renewal of outworn plant ".

triangle,[1] of which (in the form in which it is reproduced here) the lower part represents the gradual investment of input in the good while it is being made, and the upper *Jevons' investment* part represents the gradual disinvestment *figure* as it yields its services. But although this is a more realistic way of describing the life history of an individual good, it does not easily lend itself to a representation of the complete process of using and maintaining a given stock of durable goods. The only way in which we can give a schematic representation of this process is by concentrating either on all the output which is due to the investment of services at one moment (the original form of the input function), or on all the investment to which the output of one moment is due (the inverted form of the input function).

Both of these methods are, of course, artificial in the sense that they do not include the complete life history of any individual good, but only either the results of the investments made at one moment in different durable goods in *Difficulties of com-* different stages of completion, or the in- *bining the period of* vestments to which the services derived *gestation and the* *period of use in one* at any one moment from all the durable *diagram* goods then in existence are attributable. In either case this means that we split up, as it were, the natural unit which a durable good represents, and treat as belonging to one process either such parts of the different goods composing a given stock as were made at

---

[1] W. S. Jevons, *Theory of Political Economy*, 1st ed. (1871), p. 223, 4th ed. (1911), p. 231. The figure has here been turned by 90 degrees as compared with the original, in order to make it correspond with the other diagrams used in the present work. Jevons' technique has been used and developed in the excellent discussion of the problems connected with durable instruments by R. F. Fowler, **1934.**

one moment, or such parts as give their services at one moment.

All this becomes relevant immediately we try to show the combined effect of the time it takes to make a durable good and the time it takes to use it up. The actual process by which the durable good is produced could, of course, be directly shown, as in Jevons' diagram, by the inverted input function, but the result of using the good would again appear as a stream of services stretching over a further period of time. Instead of this we want a description of the range of periods for which we have to wait for the products of all the input which matures at a particular moment of time. The input which matures at any moment will have been invested in different goods and at different times. We shall have to assume that every investment made at any stage of the production of a durable good makes some contribution to the services which that good will yield at every moment of its existence. We have therefore to wait for the result of every investment, first for a period until the durable good is completed, and then for a further range of periods corresponding to the life of the good and the rate at which it yields its services at different periods of its life. (Incidentally this means that not only the durable good itself, but also the input which is invested in the durable good, has to be regarded as being at one and the same time in a number of different " stages ".) While it would not be impossible to represent this situation by a specially constructed diagram in three dimensions, it is hardly worth while to devote much more space to this point.[1]

The representation of the combined process

---

[1] If the reader wishes, he can easily construct in imagination the appropriate diagram by first conceiving the range of periods for which different quantities of input are invested in the production of a durable good represented by a solid of which the input function with its co-ordinates would give the elevation, while its base would be a square. The further range of periods for which every unit of input invested in the durable good remains invested in that good after it has been com-

Compared with the real world, of course, even this case of a durable good which is made without the help of other durable goods (*i.e.* from pure input only) and which then serves consumption directly without further co-operation from other current input, is still very much simplified. Actually all the services maturing at any one moment, as well as the results of all the investments of input made at any one moment, will as a rule be the outcome of a long chain of alternating uses of durable goods and time-consuming processes which will together form a very complicated pattern. But it is not necessary here to follow up these complications in all their details. It is quite sufficient to have elucidated the principle according to which even the most complicated patterns of this sort can be described by one input function.

pleted could then be shown by erecting on the upward-sloping surface of the solid so obtained, and at right angles to the first input function, a further solid consisting of a family of inverted input functions describing the durability of the good. The various vertical distances between the base and the top surface of the complete solid would then show the total range of complete investment periods, from the moment input is invested in the production of a durable good till the moment when the services of the durable good mature, and all the possible ways in which this total investment period can be divided between investment during the production of the durable good and investment during its life : for some parts of the total input both these periods and therefore the total investment period will be zero, for some other parts the total investment period will be equal to the sum of the total duration of the process of manufacturing the durable good plus its total lifetime, while most of the input will be invested for some other combination of intermediate periods.

CHAPTER XI

THE PRODUCTIVITY OF INVESTMENT

THE mere description of any given investment structure by means of the input (or output) function is only a preliminary, even though a very necessary preliminary, to the central problem with which we have to deal. Up to this point we have not considered the reasons why any particular structure of production should have been chosen in preference to all the other possible organisations of the available resources. That is to say, we have neglected all consideration of the different productivity of different forms of investment and their influence on the choice of a particular investment structure. In the last two chapters in particular, the exposition was based entirely on the concept of the input function which, by definition, excludes any consideration of possible variations in the size of the total output derived from a given input. It would have made little difference in this respect if we had used for this purpose of mere description of the structure of production the output function instead of the input function. Even in this case we should not have been able to investigate the relation between the way in which input is invested and the size of the output. This can only be done if we know the exact connection between particular input functions and particular output functions, and this connection is closely connected with, and in part dependent on, the rate of interest.

The rate of interest depends, however, on a relationship which we have not yet considered, namely, that between *variations* in the investment structure and changes in the size of the output. This relationship is not the same as the connection, within any given investment structure,

between the value of the various units of input and the value of the corresponding units of output, and it is important that these two things should not be confused. In
Effect of changes in the investment structure on the size of the product
this latter case we have to deal with a growth of value in time, at a given rate of interest, in the course of a given process of production. And this growth of value will be represented by the difference between a given input function and the corresponding output function. In the case we want to consider now, however, the subject of investigation is the connection between *changes* in the shape of the input function and *changes* in the shape of the output function. The question we have to answer is how the productivity of investment reacts to changes in the range of investment periods.

Now we can plainly see why it is that the theory of interest can only be correctly formulated after we have obtained an adequate understanding of the nature of the
The ranges of investment periods cannot usefully be reduced to one single time interval
investment structure. In the past certain oversimplified conceptions have led to an approach to the interest problem which is of little use in explaining the phenomena of the real world. These concepts found their way into the analysis when it was clearly recognised for the first time that there was a definite relationship between the need for capital and the time elapsing between investment and the maturing of the product, and when this relationship was first explicitly made the basis of theoretical analysis. It was assumed, by Jevons and Böhm-Bawerk, and even, though with some misgivings, by Wicksell, that the variety of different waiting periods with which we have to deal could in some way be reduced to a single time interval, and that this average or aggregate investment period of society, which was regarded as a technical datum, could be unequivocally linked up with the quantity of capital. On this assumption of a unique correlation between " the supply of capital " and some

single time dimension of investment which could be determined on purely technological grounds, it seemed possible to represent the productivity of investment as a simple function of " the " period of investment, or, what was regarded as equivalent, the quantity of capital. It was assumed that the size of the total product would increase at a decreasing rate with successive increases in this investment period (or in the quantity of capital), and that the ratio between the marginal increase of the product (due to the last extension of the average investment period) and the total product determined the rate of interest.

This approach suffers from two fundamental defects, which not only make the conclusions inapplicable to any real phenomena, but even deprive it of value as an initial simplification. For the unrealistic assumptions which it makes do not merely refer to incidental circumstances ; they touch the very core of the problem and consequently make it impossible to proceed from them to more realistic cases. The *first* of these two defects is the assumption that the variety of waiting periods which are involved in any given structure of production can be combined on a technological basis, and described in terms of a single aggregate which has an unequivocal meaning. The *second* defect is the assumption that the extent to which we are in a position to wait for part of the product of the existing resources, without reducing consumption below the level at which it can be permanently maintained, can similarly be expressed in terms of a single " amount of waiting ", a kind of product of the volume of commodities for which we have to wait and the time we have to wait for them. These two points are so important that it is necessary to deal with them separately in considerable detail.

All attempts to reduce the complex structure of waiting periods, which is described by the input functions *and*

> Neither the range of waiting periods embodied in a given investment structure nor the supply of " waiting " are one-dimensional magnitudes

the output functions, to a single aggregate or average [1]
investment period, which could be generally substituted
for these functions in the discussion of the productivity

Conditions under
which description in
terms of a single time
interval would be
valid of investment, are bound to fail, because
the different waiting periods cannot be
reduced to a common denominator in
purely technical terms. This would only
be possible provided we had to deal with only one homogeneous kind of input,[2] and provided the value of the
product were always directly proportional to the amount
of this input that was used. Of course neither of these
assumptions is true in reality. But it is such ideas as
these, dating back to the real cost theories of value, which
have until quite recent times disfigured and invalidated
much of the theory of capital.

Actually we have to deal with a situation where first
there are a great number of different kinds of input, and

The two main points
in which the tradi-
tional assumptions
are contrary to reality where, secondly, what is more important,
the value of the product due to different
units of input is variable and can be
deliberately varied by using more or less of the particular

[1] In the traditional discussions of these problems only the concept
of the average period of investment or of production has been used,
but it is of course uniquely related to the idea of an aggregate or a
sum of all the investment periods. And to make it clear that our
objections are not merely directed against the process of averaging,
but against the whole idea that the investment structure can be
adequately described by a process of summing up the individual
investment periods, the expression " aggregate or average " will be
used throughout the text. In terms of the diagram, the concept of an
aggregate of all investment periods is represented by the area enclosed
under the input curve. It is always equal to the base line of the
curvilinear triangle multiplied by its average height (representing the
average investment period). The important point is that triangles with
the same area but bounded by input curves of different shapes cannot be
regarded as representing equal quantities of capital because the shape
of the input curve possesses a special significance which must not be
neglected.

[2] This would imply also that the intermediate products resulting
from the investment of this input could not be used for any other
purpose than that for which they were originally intended, and would
not therefore have to be counted as separate resources.

kind of input in combination with given other kinds of input.

The first of these two circumstances means that in all cases where different kinds of input are applied in the different stages of any one process of production, the relative amounts of waiting involved in different processes will depend on the relative values of the different kinds of input. In order to arrive at an aggregate figure of the amount of waiting involved in each process we have to assign definite weights to the different units of input, and these weights must necessarily be expressed in terms of value. But the relative values of the different kinds of input will inevitably depend on the rate of interest, so that such an aggregate cannot be regarded as something that is independent of, or as a datum determining, the rate of interest.

Still more serious is the second difficulty. This is directly connected with the fact already noted that in some cases only the input function (*i.e.* the range of periods for which we have to wait for the products of different units of input) and in other cases only the output function (*i.e.* the range of periods for which we have to wait for the different units of output) is directly given and that the one can only be converted into the other on the assumption that the rate of interest is given. This means that in many cases (in all cases where durable goods are concerned) we cannot say in any general way, and on purely technical grounds, how long the different parts of the total amount of input invested will remain invested. But this is not all. The fact that the value of any investment grows gradually (at compound interest) into the varying value of its product means that larger and larger quantities have to be regarded as being invested at each successive period for which the given investment is continued. If, *e.g.*, the product of one year's investment of a given quantity of input is reinvested for another year, the amount that is reinvested includes the interest accrued on the original investment during the first year. And the result of investing a given quantity of input, at a given rate of interest, for two years will be larger than the result of investing twice the quantity of input for one year.

The effect of this is that the amount of waiting involved in a particular investment is not simply proportional to the length of the investment period and the value of the input invested, but is dependent

The "amount of waiting" is not directly proportional to the investment period

also on the rate of interest.[1] In consequence, when we compare two different investment structures, it will not always be possible even to say, on purely technical grounds, which of them involves the greater amount of waiting. At one set of relative values for the different kinds of input and at one rate of interest, the one structure, and at a different set of values or a different rate of interest, the other structure, will represent the greater amount of waiting, or will be " longer " in the sense in which this term has commonly been used. If, *e.g.*, we take two investment structures of processes of production in which labour and raw materials are used in different proportions but where at one set of relative prices of labour and the

---

[1] Cf. Wicksell, *Lectures*, vol. i, p. 184 : " It should perhaps be pointed out here that the assumption that the average period of investment is independent of the rate of interest (*i.e.* of simple interest) only applies, strictly speaking, where several different capital investments relate to one and the same future act of consumption (as in Böhm-Bawerk's example). In the opposite case, where one (or more) factors of production are invested in a single capital good or durable consumption good, it may easily be seen that the average investment period will be dependent on the rate of interest, even with simple interest.

" On the whole the theory of the coincidence of the rate of interest and the ' marginal productivity of waiting ' is only applicable as an exact mathematical formula on certain abstract assumptions. This is quite natural, for waiting on the part of society as a whole — and frequently also on the part of the individual — is not a simple quantity, but is, as we have just pointed out, a complex ; ' average waiting ' as a rule exists only as a mathematical concept, without direct physical or psychic significance."

raw material the average investment period for the whole input is the same, a rise in the price of labour relatively to that of raw material will make the average period of the one of the two processes longer than that of the other, and a fall in the price of labour relatively to that of the raw material will have the opposite effect.[1]

In short, there is no way in which the variety of technical periods during which we have to wait, either for the products of different kinds of input or for particular units of the product, can be combined into an aggregate or average which can be regarded as a technical datum. No matter what procedure we were to adopt, the same technical combination of different inputs

Which of two investment structures as a whole involves more waiting cannot be decided on purely technological grounds

would, under different conditions, appear to correspond to different aggregate or average periods, and from among the different combinations sometimes one and sometimes another would appear to be the " longer ". But as the size of the product will clearly depend on the technical combination of the different kinds of input, it obviously cannot be represented as a function of any such aggregate or average period of investment. All that we can say is that it depends on the combination of the different investment periods or waiting periods which are incommensurable in purely technical terms, and that *ceteris paribus* a change in any one of these periods will cause some definite change in the, size of the product. We must therefore base the following analysis on the multiplicity of data provided by our description of the investment structure, without trying to combine them into a single productivity function of waiting or of capital.

The difficulty associated with the idea that the productivity of capital is unequivocally dependent on the length of a definite aggregate or average investment period has its counterpart in a similar difficulty connected with

[1] For further discussion of the points provisionally raised in the last two paragraphs see below, Chapter XV, pp. 199-201.

the concept of a definite supply of capital which is supposed to make it possible to " wait " for a determinate aggregate or average period. Sometimes it is assumed

The corresponding difficulty in the concept of a given supply of waiting

that a given " quantity " of capital is available in a " free " form. In this context the vague concept of " free capital " can hardly mean anything else but a stock of ready consumers' goods, which, if consumed at a given rate, will enable us to wait for a definite period for the product of current productive activity. But although this is not an impossible assumption, it is not a useful one. In the first place, the supply of capital is never given in the form of consumers' goods to the extent of more than a small fraction of its total. And in the second place, the problems which would arise if it were given in this form would be very different from the problems which actually arise under the conditions that current consumption is supplied out of current output and is at least partially due to current (mixed) input.[1]

In place of this unrealistic concept of an actual stock of consumers' goods, Böhm-Bawerk introduced [2] the more refined concept of the subsistence fund, which consists,

Böhm-Bawerk's subsistence fund

not of ready consumers' goods, but of quantities of prospective or inchoate consumers' goods which are as yet only represented by intermediate products. This stock of intermediate products, however, would correspond to one definite quantity of consumers' goods, and therefore determine a single possible waiting period, only if all of the intermediate goods were completely specific in the sense that each of them could only be turned into a fixed quantity of consumers' goods maturing at a particular date. In fact it is only in exceptional cases that the goods of which the stock of capital consists are specific in this sense. As a rule the quantity of consumers' goods that is obtainable from a given intermediate product, and the date or dates when this quantity

---

[1] Cf. Chapter VII, p. 88, footnote.

[2] Cf., however, the passage from N. W. Senior quoted above, p. 85.

will become available, will depend, just as in the case of
pure input, on how the good is used, *i.e.* with what kinds
and quantities of other capital goods it is combined. A
given stock of capital goods does not represent one single
stream of potential output of definite size and time shape ;
it represents a great number of alternatively possible
streams of different time shapes and magnitudes.

In fact what is meant by the " supply of capital ", in
so far as this term refers to things of the outside world
and not simply to a psychical attitude (that is to a preference for income streams of particular time   Meaning   of   the
shapes), can be more exactly described only   " supply of capital "
in terms of the alternative ways in which the existing
stock of non-permanent resources can be used to provide
contributions to income at different dates. Each of the
constituent parts of this stock can be used in various
ways, and in various combinations with other permanent
and non-permanent resources, to provide temporary
income streams while we wait for the return from other
resources which have been invested in processes which
will not yield their product until a later date. What
we sacrifice in order to obtain an income stream of a
particular shape is always the parts of the potential
income streams of other time shapes which we might have
had instead. The datum usually called the " supply of
capital " can thus be adequately described only in terms
of the totality of all the alternative income streams between which the existence of a certain stock of non-
permanent resources (together with the expected flow of
input) enables us to choose.

This brings us back to our starting point and the correct
formulation of our main problem. Our task is to determine
the principles on which a given stock of non-permanent
resources (including, of course, any supply   The data of the prob-
of consumers' goods not needed for current   lem
consumption) can be most effectively combined with the
expected flow of input in order to give that income stream

which is preferred to all other possible income streams. The initial datum from which we must start is a full description of the results which are known to be obtainable from various combinations of the existing stock of non-permanent resources with the expected flow of pure input. This means that the data on the technical side which we require are not simply the quantity of some homogeneous substance, some given " fund " of capital, but a complete enumeration of all the different income streams which can be obtained from given resources, and of the ways in which these income streams are affected by varying the use that is made of particular resources.[1] In other words, the only technical data are the quantities of a great variety of different resources, with full information as to how they can be used, the quantities of the product which can be derived from different ways of using them, and the dates at which the product will be obtained.[2]

In addition to this we shall, of course, require definite information about the psychical attitude of the individual or individuals concerned, their preferences as between

The problem of time preference postponed by assumption that constant income stream is desired
income streams of different time shapes, or their willingness to undergo a temporary reduction in consumption in order to be able to consume more later on, or *vice versa*. To facilitate the exposition, however, we shall divide our discussion of the problem into two parts. First we shall confine our attention to the effects of the productivity of investment, on the assumption that the object is to obtain an income stream which under all circumstances remains constant in time. Then, after having analysed the effects of productivity in this comparatively simple case, we shall proceed to study the effect of the possible willingness of the people concerned to let the size of the income stream vary in time. The exact meaning of this

---

[1] Cf. Irving Fisher, *The Nature of Capital and Income*, 1906.

[2] Cf. last section of Chapter XIV below.

assumption that people aim at a constant income stream will be explained at the beginning of the next chapter in connection with certain other simplificatory assumptions, which we shall have to employ in our first approach towards a solution of the problem.

In the remainder of the present chapter we shall merely try to sum up the problems which have arisen out of this first survey of the productivity of investment, and shall re-state them in a form in which they will be more useful in the subsequent stages of the analysis.

It will be remembered that in the first diagram which we used, the curvilinear triangle, whose area represented the part of the future output stream which already existed in the form of non-permanent resources, was drawn on the assumption that a particular method of using these resources, a particular structure of production, had been decided upon. Many other ways of combining these resources with the expected stream of input would be possible, and each of these would give an output stream which would have to be represented by a triangle of different shape. We have seen that it is impossible to represent the size or shape of this output stream as being dependent on some single time interval applying to the investment of all the different kinds of input (some single aggregate or average period of investment), and that we have to start by analysing the effects of variations in those individual investment or waiting periods which can be isolated.

The general relation between the size of the output and the range of investment periods

This means that all that we can say in practice is that if the use made of all other input is already determined, changes in the investment periods of particular units or groups of input will lead to certain known changes in the size of the product. And in all cases where the lengthening of any such individual investment period needs to be taken into account as a real alternative, its effect will be to increase the product obtained from the input concerned.

But the size of the increase in the product which will be brought about by any particular extension of an individual investment period will depend on the use that is made of the whole of the rest of the input. The size of the return cannot therefore be regarded merely as a function of this particular investment period : it must be regarded as a function of all the individual investment periods of the different units of input.

This is perhaps the place where it should be expressly pointed out that while so far we have assumed that the physical product of every individual unit of input can be

Only effects of marginal changes need be known for purposes of further analysis

determined, this assumption is not essential for our further analysis. All we need to know for the purposes of what follows are the effects of marginal changes [1] and particularly the relations between the changes in the investment periods of those particular units of input which it may be advisable to use differently in the given position and the changes in the total quantity of capital. Strictly speaking it would for this purpose not even be necessary to know the total length of these investment periods. It would be quite sufficient if we knew the amount by which a particular investment period is lengthened or shortened, that is, the interval of time between the moment when (in consequence of the change in question) the output stream is decreased, and the moment when some additional output, which is substituted for it, will mature. According as the date of the new output is later or earlier than that of the output which has been sacrificed to obtain the former, the investment period would have been lengthened or shortened, and we need in this connection not refer back to the date when the input is invested. Since, however,

---

[1] Cf. Wicksell, *Lectures,* vol. i, p. 260 : " Fundamentally it is just as absurd to ask how much labour is invested in either one or the other annual use as to try to find out what part of a pasture goes into wool and what part into mutton. It is only at the margin of production that these quantities can be differentiated and have a concrete significance assigned to them."

we shall as a rule know which units of input we have used differently in order to bring about an increase of output at one date and a decrease at another, we shall normally have no more difficulty in ascertaining the total length of the investment period of a particular unit of resources than in finding the marginal change in that period.

It is, however, undeniably true that the technically given structure of investment is rarely if ever so simple in character that particular units of input can always be unequivocally ascribed to particular quan- It is not always pos-
tities of input. The popularity which the sible to connect indi-
vidual units of input
examples of the growing of trees or the with individual units
maturing of wine have enjoyed with of output
writers on this subject is due to the fact that these examples correspond pretty closely to this simplest of cases, the " point input — point output " case. But to assume that all cases of investment can be treated on these lines is to evade the main problems. As we have seen, the relationship between the product and the input used will as a rule be in the nature of a joint demand for resources to be used at different moments to produce the output of a given moment, or of a joint supply of products spread over a period of time and due to the input invested at one moment, or it will be a combination of both. Sometimes we shall be able to say only that a particular quantity of output is due to all the input invested over a period of time, without being able to decide on a technical basis what part of the output is due to the quantities of input invested at particular dates. At other times the only thing which can be regarded as a technical datum will be the fact that the input invested at a particular date brings forth a stream of output extending over a period of time, and we shall not be in a position to state in general terms what part of this stream is to be attributed to particular units of this input. And even more frequently the only technical link which we shall be able to establish will be the connection between a stream of input stretching over

a period of time and a stream of output stretching over another period of time.

In a great many cases, though not in all, the fact that the connection between these aggregates of input and aggregates of output is not absolutely rigid makes it Use of the principle of possible to analyse the connection further.
variation   Whenever the amounts of input, which are invested at particular stages of the process, can (at least within certain limits) be continuously varied, it will be possible to observe the effects of marginal variations of input on the quantity of output at particular dates. Where we have to deal with time-consuming processes of production it will as a rule be possible to invest some of the units of input at an earlier stage, *i.e.* for a longer period, or to invest more units for a given period, and to observe the effect of this variation on the magnitude of the product maturing at a given date. And in this sense it will be possible to state how the product will vary, *ceteris paribus*, with variations in the investment period of this factor. Similarly, where we have to deal with durable goods, it will often be possible to observe that changes in the amounts of particular kinds of input invested in them will bring about definite increments or decrements to the services rendered by these goods at definite dates. And then it will be possible here, too, to say that, *ceteris paribus*, the investment of an increasing proportion of the total supply of the factor in question for longer periods will bring about increases in output at a definite rate.

But even where there is this continuous variability of the investment structure which makes it possible to establish the contributions to output due to changes in the investment periods of particular factors, we have still to face the difficulty that this functional dependence of the size of the product on the investment period of the unit of input concerned is only true for a particular arrangement of all other input, and will be different for any other arrangement. And the effects of variations in the investment periods of different units of input cannot, as we have seen, be set out in any unequivocal way according to the length of the periods so that one complex investment structure can always be said to be longer than another, or so that the total size of the product can be described as being dependent on the length of the investment structure.

Finally there is the difficulty, to which we have so far only alluded by implication, that in many cases there will be whole blocks or ranges of input and similar blocks or ranges of output between the individual units of which it is impossible to establish any connection by the principle of marginal variation, because the rate at which input has to be invested at different times and *Sometimes we cannot establish any physical relationship beyond that between aggregates of input and aggregates of output* the rate at which output matures are not capable of variation but are rigidly fixed for a particular process. In these cases, as we shall see, all that we have to go upon is the variation in the value of the product concerned relative to the variation in the total quantity of input devoted to its production.

Such, then, is the variety of possible variations in the investment structure which we shall have to take into account in our search for the principles on which any stock of non-permanent resources can be combined with the expected flow of input in the most advantageous manner.

CHAPTER XII

PLANNING FOR A CONSTANT OUTPUT STREAM

WE must begin our discussion of the ways in which all
resources must be organised to obtain the best result by
stating more fully the assumptions on which we shall

Assumptions on which
the principles deter-
mining the time struc-
ture of production will
be first discussed :
(a) The supply of re-
sources
proceed. Our starting point will be a
community which is equipped from the
outset with a stock of many kinds of non-
permanent resources, and which expects
to command a constant flow of pure input
which can be combined with the capital assets in the
manifold ways already described to provide output streams
of different sizes and time shapes.

Whatever provisional plan for the combination of
these different kinds of resources we assume to be contemplated, there will always be numerous possibilities of
increasing the size of the product obtained from particular
units of input or particular capital items by using them in
such a way that the date at which they will yield their
product is postponed. The range of these possibilities will
be very wide. Investment periods which are already very
long may be lengthened further as well as those which
are comparatively short. And in some cases a relatively
small extension of an investment period or of a range of
investment periods may cause a relatively large increase
of the product, while in other cases a very considerable
extension of an investment period may result only in a
small increase of the product.

The reason why only some of these possibilities of increasing the product from particular units of input will be
turned to account is, of course, that every postponement
of the return from these units of input will cause, *ceteris*

paribus, a gap in the expected income stream at some point, and this gap will have to be filled, if the output stream is to be constant, by investing other units of input for correspondingly shorter periods. So long as there is any limitation on the extent to which the members of our society are willing to restrict their consumption for the sake of increases in output which may be obtained by investing input for longer periods, there will always be the problem of deciding what part of the available input should be invested for relatively long periods and what part should be used to provide sustenance in the interval before the product of the input invested for the longer periods accrues.

The decision as to which of the alternatively possible combinations of the resources is the most advantageous, and the question of how to proceed in every individual case in order to arrive at this best total arrangement, raises, of course, a value problem of the most general nature. It is (*b*) The general value problem will be studied for a " simple economy " a value problem which would arise independently of any possibility of exchange between different persons, since even an isolated individual would have to take account of the same factor in making his dispositions. In cases of this kind it is always useful to commence by studying the problem in its most general form, *i.e.* in the case where a single person administers all the available resources in the service of a single system of ends.[1] This assumption allows us to investigate the influence of the technological data in their simplest form, without having to take account of the differences in aims of a multiplicity of persons and the effects of a different distribution of resources between them. It is only in a second and separate stage of the analysis that we shall link up the result obtained under this assumption with the explanation of prices in an exchange economy.

[1] Cf. the passage from Marshall quoted above, Chapter II, p. 27, footnote 1.

But although we shall employ the idea of an economic system directed by a single will, we shall not go back to the case of a single individual, a Robinson Crusoe who —that is, for a com· works in complete isolation. Such an indi-
munist society — vidual would obviously be unable to make use of more than a very few of the advantages of time-consuming processes, since most of them are applicable only where production is carried on on a fairly large scale and where there is scope for a good deal of specialisation or division of labour. It will be more helpful, therefore, to consider the case of a communist society in which all economic activity is directed by the will of a single dictator or general manager. I shall retain this assumption for this and the next six chapters and shall postpone consideration of the problems of a market until Chapter XVIII.[1]

We shall assume that this communist society is equipped, at the moment when we begin to consider it, with a stock of non-permanent resources of many different — which has previ- kinds. Some of these will be the result
ously been station- of the productive activity of the past and
ary— others will be wasting natural resources of various kinds. The problem of our dictator will then be how to make the best use of this stock, *i.e.* how to derive from it the stream of income which is preferred to all the other streams that are also technically possible. We may assume that in the past the amount of these non-permanent resources, or of " capital ", which was used in each of the various industries and processes, was determined either arbitrarily or else in accordance with some traditional routine, but without any definite calculations

[1] On the significance of this methodological procedure, cf. Friedrich Wieser, *Theory of Social Economy*, New York, 1927. It need scarcely be added that such a discussion of how a communist dictator ought to act if he wanted to obtain an economic distribution of resources does in no way prejudice the question whether he could so act ; we are, in other words, assuming an omniscient dictator without, of course, believing that such a dictator could ever exist.

of profitability. We shall assume in particular that our dictator has disdained to take account of the interest factor in his calculations. But we may suppose that it has now become so evident that the traditional distribution of these resources between the different industries is wasteful that the dictator feels compelled to attempt a redistribution which will secure the use of the resources to the best advantage. On what principle will he have to act ?

We mentioned in the last chapter that, in discussing this problem, we should at first make a further simplifying assumption. We shall assume that what the dictator aims at is to produce the greatest possible income stream which remains constant in size. This means that for the present we shall exclude the possibility both of *— and now aims at producing in the future the greatest possible constant income stream* temporarily reducing the income stream in order to increase it by a larger amount at a later date, and of a temporary increase in consumption (even if advantageous because it would not entail any considerable reduction in the income stream at later dates). This assumption that under all conditions the aim will be to secure a constant income stream is, of course, highly unrealistic,[1] and will be removed at a more advanced stage of the analysis. But for the time being, and until we expressly introduce more specific assumptions about the willingness of people to sacrifice part of their present income in order to obtain additions to future income, or *vice versa*, this assumption will help us in much the same way as the hypothesis of the stationary state helps us in general economic analysis.

---

[1] This is particularly the case if we interpret our assumption in the strict sense of the dictator having to reach at once the maximum income stream which can be permanently maintained. But if we want to exclude any consideration of the sacrifice he is willing to make in order to increase future income at the expense of present income, we shall have to interpret our assumption in this strict form, and not allow him any time during which to approach this maximum rate of consumption — although output may increase more slowly if consumption in the meantime can be supplied from stocks.

But it is first of all necessary to define the concept of a constant income stream more exactly. If it is taken too literally, to mean that the income must also be of Meaning of a constant constant composition, *i.e.* that it must con-income stream sist at every moment of the same combination of the various commodities, a great many of the possible improvements in the use of the available resources will be excluded. Making better use of the existing resources will not only mean producing certain commodities in different ways ; it will also mean extending the production of some of them at the expense of the production of others. And even though we do assume that the level of total satisfaction has to be maintained constant throughout, our dictator will evidently have a much wider range of possibilities of improvement before him if he is allowed, in the course of reorganising or readapting the existing structure of production, to substitute additional quantities of some commodities at certain points for equivalent amounts of other commodities.

By admitting this possibility of changes in the composition of the income stream we are, of course, leaving the completely stationary conditions which have formed the subject of most of our discussion up to this point. Henceforth we shall deal with equilibrium conditions in the wider sense explained above in Chapter II, that is, we shall merely assume that the data given to our dictator at the beginning of the period remain unchanged ; but these data include foreseen changes in circumstances which will make him plan from the beginning for all those successive changes in his allocation of resources, which the conditions of the moment will cause to appear appropriate.

A constant income stream then has to be defined not simply in physical terms as such and such quantities of each of the commodities included, but in value terms. It need not be of The best way of describing it will, of course, constant composition be by the apparatus of indifference curves, or rather n-dimensional indifference surfaces. If we assume that the preferences of our dictator at every successive moment are represented by an identical [1] system of indifference curves, then an income stream of constant value will have to consist at every successive moment of a combination of goods which occupies a position on the same indifference surface. At successive points of time additional quantities of some commodities (or perhaps commodities which were known but not produced previously) can be substituted for some of the commodities available at earlier moments, but they must always be in such quantities that the additions just compensate for the deductions without making the total in any way more or less attractive.

We have assumed that from the date at which the rearrangement of resources is made our dictator has to keep the income stream constant. His task, subject to this condition, is to maximise the income *Every change in disposition of resources* stream by making the best possible use of *involves two shifts in* the available opportunities for increasing *opposite directions* output by investing some of his total input for longer periods and some for shorter periods. We have already seen that every attempt to improve upon the original arrangement of the resources, which also yielded a constant income stream but not one of optimum size, necessarily entails this double shifting of resources in opposite directions in time. The postponement of the date at which the return from any particular investment will become available will mean, *ceteris paribus*, that though the income stream will be swelled at this later date to a higher level than it would otherwise have reached, it will be reduced at some earlier date below that level. This

---

[1] We have to postulate identity of tastes at successive moments in this sense in order to give the concept of a constant income stream an objective meaning. The subjective views of the person in question as to what increment of income at one date just suffices to balance a decrement at another date belong to the phenomenon of time preference which we want to reserve for later treatment. See Chapter XVII below, and Hayek, **1935b**.

gap will have to be filled by some reshuffling of resources. And if the whole transaction is to be advantageous it must be possible to shift some other resources from production for the later date to production for the earlier date at a cost which is smaller than the gain from the first operation.

Let us first consider variations in the investment periods of individual units of input in a case where it is easy to follow the connection between changes in their invest-

The extension of the investment periods of individual units of input

ment periods and changes in the product, *i.e.* a case where the investment period of a single unit or a small group of units of input can be altered without at the same time altering the investment periods of other units. Under the conditions that we have assumed there will always be some instances where the profit to be obtained by lengthening the investment periods of individual units of input will be particularly conspicuous. A certain material, say a quantity of coal, which had originally been intended to heat a house during some period in the immediate future, might, if it could be made available for smelting iron ore, make possible the production of certain urgently needed tools which would at a later date make a very considerable contribution to the output stream.

But if advantage is to be taken of this opportunity and the total income stream is nevertheless to be kept constant from now onwards, two further adjustments in

The compensatory shortening of the investment periods of other input

the disposition over the available input will be necessary. First, it will be necessary to fill the gap created in the earlier segment of the income stream, at the expense of the later segment, so that the income will again be equally large at both dates but larger than it was before the rearrangement. In many instances the readjustment will have to take place in an indirect, roundabout way, involving changes in the use made of a great many different kinds of input. But to begin with a comparatively simple case, we shall assume that the change which just compensates for the extension of the investment period of our quantity of coal consists in using for current consumption certain input which under the old scheme would have gone to produce some commodity which would have matured at the time when the product of the coal is due to mature under the new scheme. Assume, for instance, that, at the time when the new increased product of the coal is due to mature, some durable consumer's good will wear out and would under the old arrangement have had to be replaced : but as it is decided not to replace this good, the input which between now and the date concerned would have been used for that purpose becomes available for current consumption.

But after this second rearrangement we shall still only have increased the income during two segments of the future income stream. And to make it constant all the time it will be necessary to make further exchanges of a similar nature in the utilisation of input accruing at all future dates. *Similar changes will have to be made in the use of input at all future dates* This means that not only the investment periods of one pair of present units of input, but also the investment periods of all the corresponding units of input accruing at later dates will have to be adjusted in like manner in order to make the future income stream constant.

Hence one effect of the change will be that, instead of the services of the durable good, we shall, from a certain date onwards, have the services of the new product of the coal. And since a corresponding quantity of coal currently produced will be used in the same manner at all future *The net effect of the double change is a new constant income stream* dates, or since the labour and other input invested in this quantity of coal will in the future always be invested for the longer period and will yield a correspondingly larger product, this change will mean a permanent addition to the future income stream. Against this we have to balance in the first place the temporary gap caused by

investing the coal for a longer period. We shall assume
for the purposes of the argument that the services which
we can expect to obtain from the product of the coal
will be just equal in value to the services which the
durable consumer's good renders while it lasts. In the
second place, we have to take account of the decrease in
the product from the input which would have been used,
under the old arrangement, to replace the durable good,
and which is now used, under the new arrangement, to
serve current consumption.

The net effect of these various changes on the size of
the income stream can be shown more easily by means of
a simple diagram (Fig. 10). The two dotted lines marked
Diagrammatic Illus-   *A* and *B* in each of the two parts of the
tration   diagram represent the streams of input
which, under the original arrangement, would have been
currently used to reproduce the quantity of coal and to
replace the durable good respectively. This original

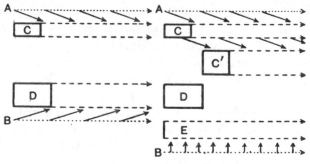

Fig. 10

arrangement is shown on the left-hand part of the diagram,
and the right-hand part represents the situation after the
change has been made. The blocks marked *C* and *D*
show the stream of services to be obtained from the coal
and the durable good respectively : the height of the
blocks represents the rate at which the services will
accrue and their length represents the period during

which they will accrue. The continuation of these blocks in dotted lines in the left-hand part of the diagram indicates the similar services which would be obtained if C and D were continually replaced. This replacement through the investment of input is indicated by arrows.

In the original position (shown on the left) the groups of input A and B would be continuously invested to reproduce goods similar to C (coal) and D (the durable consumer's good). But under the new arrangement, where the product of the investment of A (*i.e.* the coal) is invested further in order to give later a larger product, C', the flow of services B has to be used for direct consumption as it becomes available, and accordingly gives a smaller product. This decreased return from B is shown by the narrow strip E at the bottom of the right-hand half of the diagram. Since the current use of a constant stream of input will obviously give us a constant stream of output, it is clear that, in order for the total income stream to be constant also, the rate at which services will be obtained from C' will have to be exactly equal to the rate at which services will in the near future be obtained from D. In the preceding paragraph we assumed that this was so, and it will now be clear why this assumption was necessary.

This last conclusion, which may at first sound surprising, becomes plausible immediately we look at the situation in a slightly different way. It is really the existence of the stream of services embodied in the durable good (D) which makes it possible to wait (without temporarily reducing the income stream below its previous level) for the product of some other resources. In the initial situation it was the stream of input B which was invested (to reproduce goods of the type of D). In the new situation another kind of input, *i.e.* the coal, which has for the most part still to be produced by the investment of A, is invested instead and B is used for current consumption. Instead of a single good D, we might of course have taken any group or aggregate of non-permanent resources which would have served the same purpose. In order to make the further investment of C possible in the case assumed, all that is necessary is to find some group of commodities which, in the interval before the product of C becomes available, will give services that are equal in quantity to those which C will produce later.

But what decides whether the whole transaction is advantageous or not ?   The part of the total income stream which consists first of the services of D, and then

The conditions under which the rearrangement will give a net gain

of C' and the goods that replace it, is just equal in value to the part which was formerly obtained from D and which could have been continuously obtained by replacing D. The net change in the total size of the income stream will therefore depend on the relative magnitude of the return formerly obtained from the group of resources A (shown by the strip marked C on the top left-hand side of the diagram) and the return now obtained from the group of resources B (shown by the strip marked E at the bottom of the right-hand half of the diagram). If the latter is greater than the former the difference is clearly a net gain. If it were smaller the transaction would have resulted in a net decrease of the total income stream instead of an increase.

These income streams (C and E) are the product of resources either of which could equally well have produced an income stream of the size of D or C' if it had been invested to yield its product later by an interval corresponding to the duration of D. But if the product (C) of A is invested further for this period, the final product of the magnitude of D will grow from a smaller magnitude than if B is used instead, *i.e.* the rate of increase obtained by extending the investment period of A will be greater than that obtained from the extension of the investment period of B. This means that we get a given part of the output stream, of the size of D, at a smaller sacrifice of other output by investing *A* instead of *B* for the longer period and are therefore in a position to increase the size of the total output stream.

It will now be evident that whenever the rate of increase of the product which can be obtained by lengthening the investment periods of some units of input is greater than the rate of decrease of the product caused by shortening the investment periods of other units of input by the same interval of time, it will be advantageous to make the corresponding changes. So long as there are differences in the rates of return that are obtained by investing different units of input for any given period, it will be possible to go on increasing the total size of the income stream in this way. Hence the condition for maximising the total income stream which we have been seeking is that this rate of increase of the product due to an extension of the investment period by a given interval shall be the same for all investments.

We shall, however, soon see that, in the form in which it has just been stated, this condition is a necessary but not a sufficient condition for fully determining the optimum position. The rates of increase of the product which are due to the extension of the investment period by any given interval must be the same for all units of input. But this says nothing about the relationship which has to prevail between the rates of increase due to investments for different intervals. As we shall see, it is only after this question has been considered that a complete solution to our problem can be formulated. But since a full discussion of this point will take considerable time, and since it is closely connected with several other points, it must be postponed to a later chapter. In the meantime it is necessary to add some further remarks on the concept of a " rate of increase of the product " and the terms in which it is measured.

If we could assume that the relative values of the different commodities always remained the same, that is, if our constant income stream were also of constant composition, then the concept of a uniform rate of increase for all investments made at one point of time and maturing at another would present no difficulties. Whenever the sacrifice of a given quantity of one commodity at the earlier date led to the production of an increased quantity of the same commodity at the later date, the ratio between these quantities would have to be the same for all the commodities concerned. And in the probably more numerous cases where the sacrifice of a given quantity of one commodity at the earlier date led to the production of a quantity of another commodity at the later date, these two quantities would have to be such that their value equivalents in terms of any third commodity at the two dates would bear the same ratio to one another. There would then be a uniform rate of increase over the interval concerned which, in terms of no matter what commodity we expressed it, would show the same numerical value.

The rates of increase when the kind of output changes

We have already observed, however, that this sort of stationariness is not compatible with making the best use of the existing stock of non-permanent resources. During the initial rearrangement of the resources certain substitutions of one kind of commodity for another at successive dates will be part of the plan. And the same will apply, although to a lesser and rapidly diminishing degree, to all later stages of the process of change. The reason is, of course, that we start out with an assortment of non-permanent resources, which is the result of a particular historical development, and which will consist in large part of items which it is either impossible or else unprofitable to reproduce. Since the form in which these resources exist at the beginning, and at every subsequent

Why the relative values of the different commodities will usually change during the process of adjustment

stage, will exert an influence on the kind of resources by which they will be replaced, and since the resources existing at every moment are determined by past conditions, we have to deal with a process of continuous change. Even if we could assume that at the initial moment, when our dictator makes his new plan, he is in possession of complete knowledge of all future conditions, this plan would have to envisage an infinite series of changes. These changes would, it is true, rapidly decrease in magnitude as time went on, and would after a while become insignificant, but in principle they would continue in some small degree for ever.

This means that we shall have to deal with a stream of different goods whose relative values will be constantly changing, at first, perhaps, quite considerably and even later to some extent. In such a system the concept of a uniform rate of increase of all investments made from one point of time to another point of time is much less simple, but it still has a quite definite meaning. We now have to take account of the possibility of a change in the value of every single commodity relatively to the values of other commodities. But it will still be true that, measured in terms of any one commodity, the rate of increase will have to be the same for all commodities. The actual numerical value of this rate of increase will, however, be different, according as one commodity or another is chosen as the standard of comparison or "numéraire".

The rates of increase when the values of the different commodities change

This statement requires some elaboration. Let us consider two points of time of which the earlier one represents the date at which numerous investments are made and the later one the date when these investments mature. Let us assume further that the relative values of the different commodities are different at the two dates. If we now take any one commodity (defined in technical terms) which is used at both dates and of which the

quantity available at the later date can be increased at
the expense of the quantity available at the earlier date,
we shall have a definite quantitative rate of increase due
to the " investment " of that commodity. For another
commodity we shall probably find a different rate of
increase. Equilibrium (*i.e.* the most advantageous disposition over the resources) requires that these two rates
of increase between the two dates shall stand in a definite
relationship to the relative values of the two commodities
at the two dates. If we take such quantities of the two
commodities as are of equal value at the first date, and
make them increase by investment at their different
individual rates, the quantities of the two commodities
obtained at the second date must again be of equal value.
This, of course, amounts to the same thing as the statement made before, that in terms of any one commodity
(any " numéraire ") the rate of increase must be equal
for all commodities. Although the quantitative ratio
between the physical amount invested at the earlier date
and the physical amount obtained at the later date may
be different for different commodities, the value equivalents in terms of the " numéraire " at the two dates
must bear the same ratio to one another for all commodities.

It is probably unnecessary to emphasise that there is
no way in which this multitude of different " own rates of
interest " (as Mr. Keynes has called these rates of increase
in terms of particular commodities) can
be reduced to one single rate which has
a stronger claim than any other to be regarded as *the* rate of productivity of investment. To distinguish, in any particular case, between
the part which is due to circumstances affecting the value
of the particular commodity and the part which is due
to the productivity of investment is just as impossible as
to divide the change in the relative value of two commodities into the part which is due to a change in the

No one rate of increase can be regarded as " the " rate of productivity of investment

value of the one, and the part which is due to a change in the value of the other. Although the search for this philosopher's stone is probably still being pursued by some economists, nothing more need be said about it here.

CHAPTER XIII

COMPOUND INTEREST AND THE INSTANTANEOUS
RATE OF INTEREST

IN the last chapter we found one of the conditions which must be fulfilled if the maximum constant income stream is to be obtained from a given stock of non-permanent resources in collaboration with a constant

A uniform rate of increase for all investments between any two points of time is only one condition of maximum

flow of input. This is that the rate of increase of the product which is due to the investment of input from any one point of time to any other point of time shall be the same for all units of input that are invested for this particular time interval. It will be remembered that when we speak of " the rate of increase being equal " we do not mean that the rates of increase in physical terms must necessarily be equal for all the different commodities, but only that the rates of increase in value terms must be equal.

This conclusion, however, applies only to a particular interval of time. So far nothing has been said about the relationship between the rates of increase over different

Rates of increase for investments for different intervals of time

intervals of time, whether these intervals are of the same length but begin and end at different moments of time, or whether they are of different lengths. In so far as different but equidistant pairs of moments are concerned, one would be inclined to assume that the rate of increase would have to be the same. And under perfectly stationary conditions this would undoubtedly be true. But, as we have seen, a completely stationary state could be reached only gradually, and after a very long time ; therefore as long as the relative values of the different commodities con-

170

tinued to change, the rate at which any unit of investment in their production increased would necessarily change also. There would be no necessary relationship between the rates of increase over different periods in this case, except in so far as the periods overlapped, and then it would become a special instance of the problem of the rates which will rule for periods of different lengths.

This latter problem may be best considered by comparing the rates which will prevail during two or more very short periods of equal length immediately succeeding each other with the rate for the longer period to which they add up. If, for Intervals of different lengths example, we call the present moment 1 and consider two later moments which we will call 2 and 3, the question we have to answer is what will be the relationship of the rates of increase obtained by investing from 1 to 2 and from 2 to 3, to the rate of increase obtained by investing from 1 to 3. The answer will evidently depend on the conditions under which it will be impossible to increase the total product by investing more for the shorter periods and less for the longer period or *vice versa*.

At first one might be inclined to assume that this condition will be satisfied when the increase in the product obtained by investing a given quantity of input for the longer period is equal to the sum of the Rates of increase not simply proportional to length of interval increments of the product obtained if corresponding quantities of input are invested for each of the two shorter periods. But on closer examination this answer proves to be incorrect. It can easily be shown that equilibrium requires that the rate of increase over the longer period should be equal not to the sum of the (percentage) [1] rates of increase over the two shorter periods but to their *product*. If, for example, the rate of increase due to the investment over the shorter periods is the same for both periods and amounts in each

---

[1] The essential point is that the rate is expressed as a ratio and not as a simple time rate in absolute terms. Cf. below, p. 177.

case to an increase to 1·01 of the value of the input invested, then the rate of increase over the longer period will have to be such as to give a product not simply 1·02 times the value of the input invested but 1·01 × 1·01 or 1·0201 times that value. ,

The proof is as follows. Let us suppose that at first the distribution of input between the longer and the two shorter investment periods was such that the rate of increase obtained over each of the two shorter periods was just half as great as the rate of increase obtained by investing for the longer period. If now some quantity of input which used to be invested for the longer period is invested only for the shorter period, *i.e.* from 1 to 2 instead of from 1 to 3, it will give an addition to the output at 2, which, compared with the original value of the input invested, will already show an increase by half the amount by which that input would have increased by the end of the longer period. And it will be possible, without changing the amount of output originally available at 2, to invest an amount of input equivalent to the output obtained at 2, from 2 to 3. This amount, which will already represent say 1·01 times the amount first invested, will then further increase to 1·01 times its present magnitude or, that is, to 1·0201 times its original magnitude. This means that if the rate of increase obtainable by investing for the longer period were only twice as large as the rate of increase over each of the two shorter periods, a greater return could be obtained by investing for the shorter period only in the first instance, and then reinvesting an amount equivalent to the resulting product for the second short period. It would be profitable to invest for the longer period only if the rate of increase were at least equal to the product of the rates of increase obtainable over the two shorter periods.

So long as we assume completely stationary conditions and, consequently, that the rates of increase for all periods of equal length will be the same, all that this result means is that the rates of increase over periods of different lengths will have to correspond to the familiar law of compound interest. The rate of increase over any long period which is divisible into n shorter periods of equal length will in general be equal to the nth power of the rate of increase applying to any of the shorter periods. And, as will soon become apparent, it is really compound interest which is the fundamental phenomenon : " simple interest " is only a simplification which is convenient for practical purposes but is rather misleading if used in theoretical analysis. But for the present I want to emphasise the still more general concept of the rate of increase over any period being equal to the product of the rates of increase during all the shorter periods which it contains. These latter rates may, as we have seen, vary from one short interval to the next, but the rate will have to be uniform for all the input invested during any one such interval.

The rate ruling for the longer interval must be equal to the product of the rates for all the shorter intervals into which it can be divided

The relationship which has to prevail between the rates of increase over shorter and longer periods must of course apply however short we make the shorter intervals of which we suppose the longer ones to be composed. And by decreasing the length of these shorter periods further and further, until at the limit they approach mere moments of time, we finally arrive at a concept which will prove useful when we come to give a more exact formulation of the connection between the productivity of investment and interest. This concept is the instantaneous rate of interest or " rate of interest at a moment of time " (Wicksell's *Verzinsungs-energie* : literally, " force of interest ").[1]

The instantaneous rate of interest

The meaning of this concept may be best explained by comparing it with the concept of the velocity at a

---

[1] Cf. Wicksell, *Lectures*, vol. i, p. 178, and I. Fisher, *The Nature of Capital and Income* (1906), p. 359, where the same magnitude is described as the " rate of interest per annum computed continuously ".

moment of time of a body which is moving at a uniformly accelerating speed. At least for stationary conditions, where the force of interest would be the same at every moment, the case of a uniformly accelerating velocity provides a complete parallel. In this case the velocity of the body will change during any interval of time and, in consequence, the actual distance travelled during any interval will not give an exact expression of its speed at a moment of time. Similarly our rate of increase of the value of any unit of input invested will change during any interval, however short, and no actual increase during any such interval will give us an exact measure of the rate of increase at a moment of time. And because, since movement can be described only by stating the distance travelled during some finite period of time, the only way of stating the speed at a moment of time is to state the distance which would have been covered if the instantaneous speed had continued for a period of time, therefore, since growth in value can be described only by stating the amount of increase during some finite period of time, the only way of stating a rate of increase at a moment of time is to state the amount of the increase that would have taken place if the instantaneous rate of increase had prevailed for a definite period of time. And just as we speak of a velocity of so-and-so many feet per second, although the velocity of a falling body never remains constant even for a second, so we speak of an instantaneous rate of interest of so many per cent per annum, although of course this rate does not actually continue throughout the year, but applies only to a particular moment.

In more concrete terms, an instantaneous rate of interest of 5 per cent per annum will, in consequence of the continuous compounding of interest accruing at every Relationship to effect-   moment, mean an effective increase by the ive rate of interest   end of the year of 5·127 per cent, while in order to obtain an effective increase of only 5 per cent on the initial value by the end of the year, an instantaneous rate of only 4·873 per cent per annum would be required.

This relationship between the instantaneous rate (expressed per annum) and the resulting effective increase over the year if interest is compounded continuously, can best be shown by means of the familiar — Illustrated by compound interest curve. The characteristic attribute of a compound interest curve (as of all "exponential" curves of which it is a particular example)

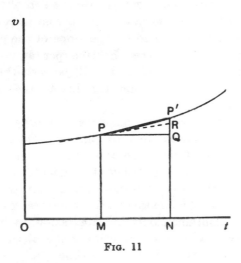

FIG. 11

is that at every point on the curve the tangent is always in the same proportion to the corresponding value of the ordinate. If, for example, the ordinate of the point P in the diagram (Fig. 11) is 2 and the slope of the tangent at this point is 2/5, then the tangent at the point P' with an ordinate of 3 will be 3/5, and so on. Now the slope of the tangent at any point divided by the ordinate represents the instantaneous rate of interest, or force of interest, at that point. Its immediate expression, a rate of increase divided by an absolute quantity, is, however, a pure number with no obvious meaning. It assumes concrete meaning only if we express it in terms of the proportional increase in the original quantity which it would have caused if it had continued to operate for a definite period, say one year. If in Fig. 11 the distance between the points M and N on the abscissa represents such an interval of one year, then the ratio of QR to RN will represent the force of interest expressed *per annum*.

It is at once apparent that the effective increase over the year is greater than this percentage. At this rate of instantaneous compound interest, the initial quantity MP will actually have increased by the end of the year to NP'. And the average rate of the actual increase during the year will be expressed by the slope of the chord PP'. This slope represents the effective per annum rate of interest in the usual sense. It will be seen that it must necessarily be greater than the instantaneous rate or force of interest.

The situation becomes considerably more complicated, of course, as soon as we drop the assumption that the force of interest is the same at every moment, which will be true only under completely stationary conditions. In cases where the instantaneous rate is not the same at every moment, the effective rate of interest can, strictly speaking, be obtained only by integrating, over the relevant interval, a function describing the absolute rate of interest at successive moments of time.

Before we proceed further it will be useful to consider Ambiguity of the in greater detail a distinction which is term "rate" implicit in the discussion of the last section, and which, if not clearly understood, is liable to cause considerable confusion.

The source of this confusion is the ambiguity of meaning, or perhaps merely the inexact use, in common parlance, of the term "rate". The rate at which anything proceeds refers in the first instance to the absolute magnitude of the movement or other change during a unit of time. It is in this sense that we speak of movement at the rate of so many feet per second, of wage payments at the rate of so many shillings per hour, etc. But when we are referring not merely to the rate of flow, but to the rate of continuous change in some magnitude, we can also express this rate as a ratio or proportion of that magnitude itself. This is, of course, what we do when we express the rate as a figure *per cent*. It is a time rate expressed as a ratio or proportion.

So long as we think of interest merely as a flow of income which is drawn and consumed continuously as it matures, there is not much danger that this particular way of expressing it will mislead. The difficulty arises only when there are periods during which interest is allowed to accumulate with the principal; this may be the case either between the dates at which interest is periodically paid, or over the longer period before a particular investment bears fruit. In such cases, where we have to deal not simply with a continuous flow but with a continuous growth of an initial magnitude at a given rate, the distinction becomes important. For a constant rate of growth in the absolute sense will be not a constant but a decreasing proportional rate (*i.e.* a rate expressed as a ratio of the magnitude which the quantity in question has reached at any moment), and a constant rate in the sense of a ratio will mean an increasing rate in the absolute sense of the term.[1]

The "rate" of interest a rate of growth expressed as a ratio

It is because the rate of interest is a time rate expressed as a ratio that, in order to obtain it, we have to divide the absolute rate of increase of the product due to a given extension of the investment period by the amount of the product. The difficulty which this seems occasionally to cause is avoided if the difference between the

[1] Cf. F. H. Knight, 1936, p. 444 : " The ambiguity of the word ' rate ' is most unfortunate. In expressions such as the ' rate of interest ' the word is inaccurately used as it combines a time rate of flow (correct meaning) with a ratio of this flow to a principal. And in addition there is really involved an instantaneous rate (ratio) of growth with reference to a continuously changing base."

concept of a rate in the absolute sense and the concept of a rate in the sense of a proportion or ratio (as used in the term " rate of interest ") is always kept in mind. The rate of increase of the product is expressed as an absolute quantity per unit of time ; it becomes a rate of interest if we express it as such-and-such a proportion (or percentage) of the total magnitude which is increasing. And the relevant total magnitude for this purpose is of course not that existing at the time the (pure) input was applied, but the magnitude to which it has grown by the point of time at which we wish to describe the rate of increase.

CHAPTER XIV

THE MARGINAL PRODUCTIVITY OF INVESTMENT
AND THE RATE OF INTEREST

THE analysis of the last chapter has provided us with a convenient means of giving numerical expression to the magnitude which in the chapter preceding it we called, rather clumsily, the " rate of increase of the product due to the extension of the investment period ". But to identify this magnitude, as we did in the last chapter, with the rate of interest was somewhat premature — even though by the rate of interest we mean here merely the general rate of return on real capital and disregard the problems of the relation between this rate and the rate at which money is lent and borrowed. Strictly speaking we can call it the rate of interest only in an equilibrium situation where the " rates of increase " have been equalised for all the different investments. So long as we are investigating the conditions of equilibrium and are talking about the rates of increase due to particular investments it will be convenient to use the expression " the marginal productivity of *an* investment ". This phrase is here introduced as a technical term with the specific meaning of the ratio of increase of output from a particular unit of input, due to an extension of the investment period of that unit of input, and expressed as a time rate.

We shall now proceed to apply the general rules governing the relationships between the marginal productivity of investments for different periods to the problem of determining the choice of the period for which any individual unit of input will be invested. We shall first confine our atten-

The distribution of investments over periods of different length

tion to the case where the investment period of the particular unit of input can be continuously varied, and where the product due to the investment of this unit of input can be clearly isolated.

This does not mean that we shall be exclusively concerned with the rather exceptional " point input — point output " case. Our conditions will be satisfied equally

Cases where the physical marginal product of units of input can be isolated

well whenever it is possible continuously to vary (at least within certain limits) the amounts of input invested at different stages of the process of production. In " continuous input — point output " cases of this kind where the shape of the input curve can be continuously varied, it is possible to change either the rate at which input is applied in particular stages of a process yielding a product at a particular date, or (what really amounts to the same thing) the periods for which units of input are invested. In such circumstances it will always be possible to observe what changes in the quantity of the product are caused by changes in the investment periods of particular units of input. On the assumption that the use to be made of all other input is given, we can then represent the size of the product as a function of the investment period of the unit of input concerned.

The cases which we shall have to exclude from consideration for the present are all cases where no such connection between particular units of input and par-

This is impossible where the input function is rigid or where it can only be derived in value terms

ticular increments of output can be established on purely technological grounds, and where all that can be regarded as a technological datum is a connection between certain aggregates of input and aggregates of output. Included under this head there are first all those cases of time-consuming processes (*i.e.* " continuous input — point output " cases) where the rates at which input is invested during the process are not continuously variable, or, that is, where the input function is more or less rigid.

Secondly, there are all cases of durable goods (*i.e.* " point input — continuous output " and " continuous input — continuous output " cases) where the variability of the individual investment periods, which is required to establish a technological link between units of input and units of output, is, if it exists at all, much more limited. These cases will have to be reserved for separate discussion in the next chapter.

Among the cases that we shall consider here, the simplest one of " point input — point output " has one great advantage for purposes of exposition which makes it advisable to consider it first. In many instances the intermediate products which arise in the different stages of the process are similar in character to the final product ; in consequence, what is being reinvested at every stage can be directly compared, in terms of physical quantities, with the final product. It is to this circumstance that such instances as the growing of timber and the maturing of wine owe the great popularity which they have long enjoyed with writers on the subject. In such instances, the addition to the product which is attributable to the extension of the period for which the input applied at the beginning of the process remains invested can be calculated by a direct comparison of the quantities of the product which result from one and the same process according as it is terminated at an earlier or a later date.

The " point input — point output " case

This assumption makes it easy to see the main point. It is clear that what is being invested for the further period by which the original period is extended is not simply the amount of input that was invested in the beginning, but the product into which that input has grown at the end of the shorter period and which could have been consumed at that time. If any such extension of the investment period is to be profitable, the proportional increase

Equalising the marginal productivity of different investments

in the product due to it must be at least equal to the proportional increase in the product due to any other input which is invested for exactly the same (additional) period. So long as the proportion in which the product already obtained will continue to grow by further investment is greater than the proportional increase for any other input invested over the same period, it will evidently be advantageous to invest the product further for that period. And all the input will be invested in the most profitable way only if none of the products maturing at any moment would increase in a greater proportion than any other maturing at the same moment if its investment were continued for a further short period. (At the limit this rate of increase during a short period of time again becomes, of course, a rate of proportional increase at a moment of time.)

Thus, if we take a particular unit of input whose investment period can be continuously varied while that of all other input remains constant, the particular investment period which will be most advantageous will be the one where the proportional rate of increase of the product is equal to the rates of increase for all other products maturing at the same moment of time. And under stationary conditions it will also have to be equal to the rates of increase for the products maturing at all other moments of time.

So much for the considerations which determine the choice of the investment period for a particular unit of input. The same considerations will, of course, also decide how a number of units of one kind of input or of different kinds of input have to be distributed between different uses. When input of any particular kind can be used in a variety of processes, the additional returns that are obtainable by lengthening the investment periods will presumably decrease at different rates in the different processes. The proportional rates of final increase will

Distribution of Investments between different "point input — point output" processes

consequently be equalised if the different units of input
are invested for periods of different lengths.

For the simple " point input — point output " cases
which we are still considering, and in which the increase
of the product during any one process can be directly
measured in terms of quantity or value, the conditions of
equilibrium as between processes of different lengths can
easily be shown in a simple diagram (Fig. 12).   In this
diagram the ordinate measures the value of the product

obtained from the in-
vestment of a unit of
input for the different
periods which are mea-
sured along the ab-
scissa.   The curves P_1,
P_2, and P_3 represent
the value of the pro-
duct obtained after
different intervals from
three different processes
starting at the moments
O, T_1, and T_2 respectively.   Equilibrium re-
quires that for all such

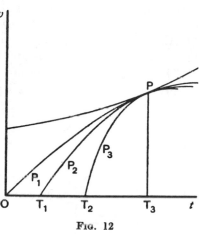

Fig. 12

processes which terminate at a given date, say T_3, the
ratio between the rate of final increase of the product
(due to the last extension of the investment period) and
the product obtained must be the same.   In the case
shown in the diagram, in which the product obtained from
each of the three processes in question at T_3 will be the
same, namely, T_3P, this condition will be satisfied if the
slope of the three productivity curves at P is the same.
(For the purpose of the diagram we have made the size
of the product maturing from the three processes at T_3
equal by assuming that the quantities of input invested
in each of the three processes will be such as to produce
the same output at that date.   As will appear presently,

this means that more input will have to be invested in the
process beginning at T_1 than in the process beginning at
O, and that still more input will be invested in the process
beginning at T_2 than in the process beginning at T_1. If
instead we had chosen to represent the curves describing
the amount of output resulting from investing equal
quantities of input at the three dates so that the output
obtained at T_3 from the processes beginning at T_2 and T_1
would be smaller than the output obtained from the process
beginning at O, the condition of equilibrium would not be
that the slopes of the curves above T_3 should be identical
but that they should stand in the same proportion to the
height of the curve at this point.)

The same condition will of course have to be satisfied
at any moment, that is, for all processes maturing at the

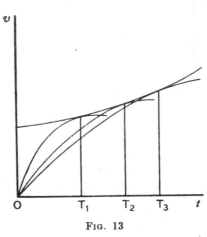

FIG. 13

same moment of time
the ratio between the
rate of increase of the
product and the size of
the product itself will
have to be the same.
This does not mean that
these ratios must also
be equal for processes
terminating at different
moments. That is true
only under stationary
conditions. It is, how-
ever, useful briefly to
follow the usual practice
and to discuss this stationary case. We can then consider
the relation between processes resulting from the investment of equal quantities of input at a given moment for
different periods. If in this case the ratio of the final increase of output to the absolute size of this output is also to
be the same for all the processes, the condition of equilibrium
will be determined by all the various productivity curves

touching the same compound interest curves at different points. This situation is represented in Fig. 13, where the process represented by the productivity curve P_1 is terminated at T_1, the process described by the productivity curve P_2 at T_2, etc.

The condition of equilibrium thus described is a necessary but not yet a sufficient condition, for there will always be not merely one but many different compound interest curves, which can be made to touch all the productivity curves and which therefore will give us different sets of equilibrium points. We shall see later that the explanation lies in the circumstance that the relative values of the different kinds of input and the different kinds of output will depend on the amounts invested in different processes and for different periods. But before we can go on to deal with this point we must first generalise the conclusions so far obtained by applying the same argument to other cases than the simplest "point input — point output" one.

We must now consider the conditions governing the investment period of input which cannot be regarded as an isolated point input, but which is applied at one point of, and as part of, a "continuous input — point output" process. Where the input function describing such a process is continuously variable, the question which arises is whether particular units of input should be invested at an earlier or a later point of the process (or whether more or less units should be invested at a particular point). Before we can answer this question, two modifications of our argument are necessary.

The first of these modifications is made necessary by the fact that in the case we are now considering the extension of the investment period of particular units of input cannot be brought about simply by continuing the same process somewhat longer; the units of input have to be invested from the beginning in an altogether different process. There will not in this case be any consumable product available after the interval at the

The marginal pro-
ductivity of invest-
ment in this case is
not the increase in
product obtained by
continuing the same
process — end of which the product would have become available in the original process. We have to deal, therefore, not with different quantities of output which would emerge from the same process at different

dates, but with quantities of output which would emerge at different dates from alternative processes in any one of which the input can be invested. And we shall have

— but the increase
obtained by choosing
an alternative, slightly
longer, process to compare not the total size of the products of the different processes but only the size of the contributions to those products

which are due to the co-operation of the particular units of input concerned. That is, we have to compare the marginal addition to the product which can be obtained by investing some small quantity of input at one point in one process with the addition which can be obtained by investing the same quantity at the same moment at a somewhat earlier stage of a similar process which will give forth its product a little later.

But although it would be impossible in this case to prolong the investment period by just continuing for a little longer a process already started, the initial decision about which of the alternative investments to undertake would have to be made on exactly the same principles as if we were dealing with products which could be obtained from one and the same process at different dates. This means that the result of an extension of the investment period of a particular unit of input would have to be *judged as if* what was being invested for the additional interval were the marginal addition which could have been obtained from that unit of input if it had been invested for the shorter period.[1] And the concept of the proportional rate of final increase of the product — the

---

[1] *I.e.* at a later stage of the same process.

magnitude which in equilibrium must be equal for all investments — would in this case refer to the difference between the marginal products which could be alternatively obtained by applying the quantity of input earlier or later in the process.

The second modification which has to be introduced at this point is a qualification which was implicit in the discussion of the earlier, simpler case, but which now becomes more obviously necessary and must therefore be made quite explicit. It was pointed out in that earlier discussion that the size of the product which is obtainable from a particular use of a given *The return from the investment of a unit of input can here no longer be regarded as a function of the investment period of that unit only —* unit of input, and the variations in the size of the product which are due to changes in the investment period of that unit of input, can be regarded as given on the assumption that the investment periods of all other units of input are determined.

There are two reasons for this in the present case. The first reason, which is the more general one and also applies, although perhaps less obviously, to the former case, is that the size of the product obtained at a particular date can be described only in terms of value, and this value will be determined only if the quantities *— partly owing to the effect of changes in the relative quantities of different products on their values —* of all other commodities available at this and all other dates are given. The second reason, which applies exclusively to the present case but is very conspicuous here, is that even the physical size of the contribution due to a particular unit of input which co-operates with many other units in any one process, is depend- *— but mainly owing to the technical complementarity between investment periods of different units of input* ent, because of technical complementarity, not merely on its own investment period, but also on the investment periods of all the units of input used in that process.

This means that we are not entitled to regard the productivity curves of the investment of different units of input, such as we drew previously, as independently and simultaneously valid. The shape of each of them is liable to change with any change in the use that is made of The productivity any other unit of input, and any one curve curves of different units of input are not will have a determinate shape only on independent the assumption that the use of all other units of input is determined. In other words, it is not really possible to start out from the notion that the product of each unit of input is a function solely of the period for which that unit is invested. We shall have to take as our initial datum a description of the way in which the total income stream and the relative values of its component items are dependent on the investment periods of all the units of input used. The value of any part of this total income stream will depend on, or will be a function of, the investment periods of all the units of input used. And the contribution due to a particular unit of input can be determined only by observing and comparing the effects, first of taking it out of a particular use, and then of applying it in a way in which it will yield its product at a slightly later date, the use made of all other units of input remaining the same.

Fundamental as is the importance of this modification, it does not deprive our earlier construction of its value as a description of the conditions of equilibrium. It still remains true that in a state of equilibrium there must be a uniform ratio, for all units of input, between the rate of increase of the marginal product of the unit, due to a slight increase in its investment period, and this marginal product. The only modification which we have to make in order that the diagram used before may still be a correct description of this equilibrium condition is that we must not regard the productivity curves as being simultaneously valid, but must consider each only as describing the change caused by a change in a particular investment period when all the other investment periods are such as to correspond to an equilibrium position.

Perhaps it would be less misleading if, instead of showing complete productivity curves, we drew only short segments in the immediate vicinity of the point of tangency with the compound interest curve. The segment may then be looked upon as indicating the rate of change of the product of a unit of input consequent upon a small change in its investment period while assuming that all the other investment periods remain unchanged (Fig. 14).

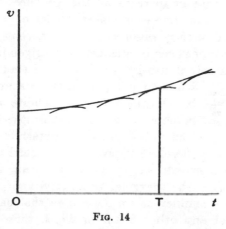

FIG. 14

The consequences of this last modification are very far-reaching. The concept of the ratio between the rate of increase of the product and the product (the ratio which must be equal to the instantaneous rate or force of interest) is of course the same as that on which W. S. Jevons' explanation of interest was based. Jevons described it as " the rate of increase of the produce divided by the whole produce ", and defined it in mathematical terms as $\dfrac{F'(t)}{F(t)}$, where the function $F(t)$ describes the size of the product as a function of the investment period of the input.[1] And both Böhm-Bawerk and Wicksell followed Jevons

Jevons' " rate of increase of the produce divided by the whole produce "

[1] W. S. Jevons, *The Theory of Political Economy*, 1st ed. (1871), p. 237; 4th ed. (1911), p. 246.

in the method he used to determine this rate. The method all three authors employed was to assume that the aggregate of waiting, or the sum of the periods for which the different units of input could be invested, was unequivocally determined by the size of the " subsistence fund ". They then concluded that the marginal productivity of waiting could be determined by so distributing the total waiting between the different units of input that the " rate of increase of the produce divided by the produce " became everywhere the same.

We have already observed, however, that the supply of capital cannot ever be assumed to be given in a " free " form as an actual subsistence fund, and that the actual stock of non-permanent resources cannot be identified in any definite and unambiguous way with quantities of future consumers' goods or determinate waiting periods. It is therefore impossible to regard the average or aggregate investment period as a datum from which we can derive the marginal productivity of investment in the same manner as we determine the marginal productivity of any other factor of which there is a given quantity available for distribution among the various uses.

The investment period not one of the data but one of the unknowns of the problem

But we see now that we do not need a description of the total time dimension of investment, an aggregate investment period, or a definite fund of capital, as an initial datum ; and that these are more in the nature of results of the forces which determine the equilibrium. The factor which limits the possible extensions of the investment periods is that as one unit of input is invested for a longer period, the output stream at the earlier date is reduced and the value of the products maturing at this earlier date is consequently raised. This means that the value of the marginal products of units of input invested for that earlier date increases, with the result that it becomes

The investment periods are not given by a determinate supply of free capital

profitable to invest more for that date. We have postulated that the available input must be used in such a way that the resulting income stream will be of constant size, *i.e.* that every gap caused by investing some units of input for longer periods must be filled by investing other units of input for correspondingly shorter periods. Therefore the condition that all input must be invested in such a way that the ratio between the marginal rate of increase of the product and the size of the whole product is the same for all units of input, also determines the period for which each of the units of input has to be invested.

The nature of our present assumption about the desired shape of the income stream, *i.e.* that under all conditions it must remain constant in time, makes it impossible for the moment to give this conclusion more exact expression. In terms of utility analysis this assumption, A final solution can be given only after the introduction of time preference which has so far been stated in only very general terms, would mean that any addition to the output at a date when the total output is smaller than at other dates would have a greater value than any addition, however large, to the output at those other dates. Apart from the obvious lack of reality of such an assumption, it is exceedingly inconvenient. We shall therefore postpone further discussion of this point until after we have made a more careful study of the possible psychological attitudes towards income streams of different shapes (cf. Chapter XVII).

But even without this more exact formulation, it will be evident by now that if we start out with a given stock of non-permanent resources, the factor which will determine the investment periods of the various items in that stock will be the condition of maximising the resulting stream, and the consequent condition of equalising the proportional rates of final increase of all the different investments. This stock of non-permanent resources in the form in which it exists as a datum is not some definite quantity of capital ; for it can be expressed as a single magnitude only after the relative values of the items of which it is composed have been determined. And these values are clearly a resultant of the same equilibrating forces as determine the investment periods. The initial datum from which we have to start is simply an enumeration of all the items of which this stock of non-permanent resources is composed, and of all their technical attributes. As will appear later in more detail, the quantity of capital as a value magnitude, no less than the different investment periods, are not data, but are among the unknowns which have to be determined.[1]

[1] Wicksell saw this quite clearly, although he proceeded in his exposition as though the investment periods or the quantity of capital were given magnitudes. It is evident that he realised that this was not so from a passage in his *Lectures* (vol. i, p. 202) already quoted, where he emphasises that " it would clearly be meaningless — if not altogether inconceivable — to maintain that the amount of capital is fixed *before* equilibrium between production and consumption has been achieved ". Wicksell did not, however, consistently follow this up. It seems that he discovered this point rather late and never fully incorporated it in his system. This is borne out by the fact that in the German translation of his *Lectures*, which was prepared from an earlier Swedish edition, the passage quoted above is much less emphatic (cf. *Vorlesungen über Nationalökonomie*, vol. i, 1913, pp. 272-273).

CHAPTER XV

INPUT, OUTPUT, AND THE STOCK OF CAPITAL
IN VALUE TERMS[1]

In the last two chapters we saw that wherever it is possible, on purely technological grounds, to attribute a definite quantity of output to the application of a definite quantity of input at a particular moment of time, the values of these quantities must bear a relationship to one another corresponding to a compound rate of interest which (in the special sense defined) is uniform throughout the system. It will be remembered that it is possible to establish such a technological or causal connection between individual units of input and individual units of output not only in the simplest " point input — point output " cases but also in some " continuous input — point output " cases. This is possible in these latter cases provided the shape of the input function can be continuously varied so that the physical marginal product of units of input applied at successive stages of the process can be isolated. In the next chapter we shall have to investigate the cases where no such unambiguous physical relationship exists between individual units of input and individual units of output, and where all that we know is that a certain aggregate of output is due to a certain aggregate of input, either or both of which may be spread over a period of time. We shall then have to seek a solution of the problems in these cases on the principle of an " imputation " of a marginal value product.

The relationship between input and output in value terms

[1] The substance of this and the following chapter, although in a different form, was the subject of an article, by the present author, which appeared some time ago in the *Economic Journal* (1934b).

Before proceeding, however, to these more complicated cases, it will be useful if we try to give a general description of the relations between aggregates of input and aggregates of output in the simpler cases where these relations can be built up, so to speak, from the known relations between the elements of which the aggregates are composed.

Our task consists essentially in devising a suitable method of adapting our earlier representations of the complete structure of production, so as to show the new factor of the growth of value of every unit of input invested, during the time for which it remains invested. For this purpose we must go back to the three-dimensional diagram which we used earlier (Fig. 6, p. 117) to represent the complete structure of production in terms of units of input. In that diagram all quantities of intermediate and final products had to be measured in terms of such quantities as were the product of equal units of investment. We neglected any change in value which the results of the investment of a unit of input underwent in the course of the process. It is, however, just this growth of value in which we are now mainly interested, and in order to be able to show it in the original diagram it would evidently be necessary to introduce an additional dimension. But since the usual diagrammatic methods do not allow us to show variations in more than three dimensions in one diagram, we shall have to make room for the additional dimension by leaving out one of the variables that were shown in that earlier diagram. The one that can be dispensed with with the least loss is that represented by the vertical or s-axis of the said diagram (*i.e.* the axis which indicates the " stages " to which the different quantities of intermediate products measured along the r-axis belong). The relationship which was indicated along this axis can be shown in another way.

Graphic representation of changes of value in time

To explain this alternative device for representing the phenomenon of "synchronisation" shown by means of the third axis in the earlier diagram, we must return for a moment to the very first diagram intro- The principle on which duced in this book (p. 101) and now re- the earlier diagram is produced, with some additions, in Fig. 15. modified

That diagram shows the part of the expected income stream which can be said already to exist at any moment in the "inchoate" form of non-permanent resources.

The curve $T_m R$ bounding this part of the future income stream (the output curve) represents the distribution in time of the product of the different units of current pure input invested at the moment O. The area under this curve may be taken to represent also all the successive stages through which the pure input invested at O will have to pass before it matures into its final product.[1]

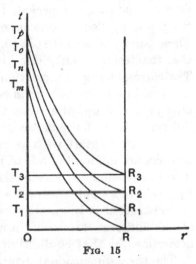

FIG. 15

But since under stationary conditions similar investments will be made at every successive moment (*i.e.* at T_1, T_2, T_3, and every other point on the t-axis), we may visualise an infinite number of similar triangles telescoped one into another. And at every point on the t-axis all these successive stages will be simultaneously present. In other words, if we conceive of this continuous series of triangles telescoped into one another, each of them will also represent the position which, under stationary conditions,

[1] Thus interpreted the curvilinear triangle of the present figure corresponds to the plane $P_3 R R_3$ in the earlier three-dimensional diagram (Fig. 6 above), the meaning of which was not explicitly discussed at that previous juncture.

would exist at any one moment. And the same will apply if, instead of two-dimensional triangles, we use a corresponding series of three-dimensional solids which are similarly telescoped into each other.

In what follows we shall start, not from the output curve, but from the input curve. Before proceeding to the construction of a diagram, however, it is necessary to

Limitations to the use of a single input curve recall once more the exact meaning of the input functions that are involved. They describe the range of periods for which different parts of the input applied at one moment of time are invested. These parts can be stated in physical terms only on condition that there is only one kind of homogeneous input. The corresponding information for a number of different kinds of input can be combined into a single input curve only on the assumption that the relative values of these different kinds of input are given. This means that we ought really to start with as many separate input curves as there are different kinds of input ; and that, although it will be possible to describe the conditions of equilibrium by means of a single composite input curve, this curve can be constructed only on the basis of given relative values of the different kinds of input, which are themselves determined by that equilibrium.

The three-dimensional diagram (Fig. 16) below depicts the growth of value in time. It is constructed by using the last diagram (Fig. 15) but interpreted as representing

The process in time in value terms the input function as base, and erecting on it a perpendicular v-axis along which are measured the changing values which the products of the various units of input obtain at successive moments of time.[1] The units of input invested at O (or at any later

---

[1] " Value " is here measured in terms of any one commodity on the assumption that identical quantities of this commodity available at different dates will be identical in value. The " growth of value in time " means that at successive dates the product of the investment of a given quantity of input at a particular date will be equal in value to increasing quantities of the commodity chosen. Under the

moment) may, of course (and if more than one kind of input is involved must), be expressed in terms of value, and the fact that values are measured along two different axes in this diagram may at first appear confusing. The explanation is simple, however, when we remember that the r-axis measures the quantities of intermediate and final products in such units as are the product of a unit of input (in factor units) and not in units of their own (commodity units). And, as we have seen, the value of

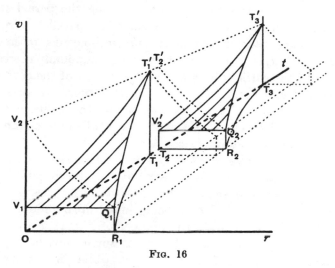

FIG. 16

the product of a given unit of input will vary in time. While therefore the value of the input necessarily remains the same throughout, and it would be superfluous to show it a second time in addition to its measurement along the r-axis, the values of the products of this input have to be indicated separately.

In the diagram, then, the total value of the input invested at any moment is represented by the rectangle $OR_1Q_1V_1$ (and $T_2R_2Q_2V'_2$ and all the similar rectangles which can be imagined at all other points on the t-axis).

stationary conditions here postulated, it is immaterial what commodity is used as the " standard of value ".

The investment periods of these units of input vary between zero and OT_1, as is indicated by the input curve R_1T_1. Over the same range of periods the value of the product of any unit of input invested will grow at a uniform compound rate of interest as indicated by the curve $V_1T''_1$. Any perpendicular cross-section of the resulting solid, parallel to the plane vOt, corresponds to Fig. 13 above ; that is, it shows how the value of the product of an infinitesimally small unit of input applied at O grows at compound interest during the period for which it remains invested. Any one of the parallel curves, which have been drawn in the upward-curving interest surface $V_1Q_1T''_1$, corresponds to the compound interest curve of the earlier diagram, and the height of the curved perpendicular surface $Q_1R_1T_1T''_1$ at the point where any one of these vertical planes ends shows the value of the product due to the investment of a small unit of input for the corresponding period.

Each of the two solids shown in the diagram — and all the others that are not shown but may be conceived to be telescoped into each other in an infinite series — can accordingly be regarded as being made up by adding all the thin slices which, in the manner of Fig. 13, show the gradual growth of the value of a single unit of input invested.[1] The difference is that while in the two-dimensional diagram it was possible to show only the growth of a single small unit invested for a particular period, the present diagram gives a simultaneous view of the growth of all the units of input invested at a moment of time for the continuous range of periods described by the input curve R_1T_1.

[1] If it did not make the diagram too complicated, we might also make it show the condition of equilibrium in the same way as Fig. 13. The condition is that, at the point where the product of every unit of input matures, the segment of the productivity curve of that unit of input (which shows the change in the size of its marginal product when its investment period is slightly changed while all other investment periods remain constant) must just touch the interest surface from below.

The three-dimensional diagram gives us a clear picture of two important relationships which, up to this point, have been left unexplained. First, it gives us a description of the total value, at a given rate of interest, of the stock of capital which corresponds to a given input function or output function. Secondly, it shows the relationship between the range of periods for which the input is invested (*i.e.* the input function) and the shape of the income stream derived from it (*i.e.* the output function). These two relationships are clearly interconnected.

The value of the stock of intermediate products existing at any moment, under stationary conditions, is represented in the diagram by the volume of each of the solids $V_1OR_1Q_1T'_1T_1$, etc. This becomes evident at once if we think of these solids

Representation of the value of the stock of capital

as being composed of an infinite series of perpendicular planes, parallel to the plane vOr, each of which represents the value of the intermediate goods belonging to the corresponding " stage " of production. The only point which needs further emphasis is, as will be seen from the diagram, that the value of the capital stock, as represented by the volume of the solid, depends not only on the shape of the input function, or the size of the area which it encloses, but also on the rate of interest. The reason is, of course, that what is being invested further at every stage is not merely the value of the original input ; it includes the interest already accrued (or the value of the product which could have been obtained if the input in question had been invested only for the shorter period).

This representation of the factors which determine the value of the stock of capital shows that there is no simple or unique correlation between the shape of the input curve and this value. It shows also that, even given the rate of interest, we could not determine the value of the stock of capital if, instead of having a full description

of the range of investment periods such as is provided by
the input function, we knew only the aggregate or average
of these periods. If such an aggregate or average were
all that were given, it would mean that
we should know only the size of the area
enclosed by the input function, and not
its shape. There will be any number of
different input functions which enclose
areas of the same size, *i.e.* which correspond to the same
aggregate or average of investment periods. And if
we take two such input curves (as for example those

Its value can be determined only if we have a full description of the range of investment periods and the rate of interest

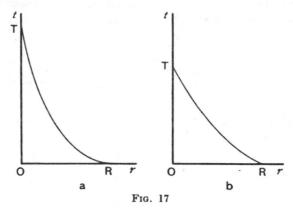

FIG. 17

shown in Fig. 17), one of which extends over a shorter
investment period and is less curved, and the other of
which extends over a longer period and is more curved,
it is clearly possible that at one rate of interest the
first, and at another rate of interest the second, will
correspond to the greater quantity of capital. Similarly,
at any given rate of interest, two input curves of different
shapes, but enclosing the same area (and therefore
representing the same average or aggregate investment
period), will correspond to different quantities of capital.

It will now be easy to derive the shape of the output
stream, in terms of units of the product (or the output
curve) which corresponds to any given input curve. In

fact, the output function in its non-cumulative form (as shown earlier in Fig. 4) is implicitly represented by the curved vertical surface $R_1Q_1T'_1T_1$ in Fig. 16. The height of this surface indicates the value of the product of a small (strictly speaking infinitesimal) unit of input ma-

Derivation of the output curve from the input curve

turing at the moment concerned. But in order to find the actual magnitude of the product maturing during any interval of time of finite length, we must also take account of the rate at which the product of such a small unit of input will be maturing at the relevant moment. This time rate is shown by the slope of the input curve R_1T_1, which forms the base of the vertical surface. Consequently the shape of the output stream is obtained by multiplying the height of the surface at each point by the slope at that point of the curve which forms its base. In this way we arrive at a non-cumulative description of the output stream as represented by the strips shown alongside the solid in Figs. 18 and 19 below. It is important to observe that the representation of the shape of the output stream thus obtained is not the usual (cumulative) form of the output function : the strips represent the non-cumulative curves, or, that is, the first derivatives of the output functions proper.[1] We shall return to the discussion of the relationship between the input and output curves, as shown in these two diagrams, in Chapter XVI below, in connection with the " point input — continuous output " cases.

---

[1] In this respect the earlier exposition of these relationships given by the author in the article quoted before (1934b) was somewhat confused.

CHAPTER XVI

THE MARGINAL VALUE PRODUCT OF INVESTMENT: THE PROBLEM OF ATTRIBUTION (IMPUTATION)

IN the cases we considered in Chapter XV we were able to build up the relationship between the input function and the output function from the connection between individual units of input and individual units of output, which were assumed to be known. Given the shape of the input function, and the marginal product of every small unit of input to which it referred, we were able to derive from it the shape of the output function. And since it was assumed that we knew the amount of input on the co-operation of which each particular part of the output depended, we were able similarly to derive the input function from the output function. This connection between the two functions was independent of the rate of interest and was based on the known physical marginal productivity of the different units of input. In these cases particular input functions and particular output functions were uniquely correlated in the sense that one, and only one, output function would fit a particular input function and *vice versa*. The rate of interest came into the discussion only to the extent that, in equilibrium, such an input function would have to be chosen that the relation between the value of any unit of input and the value of the dependent unit of output would correspond to the rate of interest ruling in the system. Changes in the output function could be brought about only by changes in the input function and if the connection between any particular input function and the corresponding output function was

Particular input functions are uniquely correlated with particular output functions only if physical marginal product of every unit of input can be isolated

202

not dependent on the rate of interest (or complex' of interest rates). And the input function (or rather the different input functions of the different kinds of input) and the output function could both be regarded as technological data which were given independently of the rate of interest or of any other value phenomenon which could only be the resultant of equilibrium.

We must now pass on to the cases where, in place of this technologically given connection between individual units of input and individual units of output, all that is given is a connection between aggregates *The case where only* of input and aggregates of output. It is *the relation between* convenient to proceed immediately to the *aggregates of input* extreme opposite of the cases so far con- *put is known* sidered, *i.e.* to the cases where nothing more than the connection between the aggregates is given. And we shall leave for later consideration the intermediate cases where it is possible, on technological grounds, to establish a connection between at least some parts of the input and some parts of the output.

There are two main cases to be considered here. The first is that of goods in process where the shape of the input function is rigidly fixed by technical conditions, and where, in consequence, we know how long *Main instances to be* we have to wait for the product of different *considered* parts of the input, but cannot say, on technological grounds, what parts of the product are due to the different units of input, or how long we have to wait for the different parts of the output. The second is that of durable goods whose durability cannot be varied, and where, accordingly, we know exactly how long we have to wait for the different parts of the services the goods will render, but do not know to what portions of the input each part of these services is to be attributed, or how long we have to wait for the product of different portions of the input. In the first case the input function is known and the output function is unknown ; in the second case the output

function is known and the input function unknown. The
problem in the first case is how to allocate a given aggregate of output among the different units of input invested
for a known range of periods, and the problem in the
second case is how to allocate a given aggregate of input
between the units of output which are due to it and which
mature at a known rate over a known period of time.

The first of these two cases presents no real difficulties.
We have a product of given size which is due to the
investment of a given aggregate of input over a given

1. Time - consuming
processes with an
input function of in-
variable shape

range of periods. Under stationary conditions the product maturing at a moment
of time as the result of a series of investments made for a range of periods preceding that moment
(described by the inverted input curve) will be equal to
the total product maturing over a range of periods and
due to the investments made at a moment of time
(described by the original input curve). We can therefore make either of these two aspects of the process the
basis of our discussion. For the sake of conformity with
the treatment of the next case we choose the second
aspect, *i.e.* the representation by means of the input
curve in its original form, which was also used for the
foundation of Fig. 16 above.

Equilibrium requires that the total value of the product shall be equal to the value of the input *plus* interest
on every unit of the input, for the known period for

The relation between
value of input and
value of output is ad-
justed by varying the
total quantity of out-
put

which it is invested, at a rate which is
equal to that ruling in the system. Since
with given technique, the quantity of the
product obtainable from investment of
given quantities of input is a datum, the
only way in which this equality can be brought about is
by varying the total quantity produced (which implies
varying the total quantity of input invested in that line
of production). Every increase in the quantity produced
in the line of production concerned will have two effects ;

it will decrease the value of a unit of output, and it will increase the value which units of input have in alternative uses. Thus, by varying the total quantity produced, any desired proportion between the total value of the input and the total value of the output can be brought about. At a given rate of interest the quantity which can profitably be invested in this line of production will therefore be uniquely determined.

But we need not assume that the rate of interest is given independently of the magnitude of the output in this particular line of production. The condition that the rate of interest here should be equal to that ruling elsewhere takes account of any possible effect of changes in the scale of production in this industry on the rates of interest elsewhere ; it therefore gives us the general condition of equilibrium.

The idea that the value of the product should be sufficient, and only just sufficient, to cover the value of all the units of input *plus* interest for their respective investment periods obviously implies some "ideal" allocation of the total product between the co-operating units of input, *i.e.* an attribution of particular "ideal" shares of the product to particular units of input. To use a concept which has been traditionally applied in economics to this sort of attribution, we may talk about the *imputation* of definite parts of the value of the product to the different units of input co-operating in its production. And this process of imputation, which enables us to connect particular quantities of input with definite quantities of output, also enables us to *construct* from a given input function the corresponding output function (*i.e.* a description of the range of periods during which we have to wait for the quantities of output which are due to the investments made at a moment of time). The output function so obtained is not, of course, in any sense a physical datum, a magnitude which can be found in the real

The general problem of attribution (imputation)

world : it is a calculating device, a " construct ", which, given equilibrium conditions, can be derived from the data. The fact that we can express the equilibrium conditions in the form of an output function is, however, not without significance. For, as we have already observed, in real life the relevant relationships are in some cases given in the form of output functions, and in others sometimes in the form of input functions, and in consequence we are only able to give a comprehensive picture if we are able to convert one into the other.

The circumstance that the problem of attributing particular parts of the output to particular units of input cannot be solved by reference to the physical dependence of the former on the latter, but has to be solved by means of imputation of value, is, of course, not peculiar to our present case. It applies generally to all cases where the proportion in which different kinds of input are combined is not continuously variable. In all such cases of fixed coefficients of production it is impossible to determine a physical marginal product, *i.e.* the quantity of the product which depends on the co-operation of a small unit of input. All that we can do is to determine a " marginal value product ", that is, that part of the value of the product which it must be possible to assign to a unit of a factor in order to render its employment profitable.

The determination of the " marginal value product " analogous to other cases of fixed coefficients of production

The case of a rigid input function, as well as the case of an invariable output function which we have still to consider, are only special instances of the general phenomenon of " constant coefficients of production ". Their only peculiarity is that it is not the proportions in which physically different factors can be used in one process of production that are rigidly fixed, but the proportions between the quantities of factors that can be applied at different stages of the process. It follows that the problems to which these cases give rise are to be solved along the same lines as other instances of the more general case of fixed coefficients.

We turn now to our second case, that of durable goods with fixed and invariable durability. In order to avoid complications arising out of the use of such durable goods in production we shall here confine our 2. Durable goods with attention to the case of durable con- fixed lengths of life sumers' goods. It will also be convenient to begin once more with the case of the " ideal " durable good, the production of which takes no time, and which therefore corresponds to the theoretical " point input — continuous output " case. In this case the investment of a given quantity of input at a particular moment yields a stream of services of a given and invariable time shape. This means that while we know how long we have to wait for each unit of the services of the good, we do not know to what portion of the input invested these units are due, and consequently how long we have to wait for the products of the different units of the input invested. In other words, the output function is given, and the input function has to be derived from it.

The question to be answered is to what " ideal " portions of the input invested at a moment of time the different segments of the resultant output stream have to be attributed. Equilibrium requires that the value of the output stream, each part being discounted for the relevant period at a rate of interest equal to that ruling elsewhere in the system, shall be equal to the value of the input invested. And the required relationship between the aggregate value of the input invested and the value of the output stream can be brought about by varying the total volume of output. The discounted value of any small part of the output stream maturing during a certain time interval gives us the " ideal " portion of the input, which may be said to be invested for the relevant period.

The principle of the solution is exactly parallel to that applying in the previous case. But the present case is so important that it is worth while illustrating its significance by considering one or two special instances in greater detail. We shall ask first, what will be the effect of a change in the rate of interest on the shape of the input function which we derive from a given output function? and, secondly, what, at a given rate of interest, will be the shapes of the input functions belonging to different output functions? Both questions can be conveniently answered by means of a diagram similar to Fig. 16 above.

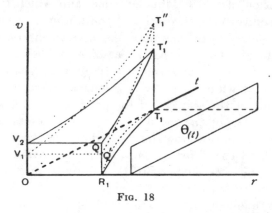

FIG. 18

In Fig. 18 the strip marked $\theta(t)$ represents the shape of the output stream (in this case assumed to be of constant volume through time) expected from a given durable good, and shown as a simple (not cumulative) frequency distribution. The amount of input used in the production of the good is indicated by the distance OR_1 along the r-axis. Values are shown, as in the former diagram, along the perpendicular v-axis, and the growth at a given rate of compound interest will therefore again be represented by an upward-sloping curve in any plane parallel to vOt. For the purposes of diagrammatic representation it is useful to assume that the value of the services of the good (the output stream) is given, although actually it is of course variable in just the same way as the value of the input.

Effect of rate of interest on shape of (constructed) Input curve

The value of the output stream at a moment of time (*i.e.* as a time rate) is then shown by the height of the strip which describes its shape.

In order for the discounted value of the output stream to be equal to the value of the input, it must be possible to exhaust the total value of the output stream by allotting to each small unit of input a segment of the output stream such that the discounted value of that segment is equal to the value of the unit of input. Or, since the value of all units of input must grow, during the time that they remain invested, at the same compound rate of interest, the product of the different units of input must be presumed to mature at such a rate that the value of the input whose product matures during any interval, plus compound interest for the period for which it has been invested, will be equal to the given value of the output stream during that interval. In geometrical terms this means that the slope of the input curve R_1T_1 at any point must be such that the product of this slope times the height of the interest surface will be equal to the given size of the output stream at this point.

As will be seen from the diagram, with a constant income stream and the given rate of interest represented by the fully drawn interest surface V_2QT_1', we obtain the concave input function represented by the fully drawn curve R_1T_1. The meaning of this is, of course, that since a greater amount of interest accrues on the "ideal" shares of the input which are invested for the longer periods than on those which are invested for the shorter periods, a larger part of the output stream has to be attributed to the former than to the latter: or, what amounts to the same thing, that where the income stream is constant the product of given units of input must be conceived to mature at a slower rate during the later part of the life of the good than during the earlier part. (The whole relationship is the same as that shown in a simpler manner in Fig. 4 (*b*) on p. 110, and the reader who finds

15

the present more complete representation difficult will do well to refer back to that earlier diagram.)

The diagram also depicts the effect of a rise in the rate of interest, the dotted curves indicating the interest surface $V_1Q'T'''_1$ corresponding to the higher rate of interest and the new input function shown as dotted curves. It will be seen that the effect is to make the input curve more concave, *i.e.* to attribute the services maturing later to a greater amount of input and the services maturing earlier to a smaller amount, and to reduce the value of the input *relatively* to the value of the output. (The diagram shows only a decrease in the value of the input, but it is clear that the decrease in its value relative to the value of its product will be brought about partly by a fall in the value of the input and partly by a rise in the value of the output.)

Lastly, Fig. 19 shows the shape of the input functions, which, at a given rate of interest, correspond to output functions of different shapes. The strips marked θ_1, θ_2, and θ_3 represent three (simple) output functions which increase at a constant rate, remain constant throughout, and decrease at a constant rate respectively. The curves marked ϕ_1, ϕ_2, and ϕ_3 represent the corresponding (cumulative) input functions. It will be noticed that a tendency for the output function to decrease makes the input function more concave, and that a tendency for the output function to increase makes the input function less concave, or may (if the output function increases at a rate greater than the rate of interest) even make it (partially or entirely) convex. In order for the input function to be linear it would be necessary for the output function to increase in geometrical progression at a rate equal to the prevailing rate of interest.

In order to complete the analysis we ought now to extend our argument to two further cases. The first is the " continuous input — continuous output " case corresponding to durable goods which are the product of a time-consuming process of production. The second case, or group of cases, includes durable goods which do not render final services directly without further The more complicated cases collaboration from other factors but give off different amounts of these services according to the amount of co-operating factors used, and durable goods which give off different amounts of final services according to the intensity with which they are used. The latter group of cases includes, of course, not only a

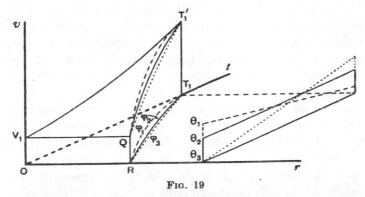

FIG. 19

great many durable consumers' goods but also all durable producers' goods. Although these cases present no really new problems, their actual analysis is so complicated that it is hardly possible to give it in any detail without resorting to an elaborate mathematical apparatus, and they are consequently best left to more specialised studies.

In order to give some indication of the kind of difficulty which arises, and of the general principle under-lying its solution, a few words may be added on the "continuous input — continuous output" The "continuous in-put—continuous out-put" case case. Here the difficulty is that it is no longer sufficient to be able to attribute definite parts of the output to "ideal" portions of the input; we require to know what part of the output is to be attributed to the concrete quantities of input that are invested at particular dates. But it is not possible to say that some particular unit of input invested in the course of the production of the durable good concerned contributes only to the services which that good renders at a particular moment or during a particular small interval of time. What we have to do in order to obtain a clear picture of the value relationship is to attribute to each of the different units of input invested at different stages of the production of the durable good some small part of the services which the durable good will render at all moments of its life. This means that, in order to distribute the value of the services rendered by the good among the units of input invested in it at different dates, we shall have, so to speak, to slice the output stream longitudinally, and to attribute to the different units of input slices of different thickness according as they have been invested earlier or later in the process of production. This relationship, which cannot be more than suggested in words, obviously transcends the possibility of diagrammatic representation even in three dimensions ; it can be adequately described only in terms of mathematics.

There remains, however, a more important problem which must be dealt with before we conclude this chapter. We have confined our attention so far in the chapter to cases where either the input function or the **Partial rigidities** output function was rigidly fixed and could not be varied in any way. It was mentioned near the beginning, as a point reserved for later consideration, that between the case of continuous variability of the input function and the case where either the input function or the output function was of an invariable shape, there were important intermediate cases. These include the case where the known input function is only partially variable, *i.e.* where the rate at which input is applied in the course of the process can be varied at certain points, or for some part of the input, but not at others. This case, although a source of additional complications, does not require any further comment. A more interesting case which merits further discussion is where the shape of the known output function allows of limited variation because the durability of the good to which it refers may be changed by altering the amount of input invested in that good. This may serve as an instance of the general case where a definite physical marginal product can be determined for some part of the input but not for all.

The peculiarity of a durable good with variable durability is that it will not usually be possible to vary the shape of the stream of services obtained from it in any arbitrary manner ; the effects of varying the amount of input invested in the good will be mainly concentrated at the end of the stream of services derived from the good. Exactly how the additions to the stream of services from any durable good which are due to the investment of additional input will be distributed in time will depend on the initial shape of this stream of services (and the change in this shape, if any, which is caused by the additional investment). If the stream is of constant shape, and simply becomes longer when more

Changing the length of life of a durable good : the time distribution of the result of a marginal investment

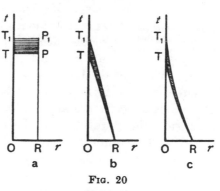

Fig. 20

input is invested in the good, the marginal increment will all be at the end of that stream, as is shown in diagram (a) of Fig. 20. The two other cases that are most likely to occur are those where the stream of services decreases at a constant rate and at a decreasing rate respectively. Assuming the general shape of the stream to remain the same with the additional input as without, the marginal additions to the stream of services will in these cases be distributed in time in the way depicted by diagrams (*b*) and (*c*) respectively of the same figure.

The essential point, however, is that in all these cases we cannot establish a marginal dependence on particular units of input for individual units of service maturing at all points during the life of the good, but only for those units of service which are due to the marginal addition total input. This means that while we cannot derive a complete input function from the given output function on a marginal productivity basis, and while in consequence it cannot be said that a particular input function is uniquely correlated with the given output function, there does exist a definite connection between the *marginal* investment in the durable good and the additions to the stream of services which that good renders.

The conclusion is that two factors now have to be taken into account in deciding how much it will be profitable to invest in any particular kind of durable good. The Combined effect of varying quantity and varying durability of durable goods marginal product of the input invested in any one such good must be equal to the value of a unit of that input, and the discounted value of all the services yielded by the good must be equal to the total value of the input invested in it. Two kinds of variation are possible in order to reach this equality : the durability of the individual good can be varied, and the number of goods of the same kind that are produced can be changed. Both these possibilities of variation will have to be used, until not only the discounted value of the variable physical marginal product of the last unit of input invested in a single good is equal to the value of that unit of input, but the discounted value of all the services of any good is equal to the value of all the input invested in it.

This case of durable goods of variable durability is the most important of the cases that are needed to supplement the earlier discussion of the connection between the productivity of investment and the rate of interest. For the " ideal " durable good (the " point input — continuous output " case), what has already been said is sufficient to indicate the complete solution. It would of course be possible to go on and apply the same kind of argument to the more complicated cases mentioned before. But though a casuistic elaboration of this kind may be necessary for certain purposes, the general principle has probably been sufficiently well illustrated, and the gain we should derive from further refinements would hardly compensate for the effort which the more detailed analysis of these highly complicated cases would require.

CHAPTER XVII

TIME PREFERENCE AND ITS EFFECTS WITH CONSTANT
RETURNS ON INVESTMENT [1]

THE assumption employed up to this point that the dictator of our economic system will under all circumstances aim at a constant income stream was only an expository device, adopted provisionally. Its purpose was to enable us to study the significance of certain factors in isolation ; but it has little relevance to the conditions existing in real life. It is extremely unlikely that anyone would want a constant income in time whatever the circumstances, and regardless in particular of the prevailing opportunities of varying the size of the returns obtainable by investment and disinvestment respectively. Our next task is therefore to introduce a technique by which we can adequately describe the possible attitudes a person may hold towards income streams of different time shapes, and which will enable us to use more realistic assumptions in this connection.

The assumption that a constant income stream is desired under all circumstances is abandoned

It will, however, not be expedient to drop at once all the simplifying assumptions hitherto employed. It will be advisable at first to study the effects of the dispositions over time on the assumption that, apart from the effects of these dispositions themselves, everything else remains unchanged. This assumption of constant data will in particular include the assumption that the tastes and the knowledge of the economic subject and the flow of services from the permanent resources which he commands remain the same.

In all other respects the assumption of stationary conditions is still retained

[1] Parts of this and the following chapter are taken verbatim from an article which appeared some time ago in the *Economic Journal* (**1936b**).

The meaning of these assumptions, especially of that of " constant tastes ", will require careful definition. It will soon become evident that the existence of constant data as just defined does not necessarily imply the existence of a stationary state in the traditional sense, since these conditions are fully compatible with actions on the part of any individual who will change his position from period to period and will therefore alter the conditions which affect the decisions he will make at successive points of time, even though we assume his tastes to remain constant.

Before we proceed, however, to define the critical concept of constant tastes, it will be useful to say a few words about the implications of the other main assumption, *i.e.* that the dictator of our communist society expects to command a constant stream of input. This assumption provisionally rules out one of the main factors which in the real world lead people to accumulate capital. If, as would follow from this assumption, people planned for an eternal life during which they would invariably command the same quantity of permanent resources, some of the main motives which govern their actions in the world as it is would be absent. Yet it is only on this assumption, together with that of constant tastes, that we are able to obtain a clear view of the significance of time preference for the decisions to save and invest, or to take advantage of opportunities for obtaining larger additions to future income by giving up a given amount of present income. In later sections of this chapter we shall supplement this preliminary analysis by considering the factors which we are here ignoring.

The idea of tastes which remain constant in time is of course again not something which is supposed to exist in reality ; it is merely an expository device and is closely connected with the concept of the stationary state. This concept is of particular importance in the theory of

The expected flow of pure input is assumed to be constant

interest because all the familiar theories concerning the psychological factors affecting interest imply the existence of constant tastes at least in this particular sense.

The significance of the assumption of constant tastes   Indeed the main reason why it is so important to have a clear grasp of this concept is that practically all the difficulties which arise in this connection are due not to any special complexity of the problem, but to the fact that the path is strewn with the effects of various confusions on this point. The blame for this rests not with the individual authors who have treated these problems in the past but with the state of the general theory of value of which they had to make use. It is only in comparatively recent times that the development of the "substitution" technique (and the connected method of representation by indifference curves) has provided us with a method which effectively avoids the dangers of the earlier utility analysis. In what follows an attempt will be made to give a straightforward statement of the relevant relationships as they appear in the light of the modern theory of value. All discussion of the relations between this positive statement and the traditional concepts or theories is relegated to Appendix I.

The assumption of constant tastes was introduced into equilibrium analysis to indicate that a person will act in the same way at different points of time if faced *The meaning of constant tastes* with the same circumstances. " Acting " here includes, of course, the distribution of resources between the present and the future,[1] and the

---

[1] There is a further difficulty arising out of the question what are to be regarded as the same time intervals ; and according as we give different answers to this question we obtain a wider or a narrower concept of constant tastes. We can define constant time preferences, as is done in the text, as a state of affairs in which at any point of time the relative values attached to a unit of present income and a unit of income a year hence are the same. But we might also include under that description the case where the relative values attached to incomes at the times $t_m, t_n, t_o \ldots$ are the same at $t_1, t_2, t_3 \ldots$ without postulating that the attitude between any pair of successive points of time $t_m, t_n,$

assumption of constant tastes therefore means that, faced with the same possibilities, a person will at different moments of time distribute his resources in the same way between present and future. The *same* distribution in this sense need *not* be an *even* distribution through time, *i.e.* a distribution which provides for the same income in the present and in the future. The attitude would still be the same if at both dates the person were equally willing to increase his future income at the expense of the present or *vice versa*. But there arises the further difficulty that if he provides for an increasing or decreasing income stream, the circumstances in which he will have to act at different moments will necessarily vary. And in order to say whether his tastes have remained the same or have changed we shall have to compare his decisions at the later moment not with the decisions he actually made at the earlier moment, but with the decisions he would have made if the choice before him at the earlier moment had been the same as it is at the later moment. Or, in other words, the fact that the tastes of a person have remained constant cannot be established merely by comparing his actual decisions at successive moments but only by comparing his (hypothetical) attitude to all possible sets of circumstances at each moment, as expressed by his complete "indifference map"

t_o ... (which are assumed to be equidistant) must be the same. As will be readily seen, this question is closely connected with the assumptions we make regarding foresight. If we assume that the person in question plans investments at the initial date t_1 for all the future dates t_2, t_3 ... t_m, t_n, t_o ..., then his tastes will have to be regarded as constant in the strict sense only if the relative importance he attaches to marginal increments at t_m and t_n (or any other pair of future points of time) is the same whether he is at t_1, t_2, t_3, or any other point, irrespective of whether at any given moment his attitude as between different pairs of future moments is the same or not. This would be the wider concept of constant tastes, and although it would satisfy the requirements of equilibrium analysis, it would complicate matters in the present context. For this reason the narrower concept is used in the text, which involves identity of the attitude as between any two moments and which, as will be easily seen, is a special case of the wider definition.

Complete " indifference maps " as we should require them for an adequate treatment of the question cannot, however, be shown by graphical methods. Each of the

The use of the indifference curve method makes considerable simplifications necessary
"indifference maps ", showing the attitude of a person at any moment of time, would have to show his relative preferences not only for all the different commodities, but also for each of these commodities at all future points of time which he considers. This means that the complete " indifference map " would have to be drawn in as many dimensions as correspond to the number of different commodities plus the number of different dates for which the person plans, or, strictly speaking, since time is continuous and infinite, in an infinite number of dimensions. But since the tastes in which we are primarily interested are the relative preferences for present and future goods, it is possible to show the essential points on a drastically simplified model.

In the first place we can provisionally ignore the existence of a variety of different commodities and speak of income as if it consisted of a single commodity,

Income conceived as a single (composite) commodity
or, what for our purposes amounts to the same thing, as if it were a composite commodity, always made up of exactly the same proportions of the different goods. This involves either or both of the assumptions that for technological reasons the different commodities can be produced only in fixed proportions, and/or that there exists such a peculiar kind of psychical complementarity between them that they are only wanted in fixed proportions. And it means that, whether the income stream is expanded or contracted, the quantity of every single commodity contained in it will be increased or decreased in the same proportion. The possibility that changes in the size of the income stream will lead to changes in its composition will be considered explicitly in later sections.

What we have to consider, then, is the attitude of the

person at successive moments of time when he has to choose between an addition to his income now and an addition at a later date. But since it will usually be possible by a given sacrifice of present income to increase future income at any one of a long continuous range of future dates (or *vice versa*), we should still have to consider many more variables than can be shown in any diagram. Our indifference map would, strictly speaking, still have to have an infinite number of dimensions — that is, as many as there are future moments of time to be considered. We can, however, obviate this difficulty by assuming that there is only one possible period of investment, say of one year, as might be the case in a purely grain-growing community, and that there will periodically occur the opportunity of deciding what part of the current input should be devoted to current consumption and what part of it should be invested for one year.

Investment assumed to be possible only for one definite period

From the assumption already introduced (*i.e.* that the tastes of the person considered remain unchanged) it follows that any investment, once it has been made, is intended to be permanent : that is, to be repeated in every successive year. For our assumption implies that in so far as he has to choose at successive moments of time between the same alternatives, he will always decide in the same way. Any question as to what he will do at successive moments arises only to the extent that, in consequence of past decisions, the opportunities now open to him have changed. This means that all that is to be regarded as the addition to next year's income due to a given investment is the *net* return : that is, the amount which is left for consumption after provision has been made for the same quantities to be invested (or reinvested) as in the previous year. In such circumstances any investment can be expected to make equal additions to the income of all future years.

Any investment once made is assumed to be intended as permanent

The choice which is described by the "indifference maps" below is, then, one between additions to this year's income and additions to the income of all future years.

In consequence, net (and not gross) returns of the investments have to be compared

It is important to remember this throughout the exposition that follows, since the maps differ in this respect from the otherwise similar diagrams made familiar by Professor Irving Fisher's discussion of the same problems.[1] The advantage of the method adopted here, as will be seen, is that it enables us to use the diagrams to describe the successive decisions of an individual, or the process of saving over time.

In the following diagram (Fig. 21) this year's income is measured along the ordinate Oy and the income of the next and all future years along the abscissa Ox. The line

The construction of the diagram

Ow is drawn across the quadrant at an angle of 45 degrees to the two axes to indicate the *locus* of all points representing an equal distribution of income between this year and all future years (corresponding to stationary conditions). It will be convenient to start the discussion from a point where no investments have yet been made, no non-permanent resources exist, and a constant stream of current input is expected. The income which could permanently be expected from the direct use of the input may be represented by the distance OL. If no investments were to be

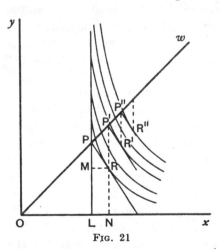

Fig. 21

[1] Cf. *The Theory of Interest* (1930), p. 237 *et seq.* The "Willingness" and "Market" lines there employed refer to gross (and not

made, and, in consequence, the expected future incomes were equal to the present income, the initial position would be represented by the point P (with the ordinates $x = y = OL$).[1] This may serve as our starting point.

The choice to be made in this initial situation is between retaining a given amount of present income and obtaining a permanent addition to the income of each period in the future. It may, perhaps, not be immediately obvious that in this situation saving will occur only if such a permanent net return is obtainable, and we must be careful not to beg this question. But it can easily be shown *Only cases where investments are expected to yield a positive return need be considered* that on our present assumptions this will be so. As we have already seen, it follows from our assumption of constant tastes and constant external data (including in particular constant technical possibilities) that the investment which is made at the first moment must be repeated at every successive moment. But if no net return were obtainable (of if the gross product obtainable from the investment were actually smaller than the amount invested), the sacrifice of present income would not be balanced by any addition to future income (or might even lead to an actual decrease in future income). And since we are here excluding the possibility of a desire to provide for uncertain contingencies (*i.e.* unforeseen changes in the net) returns. In consequence, in Professor Fisher's diagrams, " a given rate of interest is represented by the algebraic difference between the slope of a given Market line, and the 100 per cent slope of the 45° zero interest line," while in the diagrams that follow the rate of interest is directly represented by the slope of the curves.

[1] As we start out from a position in which only permanent resources are supposed to exist, an increase of present income at the expense of future income is evidently impossible, either for the isolated individual or for the community as a whole. For this reason the part of the plane yOx (Fig. 21) which lies to the left of the line LP can be neglected, since it contains no points which represent possible combinations of present and future income. Even after capital has been accumulated and, in consequence, it becomes in principle possible to increase present income at the expense of future income, it will never be possible to reduce future income below OL, since by their nature the services of the permanent factors cannot be consumed before they mature.

data), a permanent investment without the prospect of a net return would imply a desire to bring about a net decrease in total income, and may for this reason be excluded from our considerations.

The possible attitudes as between alternative marginal increments of present and future income which we shall have to consider will therefore range from one limiting case where every addition, however small,
Possible and probable rates of time preference to the permanent income stream will induce the person to give up part of his present income, to the other limiting case where no addition, however large, to the permanent income stream will induce him to give up part of his present income. It is impossible to decide on *a priori* grounds what the actual attitude of a person in any given situation will be. But it is a reasonable assumption, borne out by common experience, that in order to induce a person who, apart from this decision, would be certain of a constant income, to give up part of his present income in order to increase his future income, this permanent addition to future income would have to reach a definite minimum magnitude. And it is even more certain that in order to induce him to make larger and larger sacrifices of present income at a given moment, more than proportionately larger additions to future income will be required. Since the preservation of life requires a certain minimum of present income, no addition to future income, however large, will induce him to reduce present income below this minimum.

If we now describe this attitude by means of indifference curves, the first limiting case — that in which every permanent addition to future income is considered worth
The slope of the indifference curves some sacrifice of present income — will be represented by a curve with a perpendicular slope at the point P. If, however, some definite addition to future income is necessary in order to induce the person to give up even the smallest quantity of present income, the curve at this point will show a (negative) slope corre-

sponding to the rate of (net) return which will just leave the person indifferent as between saving and not saving. In either case any point to the right of this curve will represent a combination of present and future income which will be preferred to the constant income represented by P.

In all cases the slope of the curve will be as indicated only at the point where it crosses the line Ow, and, as we move along the curve further to the right, the slope will gradually diminish. Whether the slope at The curvature of the P is perpendicular or slightly inclined, it indifference curves will gradually turn more and more to the right with decreasing values of the ordinate : ultimately it will become horizontal at some point before present income (measured by the ordinate) has dwindled to zero. And the same will be true of all the other members of the complete family of indifference curves which may be drawn through all other points on the line Ow.

This set of curves describing the psychical attitude of the person at any moment will enable us to derive his actual behaviour if we combine it with a corresponding representation of the technical possibilities Investment opportun- of investment. The simplest assumption ities represented by to make in this respect — and the only transformation lines assumption compatible with the case where there is only one commodity and only one possible investment period — is that up to a definite limit [1] investments yield constant returns, and that at this limit the net return falls suddenly

---

[1] In this case successive investments will be made by investing successive doses of the pure input for the given investment period instead of using them for the satisfaction of current wants. And all opportunities for investment will be exhausted when all the available input is invested for that period. Up to this point we may expect constant physical returns unless we assume that some kinds of the pure input are more suitable for investment than other kinds. The point at which all input has been invested represents the absolute limit beyond which future income cannot be increased. In the diagram this is expressed by the fact that all transformation lines end (or become perpendicular) at the points corresponding to this maximum income.

to zero. This constant rate of transformation of present income into permanent additions to future income can be expressed by a family of straight transformation (or " displacement ") lines of corresponding slope, as shown in the diagram.

With this representation of the technical possibilities added to the indifference curves, the action of the individual can immediately be deduced. If he starts at the position represented by P, he can and will move in the manner indicated by the transformation line going through that point. From among the possible positions represented by all the points on this line the one that is most preferred will evidently be the position indicated by the point R where the transformation line just touches an indifference curve. This means that at the first date the person will save, out of his income LP, the amount MP, in order to increase next year's and all future years' income from OL to ON.

The first act of saving

But this is only the beginning of a process that will continue for some time. The diagram, it will be remembered, is supposed to represent the tastes of the person not only at the initial moment but at every moment, since his tastes are assumed to remain constant. Thus, as we can derive from the diagram the position in which the person will be at the second moment in consequence of his decision at the first moment, we can also derive from it what his decision will be at the second moment. As a result of the investment at the first date, the person will later find himself in command of an increased present income with an assured future income of equal magnitude, *i.e.* he will be in the position represented by P'. And he will again find it to his advantage to move along the transformation line from P' to R' on to a higher indifference curve, and so on. If, as we have assumed, the decisions to save and invest take place discontinuously at definite intervals, the person will be in successive years at the points R, R', R''.

The path of saving

There are two questions to which we must give at least provisional answers before we can go on to make more realistic assumptions concorning the shape of the transformation curve. The first is : What is the relative importance of the productivity element and the psychological attitude respectively in determining the rate of interest while the process of saving continues ? The second is : At what point will that process come to an end, and on what will the rate of interest depend in that final stationary state ?

Under the assumption made so far (*i.e.* straight transformation lines or constant — opportunity — costs) the answer to the first question is very simple. While the process of saving still continues, the rate of interest will be determined solely by the productivity of investment (the slope of the transformation curve), and the psychical attitude will merely determine how much will have to be saved at every moment in order that the marginal rate of time preference may adapt itself to the given and constant productivity rate. The only rôle " time preference " plays in this particular case is that it determines how long it will take until a stationary position is reached.[1]

The relative importance of productivity and time preference

To the second question there are two alternative answers. It is of course possible for saving to go on until there is no possibility of further investment. In this case the final equilibrium position will be represented in the diagram by the point where the end of the highest transformation line lies on the line *Ow*. Here investment comes to a standstill simply because, although possibly the person would still like to invest more, there are no further outlets for investment.

The final stationary equilibrium

---

[1] The situation here is of course exactly the same as in the more general case where the relative costs of two commodities are constant (*i.e.* independent of the quantities produced) and where, in consequence, their relative values are uniquely determined by their relative costs and cannot be affected (except in the very short run) by changes in their relative utilities.

Since this case is quite irrelevant to the problems which will arise later under more realistic assumptions, we need not consider it further.

The second possibility is that the process may come to an end before the investment opportunities are exhausted. It may be that at some point on the line *Ow* the transformation line will coincide with the tangent to the indifference curve, and that in consequence there will be no inducement to move along that line to the right, *i.e.* to invest. In the present case this is possible only if the slopes of the indifference curves at the points where they cut the line *Ow* are not the same for all the curves, but gradually increase. So far we have had no occasion to make any explicit assumption in this regard. If, however, we now introduce the assumption just mentioned (*i.e.* that the slopes of the successive indifference curves at the points where they cut the line *Ow* become continually larger), it is evidently possible that in some such position where present and future incomes are equal, the time preference may be equal to the technical productivity of capital. In this case the ultimate stationary equilibrium will be reached with a positive rate of interest equal to the constant productivity of investment. The psychical attitude will merely determine at what income this point will be reached. The rate of interest in this state of final equilibrium will be determined solely by the productivity of investment.

CHAPTER XVIII

TIME PREFERENCE AND PRODUCTIVITY : THEIR
RELATIVE IMPORTANCE

THE assumption of constant productivity of successive
investments had to be introduced, it will be remembered,
as a consequence of two other simplifying assumptions
which were necessary in order to render   The assumption of
a diagrammatic treatment of our problem   constant returns on
investments aban-
practicable.   These   assumptions   were,   doned
first, that only one commodity (or " income " conceived
as a sort of composite commodity consisting of constant
proportions of the different components) was produced,
and, secondly, that there was only one possible period of
investment.[1] As soon as we drop either of these assumptions we come to the more realistic case where successive
investments will yield decreasing returns. It will be seen,
however, that the results obtained under the less realistic
assumptions are not altogether useless or irrelevant,
since, as compared with time preference, the productivity
of investment is likely to be fairly constant.

There is, however, the serious difficulty of exposition
that as soon as we drop either of the two assumptions
concerned, the diagrammatic method so far used is no
longer strictly applicable. The reason why   Consequent difficul-
the existence of different commodities   ties of diagrammatic
makes the returns on successive invest-   representation
ments decrease is twofold. In the first place the advantage
of time-consuming processes will be different in the production of different commodities, and in the second place
if the production of some commodities is increased more

---

[1] Probably a third condition is also required in order to obtain
constant productivity, i.e. that input should be homogeneous.

than that of others the relative values of the former will fall. But in our diagram only decreases in physical returns can be properly represented. The reason why the possibility of varying the investment period implies decreasing returns is that the existence of different kinds of possible methods of production will always mean that the most profitable ones will be selected first, and the less productive ones will be taken up only gradually as the supply of capital increases. The difficulty of representing this case diagrammatically is due to the fact that if the periods of investment vary, it is no longer possible to assume that the results of the investments made at any one date will all become available after a single and constant interval of time. But while it would be difficult to take account of this factor in the diagram, the inaccuracy caused by neglecting it is not so serious as to make the simpler form of the diagram useless for the elucidation of this case. We shall therefore simply postulate that decreasing returns occur as a result of the variety of investment periods, but shall neglect the particular complication mentioned in order to be able to use the same sort of diagram as before.

The way in which the diagram (Fig. 22, p. 233) will express the fact that the returns on investment decrease is that the transformation lines will be curved and concave The shape of the towards the axes instead of being straight transformation curves as in the former case. Since the return on further investment must be assumed to depend only on the amount of investments already made (*i.e.* only on the provision made for the future) and to be independent of the size of the income left for the present, it cannot be presumed that the shapes of the different members of the complete family of transformation curves will be independent of each other. At any point corresponding to a given value on the abscissa the slope of all the transformation curves will have to be the same, and they will therefore all be similar in shape. But those further up and to the right will possess additional parts at their lower end which are missing from those further down and to the left.

Which member of this family of transformation curves will be relevant at any particular moment will depend on the size of present income. But this affects only the variety of the choice and not the size of the returns obtainable for the sacrifice of a given amount of income. What propor- tional share of current income a given quantity to be invested represents will have little if any effect on the size of the returns that will be obtained. The latter will depend almost exclusively on the aggre- gate of the investments already made, no matter whether the individual investments making up that aggregate have followed each other at long or at short intervals.

It is practically inde- pendent of the length of the period over which the invest- ments are made

But while the size of the present income, out of which we save a given amount, will have no influence on the return on the investment of a unit of that income, it will have a very considerable effect on our willingness to save any given amount. And since the aggregate of income out of which a given amour t is saved will vary in proportion to the length of the period during which that amount is saved, it follows that the shape of the indifference curve will vary with the length of the period which we regard as " the present ". As the period during which a given amount is to be saved and invested becomes shorter, this given amount becomes a proportionately larger share of the income of that period. For a person with an annual income of £600, for example, saving £25 in the course of a year is an altogether different proposi- tion from saving the same amount in the course of a month. The sacrifice in the second case amounts to reducing one's expenditure to one-half one's income. And as we make the period still shorter the reluctance to save and invest a given amount will increase further.

The willingness to save a given amount depends on the length of period during which it is to be saved

The fact that of the two relevant curves, the transformation curve and the indifference curve, the first is independent of the length of the period considered while
The relevant period the second is dependent on it, means, in terms of the diagram, that as we make the income period shorter the indifference curve will become more and more curved while the transformation curve will remain practically unchanged. For our purposes, however, the relevant periods will clearly be the comparatively short intervals at which income accrues and at which the decisions have to be made as to what part of income to consume and what part to save.[1] Compared with the totals that may be profitably invested, even the total income for a year, and still more the total income for a month, are relatively small magnitudes. But it is these relatively short periods which we have to consider if we want to understand the position of a person at different points on the path of saving.

It is, then, the ratio of the curvatures of (or the ratio of the elasticities of substitution expressed by) the two groups of curves which is of fundamental importance for
At every step in the process of saving the variable rate of time preference adapts itself to the relatively constant rate of return what follows. Perhaps it is necessary to dwell somewhat longer on this point. The above statement about the ratio of the curvatures is an expression of the fact that, if we consider a relatively short time interval, the sacrifice of successive parts of the income of

[1] New decisions of this sort are required for each date at which, in consequence of past investment, current income increases. It is irrelevant for our purpose whether we assume that the " new decision " is not made until that moment or whether we assume that the altered disposition after that moment has been decided upon from the beginning. The difficulty, as mentioned previously, concerns the date or dates when the successive fruits of investment become available. Contrary to the first case discussed, these investment periods are no longer identical with the income period. Thus, strictly speaking, it is no longer true that the decision to save made during any income period is directly affected by the result of the investment in the immediately preceding period. This is a complication which, as mentioned previously, will be deliberately neglected.

this interval of time in the interests of the future will
meet with a rapidly increasing resistance, while, on the
other hand, the investment of successive fractions of a
small total income will have quite an insignificant effect
on the rate of return obtainable from investment. The
situation will still be similar to the case discussed before
to the extent that during any short income-period the
rate of time preference (as represented by the indifference
curve) will have to adapt itself to a relatively constant
rate of return. In terms
of the diagram : If the
process starts at *P*,
then, during the first
time interval the indi-
vidual will move along
the transformation
curve until he reaches
R, where the rate of
time preference on fur-
ther doses of present
income is equal to the
rate of return, which
will have been little
affected by the com-

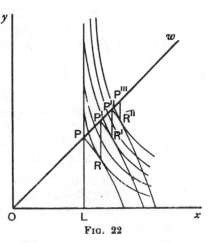

Fig. 22

paratively small amount invested.   In consequence of this
investment he will some time later find himself at *P'*, and
will again save until his time preference has been raised to
equal the comparatively constant rate of return. That is,
he will move to *R'*. And when, in consequence of this,
he finds himself in the position indicated by *P''*, he will
again save, and so on.

The imaginary curve *R*, *R'*, *R''* . . . thus again represents the path along which the saver moves in time. The
main points that are brought out by this method of representation are these : First, saving must necessarily be
treated as a process in time the effects of which continually change the actual position of the saver and thereby

his willingness to perform further saving. Secondly, at any point in this process the rate of saving is practically determined by the productivity of investment alone, and

Time preference directly affects only the rate of saving : its effect on rate of interest is indirect only time preference is important only in determining *how fast* the saver will move towards a position in which the productivity of further investment, and therefore the rate of interest, is lower.[1] It will also be seen that, so long as saving continues, the time preference of the individual as represented by his marginal rate of substitution between equal present and future income streams (the slope of the indifference curve where it crosses the line Ow) may be zero, or even negative, and there will nevertheless be a positive rate of interest.

The exact direction of the path of saving will evidently depend on the shape and position of the two sets of curves. Whether and when a stationary position will be

Positive time preference a condition for the existence of interest under stationary conditions reached depends on the rate at which the productivity of investment decreases as the amount invested increases, compared with the change in the rate of time preference consequent upon the increase in income. It is conceivable that saving might not cease until all opportunities for investment had been exhausted, because any rate of return, however small, would lead to some saving. This would mean that at the point where they cross the constant-income line Ow, the indifference curves, at least in the region of the higher incomes, would be perpendicular. In this case stationary conditions would be reached only at a zero rate of interest. But if the indifference curves have a definite slope along that line (*i.e.* if there is, in the traditional meaning, a positive time preference), saving will cease, and a stationary state will be reached, with a positive rate of interest corresponding to the rate repre-

---

[1] The credit for having made this point clear belongs to Professor F. H. Knight, with whose more recent statements on this point I find myself in complete agreement. Cf. particularly his articles **1932a** and **b.**

sented by that slope. And in this sense it can be said that the rate of time preference determines the rate of interest existing in the final stationary equilibrium, and there only.[1] Lastly, there is also the possibility that as the return on investment decreases, the rate of saving may become so small that the investment opportunities will not be exhausted within any time in which we are at all interested. In this case saving will go on indefinitely (*i.e.* the path of saving will end at the line *Ow* only after an indefinitely long time), and while it continues the rate of interest will be determined not by time preference but by the productivity of investment.

The shape of the curve describing the path of saving depends on the rate at which the willingness to save changes with a change in income, and the rate at which the returns on further investment decrease in consequence of past investment. Only Factors determining the path of saving in the case of constant returns from successive investments (see Fig. 21) will its shape depend entirely on, and be a property of, the structure of the "indifference map". In this case the curve becomes an instance of the "expenditure" curve, which is familiar from the modern expositions of the theory of value,[2] and which represents the change in the distribution of "expenditure" (in our case between present and future income) consequent upon an increase of income. In the other case we considered, shown in our second diagram (Fig. 22), this effect of an increase in income is mixed up with the effects of the decreasing returns from further investment. It will be

----

[1] "The" rate of time preference is here the rate at which a person would just be indifferent towards giving up a marginal quantity of his present income in return for a corresponding addition to his *otherwise equal* future income. Since, as will be clear from what has been said before, a positive rate of time preference in this sense is entirely compatible with the assumption of constant tastes, we have here the case of a stationary equilibrium with a positive rate of interest, which Professor Schumpeter regards as impossible (cf. Appendix I).

[2] Cf. J. R. Hicks and R. G. D. Allen, "A Reconsideration of the Theory of Value ", *Economica*, N.S., vol. i (1934).

useful to isolate this influence also, and to show how
the person in question would react if, while his income
remained unchanged, the returns on investment were
gradually altered by extraneous circumstances.

This can be done by deriving from the "indifference
map" a curve showing the demand for future income, in
terms of present income, at every possible rate of return on
The effect of the rate   investment. The phenomenon which this
of interest on saving   curve describes is, of course, identical with
that which has been widely discussed under the heading
of how the individual saver will react, *ceteris paribus*, to
changes in the rate of interest. It will immediately appear,
perhaps contrary to the first impression, that the assumptions so far made do not in any way prejudice this
question. They are
compatible with the
saver's either increas-
ing or decreasing the
amount saved in re-
sponse to a rise in the
rate of interest, and
vice versa.

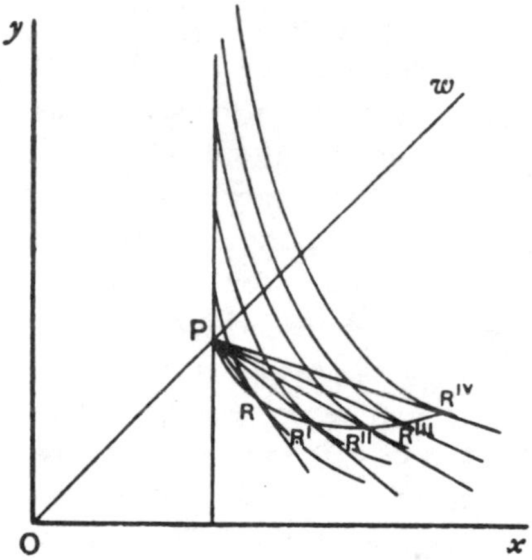

The demand curve
which we are now con-
sidering shows the effect
of a change in price on
the distribution of out-
lay between present
and future income as

FIG. 23

distinguished from the effect of a change in income (shown
The construction of   by the expenditure curve). It is constructed
the demand curve for   (Fig. 23) by rotating the price line *PQ*
future income   round the fixed point *P* (which represents
present income on the assumption that no investments
have yet been made), and connecting up all the points
(R, R', R'', R''', R^{iv}) where this line becomes tangential
to the successive indifference curves. The slopes of these

lines represent the different rates at which present income can be transformed into future income, *i.e.* the rates of return or the rates of interest. As they become less and less steep, the permanent addition to future income which can be obtained for a given sacrifice of present income becomes greater and greater.

The diagram is constructed in such a way as to show a case where, up to a point, the sacrifice of present income which the person is willing to make in order to obtain additions to future income increases as the returns on investment increase. But even if, as the assumptions underlying the diagram imply, the additions to future income which will be demanded continue to increase indefinitely with increases in the rate of return on investment, this does not mean that the demand for future income *in terms of present income* will continue to increase. As the additions to future income that are obtainable for given sacrifices of present income increase, the demand for such additions to future income may well increase less than in inverse proportion to the decrease of their price in terms of present income. That is, the amount of present income given up to obtain additions to future income may actually decrease. This is shown in the diagram by the fact that the demand curve turns upwards at some point. At this point the elasticity of the demand for future income becomes less than unity, and the supply of savings will henceforth decrease as the rate of interest increases.

The elasticity of demand for future income

We can say nothing *a priori* about the point at which in concrete cases the rate of saving will begin to decrease with further increases in the rate of interest. It will be different with different individuals, and it may conceivably be so low (although this seems very unlikely) as to make a fall in the supply of savings in response to increasing rates of interest the rule rather than the exception, at least so far as concerns those rates

No general rule as to whether the rate of saving will move in the same or in the opposite direction to the rate of interest

of interest with which we have to deal in actual practice. But for the theoretical questions with which we are dealing here our lack of certain knowledge as to which case is most likely to occur is of small consequence. All that we want to stress is that our treatment implies no particular assumptions in this respect : either of the two cases fits into our scheme. In practice we ought probably to assume that the rate of saving will increase with increasing rates of interest up to a point and decrease beyond that point. And the position of this point will be different for different individuals and at different times.

In the case of the economic dictator of a communist society on which our attention has so far been centred, it is probably most reasonable to assume that the dictator

Effect of limitation of period over which plan extends

plans for an indefinite future and expects to command a constant stream of output during that future. But it is important, in view of later applications of our argument, to drop these assumptions now, and to consider the case where the future period in which the person is actively interested is limited, and where also, perhaps, he cannot expect a stream of permanent services which will last throughout the period in which he is interested. The latter condition means, of course, that initially he does not command any really " permanent " [1] resources : all that he has are relatively durable wasting resources. Thus even if he does not want to increase (by investment) the stream of final services which he can obtain from the direct use of these resources while they last, he will be obliged to make provision for their replacement by *producing* resources for the time when they are exhausted.

The more important of the two assumptions is, however, the first, *i.e.* that the person in question plans only

[1] But since the services from these resources cannot in any way be utilised before they accrue in the course of nature, *i.e.* since they are non-anticipatable services, they may, so far as his initial plan is concerned, to a large extent possess the essential characteristics of " permanent " resources.

for a limited period beyond which he is not interested. This means, of course, that we can no longer assume that he will make provision for a permanent income stream : we have therefore to allow for the possibility of his re-converting capital that has been accumulated during the earlier part of the period into income during the later part of the period. If we make the further assumption that he has no permanent resources whatever, but is from the beginning only equipped with a stock of wasting assets of varying minimum durability, the problem becomes one of how to use this stock of capital so as to produce an income stretching over the desired period and possessing the most preferred shape. But even on this assumption we shall have to take into account that the services of some of the wasting assets are more like those of permanent resources in that they cannot be consumed before a certain date. This means that even if none of the resources are strictly permanent, the essential fact remains that some of them cannot be used before a certain date.

It is hardly possible to discuss these questions in a satisfactory manner without making allowance for one further important element. I refer to the uncertainty which will usually exist concerning both **Significance of un-** the length of the period for which provision **certainty** will be required and the time for which the resources are likely to last. Any attempt to go beyond what has already been said would therefore mean entering upon a systematic analysis of the rôle played by uncertainty in this connection. But for a number of reasons it has seemed advisable to stop short of this discussion here. One reason is that there appears to be little possibility of saying much that is worth while on the subject without making more concrete assumptions about the institutional background than are required for the more general considerations to which the bulk of this study is devoted. It seems in particular that the significance of uncertainty may be more properly discussed in connection with the monetary aspects of our problem, which we are not discussing here. Furthermore, most of what can usefully be said about the significance of uncertainty on the general plane of abstraction on which this discussion proceeds, seems to have been said by others, especially by Professor Irving Fisher.[1] Therefore, instead of adding to the length of this discussion by going over what to most readers will be familiar ground, it is perhaps preferable to refer to these other works and to confine ourselves here to the little that can be said about the topic which is our immediate concern without introducing the factor of uncertainty.

If, then, we assume that an income stream is wanted for a limited (but definite) period only, this will in general mean that any act of saving and investment will increase

Effect of anticipated length of life on willingness to save
income during the remainder of the period not only by net interest, as the term has been used above, but also by a further amount corresponding to the rate at which it will be possible gradually to use up the capital previously accumulated. Or, in other words, any given increase of one's income for the rest of one's life will be obtainable at a smaller present sacrifice than a similar increase of a perpetual income. This will probably mean that a person will be ready during the earlier years of his life to provide year by year for some addition to his future income. But since given additions to future income can in this case be obtained at a smaller present sacrifice, the effect is likely to be that he will not save as big a portion of his present income as would seem advisable if he were providing for a perpetual income. And he will certainly stop saving at an earlier age. On the whole, then, we should expect that a limitation on the time for which a person wants to provide an income — and any shortening of this time — will make him save less than he otherwise would.

[1] See also an unpublished thesis by Dr. Helen Makower on *The Theory of Value on the Capital Market* (University of London, 1937).

The effect of the second of the two factors mentioned above, an expected decrease in the stream of " permanent " services that would be available without saving, works in the opposite direction. Additions to a future income which, in the absence of present saving, would be lower than present income are likely to appear more urgent than increases of future income beyond the level of present income. An expected decrease in the stream of services of the " permanent " resources is therefore likely to increase saving and so to counteract (though not necessarily to offset, or not more than to offset) the effect of the limitation of the period for which an income has to be provided. Since we are not concerned here with the concrete magnitude of time preference, but only with the direction in which various factors are likely to affect it, we may leave this problem here.

Effect of anticipated decrease of non-anticipatable services

The last point which needs to be touched on briefly in this chapter is the possibility of the existence of different rates of time preference in respect to different commodities. Up to now we have looked upon " income " as if it were a composite commodity which was necessarily made up of constant proportions of the different goods. This involved either or both of the assumptions that the different commodities could, for technical reasons, be produced only in fixed proportions, and that there existed such a peculiar degree of complementarity between them that they were desired only in fixed proportions.

Rates of time preference for different commodities

If tastes remained constant and conditions were in all other respects stationary, we should expect the rate of interest to be the same no matter in which commodity it was expressed. But, even with constant tastes, there is no reason why people, when their total incomes increase, should not want to spend these incomes in different proportions on the various commodities. And, in addition, we shall have to take into account that at different dates the relative preferences for the various commodities may be different. This need not mean a " change in tastes " in the sense that a person has altered his intentions. He may from the beginning have anticipated that at different periods he will want his income in different forms (and made his plans accordingly), just as everyone will foresee that he will have different needs at different seasons of the year and different hours of the day.

But we may begin with the simpler case where tastes are constant in the sense that, with equal opportunities before him, the individual will always decide in the same way at the different dates. All that we Effects of accumulation of capital on relative values of commodities have to consider in this case is the effect of the gradual accumulation of capital on the relative values of commodities. This works in two ways. On the one hand, with given relative costs (*i.e.* given displacement curves) for the various commodities, relative preferences, and therefore relative values, may change in response to increases in income. On the other hand, the fall in the rate of interest accompanying the accumulation of capital will affect the relative costs of the different commodities in varying degrees according to the proportional amounts of capital [1] that can be profitably used in their production at the different rates of interest.

The general implications of such a situation were discussed above (Chapter XII, p. 167), when we dealt with the meaning of the concept of a uniform rate of interest in value terms. We know that equilibrium in these intertemporal value relationships is quite compatible with different intertemporal marginal rates of substitution for different commodities. All that need be added here is an explanation of how this situation fits into our representation of time preferences. And although the present case falls outside the field in which the graphical representa-

[1] The decisive magnitude in this connection is the " elasticity of substitution " of new capital for the concrete resources already in existence.

tions used previously are applicable, a conceptual extension of our scheme to cover this case meets with no serious difficulties.

We shall have to conceive of a structure of n-dimensional indifference surfaces where n includes the number of commodities considered *plus* the number of different points of time (or periods) for which the person plans. Similarly the different rates of transformation between the different commodities, or between commodities at different points of time, can be represented by a corresponding system of n-dimensional displacement surfaces. The relative values of the commodities, and their individual time rates of increase, will then be formally determined on exactly the same principles as those determining the relative values of a number of commodities that are assumed to be simultaneously available. Every increase or decrease in the value of any one commodity, relative to that of others, which takes place in response to an increase in total income will mean a corresponding rate of interest during the period in terms of that commodity. Suppose, *e.g.*, we take as our standard of reference the rate of interest in terms of commodity a, and consider a commodity b, the value of which increases in terms of a from one moment of time to another, so that at the second moment a smaller quantity of b corresponds to a given quantity of a than at the first moment. Then equilibrium requires that the rate of interest in terms of b should be smaller than the rate in terms of a. And the same applies, *mutatis mutandis*, to a fall in the value of one commodity in terms of another : here the rate of interest in terms of the former will have to be greater than in terms of the latter.

Fundamentally the same considerations also apply where the cause of the change in relative values is not a change in total income but a foreseen " change " in tastes. If — to add just a few words on this case — it

[sidenote: Conditions of Intertemporal equilibrium of values]

is known in advance that at a later date relatively more of commodity a will be demanded and relatively less of commodity b, and an increase in the output of a at the

Effect of foreseen changes in relative preferences for different commodities

expense of that of b is obtainable only at increasing cost, then the rate of interest in terms of a (*i.e.* the price of present a's in terms of future a's) will be smaller than the rate of interest in terms of b.

It will be seen that this description of intertemporal relationships covers not only the case of constant tastes in the narrower sense but also the case where the actual distribution of the resources is different at different dates but where it has been correctly foreseen from the initial moment when the planning for the whole period was done. This means that it covers as much as can be covered by general equilibrium analysis — *i.e.* all actions based on the knowledge possessed at one moment of time.

PART III
CAPITALISTIC PRODUCTION IN A
COMPETITIVE COMMUNITY

CHAPTER XIX

THE GENERAL CONDITIONS OF EQUILIBRIUM

WE are now ready to drop some of the special assumptions on which we have so far discussed the problems of capital and interest, and to apply the results obtained to the phenomena of the market. The case of a centrally directed communist society which we have been considering has shown us the rôle that is played by two basic factors (*i.e.* the various opportunities to invest and the time preferences of the persons concerned) under the (analytically) simplest conditions, that is when all resources are under the control of a single mind which uses them in the service of a coherent system of ends. Here we shall move one step nearer to reality by considering the case where the command over the existing resources is distributed between a multitude of independent persons, each of whom uses his share of them in the service of his individual system of ends and all of whom are in a position to exchange on a market.

This transition to a set of assumptions which are somewhat more closely related to real phenomena does not, however, mean that we shall undertake to explain the actual process on a competitive market. Still a study of equilibrium relationships As was indicated in the introductory section, this study will in the main be confined to an analysis of equilibrium relationships. The transition from .the study of equilibrium in a " simple " economy to the study of equilibrium in a competitive economy here means passing from the analysis of the plans of an individual to the analysis of the compatibility of the independent plans of a number of individuals. The question of how

247

and when such a state of competitive equilibrium will come about does not directly concern us here and will only be touched upon incidentally. But, as will be remembered, this does not mean that our discussion has to be confined to stationary conditions. In fact, this part of the book will deal largely with the readjustments of the economic system which would be necessary if an unforeseen change were to be met by the immediate establishment of a new position of equilibrium.

This will not exclude us from speaking in places, for illustrative purposes, of successive movements which will lead to an equilibrium position. This, however, will not be meant as an explanation of the actual causal process which in the real world may bring about a position of equilibrium. The successive approaches are rather to be conceived, like the *tâtonnements* in Walras' analysis or Edgeworth's construction of re-contracting, as successive attempts of the individuals to find out what the equilibrium position is. We are, in other words, deliberately discussing changes which can be brought about only through the mechanism of money and competition, yet disregard for our present purposes the exact rôle these two factors play. The reason for this is that we are here really not interested in the *process* which brings about equilibrium but merely in the *conditions* of a state of equilibrium, and when we are considering positions other than equilibrium positions it is merely to show why they are not equilibrium positions. And the approach to equilibrium of which we shall occasionally speak is not meant as a description of a process but merely as a conceptual tool which leads us, as it were, as spectators from positions which are more removed from equilibrium to positions which are closer to it, and finally to the equilibrium position itself.[1]

---

[1] The nature of the causal processes involved can be considered, in so far as this will be done at all in this volume, only after we have explicitly introduced money at the beginning of Part IV.

In discussing equilibrium in such a society we shall have to take account of the following new data. In the first place we shall have, instead of a single system of preferences, and particularly time preferences, as many independent and probably different systems of wants as there are different indi- The data of the problem: (1) individual tastes viduals. Each of these systems can be represented by an indifference map similar to that used in the preceding chapters to describe the attitude of the single dictator. In the present chapter, however, not much attention will be paid to these time preferences. At the beginning of this discussion we shall once again, and for the last time, make use of the assumption that everybody aims at a constant income stream. We shall postpone the explicit discussion of what happens when people aim at increasing or decreasing income streams.

In the second place, the resources available for the satisfaction of these wants will be unevenly distributed between the individuals. As a rule, we shall find that most individuals do not command all the resources which, with the technique actu- (2) the distribution of resources ally in use, are required to carry on the continuous production even of a single commodity. Usually we shall find that the resources required for any one process of production are divided between a number of persons. In most cases equipment belonging to different stages of one process of production will be in different hands. And some at least of the permanent resources whose services are required in the different stages, certainly human labour if no others, will be under the control of persons other than those who own the material equipment and direct and organise production. In consequence it will be necessary to exchange not only different final products but also intermediate products and the services of resources of all kinds.

It will be convenient to start by considering a society which has been working on these lines in the past, but to consider it at a point of time without inquiring how the direction of production has been determined hitherto. We may assume that at the moment at which we begin to look at this society, considerable changes in the data have just occurred, so that a new equilibrium has to be found. We can then speak of the different purposes for which the various resources had been intended before the change occurred, without begging any of the questions which are raised by the determination of the new equilibrium.

The most significant way of classifying the different resources in this connection is according to the date or dates when they can be made to yield a consumable Classification of available resources based on nearness of date when they can bring a return product. Everybody, or nearly everybody, will, of course, normally be in command of some resources which can be made to serve his needs in the immediate future. His own labour at least will as a rule fall in this category, even if no other of his resources do. But this does not mean either that this is the most profitable use that can be made of these resources or even that it could enable the individual to produce enough to keep himself alive. In modern societies, where in consequence of the accumulation of capital the growth of population has been stimulated far beyond the figures which could be maintained without that capital, it will frequently be impossible for a single individual to produce with his unaided labour even enough to subsist on. And the other resources in the possession of many individuals will often not be capable of yielding consumables until a distant date, or if they are used for immediate consumption, will bring only a small fraction of what they would yield at that later date.

In consequence of the (vertical) division of labour by far the larger part of the resources most suitable to provide consumables for the immediate future will be under the control of a comparatively small section of the members of the society. Only a relatively small propor-

tion of the society's resources will be in the form of actual
consumers' goods, ready for immediate consumption ; by
far the greater part will consist of other resources which,
either because they were originally intended to serve
consumption at later dates, or because of the changed
circumstances, are best suited to serve consumption in
the more distant future.

It becomes necessary here to give a more precise
formulation of this distinction which was implicit in most
of what has been said up to this point. There may on the
one hand be input which can be used only
in one particular " stage " of production   Specificity and versa-
or only so as to give a product at a definite   tility of different kinds
and invariable interval after its investment. Such input
we shall call completely *specific* input. Specificity in
this extreme form will probably be of very rare occurrence, but it will evidently be possible to distinguish
between lesser and greater degrees of specificity according as the use of particular kinds of input is confined to a
longer or shorter range of periods.

Most kinds of input will, however, be not specific, but
more or less " *versatile* ",[1] in the sense that they can be
used in a great many if not in nearly all stages of production. But in their case a further dis-
tinction of degree is necessary, which is   The two respects in
somewhat more complicated than the one   which specificity or
                                            versatility varies
based on the absolute possibility or impossibility of using
certain resources in particular stages. If we consider two
kinds of input which can be used over the same range of
" stages ", they may still differ with regard to the change
in the size of the products consequent upon a change in
their investment period. If we start from a given disposition of the input, the necessity of shifting some part
of one kind of input to another stage may involve a
greater loss of product than would be the case with another

---

[1] This term has been suggested by Mr. G. L. Shackle as a substitute
for the clumsy " non-specific ".

kind of input, and in this sense the former would have to be regarded as less adaptable than the latter. This distinction is, however, very much more complicated than the former one, which was based on the absolute mobility or immobility of the different kinds of input. For the change in the product which is due to any such transfer will depend not only on the proportions in which the two kinds of input in question have already been distributed between the stages but also on the use that is made of all other input. The question resolves itself into the question of the elasticity of demand for the different kinds of input at the different stages, and the answer ultimately depends on, and can only be appropriately discussed in terms of, the complete productivity function of investment for all kinds of input and the elasticities of substitution which could be derived from it.

How the versatile kinds of input (which can be used to produce income either in the nearer or in the more distant future) will actually come to be used, will evidently depend on the relative prices which they will fetch in the different uses. And for any particular individual the relative magnitude of the return which he can obtain will depend on the way in which all the other people intend to distribute their total resources between present and future uses. If all the others devoted the greater part of their resources to acquiring income for the immediate future, the product which he could obtain from his resources in the near future would become relatively more valuable and would induce him to choose this use, and *vice versa*. But the same is, of course, true of all the other people, so that it is impossible to treat this willingness of people in the aggregate to divide their resources in certain proportions between the present and the future as a datum from which we can derive the way in which they will use the different individual resources.

The difficulty which arises here can be stated in slightly

different terms as follows. Whether in any individual case it will be more profitable to use given resources to produce income in the nearer or in the more distant future, will depend on the proportion in which The danger of a cir- the community in the aggregate decides to cular argument distribute its total resources between use for the present and use for the future. But this proportion in which the total resources are distributed evidently will depend not only on the willingness of the different individuals to distribute their resources in particular ways, but also on the value of the resources in their possession. On this value of the resources in the possession of every person there will depend not only the way in which he will want to distribute them between present and future, but also the weight which attaches to his decision in making up the aggregate proportion for society. But this value depends in turn on the similar decisions of all others, and it seems therefore as if the whole argument were moving in a circle.

This apparent impasse can, however, be overcome if we focus attention on the peculiar key position held by the owners of resources which can be made to yield consumers' goods in the immediate future, and The key position of if we begin by studying the effects which the owners of ready their decisions will have on the position of consumers' goods all others. If everybody decided to consume himself all the consumable goods which he could possibly command during, say, the next month, and did not care what happened afterwards (*e.g.* because the belief in some millennium made people expect the end of the world to come at the end of this month), then, clearly, all " resources " which could not be made to give a consumable return before that date would be completely valueless and would not be used at all. And all those other resources which, in different circumstances, would have been invested for more than a month will now be used to produce the much smaller and in some cases almost negligible amounts which they can produce within the month. If the society in question has previously used a great deal of capital, this will mean that by far the greater part of the consumers' goods which can be made available during the month will be in the command of a comparatively small section of the society, while the rest of the society have little more than what their bare hands can produce during that period.

What is to be regarded as the amount of ready consumers' goods over which command is held at the time in question, largely depends of course on the period which we take as the basis of our distinction. If instead of a month we had taken a week or a day as our period of reference, a still smaller part of the total resources could have been turned into consumers' goods during that period, and the greater part of the " supply of ready consumers' goods " would probably have been in the hands of a still smaller section of the community. As we shall see [1] later, there are several traditional concepts, such as those of circulating capital and the liquidity of capital, the exact meaning of which depends entirely on what we choose as our period of reference. For present purposes we ought, strictly speaking, to begin with the supply of consumers' goods which could be made available during the smallest conceivable interval. But though this would be more exact, it would give the whole analysis a somewhat unrealistic complexion. It will therefore be better if we choose as our starting point some definite period of reasonable length, and there is no reason why we should not take the month which we have already used as a representative period.

The " command over ready consumers' goods "

Apart from the purely hypothetical case referred to above, it is, of course, very improbable that those who have direct command over the ready supply of consumers' goods will ever want to consume all of it themselves.

[1] Cf. Chapter XXIII.

For the effect of this would be that after the period in question had elapsed they would be reduced to exactly the same position as everybody else. This is so because, while everybody else was engaged in turning all that they had into consumers' goods, no other resources would *It will be in the interest of the owners of ready consumers' goods to give up part of them —* be advanced nearer to consumption, since those who were in possession of the resources best adapted for use in those earlier stages would be compelled to strain all their energies to produce enough consumers' goods, with means ill suited to the *— in order to secure replacement of their stock* purpose, in order merely to keep themselves alive. It will consequently be in the interest of those who command considerable quantities of ready consumers' goods to offer part of them to those who are willing to provide them, on the most favourable terms, with new capital goods to replace those which are used up.

On what principle will the owners of consumers' goods distribute that part of those goods which they decide not to consume themselves between the different types of capital goods in which they have the possibility of investing ? One might be inclined to assume that at first, and so long as only *Principles determining choice of resources for which consumers' goods will be offered* relatively small quantities of ready consumers' goods are available for investment, only capital goods that will bring a return in the comparatively near future will be demanded, *e.g.* that at first only resources which will bring a return during the month immediately succeeding the current one will be wanted, and that only after all investments which will yield a return in the second month are actually taken up will anybody be willing to invest in goods which will not yield a return until the third month, and so on.

This conclusion would, however, be erroneous. If the owners of the consumers' goods want to keep their income permanently above the level that would be possible if they were to consume their whole stock now without making any provision for its replacement, they will have to plan for regular re-investment of similar amounts during every future period. And if direct investment for a later date will yield a product that is larger than what could be obtained by re-investing the equivalent of the product that is obtainable from the same input at an earlier date, it will be profitable for them to invest for the longer period from the start.

Those who command ready consumers' goods will then use such part of them as they do not want to consume themselves in the immediate future, to engage such other input as will yield the relatively highest per annum rate of return on present cost. What part of their consumers' goods they will be willing to invest in this form will partly depend on the return to be obtained. The cost of the investment on the other hand will depend on the return which the input to be invested for longer periods would have yielded in the immediate future. This means that at first, so long as only a relatively small proportion of the total of ready consumers' goods is invested, that input which would help to add to the return only by very little or which would help to add to it only at a very distant date, will fetch no price at all. All the cost that is then involved is the remuneration which has to be offered in order to induce input, which could also be used to produce consumers' goods currently, to be applied instead to the provision of consumers' goods in the more distant future. It will therefore be the input which brings the lowest present return, compared with the return it might bring in the more distant future, that will be first withdrawn from current use and invested. It will be noticed that this will always mean a reduction of *current* output below the potential maximum.

If we assume that the people who have direct command over the greater part of the ready consumers' goods at first offer only a relatively small part of them to others,

(margin note: Part of command of ready consumers' goods that will be transferred)

they will probably find that the amount of resources they can obtain in return is insufficient to replace those which they are using up. It will therefore fail to assure them of a supply of consumers' goods in the future *Effect of successive* equal to that which they command in the *transfers of increasing parts of command over ready consumers' goods* present. And if they want to maintain their available income at an even level they will have to increase the share of the consumers' goods in their possession which they cede to other members of the community. We may therefore proceed to consider the effects which follow if they gradually increase the share of their ready consumers' goods which they are willing to exchange against resources with a more distant return.

One effect will evidently be that the rate of return on the investments will fall as the amount invested increases. The first small quantity of consumers' goods available for investment would have been shared out *Fall of rate of return on investments* among investments of different lengths but all bringing the same maximum rate of return. A larger quantity would similarly be distributed among investments of different lengths, but all yielding a somewhat lower rate of return. Böhm-Bawerk has described this process by saying that investments would have to be spread along contour lines corresponding to lower and lower rates of return as the amounts available for investment increased.[1]

Closely connected with this is the effect on the prices (in terms of consumers' goods) of the various resources. At first the prices which the owners of the ready consumers' goods would have to pay to obtain *Changes in relative prices of different resources* input for production for the more distant future would only just exceed the very low returns which the kinds of input least suitable to the direct production of consumers' goods could obtain in that use. But as more and more consumers' goods are used to remunerate input whose services are going to

[1] Cf. *Positive Theory of Capital*, p. 405.

be invested, two things will happen. The alternative current returns of this input will increase and, in addition, competition between the owners of the consumers' goods will drive up the prices of the resources of lower present productivity to a figure corresponding to its actual return discounted at the lower rate of interest now ruling. And in all cases where the additional supply of consumers' goods is used, not to invest input which had not been invested at all previously, but to lengthen the investment period of input which, with a smaller supply of consumers' goods, would have been invested for some shorter period, it will be necessary to pay a price higher than the (discounted) return from the shorter investment period.

Both the last two considerations apply both to resources which would have brought some return if used directly, and also to resources which would have been quite unusable, and valueless, if those in command of the ready consumers' goods had consumed all of those goods themselves. At first, indeed, such resources (which will be largely of the non-permanent kind like machines) will always be put into operation when nothing more than the remuneration of the less specific co-operating input (*i.e.* the " prime cost " of using them) is covered. But as the demand for capital goods in general (or, what is the same thing, the share of the command over ready consumers' goods devoted to investment) increases, these resources will gradually gain value and will fetch a price (in terms of consumers' goods). As more and more present consumers' goods are offered in return for the expectation of future consumers' goods which the possession of such resources warrants, the price of these resources will go on rising.

All this means that the command over a considerable share of the supply of ready consumers' goods will in the first instance be transferred from those people who directly own them to those people who can offer means of procuring future consumers' goods on the lowest terms. It is, however, not probable that this second group either will want to take out the whole of what is due to them in the form of present consumers' goods. As their potential command over consumers' goods increases, similar considerations to those which guided the first group will lead the members of the second group to invest, rather than consume, part of the final output which they command. They will, so to speak, pass on to others part of the command over ready consumers' goods which they have received, in return for resources which will enable them to procure a similar command in the future. As an effect of, and parallel with, the increasing demand for capital goods on the part of those who directly command the supply of ready consumers' goods, we shall therefore find that others, who have only a derived command over consumers' goods, will throw the weight of a part of the increasing value of their resources on to that side of the scales which favours a further increase in the demand for capital goods. That is to say, once the offer of ready consumers' goods in exchange for as yet inchoate consumers' goods has given the latter a definite value, these in turn can be used to increase the aggregate demand for capital goods and so to transmit further the value conferred upon them by the demand from the direct owners of the consumers' goods.

The sum of the potential command over ready consumers' goods of all individuals may be many times the total of ready consumers' goods in existence

We must now consider more particularly the position of the owners of non-permanent resources in the different stages of this process. We shall for the most part refer to those non-permanent resources which consist of man-made equipment, but the main conclusions will apply equally well to wasting natural resources. The main point to be considered here is the distinction between the conditions which will merely make it profitable to *use* an existing

Effects on use and replacement of existing non-permanent resources

piece of equipment and the conditions which will make it possible and profitable to *replace* it, either by a similar or by some other kind of equipment. For the present we shall again confine ourselves to the " stationary " case and shall assume that every owner of such nonpermanent resources aims at obtaining from them, or with their help, a permanent income stream of constant volume. The cases where the different individuals deliberately aim at either an increasing or a decreasing income stream will be taken up systematically in the next chapter.

The equipment existing in our community may or may not have been designed to produce a constant income stream. But since we assume in any event that immediately prior to the moment when we begin to consider this community unforeseen changes have occurred in some material respect so as to upset the original plans, this is really not relevant to our problem. What is important is that equipment is in existence which is, or can be, adapted to certain kinds of processes, whereas the equipment required for other processes (which might require less initial expenditure if the community were starting from scratch) is not in existence.

If we begin by considering the position of entrepreneurs owning equipment which belongs to a very late stage of a particular process of production, we shall find that it will become profitable for them to **Effects of existing equipment on direction of re-investment** operate the equipment as soon as the amount of consumers' goods offered in exchange for their product is just sufficient to pay the factors, which have an alternative use in a shorter process, a price slightly higher than what they could earn in that shorter process. But as the total amount of ready consumers' goods available for investment increases, these entrepreneurs will be able to extract higher prices which will leave a margin over and above mere operating cost. For those who have ready consumers' goods to offer, the opportunity of buying the products of the already existing machinery in comparatively late stages will in the majority of cases (unless the change which has occurred in the relevant conditions is very great) be by far the cheapest way of securing a supply of future consumers' goods, since at first they will have to pay little more than the mere operating costs of that machinery. And even when, in consequence of the competition between the owners of present consumers' goods, the prices of the products of the machinery rise, these products will probably still continue for some time to represent the most favourable opportunity for investment, since the cost of procuring any new products of similar utility will presumably be much nearer to the total cost (*i.e.* including the cost of creating the required equipment) than to the mere operating cost of the already existing machinery.

The income which the owner of this existing piece of equipment obtains from it as the price of its services rises is of a temporary nature, limited by the duration of that piece of equipment. And if he wants to draw a permanent income from this capital he will have to re-invest part of the gross income and to limit his consumption to such a figure that the expected return from the re-invested part of the gross income will be equal to his present consumption. How much he will re-invest will depend on the size of this gross income and the rate of return he can obtain from re-investment. And how he will invest it will depend on where he can obtain the highest return. And while, of course, in view of the changed circumstances, it is not certain that re-investment in new machinery of the same kind as that worn out will be the most profitable investment, there is at least a strong probability that in many cases this form will offer very favourable opportunities. The reasons are very similar to those discussed above.

The equipment which in the past was used by some other entrepreneur to supply the entrepreneur in the later stage with his equipment will probably still be in existence, and it will be in the interest of the second entrepreneur to use that equipment (instead of letting it stand idle), as soon as prices cover his operating costs. And as the demand for the equipment which he produces increases, he in turn will be faced with a position exactly similar to that which we have been considering in the case of the entrepreneur in the succeeding stage, *i.e.* he will find it necessary to re-invest the greater part of the excess of his receipts over his operating costs if he wants to draw a constant income from his capital. And he too will probably find that the existence of equipment designed to provide him with the kind of intermediate products which he needs in order to replace those which he uses up in production enables him to re-invest in the same sort of equipment on comparatively favourable terms. In general it may be said that to some extent the kind of equipment already in existence will determine the sort of production that will be undertaken.

In this way we see how the gradual increase in the value of the resources which are devoted, not to present consumption, but to the acquisition of means for pro-

Limits to the profit- viding for future consumption (an increase
ability of replacement which is initially due to the increased
by equipment of same amount of ready consumers' goods devoted
kind to this purpose) will gradually make it possible to use more and more of the existing equipment. And if no changes in the data had occurred in the meantime, a stationary equilibrium may conceivably be reached at the point where both all the existing equipment has been taken into use and it is also possible and profitable currently to reproduce such quantities of each of the different sorts of equipment as will just replace what is currently used up so that the total stock is maintained intact.

But on the assumption we have made, namely, that conditions have changed in material respects since the existing equipment was created, this is not likely to happen. Sooner or later in the course of the process some entrepreneur will find that in consequence of this change in circumstances it is no longer profitable either to invest the same amount in equipment of the kind he already possesses or to invest anything at all in equipment of that same kind. Wherever under the changed conditions the return obtainable from a given type of equipment, which he can buy at a price which only covers the prime cost of its production, is lower than the returns which could be obtained elsewhere, the owner of the existing equipment of this sort will find it in his interest to re-invest in capital goods of a different sort. And even where at first the existence in an earlier stage of the process of equipment which will be used, provided mere operating costs are covered, enables him to replace his own equipment at a price which covers little more than these operating costs, the situation will change as soon as that equipment in the earlier stage is worn out. Finally, the successive re-investment, in different and to some extent new types of capital goods, of funds which it is no longer profitable to use for the replacement of equipment similar to that from the amortisation of which these funds have been obtained, will gradually lead to the building up of a new and different investment structure.

The process by which such a system will tend towards a final equilibrium after any sort of change, will evidently be very slow and gradual. For at any stage part of the data, namely, the character and composi- The asymptotic ap- tion of the equipment in existence, will be proach towards a stationary equili- the result of an historical process which, brium from the point of view of present decisions, must be regarded as an historical accident which will never be repeated in identical form. And since the equipment which will exist at the end of any period will to some extent be influenced by the composition of the equipment which happened to exist at the beginning of the period, what we really have to deal with is a process of continuous change. Although the change may, if the external data (tastes, knowledge, and supply of permanent resources) remained the same, continuously decrease in magnitude, it will probably never cease entirely, so that the system will make only an asymptotic approach to the position of an ideal final equilibrium.

Since, however, the four following chapters will be explicitly concerned with the analysis of the effects of different sorts of change, the remainder of the present chapter may be devoted to summarising the conditions which have to be fulfilled for a stationary equilibrium to be possible.

The condition of stationary equilibrium in a competitive society with capitalistic production may be summarised as follows. The members of the society must distribute their total resources between use for present and use for future consumption in such a way as to make the relative values of the different types of resources exactly proportional to their relative costs of production, where " cost of production " includes the uniform timerate of return on resources invested. Or, to state the same condition differently, with given supplies of present consumers' goods and future consumers' goods, the values of the future consumers' goods (in terms of present consumers' goods) must exceed their costs (in terms of present consumers' goods) by an amount which bears a uniform relationship (*i.e.* that of an exponential function) to the time which will elapse before the future consumers' goods become available.

" Costs in terms of present consumers' goods " may mean in this connection the amount of present consumers' goods which might have been obtained directly from the resources which were used to produce the future consumers' goods. Frequently, however, resources of the kind in question are not used directly to produce present consumers' goods. Then the phrase means the amount of present consumers' goods which these resources would

have helped to produce if, instead of being invested for the
period in question, they had been invested for the next
most profitable period of shorter length and the other
resources had been redistributed in such a way as to
secure the greatest net addition to present income, while
leaving the rest of the future income stream unchanged.

In full stationary equilibrium this coincidence of
current value and cost of reproduction of capital goods
in terms of consumers' goods will have to hold, both
for the stock of capital goods in the   Unlikelihood that sta-
aggregate, and also for every individual   tionary equilibrium
                                           would ever be closely
capital good in existence. That this is,   approached
to say the least, extremely unlikely ever to be the case in
the real world, is by now only too evident. It is mentioned here only as a further illustration of the difficulty
of saying much that is useful about the general theory of
capital so long as we confine ourselves to the analysis of
the stationary state. Nearly all the problems which are
of importance arise out of the fact that at any moment
much of the capital equipment of society exists in a form
which cannot or will not be reproduced. And any
" equilibrium " that will ever be reached is necessarily
transient and limited to the life of the " wasting assets "
which constitute part of the " data " of that equilibrium.

But — and this is the final point with which we may
conclude the present discussion — in so far as we are
justified in speaking of a tendency towards an equilibrium,
that tendency is due to the fact that all   Uniform rate of in-
those who could, directly or indirectly,   terest a condition of
                                             equilibrium even in a
command ready consumers' goods which   society where there is
they do not want to consume immediately,   no lending of money
will be guided in their investment (apart from risk, etc.,
which does not concern us here) by the single consideration of obtaining the highest percentage return. And
their endeavour to distribute investment in such a way
as to bring the highest return will necessarily bring
about a uniform rate of return. This will be so quite

independently of any possibility of lending money, and consequently of obtaining interest on money loans. We might conceive a society where the lending of money (at least at interest) was prohibited and where nevertheless, so long as the possibility of spreading investments by means of partnerships, joint-stock participation, etc., existed, the rate of return on investment would be uniform throughout the system.

The rate of return on investment as determined by the price relationships between capital goods and consumers' goods is thus prior to, and in principle independent of, the interest on money loans, although, of course, where money loans are possible, the rate of interest on these money loans will tend to correspond to the rate of return on other investments. The fundamental price relationships are the result of a demand for capital goods in terms of consumers' goods or of an exchange of present consumers' goods for future consumers' goods. As those who command ready consumers' goods decide to consume less of them themselves and to offer more of them in exchange for future consumers' goods, the prices of future consumers' goods will naturally rise, and the difference between the prices of present and future consumers' goods which corresponds to the rate of interest will correspondingly fall.

It will be observed that in the determination of these price relationships no separate factor " capital " enters, apart from the concrete resources and the dates for which their owners want to use them. There is no supply of capital in the abstract, no " fund " of " waiting " or " capital disposal " (or whatever else the terms are by which this mystical quantity has been described), which would form a datum in the determination of those prices. In particular, there is no " real " magnitude called " free capital " which exists in any way apart from the concrete capital goods, and which could be regarded as being

The " supply of capital " as such not a datum of equilibrium

available for investment in, and in this sense constituting the demand for, the capital goods. There is of course the way in which all the individuals use their potential command over present consumers' goods. But while under given conditions the magnitude of this potential command is determined for every individual and is equal to the value of (nearly) all his resources, it would, as we have seen, be meaningless to sum up the command over consumers' goods of all the different individuals. The reason is that the greater part of the command held by any one person is dependent on the other people not exercising their similar command, and the sum of the potential command over consumers' goods of all the individuals would be far greater than the amount of ready consumers' goods actually available.

CHAPTER XX

THE ACCUMULATION OF CAPITAL

THE significance of the conditions of stationary equilibrium of capitalistic production which we have discussed
in the last chapter will become clearer only as we apply
the same considerations to the study of the effects of
different types of changes.   In the present and the succeeding chapters we shall therefore discuss the readjustments that will be made necessary if, after various
types of changes in the data, equilibrium is to be re-
established.

It will be convenient to divide this task into two parts.
In this and the next chapter we shall discuss those changes
which can properly be said to originate on the side of
Types of changes to   capital, that is, where what is usually called
be discussed   a change in the supply of capital is the
originating and active cause.   Under this head we shall
have to deal with the accumulation and decumulation
of capital (or with saving and dissaving), in a competitive society with otherwise stationary conditions.   In
Chapters XXII–XXVII we shall go on to discuss the
effects of other changes, and particularly of unforeseen
changes in the data.   These will include changes in the
supply of factors and in technological knowledge.   They
will also include such changes in tastes as reflect themselves in the relative values of different commodities at a
moment of time but not in the time shape of the desired
income stream.   In this second group of changes capital
plays essentially a passive rôle, although, as we shall see,
these changes too will in most cases give rise to new
processes of saving and dissaving.

This attempt to treat certain dynamic problems will

not, however, allow us to deal with all the complications
which arise under similar circumstances in the actual
world.   In particular it is necessary to remember that
the analysis still proceeds in real terms, that is, under
what amounts essentially to barter as-   Absence of unused re-
sumptions, and that this makes it impos-   sources assumed
sible to deal with the existence of unused resources due to
the rigidity of money prices.   The following analysis of
the effects of the accumulation of capital must therefore
assume that there are no unused resources in existence
in the technical sense of the term.   In other words, at
the ruling prices no more resources are obtainable than
are actually employed.

On these assumptions every increase of capital will
mean an increase of capital relatively to the quantity
of other factors of production, or what Böhm-Bawerk
called an increase in the amount of capital   Discussion confined
per head.   This is an important point, since   to changes in capital
relatively to pure in-
an increase of capital in proportion to the   put
other factors employed will have different effects from an
increase which is merely proportional to a simultaneous
increase in the amount of pure input that is employed.
It is only in the former case when the quantity of capital
increases *ceteris paribus* that it will lead to the peculiar
consequences usually connected with an increase of
capital, such as a fall in the rate of interest, a change in
the technique of production, or the adoption of longer
or more roundabout methods of production.   This first
case must be sharply distinguished from the second where
the increase in the total quantity of capital merely means
that a proportionally larger quantity of labour and other
pure input is being equipped with the same kind of
instruments, etc., as those formerly employed.

In past discussions these two cases have sometimes
been described as a growth of capital in its " time
dimension " and in its " labour dimension " respectively,
and Knut Wicksell referred to it as a distinction between

the growth of capital in " height " and in " breadth ".[1]
More recently Mr. Hawtrey has for the same distinction
suggested the terms " deepening " and " widening " of
capital.[2] The point which is relevant here is that on our
assumptions, and for the ^conomic system as a whole,
the growth of capital can take the form of a growth
in " height ", or of " deepening ", only. Although this
assumption is of course somewhat unrealistic, it has the
advantage of stressing an effect of the accumulation of
capital which will always be present to some extent, and
which, as has been amply proved by recent discussions,
is liable to be overlooked. Yet it is the changes which
are connected with this " heightening " or " deepening "
of capital in which the special characteristics of a growth
of capital are best seen, and for this reason this assumption actually helps to bring out an important point.

In the discussion of stationary conditions in the
last chapter it was generally assumed that everybody
endeavours to maintain his income stream constant.
The effects of plan- What this implies when there are changes
ning for an increasing in the other data we shall consider in some
or a decreasing in-
come stream detail in the next chapter. The question
which we have to discuss at present is what happens if
some members of the community aim either at an increasing or at a decreasing income stream, and consequently
invest either more or less than would be required to keep
their income constant.

It will be remembered that all resources except those
small marginal quantities (or fractions of the value of
some resources) which owe their value to the last increment of investment, give their owners a potential command over consumers' goods. In this sense, then, all
the resources in the possession of an individual (except

---

[1] Cf. Wicksell, *Lectures*, vol. i, pp. 163 and 266, and also *ibid*. p. 164,
where he speaks of changes in the " vertical " and the " horizontal "
dimension of capital.

[2] Hawtrey, **1937**, p. 36.

these marginal quantities) are " free capital " to him and give him an option whether to consume a corresponding quantity of consumers' goods immediately or to invest this. " free capital ".

Stationary conditions would of course exist if every individual divided this potential command over ready consumers' goods between current consumption and provision for future consumption in such a way as to ensure him a constant income stream. But this, as is well known, is not likely ever to be the case, nor is it necessary in order to create stationary conditions. The mere following on of successive generations, if nothing else, will regularly have the effect that at any one time some people will be saving and others dissaving. But it is a familiar axiom that, if the population as a whole remains stationary, these different actions may just cancel out and the supply of capital in the aggregate remain constant, although perhaps no single individual aims at a constant income stream in perpetuity.

Net changes only will be considered

We are here interested, however, merely in the net effects of the decisions of all individuals in the aggregate. And in order to avoid the complications arising out of the existence of a multitude of divergent decisions, of which only the net result is of interest to us, we shall assume for the present that the majority of people do aim at a constant income stream in perpetuity, but that there is just a small group of people all of whom aim at an increasing (or a decreasing) income stream. So that the only net change we have to take into account is due to the decisions of those comparatively few people.

When we use here the terms *saving* and *dissaving*, this will always mean, by definition, that people provide for an increasing or decreasing income stream respectively. In the earlier part of this chapter we shall concentrate mainly on the case where people aim at an increasing income stream, *i.e.* on the case of positive saving and investing. Most of the general

" Saving " and " dissaving "

conclusions arrived at in this connection apply also to the reverse case of dissaving. But certain peculiarities of this case will be discussed explicitly in Chapter XXVI.

If we assume that in a society in which up to now stationary conditions have prevailed some persons suddenly decide to consume less and to demand a greater quantity of capital goods, this cannot affect the relative quantities of the two kinds of goods available until such time as it takes for production to be adjusted to the changed relative demand for consumers' goods and capital goods. And an actual reduction of consumption will in consequence only be necessary when, as a result of the diversion of resources from the production of consumers' goods to the production of capital goods, fewer consumers' goods become available.[1] If, however, as we may assume to start with, the reduction of consumption occurs suddenly or unexpectedly, this must, as can easily be shown, lead in the first instance to an at least temporary accumulation of stocks of consumers' goods. Since there is a great deal of confusion in all the discussions of this barter mechanism of saving and investment, it is necessary to go into the matter in some detail.

Foreseen and unforeseen saving

It has often been argued, and is implicitly assumed in much of the classical doctrine on the subject, that the consumers' goods saved by one class of people are merely transferred to and consumed by another class of people *at the same time* as they would have been consumed by the first class.[2] We shall see later that this is to some extent true in the case where the amounts saved are used to employ formerly unemployed workers.[3] But this

The producers of new capital goods are not supported out of the consumers' goods saved

---

[1] For this and the following three sections, cf. Bresciani-Turroni, **1936**, and R. v. Strigl, **1934a**.

[2] Cf. Adam Smith, *Wealth of Nations*, Book II, chap. iii (ed. Cannan, vol. i, p. 320) : " What is annually saved is as regularly consumed as what is annually spent, and nearly at the same time too ; but it is consumed by a different group of people ".

[3] Cf. below, pp. 370 *et seq.*, and Hayek, **1939**, pp. 44 *et seq.*

case is here excluded by our assumptions, and it must at least appear doubtful whether it was to this case, and to this case alone, that the argument was thought to apply. The idea which underlies the argument and which has been given wide currency by the exposition of J. S. Mill,[1] appears to be that *the amounts saved* are offered to the resources which are to be diverted to the production of capital goods in order to attract them away from the current production of consumers' goods. This suggests in particular that the increased remuneration, which in consequence of the new accumulation of capital has to be paid for the services of labour and other permanent resources, is paid, or "advanced", out of the savings.

It can, however, be shown that it will be neither necessary nor profitable for the savers to use their savings to offer increased remuneration to the services of the input newly invested.[2] In fact, if they did so they would find that the transaction would end in a loss, and that they would not even be able to complete the intended investment unless they were prepared to do *further* saving.

The use of savings to pay increased remuneration to factors neither necessary nor profitable

And, as we shall also see, in this case the amounts saved in the first instance would not in any way help to bridge the gap which would occur later in the income stream in consequence of the diversion of current input to investment. The actual source of the additional amounts which unquestionably will have to be paid to labour and other resources is to be sought elsewhere than in the savings.[3]

[1] Cf. his "third fundamental proposition concerning Capital", that, although saved, and the result of saving, it is nevertheless consumed. (*Principles of Political Economy*, Book I, chap. v, § 5.)

[2] Contrast, however, the statement in Bresciani-Turroni, **1936.**

[3] If unemployed resources exist, and savings make it profitable to employ these resources, then the savings *will* be used to remunerate these additional resources. In this case current consumption will not be reduced but only redistributed in consequence of the new savings, and here, and only here, the Smith-Mill doctrine about the savings which are also consumed, but by another group of people, does apply.

output of consumption goods is reduced in consequence of the past investment, they (or perhaps somebody else) will be compelled to repeat the saving. In the second place, they will find that even if they are willing to repeat the saving, there will be no means out of which they can recover the extra expenses that have gone in paying these factors as additional remuneration the whole of what they have saved.

The same effect would also occur if the additional unforeseen saving were made by the consumers merely spending less money on buying consumers' goods. Although this might to some extent lead to an accumulation of unused stocks in the hands of the dealers, it would probably lead to some reduction of price and through it to some increase of consumption on the part of the people who did not save, and it would again happen that, by the time current output of consumers' goods was reduced, no or insufficient reserves would be left to cover the deficiency and the saving would have to be repeated.

It will be evident by now that savings are actually required only at the time when, in consequence of a past diversion of input from the production of consumers' goods to the production of capital goods, the current output of consumers' goods is falling off. And the success of any investment undertaken at a particular moment of time will generally depend, not on the amount of saving at that time, but on the rate of saving and the consequent price relationship between consumers' goods and capital goods at some date in the future. Saving which occurs unforeseen merely serves as a signal which creates the expectation that the demand for consumers' goods will be less in the future than it was in the past. And it would be quite sufficient if, without any present saving, it became known sufficiently in advance that saving would take place in the future. All this makes it necessary to

Savings are usually required only some time after new investments have been started

investigate in somewhat greater detail what will be the effect of additional investment on the flow of income.

Over-simplified conceptions of the "period of produc tion" have led to illegitimate conclusions in this sphere as in many others. If it is assumed that the average period of production is a uniform period for all the input, and if it is further assumed that only the investment periods of the pure input can be changed, while all the non-permanent resources are completely specific (and both of these assumptions have often made their way explicitly or implicitly into the analysis of problems of this kind), then the answer to our question becomes indeed very simple.[1]

Misleading effects of the idea of a uniform period of production

If, *e.g.*, the uniform investment period of all the pure input has previously been one year and is now suddenly extended to thirteen months, the effect will evidently be that a year after the change has been made the stream of consumers' goods will entirely cease for one month and will not begin to flow again until the date when the products of the input invested for thirteen months come on the market. If the investment period were lengthened for only part of the total input, we should have a proportionate reduction of the output stream during the corresponding time interval. And if we assume that the investment period, instead of being lengthened with a sudden jerk, is extended gradually and continuously, the effect on the size of the output stream can best be explained by the adjoining Fig. 24, which is a modification of Fig. 5 (see p. 115).

In this diagram the slope of the line *OP* represents the rate at which pure input is being invested, and the vertical distance between this line and the line *TQ* the period for which this input is invested. A continuous lengthening of the investment period will then be shown

[1] For an analysis based on these assumptions see Bresciani-Turroni, **1936.**

stream caused by changing the investment periods is enhanced by the second fundamental fact, namely, that not only "pure input" but also intermediate products and other non-permanent resources can be diverted from shorter to longer investment periods (and *vice versa*). For this reason it is not possible, as one might suppose, to deduce from the comparative shapes of the input functions of the old and the new structure the exact effects on the output stream of any lengthening of the investment structure. If the intermediate products were completely specific and only the investment periods of the "pure input" could be changed, this would indeed be possible, provided that both the aggregate input functions and also the input functions for the separate processes were given. It would then be possible to deduce from these functions what quantities of input would have to be changed over to other investment periods at every stage of the process, and by what amount their investment periods would have to be changed, and this would uniquely determine the effect on the shape of the output stream. Where, however, the intermediate products also can be shifted to other uses, this clearly becomes impossible and we must be satisfied with the following two general conclusions. *First*, the temporary decrease of the output stream consequent upon any new investment will be spread in some way over the whole period between the moment when the new investment begins and the moment when the new structure is completed. *Second*, the completion of any new investment structure which is begun at any one moment of time will usually require further new investment throughout the whole period until the new structure is completed.

It will be useful now to consider the effects of saving from a different angle. Let us consider what kinds of investments will appear most advantageous to entrepreneurs if they expect that in the near future there will for some time be a shift of demand away from consumers' goods and towards capital goods generally. We shall assume that the entrepreneurs regard a present increase of saving as an indication that, for a considerable time to come, saving and investing will continue at the same rate as at present. I am deliberately speaking here of entrepreneurs in general, and not merely of savers or of those people who have the newly saved funds to invest, because, as we shall see, the decisions of all entrepreneurs will be affected by the expectation of future savings. Since it is assumed that the shift of demand is foreseen and that there is in consequence time to adjust supplies, there is no reason to conclude that there will immediately be a corresponding change in relative prices. And it will be less question-begging if we describe the general situation by saying that the expected demand curves for consumers' goods and capital goods in general are being shifted, the former to the left and the latter to the right.

The effects of foreseen savings on the plans of entrepreneurs

The main question which arises is the following : Towards what kind of capital goods will the new demand be directed, and how will the relative prices of the different resources, and the quantities produced, be affected by this change in demand ? In abstract terms the situation can be described by saying that a greater potential command over consumers' goods available in the comparatively near future is offered in exchange for means to obtain consumers' goods in the more distant future. And it is reasonable to expect this to induce an expansion of production for that more distant future. Our task is to show the mechanism by which such a redirection of resources, if it actually does take place, is brought about.

The mechanism of the redirection of investment

The fact that people in general anticipate a shift to the right in the future demand curve for capital goods means that they expect to be able to sell at that future date, at given prices, a greater quantity of intermediate products than would have been possible under the old conditions. But a greater quantity of intermediate products can be provided for that date only by spreading present investments over a wider range of future maturity dates.

This clearly means that investment all round will be pushed on to a " contour line " of lower marginal returns over costs, *i.e.* all individual investments, whether they

Equalisation of all returns from investment at the new lower rate

are expected to mature before or after the date at which the change in relative demand is expected, will be extended to a point where the " rate of increase of the produce divided by the produce " is again uniform for all investments but lower than it was before.[1] And since even before the date at which the change in demand is expected, the returns on some investments will be lowered, competition will so adjust the prices of all the resources invested as to make the return on them the same in all uses.

It will be observed that all this happens before the new savings actually become available. It takes place solely as a result of the *expected* shift in demand. The capital which is used in the first instance to finance these investment changes, and which has its returns reduced, is old capital which was previously used to produce consumers' goods and which is now used to produce capital goods for the date concerned. The new capital (the savings) will not be required until, in consequence of these changes, less consumers' goods come on to the market.

We shall presently discuss certain exceptions to this general rule which are due to the fact that in many cases the investment structures cannot be varied continuously, and that, in consequence of changes in the productive technique used and the composition of the stock of capital employed in a particular line of industry, they will change

---

[1] So far as concerns the production of consumers' goods for the date at which the shift in demand is expected to take place, the reduction of the output of consumers' goods for that date will cause the return on investment to be actually larger than it would have been if the change in demand had occurred without any change in output.

only discontinuously. For present purposes it is sufficient to point out that what can be re-invested in the new and different form will be only the current pure input and the more versatile non-permanent re- Effect of investment sources. Such capital, on the other hand, on value of specific as was irrevocably sunk, before the new resources saving was foreseen, in very durable and highly specific equipment, cannot, of course, be promptly or wholly shifted to a different use. The return obtained from it will be reduced by the rise in the prices of the services of the resources which are needed to co-operate with it, and in consequence it will not be profitable to reproduce these instruments ; and in some cases it will be found that even in the course of time only part of the capital originally invested can be recovered and re-invested in a different form and that the rest has been lost.

Any additional investment (even while it is only expected) will thus cause a shrinkage in the return on all capital. This happens not because the capital has an unchanged absolute return which is dis- The source of the in- counted at a lower rate of interest, thus creased remuneration reducing the yield per cent, but because the of the services of the permanent resources magnitude of the share of the product going to the old capital is reduced. This fact also provides the answer to the question of the source out of which the increased remuneration of the services of the permanent resources is paid. It is not out of the new savings but out of the share of the product which used to go to the owners of the old capital, that this additional remuneration is provided. It has been shown that, as soon as the marginal returns which can be obtained from investment fall in response to the changed relative demand, competition between capitalists will tend to drive up the price of labour and the other services of the permanent resources, at the expense of the capitalists' own income. And this rise in the prices of these services also explains why an (expected) increase in the demand for capital goods (in terms of potential consumers' goods), and the consequent fall in the rate of interest, has the effect not only of making methods of production profitable which were previously unprofitable, but also of making methods of production unprofitable which were previously profitable.

CHAPTER XXI

THE EFFECT OF THE ACCUMULATION OF CAPITAL ON THE QUANTITIES PRODUCED AND ON RELATIVE PRICES OF DIFFERENT COMMODITIES

IT has been pointed out earlier in this Part that, in order to make the argument developed here applicable to the real world, where the investment structures are not necessarily capable of continuous variation, certain modifications have to be intro-duced. It is necessary to do this explicitly, particularly as certain real phenomena, which can undoubtedly be observed empirically, have led many economists to deny explicitly or implicitly the pro-position that the accumulation of capital will as a rule lead to a change in the methods of production. These economists have suggested that all that really happens is a mere multiplication of the equipment of the kind already in existence. This may be true in two cases. One is where there are unemployed permanent resources avail-able, the services of which can be used to produce addi-tional output by exactly the same methods of production as have been used previously. The other is where the increase in the supply of capital leads for the most part to an expansion of some industries at the expense of others. The first case has been briefly touched upon in connection with the discussion of the effects of saving (Chapter XX above), and, since it is a phenomenon which is mainly due to monetary causes, and therefore falls outside the scope of this study, it need not be further con-sidered here. The second case, however, is of immediate interest.

The phenomenon to be considered is closely connected

Capital accumulation may lead to the ex-pansion of some lines of industry at the expense of others

285

with a distinction already mentioned which the Austrian School used to describe as the difference between a growth of capital taking the form of an extension of **"Deepening" and "widening" of the structure of production** its time dimension and one taking the form of an extension of its "labour" dimension, and which Dr. Hawtrey has recently christened the "deepening" and the "widening" of capital respectively.[1] More capital can clearly be used in a given industry or a given economic system either by equipping a greater number of workers (or combining a greater quantity of "pure input") with proportionate quantities of equipment of the type used before, or by providing an unchanged number of workmen with more (or more elaborate) equipment. For the economic system as a whole the first of these alternatives is possible only if there is a labour reserve available. But in any particular industry the required additional labour may be attracted from another industry.

If, as we have assumed, the investment structure can in many or most lines of industry be changed only discontinuously, the sole effect of a change in the relative **A fall in rate of interest may affect only relative size of different industries** demand for capital goods in terms of consumers' goods may be to change the relative size of the different lines of production without (to revert for once to the traditional terms) affecting the proportions between capital and labour in any of them singly. An increase in the relative amount of consumers' goods offered for capital goods, or a fall in the rate of interest, will cause an expansion of those industries which use more capital in proportion to labour than others do, while the inverse case will favour the industries using relatively little capital. More or less capital will be used in industry as a whole, not because the proportion between capital and labour (and consequently the technique of production) has changed in any one industry, but only because the relative size of

[1] R. G. Hawtrey, **1937,** p. 36 (cf. p. 270 above).

the groups of industries using comparatively much and comparatively little capital respectively has changed. The technique of production may have changed in none of the industries. All the different products may still be produced in the same manner as before. And yet the investment periods of the individual units of input which have been transferred to the expanding industry will have increased. What has happened is simply that the industries whose costs of production have been reduced more than those of others by the fall in the rate of interest have expanded at the expense of the second group.

This effect is, of course, merely an application to industry as a whole of the general proposition which was invoked a short while ago (Chapter XVI, p. 206). Wherever the coefficients in which the different factors of production can be combined in individual industries are relatively or absolutely rigid, a change in the relative scarcity of the different factors can be met only by an expansion of the scale of output of those industries which use relatively less of the factors that have become more scarce, and a corresponding contraction on the part of those industries that use more of those factors. And what is true of that general case applies in this case also, namely, that unless the proportions in which the factors can be combined are variable at least in some industries, any change in the relative supplies of the factors is likely to cause violent changes in their relative values and may even render some factors completely valueless.

A special case of the general rule for fixed coefficients of production

The effects of changes in the relative demand for consumers' goods and capital goods on the value of input in general can be shown without great difficulty. A problem which is at least as important but much more complicated is the problem of their effects on the relative values of different kinds of input. In particular it is almost impossible to explain the changes in the relative values of different

Effects on relative values of different factors more complicated

types of capital goods without going back to the factors which determine the changes in the relative values of the different kinds of pure input. But any attempt to give an exhaustive analysis of the intricate relationships here involved would unduly expand the size of this study. All that can be attempted within its limited compass is to suggest the different considerations which have to be taken into account, without trying to show in detail how they combine to determine equilibrium.

These can best be shown by first assuming that there is only one sort of input: the homogeneous " labour " which in the traditional analysis is usually contrasted
Effects on value and with capital. On this assumption, the
distribution of a marginal productivity (in terms of con-
single kind of input
recapitulated sumers' goods) of successive quantities of
" labour " applied in the different stages of the process of production can be represented by a series of curves as shown in the following diagram. We can assume these stages *a*, *b*, *c*, etc., to be separated by equal time intervals, and to be arranged in the diagram from left to right in ascending order of maturity, so that stage *a* would be twice as far from consumption as stage *c* (*e* being the moment when the process of production is actually completed), and so on. In each of these curves the ordinate shows the addition to the product which is due to the successive quantities of input applied to that stage, the quantities being measured along the abscissa. As we know already, these different productivity curves cannot be regarded as simultaneously and independently true. They show only how the product will vary if the amount of input invested in any one of the stages is varied while the amount invested in all other stages remains fixed at a particular figure. There is, of course, no reason to assume that the shape of these curves will be the same in the different stages, though this has been assumed in the diagram in order to make the point which it is meant to illustrate come out more clearly.

The marginal product shown by these curves is, of course, the undiscounted marginal product, the total addition to the product which is due to the investment of an additional unit of the factor in question at the relevant stage. The actual share of the product to be attributed to a unit of " labour " or the demand price which entrepreneurs will be willing to pay for a unit of " labour " if employed at that stage, will be equal to the value of the marginal product discounted at the current rate of interest over the relevant investment period.

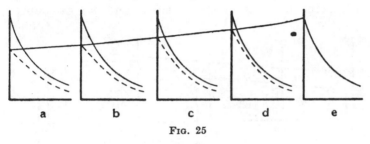

a   b   c   d   e

FIG. 25

In the diagram the effect of this discounting can be shown by lowering the different productivity curves (or, more exactly, all the individual points on these curves) by an amount corresponding to the discount appropriate to the periods for which the respective units of input are invested. Since the stages are supposed to be separated by equal time intervals, this can be shown graphically by means of a discount curve from which the individual productivity curves may be supposed to be suspended so that they will be moved upwards or downwards as the rate of interest decreases or increases. (Strictly speaking, we need a family of discount curves connecting each point of the curve on the extreme right with the corresponding points on all the other curves, so that with every change in the rate of interest not only the position, but also the shape, of the individual curves will be changed, since every point will be lowered or raised, not by the same absolute amount but in the same proportion.)

The following diagram shows two such discount curves along with the productivity curves in their corresponding position. The fully drawn set of curves corresponds to a lower rate of interest (i_1), and the dotted set to a higher rate (i_2). Since in equilib¬ium the discounted marginal product of the factor in question must be the same in all stages, the distribution of a given supply of the factor will evidently be determinate for any given rate of interest. We may suppose that, *e.g.*, at the higher rate of interest shown by the discount curve i_2 the available supply of the factor will just be exhausted, and its discounted

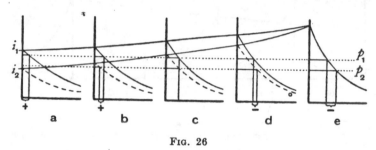

FIG. 26

marginal product will be everywhere the same, if it is distributed among the stages in the proportions indicated by the segments of the line ending at p_1 that are marked off by the corresponding productivity curves and their respective ordinates. Then if we assume that the rate of interest is lowered (represented by the discount curve i_1), the given supply of the factor in question will evidently have to be redistributed between the different stages so that more will go to the earlier and less to the later stages. The segments of the abscissa in the diagram that are marked by *plus* and *minus* signs show the changes in the quantities of input invested in the respective stages. The discounted value of the marginal product of the factor (or its price in terms of consumers' goods), indicated by the distance from the base of the line ending at p_2, will necessarily be higher than it was before.

So far this diagram is only a way of re-stating conclusions with which we are already familiar. But it can be used, although only with obvious limitations, to illustrate the factors that will determine how much the price and the distribution of any given factor will change in consequence of a given change in the rate of interest. So far it has been assumed that the shape of the productivity curve of the factor in question in the different stages is the same. But this is not at all likely in practice. And the actual effect of a change in the rate of interest on the price and the distribution of any one factor will evidently depend on what we may call the relative elasticity of its productivity in the different stages. For a factor whose productivity curves in the early stages are relatively flat, a given fall in the rate of interest will cause a much greater transfer from the late to the early stages, and a much greater rise in price, than would be the case with a factor whose productivity curves are comparatively steep in the early stages. When we remember that only a few of the different factors (the perfectly versatile ones) will be demanded in all stages, and that the majority of them will be useful only in a limited number of stages (their elasticity of productivity in the other stages being zero), it becomes at once obvious how different the effect of a given change in the rate of interest on the prices of different factors must be.

Effects on relative value of different sorts of input

We shall not follow up this point in detail. For the method adopted to give a general picture of the considerations involved is really not adequate for an exhaustive analysis. The reason for this is, of course, as in all other cases where productivity or demand curves for individual factors are regarded as given, that these curves cannot be regarded as simultaneously and independently valid. But to take account of the complicated relations of technological (and psychological) complementarity which are involved, requires another technique which has been evolved quite

Problems of complementarity involved

recently in closely related fields, and which will also have to be used in a more exhaustive investigation of our problems. Here all that we shall mention is that if we were to start from a complete statement of the substitution relationships between all the different resources concerned, all kinds of peculiaritie.s and apparent anomalies in the behaviour of individual factors would appear to be quite consistent with the general tendencies which can be deduced from the cruder type of analysis. It is, for instance, quite possible that while a fall in the rate of interest will create a tendency for the services of most of the permanent factors to be invested for longer periods and for their prices to rise, in the case of some individual factor the effect may well be that it will be invested for shorter periods, or that its price will be lowered, or both.

But all this belongs to the more complicated aspects of the subject which it is not proposed to treat here *in extenso*. After this admittedly sketchy outline of the factors that will affect the relative prices of the different kinds of input in the course of a change in the capitalistic structure of production, it is only necessary to return for a moment to one question which was raised previously but was left unanswered. How does a change in the rate of interest affect the relative prices of different capital goods which are produced and used before and after it takes place ?

The explanation just given of the difference between the changes in price of the different kinds of input also accounts for the change in the relative prices of the Effects on value of intermediate products at the successive different capital goods stages. At first it might seem as if, since in the long run the relative prices of the different intermediate products must correspond to their respective costs, these prices could change permanently only to the relatively small extent to which the direct interest element in their cost changed. But to think of interest only as a direct cost factor is to overlook its main influence on production.[1] What is much more important is its effect on prices through its effect on the demand for the intermediate products and for the factors from which they are produced. It is in consequence of these changes in demand, and the changes in relative costs which they bring about by raising the prices of those factors which are in strong demand in the early stages relatively to the prices of those factors which are less demanded in those stages, that the prices of the intermediate products are adjusted.

The point, which in this connection is so frequently overlooked and which at the same time is so very important for the understanding of the effect of changes in the interest rates, is that the change in the price of a particular factor consequent upon a change in the rate of interest may stand in no direct relation to the changed value of the particular factor at the point where it is used. The change in its price may be many times greater than would be due merely to its particular marginal product being discounted at a different rate of interest. The cause of this is, of course, that the price of a particular factor will not depend solely on its productivity in the particular use in question and that the demand for it elsewhere may be affected much more strongly by the change in the rate of interest. The rise in the value of labour and the immediate fall in the cost of machinery in a particular industry consequent upon a fall in the rate of interest may be very small, yet the increase in the demand for labour elsewhere caused by the same fall in the rate of interest may drive up the price of labour to such an extent as to enforce an extensive substitution of machinery for labour. We shall come back to this important point in Part IV of this book when we discuss the effect of changes in demand on the profitability of different kinds of investment (see Chapter XXVII below).

[1] Cf. Machlup, **1935a.**

CHAPTER XXII

THE ADJUSTMENT OF THE CAPITAL STRUCTURE
TO FORESEEN CHANGES

THE term " capital " is a convenient description of the
aggregate of non-permanent resources and one difficult to
dispense with entirely. Its use is, however, as we have
Dangers of conceiving observed before, beset with dangers. Not
capital as a " fund " the least serious of these, and one to which
of quantitatively de-
termined magnitude the majority of economists have succumbed
at one time or another, is the temptation to regard
the stock of " capital " as a quasi-homogeneous, quantitatively determined magnitude which can, like the supply
of any other factor of production, be treated as a datum
of economic analysis. One of the main conclusions of the
whole of the preceding discussion is that the supply of
capital can *not* be treated as a single quantity in this
sense. Nevertheless, in view of the established position
which this idea occupies in economic theory, it seems
advisable to examine it further.

The idea that capital is a quantitatively determined fund
which has some existence apart from and beyond the concrete non-permanent resources in which it is " embodied ",
that it is " an entity capable of maintaining its quantity
while altering its form ",[1] pervades in greater or lesser
degree almost all the literature on the subject. Indeed
it may be said that in the usual treatment of dynamic
problems, the idea of a given stock, or a given supply, of
capital occupies a central position. It is usually taken for
granted that capitalists will normally aim at keeping
their capital stock constant in some quantitative sense,
and that they will succeed in doing so. Any serious

---

[1] A. C. Pigou, 1935, p. 239.

attempt to analyse what is meant by " maintaining
capital intact " ought soon to have shown that behind
the specious simplicity of the idea there lurked a host
of confusions and illegitimate assumptions. But most
economists seem to have been unaware of these difficulties and have made no such attempt.[1] The term
" capital " was applied to the stock of non-permanent
resources, because it was felt that all the items in that
stock had certain common qualities. This led to the
idea that they might be treated as a homogeneous mass,
that in the heterogeneous components of this aggregate
was embodied some common substance which could be
preserved irrespective of changes in its composition.

The consequence of the introduction of this fictitious
magnitude becomes evident as soon as it is used as a
supposed " datum " in the analysis of the effects of any
sort of change. In the mere description of *The quantity of capital*
a stationary state which was regarded as *cannot be treated as given in the analysis*
being already in existence it mattered little. *of dynamic changes*
If everything had always been correctly foreseen, and
conditions always turned out to be what they were
expected to be when the capital goods were created, there
would never arise any problem of deciding how to use
the existing capital goods.[2] They would simply be put
to the use for which they were made. It is only in connection with adjustment to unforeseen changes that the
stock of capital goods has to be treated as a datum. But
clearly it is precisely in this connection that it is not per-
missible to describe the stock as a single magnitude, or

[1] The only systematic attempt to clear up the meaning of this
concept, that made by Professor Pigou, I have discussed in some
detail on another occasion (cf. **1935b**). Parts of this as well as of a
later article (**1936a**) on a related topic have been incorporated in the
present chapter.

[2] This is strictly true only of capital goods in the narrower (or in
some respects wider) traditional sense of " produced means of production ", but not of the wasting natural resources which are included
in our definition of capital. On this point see my article just quoted
(**1936a**, p. 226).

in terms of some common unit of measurement. It is essential to go back to its real components and to describe it by a full enumeration and description of all its constituent parts.[1]

It also becomes necessary to make a systematic study of how those in command of capital goods will behave when they find that events are turning out differently from what they expected. Here we should begin with a consideration of the concrete opportunities which will be open to them under the new conditions, and of their preferences for the income streams of different shapes between which they can now choose.

Nor is there a clearly defined neutral attitude of entrepreneurs which can be said to represent the normal, involving neither additions to, nor subtractions from, their capital stock

In discussions of this problem it is usually implied that there is a clear line between the normal process of maintaining and replacing the existing capital, and making a net addition to it. It is assumed that it is always possible to decide in an unequivocal way whether the amount of capital remains constant, increases, or decreases, and that there are typical phenomena connected with each of these processes which, at least conceptually, can be clearly separated. But as soon as one tries to apply these categories to a world where things are changing, all these alluringly simple concepts become dependent in more than one way on the answer to the following question : Exactly what is meant by a constant stock of capital ? It is impossible to define net income (or " earnings "), and therefore savings, before one has separated from the gross produce those quantities which are required for capital maintenance. It is equally impossible to say what are additions to the stock of real capital before one knows what capital goods are required to make up for current depreciation. All this is one

---

[1] The only author who, to my knowledge, has clearly seen that the traditional way of treating a quantitatively determined stock of capital as a datum is illegitimate, was Knut Wicksell. Cf. his statement quoted above, Chapter I, p. 8.

of those problems where it becomes particularly clear that the real problems of capital arise only when we go beyond the limits of the construction of a stationary state. As has been pointed out before, the very existence of non-permanent resources which will not or cannot be reproduced in an identical form is incompatible with the idea of a strictly stationary, repetitive process. It will always cause a process of continuous change in which each step is determined by the historical accident of the existence of a certain collection of non-permanent resources.

Before we can proceed, however, to discuss the reactions of the capitalist entrepreneur [1] to unforeseen changes, we must clear away certain widespread confusions concerning the appropriate attitude towards changes which can be foreseen. The points to be brought out here *The reaction of the capitalists to foreseen changes* are all implicit in the discussions of the preceding chapters, but they will be a useful introduction to the problems of the next chapter if we re-state them systematically. There are two main sources of confusion, both connected with practices widely adopted by entrepreneurs in their depreciation and amortisation policies. The one is the practice of considering the capital stock mainly as representing a certain money value and of aiming at keeping this money value constant. The other is the habit of regarding depreciation in the narrower sense, as caused by wear and tear, as being something more fundamental and important than a " mere " loss of value through " obsolescence ".

The first of these two practices represents a sort of abbreviated or simplified method, a kind of mechanical rule-of-thumb for obtaining an approximate solution to problems which are — as we shall see — sometimes extremely intricate. The historical explanation of this practice of capital accounting in terms of money is to be

---

[1] In this connection the functions of the capitalist and of the entrepreneur cannot be clearly distinguished and the two terms will therefore be used interchangeably.

found in the technique of double-entry book-keeping. And the practice derives a certain justification from the fact that a large part of the capital of many firms is pro-

Maintaining the money value of capital constant vided in the form of loans of money, and that one of the chief purposes of book-keeping is to make certain that these "liabilities" are covered by "assets". This is also, of course, the chief source of the conception of capital as a "fund".

That such is, in rough outline, the actual practice of entrepreneurs has important consequences which would require careful consideration in a more realistic investiga-

The rationale of maintaining capital intact tion. As monetary problems, however, they largely fall outside the scope of the present study. But there is a preliminary task which is germane to the present investigation, and that is to determine what will be the most appropriate action of entrepreneurs who wish to preserve their stock of non-permanent resources, given the ultimate ends which this stock serves. It is only against the background of some such set of principles deduced from the rationale of " maintaining capital intact " that it will be possible, in more realistic studies, to judge the significance and consequences of the practices actually followed.

The " maintenance of capital intact " is, of course, not an aim in itself. It is desired only because of certain consequences which are known to follow from the failure to maintain capital. We shall see, moreover, that once it is applied to a changing world the phrase has no definite meaning independently of the reason *why* entrepreneurs want to maintain their capital. We are not interested in the magnitude of capital because there is any inherent advantage in any of its conceivable absolute measurements. We are interested in it because, *ceteris paribus*, a change in it will cause a change in the income to be expected from it, and because in consequence every change in it may be regarded as a symptom of such a change in the really relevant magnitude : income.

What, then, are the reasons why we wish capital to behave in a particular way? The main reason is evidently that the persons who draw an income from capital want to avoid using up unintentionally parts of the sources of this income. They believe that these must be preserved if income is to be kept at the present level. They want to avoid unintentional "splashing" or "stinting" (to borrow Professor D. H. Robertson's terms) which would have the effect of later reducing income below (or raising it above) the level at which they aim. Capital accounting in this sense is simply a shorthand device for preventing involuntary encroachments upon future income. Whatever the time shape of the future income stream, derived from the capital in his possession, at which an individual aims, there still remains the problem of deciding what is the appropriate disposition over the individual assets in his possession. And although we certainly have no right to assume that every person will normally aim at a permanent constant stream of income from his capital, there is probably some justification for regarding this case as one of special interest. Moreover, even when a capitalist aims at some other shape of income stream, the problem remains essentially the same, and the case of the constant income stream may simply be regarded as a standard with which the others may be compared.

The significant magnitude is the time shape of the income to be obtained

Will this aim always be achieved if the immediate goal followed from moment to moment is to maintain the money value of the capital stock constant? The answer is no. Quite apart from the possibility of general changes in prices, due to monetary causes which do not concern us here, it is obvious that, under changing conditions, the money value of the stock of non-permanent resources which is required at successive moments in order to secure a constant stream of real income, need not be constant even if all changes have been foreseen.

Keeping the composition or the money value of the stock of capital constant will not secure a constant income stream

If it were known beforehand that from a certain date onward a stock consisting of the same capital goods would bring a smaller return than before, a policy which aimed merely at maintaining a stock of goods of the same kind would fail to yield a constant income. The consumption of the larger income during the earlier period would be at the expense of a later reduction to a lower figure. A policy aiming at a constant income stream would have to use parts of the higher " return " during the earlier period to build up a larger stock of non-permanent resources such that the return obtained after the change would be equal to the income actually consumed before the change. And the same is true, *mutatis mutandis*, of an expected increase in the return from a given stock of capital goods. It will be seen that a series of such changes in either direction, if correctly foreseen from the beginning, will make it necessary, if the income obtained is to be kept constant, for the stock of non-permanent resources sometimes to increase and sometimes to decrease, no matter in what terms we measure that stock. And no conceivable sort of monetary policy could make prices behave in such a way that a policy which aimed merely at keeping the money value of the capital stock constant would simultaneously secure a constant real income from that stock.

The main point, as will become clearer when we proceed to consider in detail the reactions of capitalists to unforeseen changes, is that as soon as we go back to the *rationale* of maintaining capital intact, the quantity of capital drops right out of the picture as a directly relevant magnitude. Its place is taken by a direct consideration of the size of the income streams that may be

Changes in the measurable dimension of the capital stock itself play no essential rôle in the complete economic calculus

expected at different dates. What is relevant is whether a person maintains a stock of non-permanent resources which will secure him an increasing, constant, or decreasing income stream, not whether this stock itself increases, remains constant, or decreases in any of its directly measurable dimensions. And — as will also be discussed in some detail later — it is these changes of income at different dates, and not changes in some absolute size of the capital stock, which must be made the basis of the common distinction between current consumption and saving on the one hand, and between current production and investment on the other hand, if these distinctions are to have a definite and useful meaning.

There is also a second point with respect to which the materialist conception of capital as a measurable substance leads to erroneous views. It relates to the distinction between depreciation in the narrower sense, or physical depletion through wear Obsolescence and tear, and " mere " obsolescence, or the losses in value which occur without a corresponding change in physical substance. In the light of our whole approach it will be obvious that any suggestion that the former is in any sense more fundamental than the latter is baseless, and we may deal with this point more briefly. We need only remind ourselves that the entrepreneurs are quite as likely to foresee that a capital good will become useless long before it is physically worn out or decayed, as they are to know that its useful life will be terminated only by its physical breakdown.[1] We then see immediately that in the one case just as in the other, if a constant income

---

[1] There can be no doubt that in actual life many investments are made with complete awareness of the fact that the period during which the instrument concerned will be useful will be much shorter than its possible physical duration. In the case of most very durable constructions, like the permanent way of a railroad, the prospective " economic life " ought to be regarded as much shorter than the possible " physical life ". In many cases it lies in the very nature of a product that it must be made almost infinitely durable, although it is needed only for a very transient purpose. It is impossible to adjust the durability of a machine to the short period during which it may be needed, and in many other cases the strength needed from a construction while it is used necessitates its being made in a form which will last much longer than the period during which it will be needed.

stream is to be maintained, only such parts of the expected services may be regarded as net income as are compatible with the reproduction of new non-permanent resources which will secure an equal income in the future. This means in particular that investment in capital goods liable to obsolescence must be ِo restricted that the prices of their services, or their gross return, will include an amortisation quota sufficient to replace them ultimately by new capital goods which will yield a future income equal in value to the net return of the old ones which are being consumed.[1] But it should be borne in mind that the concept of amortisation itself suggests the misleading idea that a certain quantity of capital has to be recovered and re-invested. The essential point, of course, is not that the new capital good (by which the one that has become

---

[1] The significance of such a decision on the part of the capitalist becomes particularly clear if we consider the following case. Suppose that the capitalist has to choose between two investments of equal cost, both represented by instruments of equal physical durability, but one of which is expected to remain useful so long as it lasts physically, and the other of which serves only a very transient purpose. Under what conditions will he regard the two investments as equally attractive ? The first answer is, of course, if they promise him the same permanent income. But under what conditions do they promise him the same permanent income ? Suppose that the gross receipts from the investments while they yield a return are equal in both cases, and are just sufficient to provide the same income *plus* an allowance for depreciation proportional to the physical deterioration. The effect will then clearly be that in the case where the instrument ceases to be useful long before it is worn out physically only a fraction of the sum originally invested will have been recovered, which of course will bring only a much lower income in the future. To decide in favour of this alternative would mean treating an income stream which starts at a given magnitude but decreases later, as equal to an income stream which is permanently kept at the initial magnitude of the former. In order that investment in the instrument of only transitory usefulness may appear equally attractive to that in the instrument of more lasting usefulness, it will be necessary for the former, while it remains in use, to produce gross returns sufficiently large to allow for full replacement of its original income-earning power. In other words, in order for the two investments to be regarded as equally attractive, the expected return must be sufficient to cover, in addition to the same income, not only depreciation in the narrower sense, but also obsolescence.

obsolete is replaced) should be of the same magnitude, but only that it should promise to provide the same income.

There is still a further question of considerable import- Differences according as only income from capital or all income is regarded as relevant ance which we must consider explicitly : What income is it that the capitalist is supposed to consider when he decides about the use of his non-permanent resources ? Is it solely the income which he derives from capital or is it his total income, derived from all his resources, permanent and non-permanent ?

The answer to this question assumes special significance when we go on to apply these considerations to the case, which will be the rule in a competitive society, where the non-permanent resources and the permanent resources with which they co-operate belong to different groups of people. In every society it is, of course, only a fraction of the people who deliberately regulate — or are in a position deliberately to regulate — the shape of their future income streams, and by so doing become capitalists. But, as we have seen, any decision about capital will affect not merely the income from capital. It will also affect the income from the permanent resources and, therefore, in a competitive society, the income of people other than the capitalists making the decision.

So far as concerns the isolated capitalist there can be no doubt that the dominant consideration influencing his decision will be the income to be derived from all his resources. But are we to regard him as maintaining capital intact if he keeps his total income constant, or if he keeps only his income from capital constant ? The difficulty arises from the fact that in view of the limited life of any individual all his resources are in a sense non-permanent from his point of view, and any rigid distinction between permanent and non-permanent resources becomes impossible. If we applied our definition of capital strictly and included all non-permanent resources, including human labour, the difficulty would of course disappear. Yet the fact that the total supply of labour is not provided merely from economic motives makes this practice inadvisable. From the point of view of society the distinction between the non-permanent resources and resources which are either really permanent or which, like human labour, are replaced irrespective of their productive capacity, remains important. It is therefore convenient in this connection to follow traditional usage and to look upon the capitalist, *qua* capitalist, as if he drew income from capital only, so that in his case aiming at a constant income stream from capital and aiming at a constant total income stream become one and the same thing. Then any consideration of the probable fate of any income which the capitalist of the real world may draw from sources other than his capital, and which will influence his decisions concerning this capital, will, for theoretical purposes, and in conformity with traditional usage, have to be classed among the motives which will lead him to save or dissave, that is, to aim at an increasing or decreasing income stream from his capital.[1]

This must conclude this admittedly sketchy and incomplete discussion of the attitude of the capitalist to changes which are completely foreseen. But this assumption of complete foresight is in any case so unrealistic

---

[1] The interesting fact about such a policy on the part of capitalists is that it tends to accentuate the fluctuations in the income of other resources. At least this is so in what is usually considered as the " normal " case, where the capitalists keep the quantity of capital in some sense constant. If we take, for instance, the case where a foreseen change tends to increase the income of the permanent resources at the expense of the income from capital, the attempts of the capitalists to provide against a decrease of their income by building up a larger stock of capital will further increase the marginal productivity of the permanent resources. And, *vice versa*, if capitalists foresee that an impending change will tend to increase their income at the expense of that of the permanent resources, and consequently start to decumulate capital, this will have the effect of reducing the marginal productivity, and consequently the income, of the permanent resources, even below the figure at which it would have been kept if the stock of capital had been held constant in some quantitative sense.

that the only justification for any detailed consideration of it is that it illustrates certain general principles. The more important question is the reaction of the capitalists to unforeseen changes. This will be considered in the following chapters.

CHAPTER XXIII

THE EFFECTS OF UNFORESEEN CHANGES AND IN PARTICULAR OF INVENTIONS

In considering the alterations which capitalists will have to make in their amortisation policy in face of a change in circumstances which they did not foresee at the time

Reactions of the capitalists to unforeseen changes
of making some particular investment which is affected by this change, it makes little difference whether we assume that the unforeseen event occurs quite unexpectedly or whether we assume that its imminence becomes known some time after the investment has been made. In both cases the capitalists learn that from a given (present or future) date onwards gross returns from their investment will be smaller or larger than what they expected when the investments were made, and that consequently the amortisation and re-investment plan on which they had originally decided will not secure them a constant income stream for the future. To go on consuming as much as they had planned has become incompatible with maintaining consumption permanently at the present level.

The gross returns during the remainder of the life of the capital good in question will now be likely to be greater or smaller than had been anticipated, either

Factors to be considered
because these returns will now accrue at a different rate, or because they will continue for a longer or shorter period than was expected before. In addition new alternative uses for the asset in question may have to be taken into consideration. To what extent this will be so will depend on the degree of specificity or versatility of the asset. For some assets, e.g. most stocks of raw materials, the alternative uses will be very numerous

306

and the usefulness of the good in these other uses will not be very much less than in that originally contemplated. Other assets such as specialised machinery may be highly specific; that is, there may be no other uses at all or only such as will yield a very much smaller return.

The availability of alternative uses to which the good may now be turned is a factor of great importance. But in considering it we must clearly realise from the beginning that there is no necessary connection between its possible usefulness for other purposes and the function it was originally destined to serve. This possibility of using it for another purpose is, so to speak, an accident, and not a necessary consequence of, or identical with, its original function. What we can transfer to other purposes is in particular not the same " waiting power " which it represented while it was regarded as useful for the original purpose, but another and probably different contribution of which it happens to be capable in the new situation.

Usefulness in alternative employments not necessarily connected with original value

In order to clarify some of the main points it will be useful to look first at the case of capital goods which are completely specific and for which therefore no alternative use need be considered.[1] Suppose that the capitalist whose property is affected by the unforeseen change aims at keeping his income stream in all circumstances constant, so that whatever happens to him, he wants no more than to keep his income permanently at the constant level which seems obtainable on the basis of his present knowledge. Then

" Windfall profits " (and losses) made on specific assets

---

[1] As a rule, even in the case of the most specific type of plant or machinery its scrap value will, of course, have to be considered as an alternative return. We can, however, neglect this so long as we either ignore cases where the value of the capital good in question in its present use has not been lowered below its scrap value, or if we assume that the scrap value of the material is no higher than the cost of scrapping (as is often the case with houses).

he will have to treat the remaining gross returns of the
asset as a terminable annuity of which he must consume no
more than will enable him to build up a reserve from which,
after the asset ceases to yield a return, he will be able
to draw an income equal to that previously derived from
that asset. Whether the particular unforeseen change is
favourable or unfavourable to him, this will mean that as
soon as he learns about its occurrence or imminence he
will have to change his rate of consumption to the level at
which it can now be permanently kept. If, for instance,
his receipts increase in consequence of the change by
£210, and the rate of return which he can obtain on re-
investment is 5 per cent, he must consume only £10, and
must re-invest the remaining £200, which at 5 per cent
will give him the same return in every future year. Such
windfall profits are, therefore, not income in the sense
that their consumption is compatible with "maintaining capital intact". Nor need consumption be reduced
by the amount of corresponding *windfall losses*. In both
cases only the current interest on the (positive or negative)
capital gains ought to be counted as income.[1]

After such a change, the capitalist who was previously
in a state of individual equilibrium in which he merely
Effects on time pre-   wanted his income to continue constant,
ference   may very well change his attitude. The two
most important data for his decision will have changed.
Not only will his income be different from what it was

---

[1] In the case of "windfall losses" it would, of course, often be
possible gradually to recuperate the value of the capital originally
invested. In order to do this the owner of the capital would have to
decide, after the unfavourable change had occurred, to make the same
allowance for depreciation as before and to reduce current consumption
by the full amount of the loss. But this could hardly be described as
"maintaining capital intact". It would mean that the owner would
have to reduce consumption for a period below the level at which it
could be permanently kept, in order to raise it later above that level.
It seems that this would more appropriately be regarded as new saving
— saving, it is true, to make up for a loss, but for a loss which has
already occurred. This loss was irrevocably incurred when the investment was made in ignorance of the impending change.

before, but the returns to be expected from new saving will also be different from what they were before. In all probability, if the income from his old investment has increased, the return to be expected from the new investment will now also be greater. And this, as a rule, will encourage him to aim at a further increase of his income ; that is, it will make him save. A decrease of the return on the old investment, on the other hand, will also frequently be accompanied by an increase of the returns to be expected from new investments, and therefore will also often lead to new saving. But the reverse effect, namely a reduction of income from the old investment, coupled with a decrease in returns to be expected from new investments, leading capitalists to aim at a decreasing income stream (that is to dissave), is by no means impossible.

The nature and significance of the reactions of the capitalist entrepreneur to unexpected changes will become clearer if we consider in somewhat more detail the effects of a particular type of change. In many respects the effects due to changes in technological knowledge or inventions are the most interesting, and they may therefore serve here as a concrete example of the general class of phenomena under consideration. The application of the argument to the other main types of change which are relevant here, *i.e.* shifts in demand between different types of consumers' goods, or changes in the supply of factors, will present no difficulty.

Effects of Inventions to be discussed as special instance

For the case of inventions, two kinds of effects will have to be considered : on the one hand the possibility of a loss of capital invested in plant that is made obsolete by an invention, and on the other hand, the possibility of a gain on plant and stock which, at least during a transition period, may bring higher returns than was expected. Although there is some reason to suppose that any unexpected change is much more likely to lead to considerable capital losses

Two cases to be considered

than to capital gains, it is not impossible that in particular instances the gains may exceed the losses.

The case of capital gains can be treated more shortly and may therefore be taken up first. Capital gains consequent upon an invention will mainly occur during such

(*a*) capital gains

transition periods as will elapse until it is possible to increase the supply of particular instruments which are now required in the newly invented process.[1] If, for instance, the new machinery required can be produced only in a particular plant, which before was expected to be used only little or discontinuously, and if it takes a long time to erect an additional plant of the same sort, the owner of the existing plant will clearly be able to make considerable and unexpected profits during the interval. Since these profits will be of a temporary character, he ought not to regard them as ordinary income. He ought to re-invest such part of them as will secure him an additional income in the future equal to that which he consumes during the transition period.

Losses due to technological progress require somewhat more careful consideration, since they are closely connected with questions which have been the subject of wide dis-

(*b*) capital losses: an example of "capital-saving" inventions

cussion and some considerable confusion. It is again advantageous to begin by supposing that the old equipment which, in consequence of an invention, will no longer be reproduced, is of a highly specific character. Since the example of the displacement of the long-distance cables by wireless telegraphy has often been used as an instance of what was regarded as a " capital saving " invention,[2] we may keep this in mind

---

[1] We are here neglecting increases in the capital values of wasting natural resources.

[2] Cf. A. C. Pigou, *The Economics of Welfare* (4th ed., 1932), p. 675. The terms " labour saving " and " capital saving " inventions are here used in the older, more popular sense in which they are used by Professor Pigou, who defines a capital saving invention (*ibid.* p. 674) as one " which reduces the ratio of capital to labour in the industry where it applies ". Professor Hicks (*The Theory of Wages*, 1932, pp. 121 *et*

as a concrete instance, without troubling too much about the actual technical details. We shall feel free to make successively different hypothetical assumptions about the extent to which we suppose the introduction of wireless telegraphy to reduce the cost of transmitting telegrams, and about the relative share which prime and supplementary costs constitute in either kind of telegraphy.

Consider first the position of the owners of the old type of equipment, that is, in our case of the cables. Their position will, of course, be affected only if the new. method makes it possible to provide the Effects on owners of old equipment same services at lower cost. But the fact that it has become possible to provide these services at a lower total cost does not necessarily mean that it will have become unprofitable to use the already existing equipment. If we assume the scrap value of the existing equipment to be practically zero (because, for instance, it may cost more to raise a submarine cable than can be realised for the material contained in it), then providing at least that mere operating costs are covered, it will clearly be more profitable to continue operating it than to shut down completely. The increased demand for the services, at the lower cost at which they can now be provided, will make it profitable to install so many wireless stations in addition to the existing cables that the price of a telegram will fall relatively to the cost of transmission by the new service. But, at the beginning at any rate, and until they are worn out and need replacement, the existing cables will remain in use.

Although this is rather familiar ground [1] it is necessary to give a more exact statement of the conditions under

seq.) has refined this original concept, but, as we shall see, he has not altogether escaped the consequence of the use of the " fund " concept of capital.

[1] Cf. A. C. Pigou, *The Economics of Welfare* (4th ed., 1932), p. 188 ; L. C. Robbins, *An Essay on the Nature and Significance of Economic Science* (1932), pp. 50 *et seq.* ; Hayek, " The Trend of Economic Thinking ", *Economica* (May 1933), and **1936c.**

which it will be profitable to operate equipment of the old type and equipment of the new type side by side, and the conditions under which the new type of equipment General conditions will immediately supplant the old one. The under which intro- duction of invention relevant magnitudes for both types of equip- will prove profitable ment are as follows. First, there is interest and amortisation on the capital which would *now* be required to create the equipment in question ; this we shall call " capital cost " and shall designate by c_1 for the old equipment and c_2 for the new equipment. Secondly, there are the operating costs of the old and the new equipment, which will be designated by o_1 and o_2 respectively.[1] The condition, then, for it to be at all profitable to introduce the newly invented process is that $c_2 + o_2 < c_1 + o_1$. So long, however, as $c_2 + o_2 > o_1$ it will still be profitable to use the old equipment. The return on this old equipment will have fallen below c_1, the figure necessary to make its replacement profitable, but it will still be a positive figure, namely $c_2 + o_2 - o_1$. Only when the total cost of the new process becomes as low as the mere operating cost of the old process, that is when $c_2 + o_2 = o_1$, will the old equipment cease to give any return and lose all value. And if $c_2 + o_2 < o_1$ it will be altogether unprofitable to use the old equipment, since its mere operating cost will be higher than the price which is determined by the total cost of the new process.

The owners of the old equipment, finding the gross return from it reduced, will in the first instance have to decide what part of the return to re-invest and what part of it to consume. Let us suppose that they act in con-

---

[1] " Capital cost " and " operating cost " as here used, although closely related to, are not necessarily identical with, the concepts of " supplementary cost " and " prime cost " as generally used. The reason why we prefer the terms used in the text is that for the purpose in hand the distinction between the two kinds of costs will have to be made with respect to the use of the particular piece of equipment in question and may be different from any such distinctions made from the point of view of the firm as a whole.

formity with a rational policy of maintaining capital intact, that is, that they aim at whatever constant income stream they can continue to obtain in the future. Then, as soon as they learn about the effects of the new invention, they will reduce their consumption to a level such that what they re-invest will secure them the same net income in perpetuity. They will, of course, re-invest not in the old type of equipment which it has become unprofitable to replace, but either in the new equipment or in an altogether different line of business. Since, as the old type of equipment wears out, there will be opportunities for further investment in the new type of equipment and the owners of the old type will presumably have more scope for using their knowledge here than elsewhere, it is at least probable that they will attempt to invest as much as they can in this form. But how much will they have to invest ? Is it possible that what they gradually recover now will be more than what can still be profitably invested in the new process, so that capital will be released for other purposes ? If this excess which would now overflow into other lines of industry were greater than the amount which was initially brought into our industry from outside to start the additional new services, we should have the case which has usually been treated as a capital-saving invention. Is this a possible case ? And, on the other hand, may it not also happen that so little capital is recovered as to be insufficient to replace the old equipment which is being worn out by new equipment which will render equivalent services, and that in consequence, as the old equipment wears out, further and further doses of new capital will be attracted from outside ?

The answer depends in general not on the absolute amounts of the two kinds of cost, but on the proportions in which they can be most profitably expended in order to produce a unit of the service in question. But it can

Amortisation policy of owners of old equipment

be shown that where there is complete specificity of the old equipment, the first case, that of the so-called capital-saving invention, will occur only under very special and rather unlikely conditions. In such cases, where less capital is required for the new process than was required for the old one, it is distinctly more likely that there will still be a need for additional capital from outside sources than that it will be possible to create all the new equipment out of the amortisation quotas of the old. The reason for this is of course that very often as much, or more, of the value of the old capital will be destroyed by obsolescence than is being " saved " by the invention. The additional amount of capital embodied in the now antiquated machinery will be lost at the same time as it becomes " superfluous ". This has, however, yet to be shown to apply to each of the various conceivable cases.

Significance of proportions between operating and capital costs

Let us begin with the case most favourable to " saving " of capital, that is, the case where the absolute amount of operating costs, as well as their relative share in the total cost of a unit of the product, is greater in the case of the new process than in the case of the old process. This is perfectly compatible with the total costs of the new process being lower than those of the old process, the saving on capital cost being greater than the extra expense on operating cost. The conditions of our case can then be stated thus :

Case 1 : operating costs of the new process greater than in old process

$$c_1 + o_1 > c_2 + o_2,$$
$$o_1 < o_2$$
$$\frac{o_1}{c_1 + o_1} < \frac{o_2}{c_2 + o_2},$$

from which it follows that

$$c_1 - c_2 > o_2 - o_1$$

and

$$\frac{c_1}{c_1 + o_1} > \frac{c_2}{c_2 + o_2}.$$

The gross returns of the old equipment will be reduced by the introduction of the new process to $c_2 + o_2 - o_1 < c_1$, but this may still be greater than c_2. That is to say, the amortisation quotas recovered from the old equipment may be larger than what is required to replace it by a piece of new equipment which (with a greater expenditure on operating cost) will provide the same services for the same period.[1] In this case, where the value of the old capital is preserved to an amount greater than the amount of the new capital required, in addition to the new equipment, a further amount of input will be required to produce the same final services. The owner of the old equipment will, it is true, find himself in command only of such a reduced total of resources as is now required to produce the same amount of final services. But as he will now find it profitable to use a greater quantity of input than before, he will substitute such input for capital and will actually be able to release capital for other purposes.

It is essential, however, to be quite clear about the way in which "capital" in this sense can be released from one use and transferred to another. What actually happens is that, as the old equipment wears out and is replaced by equipment requiring the investment of a smaller amount of input, but co-operating with a greater amount of current input, the aggregate of the investment periods of this input is shortened. If this were not compensated by the lengthening of the investment period of some other input, the effect would be that during some period the amount of output currently maturing would be due to a greater

The "release" of capital for other purposes

---

[1] In this case, where the mere operating cost of the new process is larger than the operating cost of the old process, it is of course impossible for the total cost of the new process to be smaller than the operating cost of the old process, and therefore for the invention of the new process to lead to the instantaneous abandonment of the old one and the complete destruction of the value of the old equipment. The new kind of equipment will in this case be installed only to satisfy the additional demand, called forth by the lower price of the product, but it will replace the old equipment only as the latter wears out.

quantity of input than is currently applied. In fact, if a total amount of input equal in value to the amortisation quotas currently earned from the old equipment *plus* input (the operating cost) used in conjunction with it were currently used to provide for the supply of the final services by the new process, the effect would necessarily be that the supply of such services would temporarily be increased beyond the level at which it could be permanently maintained. For, since in the aggregate (or on the average) this input would mature sooner than it did in the past, the flow of the final services obtained from it would not dovetail but would partly overlap with those of the old equipment. To make up for this fact that the old equipment wears out more slowly than the new, it will be necessary to re-invest in the new equipment at a slower rate but over a longer period.[1] This means that for a time resources can, as it were, be lent to other industries, which will be enabled to start the production of the products which are to be ready at a particular date earlier than would otherwise have been the case.

The case where the newly invented process makes it profitable to expend a greater absolute amount of operating cost to produce a given amount of services is, however, probably not of very frequent occurrence, and is certainly not the only case which is usually regarded as capital-saving. But it is easy to show that as soon as the amount of operating cost required to produce a unit of the final services is no more (or is less even) than in the old process, even if it is higher relatively to the capital cost with which it is combined, no capital will be " saved ". That is, no

Case 2: operating costs in new process smaller absolutely; but larger in proportion to capital cost

---

[1] I am here neglecting the case where, in consequence of a fall in price, the demand for the product increases fully in proportion or more (that is where the elasticity of demand for the final product is greater than unity). In this case re-investment may proceed at the same rate as or faster than amortisation, and the additional input required will have to be attracted away from other uses.

capital will be made available to produce additional quantities either of the same, or of some other product.

The conditions of these cases which we now have to consider can be stated shortly, in the notation used before, as follows :

$$c_1 + o_1 > c_2 + o_2,$$
$$c_1 > c_2,$$
$$o_1 \gtreqless o_2,$$
$$\frac{o_1}{c_1 + o_1} \gtreqless \frac{o_2}{c_2 + o_2}.$$

In this case the gross return on the old equipment, *i.e.* the difference between the prices of the final services as determined by the total cost of the new process, and the operating cost of the old equipment $(c_2 + o_2 - o_1)$, can at most (if $o_1 = o_2$) be equal to the capital cost of the new equipment, and may (if $o_1 > o_2$) be smaller than the capital cost of producing with the new equipment. This means that, whatever the original value of the capital equipment which was required for the old process, no more and perhaps less will be recovered than is required for the construction of such new equipment as will provide the same services. If the operating costs of the old and the new processes are the same, no input of any sort will be released, nor will any additional input be required to produce the same volume of output as was produced previously. For the additional output which it will now be profitable to produce at the lower cost, capital as well as current input will have to be attracted from elsewhere. But no general statements can be made about the effect of this on the proportions between capital and labour in the rest of the system. For this will depend, not on the relation between the proportions in which the two sorts of resources are now required in the particular industry concerned and the proportions in which they were formerly required, but on the relation between the proportions in which they are now required in that industry and those existing in the rest of the general economic system.

If the operating cost, that is the amount of input required to produce a given amount of final output, is lower in the new process than in the old, less capital will

Case 3 : operating costs absolutely and proportionately smaller in the new process

be recovered from the old equipment than is required to produce the new, and it will be necessary to attract new capital from outside the industry. But, on the other hand, some quantity of input will be released. What will happen, therefore, is that in the industry in question capital will be substituted for " labour " (*i.e.* pure input), and that consequently in the rest of the economic system capital will become relatively more scarce compared with pure input. This, as will now be clear, will very often be the effect of an invention, even though the invention causes a much smaller absolute amount of capital to be used in the industry directly affected.

It might be concluded from the above that inventions which are actually capital-saving have to be regarded as a rather exceptional case, confined to inventions which,

Effects where durable instruments are not completely specific

while decreasing the absolute amount of capital required to produce a given output, actually increase (although, of course, to a lesser extent) the amount of input required to co-operate with that capital. But we must remember that we have as yet only considered the case where the old equipment, which became obsolete because of the invention, was of a highly specific type. This means that we have still to consider the cases where the concrete non-permanent resources, which became less useful in their original use because of the invention, can easily be turned to other uses. So long as we are thinking mainly of machinery these cases are not very likely to occur, although they are by no means impossible. If an industry which in the past had used a great number of electromotors could, because of an invention, suddenly dispense with the greater part of them, these could probably without great

loss of value be absorbed in other industries.[1] But of
much greater importance in this connection is what is
commonly known as working or circulating capital such
as stocks of materials, fuels, etc.

If, to give only one example, the paper industry, owing
to some invention, no longer requires timber as raw
material, the stocks of standing trees raised in the
expectation that they would be needed as raw material
for paper-making, will not simply become superfluous.
The timber may, for instance, be used in the production
of artificial silk. This does not, of course, mean that it
will represent the same value, *i.e.* produce the same
income. Even in a highly favourable case like the one
mentioned (*i.e.* where the identical material has already
been used before in another extensive industry) the
increase in supply relative to the now more restricted
use will cause a considerable reduction in value. What
can be transferred to other uses is, of course, not the
" abstract quantity of value " or the " command over
resources " which that stock represented before the
invention occurred, but only the utility which it possesses
in these other uses. This will probably mean (unless the
input used in the reproduction of these raw materials is
highly specific) that it will not be profitable to reproduce
the full quantity of these non-permanent resources when
they are used up. In that case the other industry will
enjoy the advantages of a cheap additional supply of one
of its raw materials only temporarily. But even this does
not prove that the capital value which this stock of
raw material temporarily represented for the industry
to which it became unexpectedly available will not be
preserved in some form. The situation is here exactly
analogous to the case of wasting natural resources, which,
of course, can never be reproduced in identical form.

---

[1] That the mobility of many individual capital goods is considerably
greater than is commonly supposed, is shown in the interesting article
by L. H. Seltzer, 1932.

Yet a policy which aims at keeping the future income stream at a given level will have to see that such resources are replaced by some produced means of production which will provide services that are completely equivalent to the former ones. And, as has already been pointed out several times, the existence of such wasting resources always makes it possible to provide for such replacement.

It is difficult to estimate the extent to which it is likely that inventions directly affecting a particular industry will in this way increase the supply of capital available to the rest of industry. That in some par-

The probability of capital-saving effects of inventions

ticular cases it may be not inconsiderable can hardly be denied. But on the whole it seems that, even if we add the cases now being discussed to the more exceptional cases discussed before, capital-saving inventions are distinctly less likely to occur than is usually supposed. It may be added here that what has been said about inventions as a typical example of unforeseen changes in the conditions of production, applies equally well to unforeseen changes in the supply of pure input, or to unforeseen changes in tastes. Both might be treated on exactly the same lines and classified according to their capital-saving or labour-saving tendencies.

If we conclude from the preceding discussion that capital-saving inventions are on *a priori* grounds unlikely to be more than comparatively rare exceptions, must we

Effects of inventions on wages

also draw the same pessimistic conclusions as have been drawn by others concerning the probable effect of technological progress on the income of labour ? It seems that here too the concept of capital as a fund of fixed magnitude has led to erroneous conclusions. It has been argued that if on the whole inventions are likely to make capital relatively more scarce in comparison with labour, and therefore to increase the return on a unit of capital relatively to the return on a unit of labour, the absolute and the relative share in the national income of the capitalists as a class will as a rule be increased by an invention, while the relative and sometimes even the absolute share of labour will be decreased. But this argument seems unconsciously to assume that in the course of these changes the aggregate value of capital always remains the same, and that in consequence a higher percentage return on capital must also mean an increase in the aggregate income of capital.

We may here take it for granted, without explicit proof,[1] that it will only be profitable to introduce an invention if aggregate output is thereby increased. But if at the same time the supply of capital and the supply of labour remained the same, but the remuneration of a unit of capital increased relatively to that of a unit of labour, it would appear that in any case the capitalists as a class would draw an increased product, and that what was left to labour would be a smaller relative share and perhaps even a smaller absolute amount.

But, as we know, there is no reason to assume that in the course of such changes the aggregate value of capital will remain the same. In fact, to say the least, this is rather unlikely to be the case. Inventions will indeed as a rule tend to increase the return on the capital available for investment, but they will also decrease or destroy the return on some of the existing capital equipment. The increase in the percentage return on new capital available for investment does not therefore in any way prove that the aggregate income of capitalists will increase. It is not at all unlikely that the decrease in the absolute returns on the old capital goods will exceed the additional return on the capital which can be invested in new forms. In this case, although the invention is labour-saving in the ordinary sense, it may very well decrease not merely the

[margin note: Unlikelihood that inventions will decrease the relative share of labour]

---

[1] Cf. Wicksell, *Lectures*, vol. i, pp. 133-143 ; J. R. Hicks, **1933**, p. 121 ; and Kaldor, " A Case against Technical Progress ? " *Economica*, No. 36 (May 1932).

relative share but even the absolute share of the capitalists. And there is in any event little reason to suppose that the return on the old capital goods will increase as the rate of interest increases ; consequently the share of the capitalists will hardly ever increase in proportion to the increase in the rate of interest.

CHAPTER XXIV

THE MOBILITY OF CAPITAL

IN the preceding chapter we have seen that competition will enforce, without respect for existing capital values, such a reorganisation of production as will, under the given circumstances, make the most profit-
able use of all available resources. This, however, does not tell us much about the circumstances that will determine how useful the results of past accumulation will prove to be at any moment. In general, however, it will be obvious from what has already been said that two factors are of decisive importance in this connection : first, the foresight of the entrepreneurs ; and secondly, and particularly where this foresight is of necessity imperfect, the degree of mobility or versatility of the existing capital assets. We shall begin with the consideration of the second of these two factors and reserve the discussion of the rôle of foresight to the end, since it leads on to the problems with which we propose to conclude this part of our investigation.

The one distinction in general use which refers to differences of mobility between different capital goods is that between *fixed and circulating* (or " working ") *capital.* But although this distinction seems to aim at what is at least one important difference, the two kinds of capital are usually so defined as to stress only one, and perhaps not the most important cause of the different degrees of mobility. And, in addition, any simple dichotomy like this probably does almost more harm than good, by suggesting what appears to be almost a difference in kind instead of stressing the continuous

Circumstances on which preservation of capital will depend

" Fixed " and " circulating " capital

variation over a wide range of the relevant attributes of the various capital goods.

The customary definition identifies " fixed " capital with durable goods and " circulating " (or " working ") capital with what have here been described as goods in process. But parallel with this distinction, which is based on the length of the period during which a good will retain a particular physical shape, runs another distinction based on the time during which a particular good will remain within the precincts of a particular enterprise.[1] According to this distinction one and the same good, for instance a machine, would have to be regarded as circulating capital in the factory of its maker but as fixed capital in the factory where it is used.[2]

Conflicting definitions

The first of these two distinctions, if it were strictly adhered to, would give us a classification based on one of the reasons why different capital goods are of different mobility, but not a classification based on the degree of mobility itself, since this, as we shall see, depends on other factors besides the mobility of the individual capital good. The second distinction is based on the essentially accidental degree to which the complete process of production of any commodity is divided between a number of separate enterprises. This is a distinction which is highly important from the point of view of the individual entrepreneur,

Neither of the traditional distinctions is based on the mobility of capital

---

[1] Cf. Machlup, **1932**, p. 272.

[2] The first distinction mentioned in the text is that of Ricardo, the second that of Adam Smith. Cf. D. Ricardo, *Principles of Political Economy* (3rd ed.), chap. i, sec. 4 (*Works*, ed. McCulloch), p. 21, where he says that " according as capital is rapidly perishable and requires to be frequently reproduced, or is of slow consumption, it is classed under the heads of circulating or of fixed capital ", and he adds in a footnote, " A division not essential, and in which the line of demarcation cannot be accurately drawn ". Adam Smith, *Wealth of Nations*, Book II, chap. i, ed. Cannan, vol. i, pp. 262 *et seq.* The difference between the two authors is discussed at some length in N. W. Senior, *Political Economy*, p. 62.

but need not have the same significance from the point
of view of society as a whole. The " period of circulation "
at the end of which the individual entrepreneur expects
to recover his capital in a " free " form, that is as money,
need by no means be identical with the period for which
the investment in question remains committed to a particular purpose. In many instances the possibility of
" turning over " the capital of one enterprise will depend
on the willingness of some other entrepreneur to invest
in the product of the first enterprise.

But the use made of this distinction by many of the
classical writers shows that, although it was arrived at and
defined from the point of view of the individual entrepreneur, what they really had in mind was   Circulating   capital
a distinction from the point of view of   and the income fund
society as a whole. This, however, would coincide with
the distinction as actually drawn only under very special
assumptions. This is particularly evident where the
concept of circulating capital is used as equivalent to the
" fund " out of which incomes, and particularly wages,
will be paid during the current period. In most discussions of these problems the term " circulating capital "
is used to describe the part of the existing capital stock
which during the current period will be turned into consumers' goods.[1] It is clear that what is circulating
capital from the point of view of the individual entrepreneur would be identical with circulating capital in
this social sense only if production were completely integrated, that is if different entrepreneurs bought no products from one another but carried out the complete
process of production of any commodity they produced,
including the manufacture of any tools, etc., in their own
enterprise. Since in this case all sales would be sales to

[1] This meaning of the term comes out particularly clearly in the
protracted discussion on the effects of a conversion of circulating
capital into fixed capital which began with the celebrated chapter on
Machinery which Ricardo added to the third edition of his *Principles*.
A short sketch of these discussions will be found in Appendix II.

the final consumer, the part of the capital stock which would be sold within any given period and the part which would become available for consumption within that period would necessarily be identical.

It is obvious that a classification of this sort, based on the remoteness from ultimate consumption of a particular capital good, is of considerable importance in any discussion of the mobility of capital. And it will also be clear that the durability of particular goods will be one of the factors, but not the sole factor, which will determine how remote from the date of consumption are different parts of the existing stock of non-permanent resources. Part of the services to be obtained from a very durable good cannot accrue until some distant date. But obviously the services to be expected from some material which can be used only in the production of that durable good are even more remote from consumption, and the material in question, although less durable than the product made from it, would have to be regarded as more " fixed ". Bricks, *e.g.*, would in this sense have to be considered as being more fixed than the houses built with them. Similarly, if a machine were used to make a second machine which in turn were to serve in the production of a third machine, and if each of these three machines lasted for two years, the capital represented by the first of the three machines would be considerably more fixed than the capital represented by another machine which lasted for six years but served consumption more directly, and produced an even stream of consumable services.

The reason why the rapidity with which a given capital good can be converted into consumers' goods is so important in connection with the question of how a given capital structure can be adapted to an unforeseen change, is that it is, as we have seen (see Chap. XII), only via the income stream which a concrete capital good will produce that it is possible to replace it by a capital good

Significance of distance from consumption

of a different sort. And, if the unforeseen change occurs
not suddenly, but gradually, a substantial part of the
income stream expected from a particular non-permanent
good is more likely still to be obtained if the good will
yield this income within a comparatively short time than
if it yields it over a rather long period stretching into the
distant future.

It becomes necessary here, before we proceed further,
to introduce two distinctions which are essential to the
understanding of the effects of different types of change.
The first concerns the nature of the change   Further factors affect-
considered. On the one hand there may be   ing mobility :   (a)
                                             mobility between lines
changes, such as certain shifts in demand   of production
between different products, which do not in themselves
make it desirable for the consumable returns of the
existing resources to become available earlier than would
otherwise have been the case, but only for them to
become available in a different form. This will be so
if no more profitable uses for investment exist under the
new conditions than under the old. If in these circumstances the equipment formerly used in the branch of
production *from* which demand has shifted is equally
useful in the branch *to* which it has shifted, this mobility
of the concrete instruments between the different lines
of production may in itself enable the necessary adjustment to the new conditions to take place.

The situation is, however, different if the change
evokes an additional demand for capital which tends to
attract capital to an industry more than in proportion
to the relative increase in demand for the   (b) possibility of
product of that industry, and consequently   speeding up amort-
                                              isation
to drive up the rate of interest. It will
then be necessary to withdraw capital to some extent
from all the other lines of production. In so far as this
cannot be effected by transferring concrete instruments
from those other industries to the industry which now
needs more capital, the possibility of a withdrawal will

be limited to the amount of the non-permanent resources used in those other industries which can be turned into consumers' goods sooner than was originally intended. We have seen before that where this possibility is excluded because the non-permanent equipment concerned is completely specific, the value of the equipment will simply be adjusted to the new rate of interest, and it will not be possible to withdraw any capital at all.

It is clear, then, that the mobility of capital depends not so much on how far distant in the future is the moment when the concrete instruments were originally expected **Magnitude of loss** to bring a consumable return as on how **involved** early is the moment when they can be made to give an alternative return. And the question will not be so much a problem of physical possibility as one of the size of the alternative return compared with that of the return which had been originally expected. The mobility of capital, then (like the closely connected concept of liquidity), is a magnitude which can be adequately represented only in two dimensions, one giving the range of dates at which the alternative returns from a given resource are obtainable and the other the magnitudes of these alternative returns.

The problem of mobility becomes, however, still more complex by the fact that, in view of the extremely intricate relationships of complementarity between **Consequences of com-** different capital goods, it is practically **plementarity** impossible to speak of the mobility of a particular capital good in isolation. What effect any particular sort of change will have on its value will always depend not only on the alternative uses to which it can be turned, but also on the degree of mobility of the other resources with which it might co-operate in its former and in its alternative uses. It is really a question not of how, *ceteris paribus*, the particular unit of resources can be used elsewhere in the system, but of what its significance will be in any of the different combinations of all the existing resources which will be most advantageous under the new circumstances.

The lesson to be drawn from all this is mainly that no division based solely on the attributes of a particular good (such as its individual durability or distance from the intended date of consumption) will adequately describe the differences which we have to take into account. It is necessary to consider the position of the good in the whole process, its use in the organisation of production which is most appropriate under the present circumstances, as well as its most appropriate use after a particular kind of change has occurred.

No simple classification sufficient

There is no way of evading detailed consideration of these complex relationships in each particular case. And probably very few useful generalisations can be made about the problem as a whole, except for the negative statement that any sharp division into two distinct categories of capital goods, such as circulating capital and fixed capital, is likely to do more harm than good. It becomes particularly harmful when it creates the impression, as it seems frequently to have done, that the material structure of production may be regarded as consisting of two distinct parts : that we have on the one hand an absolutely rigid skeleton which, for all considerations of a fairly short-run character, must be regarded as given in unalterable form, and on the other hand a completely flexible stream of circulating capital which adapts itself practically instantaneously to any change in conditions and which therefore need not be treated as something separate from the pure input which is required to produce it. It is of course true that, whatever the period considered, some of the more durable equipment will be in the position of a quasi-permanent resource, and will therefore not have to be treated as capital but as a *Rentengut*. But this means only that for comparatively short-period problems the significant items

Distinctions between fixed and circulating capital often misleading

are those parts of the capital structure which can be made to yield consumable services during the relevant period. The division into two separate groups becomes seriously misleading if it treats one part of capital as being permanent, and the other part as involving no waiting whatever : all the problems of capital are then evaded.[1] The fact is rather that even in the shortest of short runs the capital equipment is not given but is eminently variable, since every act of production draws on existing stocks and leads to the creation of new stocks, and that the direction of production is largely determined by the relative quantities of different types of " circulating capital " (in the sense of goods in process) which happen to be available, and by their prices. It is for this reason that we have persistently argued that circulating capital in this ordinary sense of the term possesses the characteristic attributes of capital in a higher degree than fixed capital, and that in consequence those theories which tend to stress the importance of goods in process rather than of durable goods have contributed more to the understanding of the important problems in this field.

The second point which now requires consideration is the significance attaching to the foresight of the capitalist entrepreneurs in connection with the maintenance of capital. It will probably be obvious by **The rôle of foresight** now that the degree of mobility of capital, the extent to which it can be maintained in a changing world, will largely depend on the extent to which entrepreneurs correctly foresee impending changes. If we consider for a moment what would happen if entrepreneurs always acted as if things were going to remain for ever as they are at present, and if they never altered their plans

---

[1] This kind of treatment, widely used by economists of the Cambridge School, is evidently an effect of the unfortunate extension of the Marshallian concept of short-period equilibrium from the case of particular equilibria (where it is legitimate enough) to a position of general equilibrium, where it has no meaning. See on this above, Chapter II, p. 14.

until after a change in final demand (or any other change) had actually occurred, we can easily see what would be the effect on general productivity. Every change would mean an enormous loss, or rather, the adaptation of production to the change would be so expensive as to make it in many cases impossible. This is not because the loss on old investments would have to be regarded as a cost, but because the capital available for investment in new forms would be so scarce. How rich, on the other hand, should we now be if all past changes had been correctly foreseen from the beginning of things!

But if this dependence on the foresight of entrepreneurs of the extent to which society will at any moment be provided with capital is little more than a commonplace, it is certainly a commonplace to which far too little attention is paid in ordinary reasoning. It probably means **Main factor affecting the supply of capital at any given moment** that the amount of capital available at any moment in a dynamic society depends much more on the amount of foresight which has been shown by entrepreneurs than on current saving or " time preference ". This is of course only a corollary to the equally obvious but similarly neglected fact that, even in the comparatively short run, " capital " is *not* a factor the quantity of which is given independently of human action. How great a part of the potential satisfaction to be derived from a given stock of capital goods will still be available some time later will largely depend on how correctly the entrepreneurs foresee what the situation will be at that future moment. Their anticipations in this respect are quite as important a " datum " for the explanation of the dynamic process as the " stock of capital ". The latter concept has in fact little meaning without the former. As an enumeration of the individual capital goods existing at the start, the " stock of capital " is of course an important datum, but the form in which this capital will still exist some time afterwards, and how much of it will still exist, will mainly depend on the foresight of the entrepreneur capitalists. It would probably be no exaggeration to say that it is the main function of the entrepreneur to attempt to maintain his capital so that it will yield the greatest possible lasting return.

But not only is the size of the productive equipment of society dependent in this sense on the success of the entrepreneur ; it is also dependent, in a world of un-

Capitalised windfall gains — an important source of capital supply in a dynamic system

certainty, on his capitalising capital gains (" windfall profits "). It should be recognised that much of the new formation of capital equipment (which need not represent net additions to capital in the traditional sense) does not arise out of savings proper, but out of those gains of individual capitalists which are part of the process of capital maintenance. This process will, as was shown above, always involve unforeseen profits on the part of some entrepreneurs and unforeseen losses on the part of others. It involves changes on capital account, which are part of a continual process of redistribution of property (not to be confused with the distribution of income). The entrepreneur who finds that a risky undertaking succeeds, and for a time makes extraordinary profits because he has restricted the amount of investment so that in case of success it will yield a margin of profit which is proportional to the risk, will not be justified in regarding the whole profit as income. If he aims at a constant income stream from investment, he will have to re-invest enough of his profits to give him continuously an income equal to the part of his profit which he allocates to immediate consumption, after the rate of profit in what has now proved to be an exceptionally profitable line of business falls to normal.[1]

---

[1] It is of course possible that he may regard himself as being so much more clever than his competitors that he will count on being able to make supernormal profits of this kind permanently. To this extent he will be quite justified in regarding these profits as income.

It is in this way that, as a result of changes of demand, technological progress, etc., some capital is newly formed without new saving while other capital is lost. There is of course no reason to assume that the Capitalised windfall capital that is lost will correspond in any gains not saving quantitative sense to that which is newly formed out of windfall profits. And it is precisely for this reason that the customary concept of a net change in the quantity of capital, which is supposed to correspond in some way to saving, is of little value. There has in this case been no abstention from consumption at a rate which could have been permanently maintained. If anybody can be said to have refrained from consumption which would have been compatible with enjoying the same income permanently, it is not the entrepreneurs, but the consumers who for a time had to pay a price in excess of the cost which the production of the commodity entails after it has proved a success. But this " saving " is of course not deliberate, nor does it represent an abstention from consumption which could have been regarded as permanently possible while the outcome of the venture was still uncertain. It can hardly be questioned that in the actual world a great deal of the equipment which comes to be needed in consequence of some change is financed out of such temporary differences between cost and price. It may appear somewhat paradoxical that where it is provided in this way, its source should be regarded not as saving but as a capital gain, a kind of transfer of capital which means not only that new capital is formed in place of that lost elsewhere, but that it is formed exactly where it is most needed, and placed in the hands of those most qualified to use it. Yet this follows as a matter of course from the only definitions of maintaining capital, and of saving, which have a clear meaning. It will be shown in the next chapter that this use of these terms proves convenient in other connections also.

CHAPTER XXV

" SAVING ", " INVESTMENT ", AND THE
" CONSUMPTION OF CAPITAL "

THERE are certain consequences which follow from the considerations advanced in the last three chapters which, although they fall for the most part outside the scope of

Changes in data lead to spontaneous changes in the quantity of capital
pure equilibrium analysis, may be briefly commented upon here. The main result of these last discussions is that if unforeseen changes in the data occur, the value of the stock of capital that exists and will have to be maintained if income is to be kept constant from now onwards will also change,[1] and that consequently there is no reason to expect that in a dynamic world any of the conceivable dimensions of capital will remain constant. It remains true, of course, that *ceteris paribus* it is necessary to maintain a reservoir of goods of constant size in order to maintain a given output. But when conditions change so as to make a smaller or larger reservoir necessary for the same purpose, its contents will tend to change spontaneously in such a way as to make provision, from the moment when the change becomes known, for the particular new income stream which is now most preferred from among all the income streams of different time shapes which are now obtainable. The fact that an impending change is likely to become known to different people at different times will lead to capital gains and capital losses on the part of individuals, with the result

---

[1] The same applies whether we measure the stock of capital in value terms or in any other way, say as a certain multiple of the income of a given period, or as the result of a certain " average " waiting period or in any other way.

334

that the persons who have shown the greatest foresight will command the greatest amount of resources. But in a world of imperfect foresight, not only the size of the capital stock, but also the income derived from it, will inevitably be subject to unintended and unpredictable changes which depend on the extent and distribution of foresight, and there will be no possibility of distinguishing any particular movements of these magnitudes as normal.

These conclusions have rather far-reaching consequences with respect to the much used, or much abused, concepts of *saving* and *investment*. If the stock of capital which will be required in a changing society to keep income constant at successive moments cannot in any sense be defined as a constant magnitude, it is also impossible to say that any sacrifice of present income in order to increase future income (or the reverse) will necessarily lead to any net change in the amount of capital. Though saving and investment in the ordinary sense of those terms are of course one of the factors which affect the magnitude of capital (in any conceivable quantitative sense), they are by no means the only such factor. The changes in the size of the capital stock cannot therefore be regarded as indications of what sacrifices of present income have been or are being made in the interest of future income. This idea, which is appropriate enough for the analysis of the effects of a change under otherwise stationary conditions, has to be entirely abandoned in the analysis of a dynamic process. If we want to retain the connection between the concept of saving and investment, and the concept of a sacrifice of potential present income in the interest of future income,[1] we cannot determine the size of either saving or investment by any reference to changes

Changes in value of capital need not correspond to saving or investment

---

[1] It will be shown later that it is this latter concept which is of importance in the connections in which the terms saving and investment are commonly used.

in the quantity of capital. And with the abandonment of this basis for the distinction there must go the economists' habitual practice of separating out the part of general investment activity which happens to leave the capital stock in some sense constant, as something different from activities which add to that stock. This distinction has no relationship to anything in the real world.[1]

To deny that the usual distinctions between new investment and merely renewed investment, and between new savings out of net income and merely maintained **Possible divergence** savings, as distinctions based on the idea **between plans of in-** of quantitative increases or decreases of **vestors and the inten-** **tions of consumers** capital, have any definite meaning, is not to deny that they aim at a distinction of real importance. There can be no doubt that the decisions of the consumers as to the distribution of consumption over time are something separate from the decisions of the entrepreneur capitalist as to what quantities of consumers' goods he should provide for different moments of time. And the two sets of decisions may or may not coincide. All that is denied here is that the correspondence or non-correspondence between these two sets of conditions can be adequately expressed in terms of a quantitative correspondence between (net) saving and (net) investment.[2] But if this distinction is not to be formulated in

---

[1] The same applies, of course, in even more marked degree to the assumption implied in the distinction according to which the activities which lead to such net increases of capital are in some way subject to a different set of determining influences from those which lead to a mere quantitative maintenance. This ought always to have been obvious from the mere·fact that when additions in this sense are made (*i.e.* if capital increases in the usual terminology) this will always affect the concrete form of the new capital goods by which the old ones are replaced.

[2] This is of course not to suggest that the difficulty can be avoided by using gross concepts instead, as Mr. Keynes believes (**1936,** p. 60). The whole concept of gross saving and gross investment is closely connected with the view that treats durable goods only as capital, and proceeds as if there were a fundamental difference between fixed capital and circulating capital and as if these two categories were

this particular way, what are we to put in its place ? In general terms the answer is not difficult. If we can no longer speak in terms of absolute increases and decreases of capital we must attempt a more direct comparison of the time distribution of income. Capital accounting, as has been shown before, is itself only an abbreviated method of effecting this comparison in an indirect way. And if this indirect method fails, it is only natural to go back to its rationale, and to carry out the comparison explicitly. The indirect method consists in comparing the increase or decrease with the supposed standard case where capital remains " constant ", and thus arriving at the concepts of net saving (net income *minus* consumption) and net investment, and then placing these derived concepts in juxtaposition. Instead of this we need to make a direct comparison of the intentions of the consumers and the intentions of the producers with regard to the shape of the income streams they want to consume and to produce respectively.

The question, then, is essentially whether the demand for consumers' goods tends to keep ahead of, to coincide with, or to fall behind the output of consumers' goods, irrespective of whether either of the two magnitudes is increasing, remaining constant, or decreasing in any absolute sense. *Comparison between shape of income streams provided and demanded* But in order to give this question a clear meaning we have still to decide upon a unit in terms of which the demand for and the supply of consumers' goods can be measured. Otherwise we have no means of determining whether they coincide or whether the one exceeds the

subject to different laws. In fact, of course, the point where we draw the line between the two is not only purely arbitrary, and any classification based on these two concepts of little significance, but it is definitely misleading, because it suggests that the factors guiding investment in fixed capital are different from those influencing investment in circulating capital. The concepts of gross saving and gross investment ought to disappear from economic analysis with the sharp division between fixed and circulating capital (or, for that matter, between *the* short and *the* long period).

other. In a sense, of course, demand and supply are always equal, or are made equal by the pricing process. Thus to speak of their comparative magnitudes presupposes the existence of some unit in terms of which their magnitude is measured independently of the prices formed on the market.

Consider first the decisions of the " savers " or the body of consumers as a whole. The assumption which we must make regarding their behaviour is clearly not that they will under all conditions aim at an income stream of a particular shape, but that if they are offered a present income of a given magnitude *plus* the sources of a future income of a certain magnitude, they will attach certain relative values to these incomes. For every such combination of a given present income and the sources of a certain future income we must assume these relative valuations to be determined. Now these relative values which people in general will attach to given supplies of present income relative to the given sources of future income may clearly be either greater or smaller than the cost of the former in terms of the latter.

Relative values of present and future incomes —

If the values consumers attach to the sources of future income (in terms of present income) is higher than the cost (in terms of present income) of reproducing new sources of future income of the same magnitude, more such sources will be produced and *vice versa*. And assuming that the relative valuations of the consumers do not change abruptly — as they are unlikely to do if the income that becomes available in each successive period is equal to the income and sources of future income for which they have planned — the amounts of present income and sources of future income which production will provide in each successive period will tend to be such that their relative costs (in terms of each other) will approximately correspond to the relative values attached to them by the consumers.

— compared with their relative costs

But if, for some reason, the prices of the sources of future income have been raised out of correspondence with the valuations of the consumers, the result will be that more sources of future income will be provided for the next period than consumers will then be willing to take at prices corresponding to the relative costs. Consumers will find themselves getting less current real income, and consequently will attach a greater value to it compared with the sources of future income.

In spite of the special senses recently attached to the idea of differences of saving and investment it is difficult not to describe this case as one in which saving exceeds investment (or *vice versa*). And we shall indeed see later that the special cases to which these terms have recently been generally applied are only particular instances of the general case we are now considering. They differ from the general case only through the cause which brings about the difference between saving and investment, which in the special case is a monetary cause. But the effects are the same and they are in turn instances of an even more general case, that of demand exceeding or falling short of supply : when investment exceeds the saving that will be available at the time when it will be required because of the previous investment,[1] the result will be that the supply of capital goods will exceed the demand, and the supply of consumers' goods will fall short of the demand for them ; and when investment falls short of the saving that will be performed at the relevant dates, the effect will be that the current output of capital goods will be valued at less and the current output of consumers' goods at more than their costs. The case is simply one where, because of wrong expectations on the part of the producers, the supply of certain types of

Differences between saving and investment in real terms

[1] On the relation between the dates when the direction and volume of investment is changed and the date when the saving will be required see above, Chapter XX, pp. 279-281.

commodities will exceed, and the supply of other kinds of commodities will fall short of, demand. And the changes of prices relatively to cost will be exactly of the kind which will be necessary to bring about the appropriate changes of production. We shall see later why monetary changes are particularly apt to cause this sort of wrong expectation.

But although it is possible, as a first approximation, to treat this problem in terms of the relations between saving and investment, this terminology creates consider-
" Net " Investment able difficulties as soon as we apply it
need not Increase to any except the simplest *ceteris paribus*
quantity of capital cases. Under the assumption of other-
wise constant conditions (*i.e.* unchanged knowledge, tastes, etc.) we could deal with the changes on the investment side in terms of changes of the investment periods and the changes in the quantity of capital[1] caused by them. We could say that, by increasing the waiting periods and thereby accumulating more capital, producers cause a temporary gap in the income stream which leads to a relative scarcity of consumers' goods unless consumers restrict their consumption by a corresponding amount. And the same *mutatis mutandis* for a shortening of the investment periods and a decrease of capital. But as soon as we drop the *ceteris paribus* assumption this ceases to be a correct formulation. The correspondence between the values attached to the sources of future income and their costs is then no longer dependent on the cost of reproducing the same amounts and types of capital goods as previously made it possible to produce a certain future income.

Additional investment, in the sense that total output is reduced for a time in order to increase it at a later date, may take place, even though the quantity of capital is simultaneously reduced. Breaks in the even flow of con-

[1] Expressed as a multiple of the income of any arbitrarily chosen period.

sumers' goods, which, if disturbances are to be avoided, necessitate corresponding changes in the attitudes of the consumers, will occur only if the quantity of capital is not maintained at whatever level is required, under the conditions prevailing at the moment, to provide such a constant flow of income.

As will be easily seen, the ultimate test for the correspondence between saving and investment in the relevant sense is really whether the current demand and the current supply of consumers' goods are so Re-statement of conditions when " saving " will be equal to " Investment " matched that there is no inducement either to increase or to decrease this current supply at the expense or in favour of the provision of the future. And this correspondence between the supply of current consumers' goods and the demand for them will therefore have to be expressed by measuring them both in terms of the alternatives open to consumers and producers in the given circumstances of the moment.[1] To do this it seems necessary entirely to abandon the concepts of saving and investment as referring to something beyond and outside the normal process of maintaining capital quantitatively intact. We need to substitute an analysis which does not try to separate " old " and " new " investment and " new " and " maintained " saving as distinguishable phenomena.[2] Or, if we want to

---

[1] It might appear that all this could have been explained in simpler fashion by comparing the cost of output of consumers' goods coming on the market during a given period with the expenditure on this output (or by comparing the share of all the factors of production which have contributed to the output of a given period with the share of their income which they spend on the output). This would be quite satisfactory if it were not for the fact that the concept of cost (and, of course, income) is itself dependent on the concept of maintaining capital intact. This way of stating the relation would be adequate only if we counted the cost (in terms of present consumption) which is required, *not* to keep capital intact in some quantitative sense, but to provide sources of just so much future income as consumers wish to buy at prices covering costs.

[2] It should perhaps again be pointed out that the concepts of " gross " saving and investment as commonly used provide no way

retain the familiar terms and to use them without any reference to changes in the quantity of capital, we might formulate the condition of equality as follows : " savings " correspond to " investment " when the value of existing capital goods (in terms of existing consumers' goods) is such that it becomes profitable to replace them by the capital goods that are required to produce the income in the expectation of which people have decided currently to consume as much as they do.

It is perhaps necessary to remind the reader that we are here not yet concerned with differences between savings and investment which are brought about by monetary causes. Just as differences be-

Causes that will disturb this correspondence

tween the demand for and the supply of any commodity may be brought about either by a mere shift in demand or by the appearance of an entirely new monetary demand, thus differences in the demand for and supply of present (or future) goods generally may be brought about either by shifts in demand or by monetary changes. And just as in the case of a change in the demand for any commodity the effects will be different according to whether this change is due to a mere shift in demand or whether it is due to a monetary change, so the consequences of a difference between " saving " and " investing " will be different according

out of this difficulty. There is no reason why the amounts of particular kinds of goods produced, in particular of durable goods, should move in any strict proportion with the part of current resources which are devoted to provide for future as distinguished from present needs ; nor is there any reason why that part of gross money receipts (" gross income ") of the members of society which they do not devote to current consumption should always move in the same way as that part of their total resources which they want to devote to provision for the future. In order to give these concepts of gross saving and gross investment any definite meaning, one would have to make explicitly some very definite and unrealistic assumptions about the relations between the stream of money payments and the flow of goods, somewhat on the lines of the assumptions which underlie my own analysis in *Prices and Production* (2nd ed., 1935, pp. 43-45 and 120-122).

as they are caused by a real or a monetary change. The essence of the difference, to mention it here briefly, is that monetary changes are bound to set up expectations which will inevitably be disappointed. This, however, is not the place to consider more fully the errors of entrepreneurs which will be caused by such monetary changes and which are probably the main cause of industrial fluctuations. These problems will be briefly considered in the final part of the present study.

While, however, disturbances of this sort which are specially connected with monetary causes can be adequately discussed only against the background of a systematic consideration of the whole monetary mechanism such as cannot be provided here, there are certain other causes which may bring about somewhat similar results. A short discussion of these may therefore fittingly conclude our consideration of the " real " aspects of these phenomena.

Entrepreneurs will on the whole base their anticipations about the relative demand for consumers' goods and capital goods in the future on their observations of the situation in the present. Among the factors which may bring about changes, and therefore make their expectations false, is the *willingness* of people to save certain proportions of a given income ; but this is not very likely to change abruptly and unexpectedly. It is more probable that there may be a rather abrupt change in the *ability* to save of certain classes of people. This may result from a change in the distribution of incomes brought about either by a change in the external data or — and this is the factor which is more likely to affect a very substantial part of the population — by the action of the Government or of monopolistic groups. Any considerable redistribution of the command over the existing resources [1] will

---

[1] We shall see presently that it is not only a redistribution of net income in the usual sense which is likely to be of importance in this connection.

cause a change in the proportion in which consumers'
goods and capital assets (or present income and sources
of future income) will be demanded.

A disproportion in the way in which consumers divide
their incomes and the way in which entrepreneurs have
divided their resources between the provision of consumers' goods and the provision of capital
goods may of course arise in either direction. The case where the demand for consumers' goods
proves to be lower, and the supply of funds for investment
higher, than entrepreneurs expected seems on the whole
to be the one that is less likely to occur and certainly the
one which is less apt to create serious difficulties. This is
not the place to go into all the arguments of the under-
consumption theories which attempt to prove that a
reduction in the demand for consumers' goods is bound
to block the outlets for further investment. Even if we
consider the most unfavourable (and most unlikely) case
where the reduction in the demand for consumers' goods
affects all kinds of consumers' goods simultaneously and
to the same extent, there is no reason why this should
make further investment generally unprofitable. We have
already observed that any saving which has not been
foreseen, and therefore has not led to a corresponding
anticipatory rearrangement of resources, will lead to a
temporary accumulation of stocks. But there seems to be
no reason why an increase in the rate of saving, within
that order of magnitude which merits practical consideration, should reduce the receipts that may be expected from
the sale of consumers' goods by an amount which cannot
be more than offset by a reduction of the rate of interest
and the changes in the technique of production which this
makes profitable. No doubt there will always be some
goods, like stocks of perishable products, which, because
of their high specificity, cannot be shifted to production
for later dates, and on which, therefore, considerable
loss will be made. But on the whole it is nearly always

*Savings exceeding
expectations*

possible to change from shorter to longer processes of production, even if only by keeping larger stocks, without incurring any substantial expense ; and one of the most important cost elements in this connection, the rate of interest, will be reduced in consequence of this very increase in saving.

The situation is, however, very different in the opposite case where the demand for consumers' goods proves to be higher, and the willingness to hold capital assets lower, than corresponds to the relative costs of Savings falling short
of expectations — the quantities of these two kinds of assets which entrepreneurs have actually provided. It is here that the irreversibility of time, which at the beginning of this study we found to be the source of all the peculiar difficulties connected with capital, creates considerable differences between what seem formally to be very similar cases. The crux of the whole capital problem is that while it is almost always possible to postpone the use of things now ready or almost ready for consumption, it is in many cases impossible to anticipate returns which were intended to become available at a later date. The consequence is that, while a relative deficiency in the demand for consumers' goods compared with supply will cause only comparatively minor losses, a relative excess of this demand is apt to have much more serious effects.[1] It will make it altogether impossible to use some resources which are destined to give a consumable return only in the more distant future but will do so only in collaboration with other resources which are now more profitably

---

[1] Cf. Wicksell, *Lectures*, vol. i, pp. 186-187 : " The volume of fixed capital, on the other hand, can, in the long run, be *increased* by the conversion of circulating into fixed capital — in so far as this is generally profitable — but it cannot be appreciably diminished — the reverse operation being usually impossible. Hence it is, in most respects, on the same level as the unchanging original productive factors, labour and land. This circumstance is sometimes in evidence during booms, when large quantities of circulating capital are converted into fixed capital, and it is not possible to replace the former quickly enough."

used to provide consumables for the more immediate future.

This case of an unforeseen relative increase in the demand for consumers' goods is not only the more disturbing case ; it is (apart from monetary complications) also the case much more likely to occur and —may mean an to assume considerable proportions. In the actual consumption of capital modern world the two causes of more or less sudden changes in the distribution of income (Government interference and monopolistic extortion), to which we referred previously as likely to affect the relative demand for consumers' goods and capital goods, are apt to operate on a large scale against the capitalist class, and may effect a redistribution of much more than net income proper. This means that they will on the whole tend not only to decrease the rate of net saving in the usual sense, but may actually lead to a transfer to consumption of funds which ought to be re-invested if income is to be kept on the present level.

For the understanding of such a process of " capital consumption " it is essential to bear in mind that it is not only the capitalists who may be responsible for the consumption of their capital. Once capital is definitely and irrevocably committed to a certain purpose, any of the co-operating factors are capable, through monopolistic combination, of forcing the capitalists to pass on to them part of the gross returns which ought to be re-invested but which, if paid out as income to non-capitalists, will be mostly consumed. This as well as a considerable compulsory transfer of income from capitalists to other classes will tend to increase the demand for consumers' goods and to decrease the funds that will be available for investment relatively to the costs (in terms of each other) of the quantities of consumers' goods and of capital goods which will be available.

A rise of wages enforced by combinations of labour gives rise to exceedingly complicated problems which are

better left to more specialised studies.[1]   It sets up conflicting tendencies which are very difficult to disentangle.
In so far as it leads to an increase in the aggregate
demand for consumers' goods it tends to   The effect of an en-
bring about a consumption of capital.   forced rise of wages
But in so far as labour succeeds in securing for itself a
larger share of the output and in raising real wages it
will tend to bring about a substitution of capital for
labour or a transition to more capitalistic methods of
production.   The net effect would probably be that fewer
workmen would be employed with more capital per head,
that is, that the capital structure would grow in height
but shrink in breadth at the same time.   Although this
would probably be accompanied by some destruction of
capital, that is, by a reduction of the level at which output
could be permanently kept, it would scarcely show the
typical symptoms of a simple " consumption of capital ".
For our present purposes it will be better to leave this
special case out of account and to concentrate on the
effects of an unexpected increase in the aggregate consumers' demand which is not accompanied by an increase
in the rate of real wages, but which is caused either by a
compulsory transfer of income from saving to non-saving
classes, or by an increase of aggregate money incomes
financed by credit expansion.

There is no need at this stage of our exposition to re-
state why an increase in the demand for consumers'
goods (which on our assumptions can only mean an
increase of demand and of their prices in terms of all
other resources and of capital goods in particular) will
make some investment activities unprofitable and will

---

[1] An attempt which the present author made some years ago in
this direction (1932b) has not really taken account of the difficulty
mentioned in the text — apart from its being still made in terms of
changes in the absolute quantity of capital instead of, as it ought to
be, in terms of correspondence or non-correspondence between the
proportions in which capital goods and consumers' goods are supplied
and demanded.   Cf. also Machlup, 1935d, and E. Schiff, 1933.

lead to a transition to less capitalistic methods of production. The only point which we want to stress here is that nearly all the characteristic phenomena of such a process will appear whenever the demand for consumers' goods increases relatively to the supply, whether this demand is actually higher than is compatible with maintaining income permanently at the present level, or whether it is merely above the level for which entrepreneurs have planned. Losses on old investments will occur on a large scale, and production of capital goods will have to be reduced irrespective of whether we have what might be described as an actual consumption of capital, or whether people are merely unwilling to reduce consumption sufficiently to enable entrepreneurs to complete the investment processes upon which they have embarked.

The symptoms usually associated with a "consumption of capital" independent of absolute changes of quantity of capital

The only peculiarity of a process of capital consumption proper, that is, where consumption is in excess of the level which can be permanently maintained, is that such a process has a tendency to become cumulative. Once a community has started to live beyond its income and thereby to reduce its non-permanent resources below what is required to maintain the present level of income permanently, every day this process continues means that, in order to bring it to a stop, consumption will have to be lowered further. And a community which has at first resisted a reduction of its standard of life, made necessary by events such as the destruction of a war, is very unlikely, once it becomes aware of the inevitability of such a reduction, to make it to the increased extent which has become necessary because of the delay. I believe that the history of Europe since the last war offers important examples of countries which have been caught in this vicious spiral of delay in a necessary adjustment of their standard of life, and which consequently have passed

But an absolute reduction of capital has a tendency to become cumulative

through prolonged periods of consumption of capital in the absolute sense of the term.

In the discussion of long-term developments of this kind the use of the concept of absolute increases and decreases of the quantity of capital is comparatively innocuous and will lead to more or less the same results as the more correct analysis. It is in connection with more short-term changes, like those occurring in the course of industrial fluctuations, that

Although useful in certain contexts, the concepts of accumulation and decumulation of capital have to be used with caution

the difference between the analysis in terms of absolute and in terms of relative concepts is likely to be most significant. We could in this connection certainly not do more than speak of changes which *ceteris paribus* would lead to increases or decreases of the quantity of capital. But this way of speaking is rather misleading since it inevitably tempts one to assume that even in a changing world they will normally have that effect. And it certainly seems advisable to refrain from basing any distinction used in the explanation of dynamic phenomena on supposed net changes in the quantity of capital.

The phenomenon of the trade cycle in particular is probably largely connected with changes in that region of indeterminateness between clear increases and decreases of the quantity of capital where the concept of an absolute change has no meaning. But it probably remains true that net accumulations and net decumulations of capital in the usual sense are likely to cause phenomena similar to booms and depressions. At any rate this will be so if — as is very likely to happen — real accumulation proceeds faster, and real decumulation proceeds more slowly, than corresponds to the rate of saving and dissaving respectively. It appears that the difficulties facing analysis of these problems were already seen by Ricardo when he wrote that " the distress which proceeds from a revulsion of trade is often mistaken for that which accompanies a diminution of the national capital and a retrograde state of society ; and it would perhaps be difficult to point out any marks by which they may be accurately distinguished ".[1]

[1] *Principles*, chap. xix, in *Works*, edition McCulloch, p. 160.

PART IV

THE RATE OF INTEREST IN A
MONEY ECONOMY

CHAPTER XXVI

FACTORS AFFECTING THE RATE OF INTEREST
IN THE SHORT RUN

THE task of the first three Parts of this book has been to
show, by the same general method as is used by equilibrium analysis to explain the prices of different commodities at a given moment, why there   The "rate of inter-
will be certain differences between the   est" in equilibrium
prices of the factors of production and the   money rate of interest
expected prices of the products, and why these differences
will stand in a certain uniform relationship to the time
intervals which separate the dates when these prices are
paid. In conformity with an old-established practice, we
have described these price differences, which can be expressed in terms of a time rate, as the rate of interest.
But, as we have warned the reader early in this book,
this " rate of interest " is not identical with the price for
money loans to which this term is applied in a money
economy. It is not a price paid for any particular thing,
but a rate of differences between prices which pervades
the whole price structure. In so far as the money rate
of interest is concerned, our rate of interest is merely one
of the factors which helps to determine it, and is the phenomenon most nearly corresponding to it which we can find
in our imaginary moneyless economy. But if it were not
for the well-established usage, it would probably have
been better to refer to this " real " phenomenon either,
as the English classical economists did, as the rate of
profit, or by some such term as the German *Urzins*.

Although a full discussion of the monetary problems
to which the existence of the " real " rate of interest gives
rise lies outside the scope of the present book, it would

353

24

hardly be appropriate to leave our subject without giving a somewhat more definite indication of how the rate of interest we have been discussing and the money rate of interest are related. At this point we can give no more than an outline of the answers to the main problems. A full discussion of the whole complex of problems involved would require another book of about the same size as this one — even supposing that, in the present state of our knowledge, any such systematic and exhaustive treatment of these as yet imperfectly explored problems could be attempted successfully. As has been explained earlier in this volume, its task is to lay the foundations for the treatment of these problems, not to discuss them in any detail. And we shall confine ourselves in this final Part to the task of showing how these theoretical foundations can be used for the elucidation of certain salient points in the discussion of these more complex problems. We shall not attempt to follow all the possible complications or to explore the consequences of the different possible assumptions with any microscopic accuracy.

Limited scope of present discussion of money rate of interest

For the purposes of this discussion it will be necessary to alter the terminology used in the earlier Parts of this book. As the traditional terminology which we have followed up to this point clearly creates the danger of some confusion if it is retained in the discussion of monetary problems, it will probably be best if, for the purposes of this final Part, we reserve the term " rate of interest " exclusively for the money rate of interest, that is, the price paid for loans of money, and describe the real rate of return as the *rate of profit*.

Use of the term " rate of interest "

Our main problem, then, is to explain how the existence of a system of rates of profit, which in terms of any one commodity will tend to correspond to a uniform time rate,[1]

---

[1] For the exact meaning of the concept of a uniform time rate of return (measured in terms of any one commodity) compare above, p. 167.

will affect the terms on which money will be lent and borrowed. There can be no doubt that the existence of such a rate of profit on investments is the main source of the demand for loans of money, since command over present money is command over present resources which can be turned into future commodities at a profit. And there can also be little doubt that the existence of such a rate of profit is at least·one of the reasons why people who might themselves employ the money profitably, will not be willing to lend it without special remuneration, and that therefore the rate of profit will also affect the supply of loanable money funds. If the rate of money expenditure always remained constant, so that the money expenditure during any period was always equal to the amount of money spent during the preceding period of equal length, and if consequently we could assume that all the money received during any period would be re-spent, after an (on the average) constant interval, either on consumers' goods or on some income-bearing assets, it would clearly be justifiable to assume that the rate of interest would be directly determined by the rate of profit. To every increase in the demand for one commodity (or other type of asset) there would correspond an exactly equal decrease in the demand for another kind of commodity. That is, prices would be determined in the same way as in the imaginary barter economy. And, in particular, the demand for investment goods would be exactly equal to that part of their assets which people did not want to have in the form of consumers' goods. The supply of funds not spent on consumers' goods would become equal to the demand for such funds at a rate of interest corresponding to the rate of profit as determined by the given prices. There would be differences between the rates of profit people expected to earn in their own businesses and the rates of interest at which they would be willing to lend and to borrow, correspond-

Relation between the rate of profit and the rate of interest in equilibrium

ing to the different degrees of risk. But the net rate of interest would tend to be equal to the net rate of profit. And the relative prices of the various types of goods, and therefore the price differences, would depend solely on the relation of the proportions in which people distributed their money expenditure between consumers' goods and capital goods to the proportions in which these two types of goods were available.

While this would undoubtedly be the position once equilibrium had been established, it is one of the oldest facts known to economic theory that changes in the quantity of money, or changes in its "velocity of circulation" (or the "demand for money"), will deflect the rate of interest from this equilibrium position and may keep it for considerable periods above or below the figure determined by the real factors. This fact has scarcely ever been denied by economists, and since the time of Richard Cantillon and David Hume [1] it has been the subject of theoretical analysis which has been further developed in more recent times, particularly by Knut Wicksell and his followers.[2] But it has also given rise to a recurrent scientific fashion, from John Law down to L. A. Hahn[3] and J. M. Keynes, of regarding the rate of interest as being solely dependent on the quantity of money and the varying desires of people to keep certain balances of money in hand.

Influence of monetary changes on rate of interest

[1] Cf. R. Cantillon, *Essai sur la nature du commerce en général* (1754), Part III, chaps. 7 and 8 ; and D. Hume, *Essays Moral, Political, and Literary* (1752), Part II, Essay IV, " On Interest ".

[2] In view of the apparently widespread impression that the influence of liquidity considerations on the rate of interest is a new discovery, the present author may perhaps be excused for pointing out that more than ten years ago he described cyclical fluctuations as largely due to the fact that the rate of interest is in the short run " *determined by considerations of banking liquidity* " (*Geldtheorie und Konjunkturtheorie*, Vienna, 1929, p. 103 ; English edition, *Monetary Theory and the Trade Cycle*, London, 1933, p. 180).

[3] See L. A. Hahn, *Volkswirtschaftliche Theorie des Bankkredits*, Tübingen, 1920, pp. 102 *et seq.*, chapter headed " Der Zins als Preis des Liquiditätsverlustes."

We are here not primarily concerned with the transitory or purely dynamic effects of monetary changes on the rate of interest. But if it is true — as we must assume in the light of all evidence — that changes in the quantity of money affect the rate of interest, there must exist, even in equilibrium conditions, some relationship between the quantity of money people want to hold and the rate of interest. It is this relationship which we must first try to elucidate.

Now, as has been pointed out in an earlier chapter,[1] the desire of people to hold money cannot readily be fitted into the rigid definition of equilibrium we have used up to this point. At least, in an *Extension of concept* economy in which people were absolutely *of equilibrium used* certain about the future, there would be no need to hold any money beyond the comparatively small quantities necessitated by the discontinuity of transactions and the inconvenience and cost of investing such small amounts for very short periods. But the assumption of certainty about the more distant future, although we have so far based our argument on it, is not really essential for our concept of equilibrium. The plans of the various individuals may be compatible with the extent to which they are definite,[2] and yet the individuals may at the same time be uncertain about what will happen after a certain date and may wish to keep some general reserve against whatever may happen in that more uncertain future. In this way our system can be made to include the desire of the individuals to hold money as a general reserve of command over resources.

It is clear that to the individual the holding of money

---

[1] Cf. above, Chapter III.

[2] The interesting problem of how far, despite the fact that the plans of the different individuals are somewhat vague, the " law of large numbers " may yet create sufficient regularity so that the vagaries of the individual decisions will not disappoint expectations, cannot be considered here.

is one form of holding his *assets* [1] and will compete with other forms of investment for the resources at his command. Although holding money yields no direct return,

To the Individual the holding of money is one form of investment

it may, by enabling the holder to take advantage of unforeseen opportunities, be as much a means of reaping a return as any factor of production. And changes in the relative attractiveness of holding money or holding other resources will induce him to keep at different times different proportions of his total assets in the one form or the other. Just as his endeavour to maximise his income will make him distribute his resources between the various forms of investment in the narrower sense in such a way as to equalise their returns, so he will also distribute his assets between investment in goods, in money loans, and in cash balances in such a way as to equalise the advantage he expects to derive from these kinds of assets. If we assume, as we shall do to begin with, that only money is regarded as really liquid, and that all investments in goods and loans of money are considered equally illiquid, the equilibrium position between investments in goods and investments in loans of money will be reached when the net returns, *i.e.* the expected physical returns less compensation for risk and incident trouble or effort, are equal. The return from the holding of cash, being by its nature not so much an expectation of a definite return as an expectation of various uncertain possibilities, is less easily measured. We might perhaps speak of a mean return expected to be derived from the holding of a certain amount of money. But it is probably more convenient not to concentrate on this somewhat intangible return, but to relate the quantity of money a person is willing to hold to the amount of profit or interest which he could

---

[1] Henceforth we shall use the term " assets " whenever we want to describe the aggregate of real capital, money, and securities, which from the point of view of any individual would be regarded as his " capital ".

expect to earn if he invested that money now in goods or loans, and which he consequently sacrifices in order to keep himself in a position to take advantage of more uncertain possibilities.

Any change in the relative attractiveness of holding money and holding investments respectively and any change in the supply of money and investments is therefore likely to change the way in which any person will distribute his assets between these two outlets. It is not difficult to see that any tendency toward such a change in the distribution of assets is bound to affect the rate of interest and the rate of profit. And it follows that changes in these rates may occur even when the factors which we have so far treated as their sole determinants, *i.e.* the profitability of investment and the willingness to save, remain unchanged, and that the affect of any changes in these latter factors may be modified by a new element, the changes in the demand for the different kinds of assets, to which they may give rise.

Changes in the distribution of assets will affect the rate of interest and the rate of profit

In a general manner this effect of "liquidity preference" and the quantity of money on the rate of interest may be described by saying that the rate of interest must be such that people in general will be induced to keep as liquidity reserves just that part of the existing amount of money which is not required to transact current business. It is undoubtedly true that in this sense the quantity of money and liquidity preference will influence the rate of interest. However, this is very far from saying, as Mr. Keynes and his school do, that, even in the short run, the rate of interest is determined solely by the quantity of money and people's liquidity preferences, and still less that in the long run the rate of interest is primarily determined by these monetary factors.

The short-run determination of the rate of interest : assumptions on which considered

In the present chapter we shall be concerned merely with the effects which these monetary factors will have on the determination of the rate of interest in the very short run, postponing the discussion of the slower repercussions of any change till the next chapter. This means in particular that we shall here consider only the temporary equilibrium which will be established after a change has taken place in the market for money loans, and before the consequent changes in income and final demand have had time to affect expected returns. In order to simplify the argument in this first stage, we shall assume that there is only one homogeneous kind of money in existence, the quantity of which is fixed, and which is clearly demarcated in respect to its liquidity from all other assets, whether money loans or real assets, these other assets being regarded for present purposes as all equally illiquid. The most important consequence of this assumption is that in the present context we can disregard any differences between the different rates of return on funds that are in any sense invested, and particularly between the rate of interest and the rate of profit. So we can confine ourselves to the relation between the purely psychical return from holding money and all other physical returns from investments of every kind.

We may begin by considering the argument which is at the back of the assertion that, at least in the short run, the rate of interest is determined solely by the quantity of money and liquidity preference. It can be shown without great difficulty that this view is due to the treatment of one source of the demand for money as if it were the sole determinant of its price, an error which is rather similar to the older belief that, since the industrial demand for gold has some influence on the value of gold, the value of monetary gold depends solely on its industrial uses. The case of the relationship between the demand for money, liquidity preference, and the rate of interest, appears only superficially more plausible because it is,

Cause of erroneous belief that rate of interest is determined solely by quantity of money and liquidity preference

of course, true that the whole demand for money is
derived from a desire for holding money. But not all
the desire to hold money is due to liquidity preference,
nor can it be assumed that the demand for money due to
other circumstances can in the short run be considered as
constant. Only if one or the other of these two conditions were satisfied could it be said that the price of
money depended solely on liquidity preference and the
quantity of money in existence. In fact, of course, we
hold money not only because we do not know what to
do with it, but also, and in normal times probably to a
much greater extent, because we intend to use it for
particular purposes some time later and cannot conveniently invest it in the meantime. And while a rise
in the expected rate of return on investments will make
it relatively less attractive to hold money merely in the
hope that it will prove more useful at some uncertain
later date, it will at the same time increase the amount
of money that will be needed to transact the business
promising any given rate of return.

The misleading impression that the rate of interest is
determined solely by the quantity of money and liquidity
preference is based on the wrong suggestion, implied in
this type of analysis, that the demand for   The influence of pro-
money is dependent solely on liquidity   ductivity concealed in
"liquidity preference
preference. But the description of the   function"
demand for money in terms of a curve or function, which
is called a liquidity preference curve or function, simply
means that under this name all sorts of influences, including in particular the productivity of investment, have
been lumped together. It is, of course, always possible so
to define the terms used in an argument as to make the
conclusions purely analytical and necessarily true. And
this is exactly what is being done when liquidity preference is so defined as to include all factors which determine
the demand for money, and it is then concluded that the
price of money loans depends exclusively on the quantity

of money and liquidity preference. But in this form the statement amounts to no more than saying that the rate of interest depends on the demand for and supply of money without telling us anything as to which factor on the demand side is of most importance.

In order to show that in fact the liquidity preference curve cannot be regarded as independent of the productivity of investment but merely conceals or rather includes the productivity element, and consequently that the demonstration that the rate of interest is completely determined by this curve and the quantity of money does not prove that it is independent of the productivity of investment, we need ask only one question : Are the amounts which people are assumed to be willing to hold for reasons of liquidity at any given rate of interest supposed to be independent of the *amounts* which they can invest at that rate ? Only if this question could reasonably be answered in the affirmative could the liquidity preference curve be regarded as independent of the productivity of investment. But even if this were the case, it could surely apply only to the amounts of money held as liquidity reserves and would therefore not enable us to derive the rate of interest from the total supply of money. If, however, as is almost certainly always the case, the answer to our question is in the negative, that is, if the amount of money people are willing to hold as liquidity reserves depends *inter alia* on *how much* they can invest at a given rate of return, this means that the whole productivity element has been smuggled into the so-called liquidity preference curve. In this way the assertion that the rate of interest depends solely on liquidity preference and not on the productivity of investment is deprived of all foundation.[1]

---

[1] There has probably been some confusion with the idea that under perfect competition the investment demand schedule which any individual faces must be horizontal, that is that the amount which any individual can invest at a given rate of interest is unlimited. But,

The real position can be illustrated by slightly modifying a diagram used by Professor Hicks in this connection.[1] It is based on the assumption that the quantity of money is fixed, and it has two curves, one showing the amounts of money people will be willing to spend during any given period at various rates of interest out of their given cash holdings, and the other showing the rates

Diagrammatic illustration of relation between productivity and liquidity preference

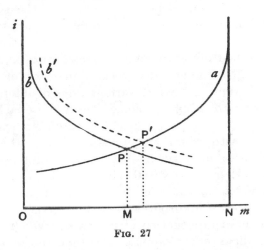

FIG. 27

of return which people expect to get on given amounts of expenditure. Thus in Fig. 27 the curve marked *a* shows that with a rise in the rate of interest (measured along the ordinate *Oi*) people will be willing to spend increasing amounts out of their given money holdings on investments (the amounts spent are measured along the abscissa *Om*), while the curve marked *b* shows that as this expenditure increases the expected rate of return falls. Since for the moment we are concerned merely

quite apart from the fact that perfect competition merely requires that no person counts on his action affecting prices, we have to deal here, not with the investment opportunities open to an individual, but with the investment demand schedule of society as a whole.

[1] Cf. J. R. Hicks, 1937, p. 153.

with the very short-term effects, this expenditure induced
by changes in the expected returns will refer only to
direct investments and will not include the further
changes in expenditure on the part of the people whose
receipts are increased by the investments. In this respect
our diagram differs from the similar diagram used by
Professor Hicks, who includes all the indirect effects on
income. Our curve represents simply what Mr. Keynes
calls the investment demand schedule, or the schedule
of the marginal efficiency of capital, at the moment
concerned.

This method of representation means that instead of
asking, as Mr. Keynes does, what quantity of money
people will want to hold at various rates of interest and
profit and with a given money income, we ask what
amounts of money people will be willing to spend on
investment with given money balances but at various
expected rates of return. This means that we treat
income as a dependent variable.

It follows from the definition of our curves that the
rate of interest and profit will at any moment be fixed
at the point of intersection of the two curves (the point
P in the diagram). Suppose now that the investment
demand schedule (our curve b) is raised, say by an
invention. If cash balances were rigidly fixed so that
the increase of expected returns would not induce people
to release any money out of their balances (*i.e.* if the
a-curve were a vertical line), the rate of interest would
rise by the full amount of the rise in the investment
demand schedule. Or, in other words, if the demand
for money were perfectly inelastic with respect to the
rate of interest, the rate of interest would depend solely
on the productivity of investment (and the rate of saving,
which, however, for our present short-term analysis we
can treat as constant) and would closely follow any change
in the productivity of investment. This is, of course, the
case mentioned at the beginning of this chapter and the

one that was traditionally discussed in the pure (as distinguished from the monetary) theory of interest.

If, however, as is more likely, a rise in the expected rate of return will induce people to release some money from their cash balances (so that our *a*-curve slopes upwards to the right), a rise of the *b*-curve will not raise the point of intersection of the two curves or therefore the rate of interest by the full amount by which the *b*-curve has risen, but only by somewhat less ; how much less, will depend on the slope of the *a*-curve. This means that the release of money from the liquidity reserves will increase the supply of funds at the same time as the demand for funds is increased, and the rate of interest will therefore rise less than if the supply were fixed. We might even theoretically conceive of an extreme case where within certain limits the desire to hold cash is perfectly elastic (*i.e.* our *a*-curve horizontal), so that in consequence of a rise of the *b*-curve, just enough cash will be released from idle balances to keep the rate of interest at its former level. In this case it might indeed be said that the rate of interest was determined solely by liquidity preference, *i.e.* the desire to hold money. For so long as our *b*-curve intersects the *a*-curve in its horizontal part, shifts of the *b*-curve will in the short run have no influence on the height of the rate of interest.

It is instructive to consider somewhat more closely the conditions under which this may be true. This will show how extremely limited an application this theoretically possible case has. A horizontal *a*-curve, as we have seen, would mean that people would in all circumstances invest just as much as could be invested at a fixed rate of return, no matter how large the amounts were. The only condition under which this would appear at all likely is that the rate of return should already have fallen so low as only just to

Conditions under which liquidity preference could be regarded as sole short-run determinant of rate of interest

compensate for the extra risk of lending or investing in real assets compared with holding money. In such a situation people would indeed invest just as much as they could invest at that minimum rate, and would hoard all the rest. But since we know that people actually do lend even at a fraction of one per cent, this minimum is evidently very low. All that the contention would therefore appear to imply is that there is some minimum figure for the rate of return below which it would never fall, and that if that figure has been reached all changes in the amount of investment will be financed by exactly equal changes in idle money balances. But even this would be strictly true in actual life only if we could regard the holding of money, as we do here, as subject to no risk either of loss or of depreciation. In fact we do know that this is not so and that in some circumstances people will even pay something for having their money kept in some form other than cash (or even bank balances), *i.e.* that they will sometimes prefer to invest even at a negative rate of return. It seems therefore that we must assume that the amounts of money people are willing to hold will decrease with every rise in the expected rate of return, from zero or even below zero upwards, and that therefore our *a*-curve will throughout be upward-sloping in greater or lesser degree.

We can therefore dismiss from our mind the case of an *a*-curve which is absolutely horizontal even in parts, and may confine our attention to the case where it is more **Probable shape of** or less upward-sloping. It still remains **a-curve** probable, however, that with a very low rate of return its slope will be slight. But it will clearly rise with rising rates of return, since the greater the reduction which has already taken place in idle balances the greater will the further rise of the rate of return have to be in order to induce the release of a further amount of given magnitude from those balances. And since there is clearly a maximum beyond which, for technical reasons, the velocity of circulation cannot be increased (because there are no " idle " balances left), the curve must tend to become vertical for very high rates of return.

The significance for the determination of the rate of interest of this conclusion (that our a-curve will slope upwards to the right) is that a shifting of the curve of return upwards or downwards will lead to the release or absorption of varying amounts of money from idle balances, and that the immediate effect of a change of the curve of return on the rate of interest will be modified to that extent.

The nature of this process can be further illustrated by means of our diagram if we introduce one further simplifying assumption which enables us to interpret it in a second way.   The assumption which we   The two sources of the have to make for this purpose is that the   demand for money amount of money that will be held by entrepreneurs in connection with investments for which they have definite plans, and by the recipients of the income created by all investments (the total of " transaction balances "), will change in exact proportion to the total of these payments. On this assumption the distance OM in our diagram, which expresses expenditure on investment, can also be interpreted as representing the amount of transaction balances held ; and since the total quantity of money in the hands of all concerned is assumed to be constant, and ON represents the case where idle balances are zero and all the money is held in transaction balances, MN measures the amount of idle balances held at any moment.

Thus interpreted the diagram shows how the given supply of money will in various circumstances be distributed between active balances and idle balances. It shows us how the two competing uses of money will in the short run jointly determine the rate of return on all kinds of investment and how misleading any assertion must be that the rate of interest will always depend either on liquidity preference only or on productivity only.

The theory that the rate of interest depends solely on liquidity preference is an inference from the implicit assumption that the whole demand for money is due to liquidity preference — or at least that the demand for money for other purposes may be treated as constant. It will now also be clear that it is not sufficient, as Professors Hicks and Lange have done,[1] merely to add the volume of money income to liquidity preference as a second determinant. For before incomes can rise with a given quantity of money a rise in returns must occur in order to induce somebody to reduce his idle balances. And it is only in consequence of a previous increase in investments, which, unless our a-curve is horizontal, will mean a higher rate of interest, that incomes and final demand will increase and in turn affect the investment demand schedule. This is, however, already outside the very short-term effects which we are considering in the present chapter. It cannot be denied, therefore, that even in the shortest of short runs the investment demand schedule has a direct influence on the rate of interest and that any change in the former will directly lead to a change in the latter.

[1] O. Lange, **1938,** pp. 16 *et seq.*

CHAPTER XXVII

LONG-RUN FORCES AFFECTING THE RATE OF INTEREST

HAVING considered in the last chapter the impact effect of any change in investment demand, we must now turn to the further repercussions of the changes we have observed. We have seen that, in a money economy, one of the effects of a change in the profitability of investment will be a release of money from (or an absorption of money into) idle balances and a consequent change in the size of the money stream which meets the stream of goods. We have not yet considered the effects on returns of this change in the money stream, since they will make themselves felt only after the short period with which we were concerned in the last chapter.

The returns curve or investment demand schedule which then we treated as a given magnitude, or as an independent variable, will clearly be affected by changes in the size of the money stream. Before we can analyse these effects it will be necessary to make a somewhat closer examination of the factors which determine the shape of this curve in general, and at the same time to distinguish between the different ways in which the amount of investment can change and the effects of such changes on the returns curve.

Influences determining the shape of the investment demand curve

So far we have not explicitly discussed the relation between the returns curve as used in the last chapter, which refers to the returns from successive amounts of money invested, and our earlier discussion of the productivity of investment in real terms. But so long as we treat prices as given, as we were able to do for the purpose of the analysis of the last chapter, the relationship is so

369

obvious that it hardly needs further explanation. Just as successive amounts of investment expressed in terms of any other unit will bring decreasing returns, so the investment of successive doses of such quantities of input as can be obtained for a given amount of money will also bring decreasing returns.

Somewhat more careful consideration is needed of what exactly we mean here when we speak of an increase in investment. Strictly speaking, if we start from an initial equilibrium position where the existence of unused resources [1] is excluded by definition, an increase or decrease of investment should always mean a transfer of input from the production of consumers' goods for a nearer date to the production of consumers' goods for a more distant date, or *vice versa*. But where we assume that this diversion of input from one kind of production to another is accompanied, and in part brought about, by changes in total money expenditure, we cannot at the same time assume that prices will remain unchanged. It is, however, neither necessary nor advisable to adhere for our present purposes to so rigid a type of equilibrium assumption. At any rate, so far as concerns the impact effects of a rise in investment demand which we discussed in the last chapter, there is no reason why we should not assume that the additional input which is being invested has previously been unemployed, so that the increase in investment means a corresponding increase in the employment of all sorts of resources without any increase of prices and without a decrease in the production of consumers' goods. This assumption simply means that there are certain limited quantities of various resources available which have been offered but not bought at current prices, but which would be employed as soon as

Meaning of changes in the "amount of investment"

---

[1] This means unused resources which could be had at the ruling market price. There will of course always be further reserves which will be offered only if prices rise.

demand at existing prices rose. And since the amount of such resources will always be limited, the effect of making this assumption will be that we must distinguish between the effects which an increase of investments and income will have while there are unused resources of all kinds available and the effects which such an increase will have after the various resources become successively scarce and their prices begin to rise.

The initial change from which we started our discussion in the last chapter, an invention which gives rise to a new demand for capital, means that with given prices the margin between the cost of production and the price of the product produced with the new process will be higher than the ruling rate of profit, *i.e.* that the marginal rate of profit on the former volume of production will have risen. The first result of this, as we have seen, will be that investment will increase, the marginal rate of profit will fall, and the cash balances will decrease till the desire for holding the marginal units of the decreased cash balances is again just balanced by the higher profits which may be obtained by investing them. This new rate of profit will be somewhere between the old rate and the higher rate which would exist if investment had not increased. But since this additional investment has been financed by a release of money out of idle balances, incomes will have increased, and as a consequence the demand for consumers' goods will also increase, although probably not to the full extent, as some of the additional income is likely to be saved.

Effect of a rise in investment demand on incomes

If we assume that there are unused resources available not only in the form of factors of production but also in the form of consumers' goods in all stages of completion, and so long as this is the case, the increase in the demand for consumers' goods will for some time lead merely to an increase in sales without an increase of prices. Such an increase of the quantity of output which can be sold at given

Effect of a rise in incomes on investment demand

prices will have the effect of raising the investment demand further, or, more exactly, of shifting our returns curve to the right without changing its shape. The amount that it will appear profitable to borrow and invest at any given rate of interest will accordingly increase ; and this in turn will mean that, though some more money will be released from idle balances, the rate of interest and the rate of profit will be raised further. And since this process will have raised incomes still further, it will be repeated : that is, every further increase in the demand for consumers' goods will lead to some further increase of investment and some further increase of the rate of profit. But at every stage of this process some part of the additional income will be saved, and as rates of interest rise, any given increase in final demand will lead to proportionally less investment. (Or, what is really the same phenomenon, only seen from a different angle, successive increases of investment demand will lead to the release of decreasing amounts of money from idle balances.) So the process will gradually slow down and finally come to a stop.

Where will the rate of interest be fixed in this final equilibrium ? If we assume the quantity of money to have remained constant, it will evidently be above the Final position of rate rate which ruled before the initial change of return occurred and even above the somewhat higher impact rate which ruled immediately after the change occurred, since every revolution of the process we have been considering will have raised it a little further. But under our present assumptions there is no reason why, even when this process comes to an end, the rate of interest need have risen to the full extent to which it would have risen in the beginning had the supply of investible funds been entirely inelastic. Thus, under the conditions we have considered, the release of money from idle balances (and the same would of course be true of an increase in the quantity of money) may keep the rate of profit and interest lastingly below the figure to which it would have risen without any such monetary change.

Let us be quite clear, however, about which of our assumptions this somewhat surprising result is due to. We have assumed that not only the supply of pure input but also the supply of final and inter- Nature of assumptions mediate products and of instruments of underlying this ana- all kinds was infinitely elastic, so that lysis every increase in demand could be satisfied without any increase of price, or, in other words, that the increase of investment (or we should rather say output) was possible without society in the aggregate or even any single individual having to reduce consumption in order to provide an income for the additional people now employed. Or, in other words, we have been considering an economic system in which not only the permanent resources but also all kinds of non-permanent resources, that is, all forms of capital, were not scarce. There is indeed no reason why the price of capital should rise if there are such unused reserves of capital available, there is even no reason why capital should have a price at all if it were abundant in all its forms. The existence of interest in such a world would indeed be due merely to the scarcity of money, although even money would not be scarce in any absolute sense; it would be scarce only relatively to given prices on which people were assumed to insist. By an appropriate adjustment of the quantity of money the rate of interest could, in such a system, be reduced to practically any level.

Now such a situation, in which abundant unused reserves of all kinds of resources, including all intermediate products, exist, may occasionally prevail in the depths of a depression. But it is certainly Mr. Keynes' eco- not a normal position on which a theory nomics of abundance claiming general applicability could be based. Yet it is some such world as this which is treated in Mr. Keynes'

General Theory of Employment, Interest and Money, which
in recent years has created so much stir and confusion
among economists and even the wider public. Although
the technocrats, and other believers in the unbounded
productive capacity of our economic system, do not yet
appear to have realised it, what he has given us is really
that economics of abundance for which they have been
clamouring so long. Or rather, he has given us a system
of economics which is based on the assumption that no
real scarcity exists, and that the only scarcity with which
we need concern ourselves is the artificial scarcity created
by the determination of people not to sell their services
and products below certain arbitrarily fixed prices. These
prices are in no way explained, but are simply assumed
to remain at their historically given level, except at rare
intervals when " full employment " is approached and
the different goods begin successively to become scarce
and to rise in price.

Now if there is a well-established fact which dominates
economic life, it is the incessant, even hourly, variation in
the prices of most of the important raw materials and of
the wholesale prices of nearly all foodstuffs. But the
reader of Mr. Keynes' theory is left with the impression
that these fluctuations of prices are entirely unmotivated
and irrelevant, except towards the end of a boom, when
the fact of scarcity is readmitted into the analysis, as an
apparent exception, under the designation of " bottlenecks ".[1] And not only are the factors which determine
the relative prices of the various commodities systematic-

---

[1] I should have thought that the abandonment of the sharp distinction between the " freely reproducible goods " and goods of absolute
scarcity and the substitution for this distinction of the concept of varying degrees of scarcity (according to the increasing costs of reproduction)
was one of the major advances of modern economics. But Mr. Keynes
evidently wishes us to return to the older way of thinking. This at any
rate seems to be what his use of the concept of " bottlenecks " means ;
a concept which seems to me to belong essentially to a naïve early stage
of economic thinking and the introduction of which into economic theory
can hardly be regarded as an improvement.

ally disregarded ; [1] it is even explicitly argued that, apart
from the purely monetary factors which are supposed
to be the sole determinants of the rate of interest, the
prices of the majority of goods would be indeterminate.
Although this is expressly stated only for capital assets in
the special narrow sense in which Mr. Keynes uses this
term, that is, for durable goods and securities, the same
reasoning would apply to all factors of production. In so
far as " assets " in general are concerned the whole argument of the *General Theory* rests on the assumption that
their yield only is determined by real factors (*i.e.* that it
is determined by the given prices of their products), and
that their price can be determined only by capitalising
this yield at a given rate of interest determined solely by
monetary factors.[2] This argument, if it were correct,
would clearly have to be extended to the prices of all
factors of production the price of which is not arbitrarily
fixed by monopolists, for their prices would have to be
equal to the value of their contribution to the product
less interest for the interval for which the factors remained
invested.[3] That is, the difference between costs and prices
would not be a source of the demand for capital but would
be unilaterally determined by a rate of interest which was
entirely dependent on monetary influences.

[1] It is characteristic that when at last, towards the end of his book,
Mr. Keynes comes to discuss prices, the " Theory of Price " is to him
merely " the analysis of the relations between changes in the quantity
of money and changes in the price level " (*General Theory*, p. 296).

[2] Cf. *General Theory*, p. 137 : " We must ascertain the rate of
interest from some other source and only then can we value the asset
by ' capitalising ' its prospective yield ".

[3] The reason why Mr. Keynes does not draw this conclusion, and
the general explanation of his peculiar attitude towards the problem
of the determination of relative prices, is presumably that under the
influence of the " real cost " doctrine which to the present day plays
such a large rôle in the Cambridge tradition, he assumes that the prices
of all goods except the more durable ones are even in the short run
determined by costs. But whatever one may think about the usefulness of a cost explanation of relative prices in equilibrium analysis, it
should be clear that it is altogether useless in any discussion of problems
of the short period.

We need not follow this argument much further to see that it leads to contradictory conclusions. Even in the case we have considered before of an increase in the **Basic Importance of** investment demand due to an invention, **scarcity** the mechanism which restores the equality between profits and interest would be inconceivable without an independent determinant of the prices of the factors of production, namely their scarcity. For, if the prices of the factors were directly dependent on the given rate of interest, no increase in profits could appear, and no expansion of investment would take place, since prices would be automatically marked to make the rate of profit equal to the given rate of interest. Or, if the initial prices were regarded as unchangeable and unlimited supplies of factors were assumed to be available at these prices, nothing could reduce the increased rate of profit to the level of the unchanged rate of interest. It is clear that, if we want to understand at all the mechanism which determines the relation between costs and prices, and therefore the rate of profit, it is to the relative scarcity of the various types of capital goods and of the other factors of production that we must direct our attention, for it is this scarcity which determines their prices. And although there may be, at most times, some goods an increase in demand for which may bring forth some increase in supply without an increase of their prices, it will on the whole be more useful and realistic to assume for the purposes of this investigation that most commodities are scarce, in the sense that any rise of demand will, *ceteris paribus*, lead to a rise in their prices. We must leave the consideration of the existence of unemployed resources of certain kinds to more specialised investigations of dynamic problems.

This critical excursion was unfortunately made necessary by the confusion which has reigned on this subject since the appearance of Mr. Keynes' *General Theory*. We may now return to our main subject, the effect of a rise

in incomes and final demand on the investment demand
schedule and the rate of interest.   The case which we shall
now take up is the situation that will arise once the increased demand for consumers' goods can no
longer be satisfied at constant costs because
at least some of the factors from which
additional consumers' goods would have to be produced
become definitely scarce.   It does not matter for our
purpose whether this occurs immediately, as soon as
incomes and the demand for consumers' goods increase,
or not until later, for, as we have seen, the process by
which increased investment increases final demand, and
increased final demand increases investment further, will
go on for some time.   We are now concerned not with
the transitory effects which occur while any unused
capacity caused by a previous slump is being absorbed —
the analysis of this is the proper subject of dynamic
studies — but with the way in which the influence of
scarcity will reassert itself once this slack in the system
has been taken up.

Sooner or later, then, the increase in the demand for
consumers' goods will lead to an increase of their prices [1]
and of the profits made on the production of consumers'
goods.   But once prices begin to rise, the additional
demand for funds will no longer be confined to the purposes of new additional investment intended to satisfy the

*Effect of an increase
of final demand on
profit schedule*

---

[1] We must not allow ourselves to be misled by the fact that for
special reasons connected with the imperfectly competitive character
of many retail markets, retail prices of consumers' goods are notoriously
sluggish in their movements.   The fact apparently is that for the
individual retailer the price elasticity of the demand for his products
is too low (and selling costs, so long as incomes of his customers are
constant, too high) to make it worth his while to increase sales by
lowering prices, although (if we exclude selling costs) he may be
operating under decreasing costs.   But this does not exclude the
possibility that when demand increases he may be able to expand his
sales at decreasing costs and increasing profits and that he will therefore be able to offer higher prices to the wholesalers.   For this reason it
is probably wholesale prices and not retail prices of consumers' goods
which are relevant for the purposes of the present discussion.

new demand. At first — and this is a point of importance which is often overlooked — only the prices of consumers' goods, and of such other goods as can rapidly be turned At first the rate of into consumers' goods, will rise, and conse- profit will rise in the late stages of produc- quently profits also will increase only in tion only the late stages of production. In order that the rise of prices should become general and should exert a proportional effect on the prices of all the various factors of production, as appears commonly to be assumed to be the normal case, it would not only be necessary that producers in all stages should be put in a position at one and the same time to spend proportionately more; it would also be necessary that the increase in incomes which would be caused by this increased spending should not lead to any further increase in the demand for consumers' goods and a further increase of their prices. Otherwise the prices of consumers' goods would always keep a step ahead of the prices of factors. That is, so long as any part of the additional income thus created is spent on consumers' goods (*i.e.* unless all of it is saved), the prices of consumers' goods must rise permanently in relation to those of the various kinds of input. And this, as will by now be evident, cannot be lastingly without effect on the relative prices of the various kinds of input and on the methods of production that will appear profitable.

The general nature of the price mechanism that will be set in operation, and of the effects this kind of change will have on the volume of investment generally, is The rise of the rate of already familiar to us from discussion profit cannot be wiped out by a proportional in an earlier Part of this book. It will, rise of all other prices however, be useful to re-state it now in monetary terms. The starting point for this analysis must be the fact that, whether the increase in investment [1] is

---

[1] The reason why throughout the following argument we shall con-centrate on an *increase* in the demand for consumers' goods is that we want to bring out the significance of the scarcity of consumers' goods (or of " capital " — which amounts to the same thing) as clearly as possible. But the argument would of course, *mutatis mutandis*,

brought about by employing, in the production of investment goods, formerly unemployed input, or by employing
apply equally to the case of a fall in the demand for consumers'
goods.

The main source of the erroneous conceptions which rule in this
field is a false analogy to the effect of changes in the expected return
and the rate of interest on the price of assets (mainly securities) which
are capable of giving only one particular kind of return. The price of
a fixed interest-bearing bond, e.g., will (disregarding for our purpose
the effects of various degrees of risk) always be equal to the value of
the expected yield, discounted at the current rate of interest ; and its
price will therefore change in inverse proportion to the rate of interest
and in direct proportion to any change in returns if such should occur.

The situation is, however, altogether different with regard to factors
of production which can be used in various ways so as to give
different returns at different dates. And this holds even for completely specific factors of production which can be used only for one
particular purpose, provided they co-operate with other factors which
fall in the former category. (The only kinds of real assets which in
effect would be similar to securities in this respect would be durable
consumers' goods which neither need the co-operation of any other
factors to yield their services nor can be used more or less intensively
so as to last a shorter or longer time.)

In order to obtain a valid analogy to the determination of the prices
of capital goods in the field of securities, we should have to conceive
of securities which not only entitled the owner to different options
of various sorts (corresponding to different uses to which productive
resources can be put), but some at least of which would bring a return
only if owned in certain combinations with other securities. If this
were the case it would clearly be possible for, e.g., a given rise of the
rate of interest to reduce the price of one group of securities which
carried a title only to one fixed series of returns by much more than it
reduced the price of another group which conferred an option on a
shorter series of larger returns as an alternative to the same series of
fixed returns. And if some securities could be used only in combination with others so as jointly to entitle the owner to a certain return,
it might well be the case that a rise in the rate of interest would lower
the price of the first kind of securities a great deal and at the same time
raise the value of the second kind of securities. This would happen if
the value of the first kind largely depended on a long series of small
returns which could be obtained as an alternative to the use in combination with the second kind of security, this latter use providing an
outlet for only a very small part of the total amount of the first kind.
In this case the value of the first kind of security would depend almost
exclusively on this independent use and would be reduced a great deal
by a rise in the rate of interest. If, on the other hand, the return from
the joint use of both kinds of security were one large sum in the near
future, a rise in the rate of interest would affect the present value of

input formerly used in the production of consumers' goods, the remuneration of input in general in terms of consumers' goods must fall *unless* the owners of the input voluntarily reduce their consumption. In the first case a given output of consumers' goods will have to be divided among a greater number of income-receivers, while in the second case a reduced output of consumers' goods will have to be divided among the same number of income-receivers. In such a situation no monetary change can alter the fact that relatively to every unit of input employed there is less output available, and that, therefore, unless people spontaneously decide to save correspondingly more, the price of input in terms of final output must fall.[1]

But if it is impossible in such a situation for the prices of all kinds of input to rise in proportion to the rise in the price of output, and as the value of nearly all input

this joint return very little. But as the part of this joint return that would have to go to the first kind of security (determined by its value in other uses) would be reduced much more, the value of the second kind of security would increase.

Now this sort of thing, which in the realm of securities would be a freak case and very unlikely to be of any importance, may well occur with productive resources. And even if here too the rule should prove to be that a rise in the rate of interest will reduce the value of income-bearing assets, this will be true to so varying an extent and subject to so many exceptions, that the analogy to the normal case of securities will be very misleading. The point to keep in mind is that, with real productive resources, the yield can as a rule be varied and will be deliberately varied in response to changes in their prices, and that it will not be the greatest absolute yield but the highest time rate of yield which will guide their use. We shall later see that on this last point, which of course distinguishes the theory of capital from timeless productivity analysis, it is analogies to the latter which have provided the second important source of error.

[1] Even if present money prices were instantaneously " marked up " in full proportion to the rise in the price of the product (or even the expected rise in the price of the output), this could lead only to a continuous and progressive rise in the price of output which would always exceed entrepreneurs' expectations till they realised that, however great the increase in the prices paid for the input, they could not prevent these prices from falling relatively to the price of output, and that therefore it would be better to adapt their methods of production to the new price relations.

in terms of output must fall to some extent, it is also impossible for the rise in the price of output to leave the relative prices of the different kinds of input unaffected. If this were so, *i.e.* if the pre-existing prices of the different kinds of input continued to prevail, the given rise in the price of output would mean very different changes in the rates of profit earned on different kinds of input. For, although a given rise in the The increase in the difference between the price of output and the prices of input generally must lead to changes in the relative prices of different kinds of input price of all output would, of course, increase the difference between the price of any unit of input producing a given marginal product and the price of that marginal product by the same amount, it would clearly change the *time rate* of profit earned on different units of input to very different degrees according to the periods for which the different units of input were invested.[1] If in the previous

---

[1] The argument can be illustrated by a simple diagram. If along the abscissa Ot we represent investment periods, and along the ordinate

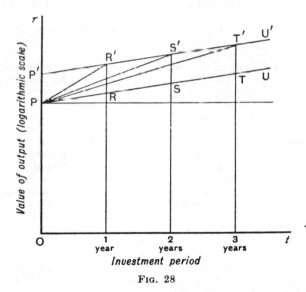

Fig. 28

Or values of units of input and of their marginal products (using for this axis a logarithmic scale), we can represent the value of the

equilibrium position the margin between the price of a unit of input and the price of its marginal product corresponded everywhere to a uniform time rate of 6 per cent, the difference between the price of a unit of input invested two years before the completion of the product and the price of its marginal product would be 12 per cent,[1] while the difference between the price of a unit of input invested only one month before the completion of the product and the price of its marginal product would be only one-half of 1 per cent. A rise in the price of the product by 2 per cent, which would increase these margins to 14 and 2½ per cent respectively, would increase the per annum rate of profit on the former to only 7 per cent but would increase the per annum rate of profit on the latter to 30 per cent.[2]

marginal products of equal units of input invested for various periods by an upward sloping line PU. The difference between the price of a unit of input (OP) and the value of its marginal product corresponds in all cases to a uniform rate of interest represented by the slope of the line PU.

Assume now that the price of all output is raised by a given proportion while the price of the input remains unchanged. The increase in the price of the unchanged quantities of output due to the various inputs can be shown in the diagram by raising the line PU, without changing its slope, to some position such as $P'U'$. The time rates of profit that will now be earned on input invested for various periods are shown by the slopes of the lines PR', PS', PT', etc., and it will be seen that the rate of profit now earned on one year's investment will be greater than that earned on two years' investment, the latter greater than that on three years' investment, and so on, all these rates being higher than the previous uniform rate of profit represented by the slopes of the lines PU and $P'U'$. And as the rate of profit on investment for different periods will have changed to a different extent, so the demand for input for investment for different periods will have changed.

If the price of input had risen in proportion to the rise in the price of output, *i.e.* to OP', the rate of profit earned on the different investment periods would still be uniform and the same as that which was earned before the rise in the price of the output. And the relative demand for input for these various forms of investment would have been unchanged. But although this assumption is implicitly contained in the usual analysis of these phenomena, it is, as we have seen, an illegitimate assumption to make.

[1] Disregarding compound interest.

[2] The example is worked out more fully in Hayek, **1939**, p. 8.

If we assume that at first the rate of interest at which money can be borrowed remains unchanged or rises only very little, it is clear that we have here a state of affairs which cannot last. And we have already seen that the situation cannot be remedied by simply raising the prices of all input in proportion to the rise in the price of the output, for there is not enough output

Effect of difference of various magnitudes between the value of input and the discounted value of its marginal product

to go round. The given output which has now to be distributed among a larger number of claimants (or the decreased output which has now to be distributed among an unchanged number of claimants) will still have to be distributed according to the discounted marginal productivity of the various kinds of input. Entrepreneurs will still tend to bid up the prices of the various kinds of input to the discounted value of their respective marginal products, and, if the rate at which they can borrow money remains unchanged, the only way in which this equality between the price of the input and the discounted value of its marginal product can be restored, is evidently by reducing that marginal product.

This conclusion may at first appear paradoxical because it means, *firstly*, that input will have to be switched from uses where its marginal product is higher to uses where its marginal product is lower, and, *secondly*, that the marginal productivity of all kinds, or of nearly all kinds, of input will have to be lowered at the same time. But if we cling to the

Changes in productive combinations (methods of production) in order to adjust marginal productivities

two basic considerations : (*a*) that it is impossible under the conditions considered for prices of all input to rise in proportion to the prices of output, and (*b*) that until equality between the price of input and the discounted price of its marginal products is restored, it will be the rate of profit earned on the various uses of the input which will guide entrepreneurs in making their decision, the answer is not difficult to find. Perhaps we may begin by pointing out that, although this case is not usually considered in elementary marginal productivity analysis, the marginal productivity of *all* kinds of concrete input can of course be lowered at the same time by changing over to less capitalistic, and therefore less productive, methods of production. And to this consideration we need only add that, as we have already seen, if the difference between the price of a unit of input and the price of a unit of output increases, a smaller marginal product maturing at a nearer date may well represent a higher time rate of profit, and therefore appear more attractive, than the larger marginal product in the more distant future which, before the rise in the price of the product, promised the higher rate of return.

With the help of these general considerations we can now show in more detail what will happen to the prices of the different kinds of input. The rate of profit to be earned at the pre-existing prices will have increased most, and demand will therefore increase most, for those kinds of input which can be rapidly turned into consumers' goods. Whether and to what extent their prices will be raised in consequence, will depend on how easily the quantity of these kinds of input available for the rapid production of consumers' goods can be increased by transfers from other uses where demand is less urgent, from unused reserves, etc. Those kinds of input of which the supply for these purposes is very elastic will be used in very much greater quantities in proportion to others, so that their marginal productivity will be much reduced, and the gap between their price and the discounted price of their marginal product will be closed mainly by a decrease of that marginal product. For others, of which the quantity used for the production of consumers' goods in the near future cannot be easily increased, the marginal productivity may be decreased only a little, and the gap will be mainly closed by a rise in their price, although this rise

Influence on relative prices of different kinds of Input

will be smaller than that of the final product. And for still others, the quantity of which cannot be increased at all in the short run, the marginal productivity may actually be raised by the increased use of other co-operating factors, and in order to adjust the margin between their price and the increased price of their marginal product their price may have to rise a great deal. Experience shows that this happens during booms with respect to some raw materials, the price of which rises proportionately more than the price of the final product in the production of which they are used.

Generally speaking, we may say that resources of which the greater part has already been used before in what we have called late stages of production will rise the more in price the nearer they are to the final output, and will have to be economised to a correspondingly greater extent. And in so far as such resources can be reproduced, their production will become relatively more or less profitable according as they are nearer to, or further from, final output. Resources which can be directly transferred nearer to the consumption stage will generally be used in a much greater proportion for investments for shorter periods than for investments for longer periods. In the end we shall find that, for nearly all factors, the productivity has been reduced by changing to productive combinations where they bring a smaller marginal product at a nearer date. And, in general, the demand will have increased for those factors which can be made to yield in the nearer future a return not very much smaller than that they yielded before, while the demand will actually have fallen for those which in the near future can bring no return, or only one which is very small compared with that which they can bring in the distant future. And while all these changes have been brought about by the increase in the margin between the price of a given unit of input and the price of a given unit of output (or the rate of profit), in consequence of these adjustments the marginal rate of profit (or the marginal price margins) will have been reduced again so as to correspond to the given rate of interest.

At this stage of the exposition it is scarcely necessary to explain at length why such an increase in the demand for investments for short periods, combined with a decrease in the demand for investments for long periods, will decrease the total *amount* of investment that will be made to provide a given output. But as one is easily misled by considerations which apply only to stationary conditions — where of course the current input that is required to maintain a given output is smaller with a large stock of capital than with a small one — it may be useful briefly to re-state the reasons why, *during the transition* from more to less capitalistic methods of production, the amount of input that will be demanded for investment purposes will fall. That this must be so is easy enough to see in simple cases. If a given amount of machine service, which in the past has been provided by machines lasting ten years, is from a certain date onwards maintained by replacing every machine that wears out by a cheaper one that lasts only five years, this will for a time reduce the amount of input that has to be invested in machines in order to maintain the stream of machine service at an unchanged level. The same applies to every other kind of investment, no matter whether we have to deal with the substitution of less for more durable goods, of less labour-saving machinery for more labour-saving machinery, or of shorter for longer processes of production in the literal sense of the term. In all these cases the amount of investment for short periods that is made more profitable by this transition will for some time be smaller than the amount of investment for long periods that is made less profitable.

We can describe this effect in terms of the investment demand schedule by saying that the curve describing the

Effect on the proportional amount of Investment

demand for real input for investment purposes as a
function of the rate of interest is tilted so that its upper
end is raised and its lower end is lowered. It is difficult to express this exactly, since we are
not dealing with one homogeneous kind
of input and since the relative values of
the different kinds of input will necessarily change in the
course of the process. But in terms of any given system

The "tilting" of the investment demand schedule

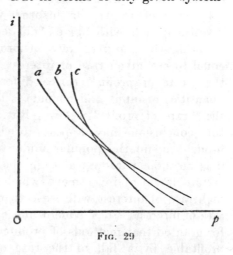

FIG. 29

of prices (or if we
assume that there is
only one homogeneous
kind of input) we can
say that as a conse-
quence of the rise in
price margins (and
therefore of the rate
of profit on the given
volume and method of
production) the curve
describing the amount
of input (measured
along *Op*), which will
be demanded at any
rate of interest (measured along *Oi*), will shift from a position like the one represented by curve *a* in the diagram, to
a position like that represented by curve *b* or *c*. The reason
for this tilting of the curve is that for every quantity of
input that is more intensely demanded at a given rate of
interest, a larger quantity of input will be less intensely
demanded. The change in the relative profitability of the
different kinds of investment will mean that the various
investment opportunities will change their relative position
on the investment demand schedule, and since for every
quantity of input for which the demand increases there
will be a larger quantity for which the demand decreases,
the shape of the whole curve will be altered in the way
indicated in the diagram.

The conclusion which we must draw from these considerations may at first appear somewhat paradoxical. It is that at any given rate of interest (except a very high

The amount of investment per unit of output changes inversely with rate of profit

one) the proportional amount of investment that will be called forth by any given final demand will be smaller with a high " rate of profit " (that is, large price margins or a low value of input in terms of output) and larger with a low rate of profit. Or, in other words, the amount of investment that, with a given final demand, will be required to bring the *marginal* rate of profit down to a figure equal to any given rate of interest, will be smaller when the " rate of profit " (price differences between given quantities of input and output) is high, and larger when the " rate of profit " is low. But, however paradoxical this conclusion may appear to those who have been brought up in the popular under-consumptionist views, it is no more paradoxical than the undeniable fact that certain kinds of investment which were profitable at a high rate of interest will cease to be profitable at a low rate of interest. It is evident and has usually been taken for granted that methods of production which were made profitable by a fall of the rate of interest from 7 to 5 per cent may be made unprofitable by a further fall from 5 per cent to 3 per cent, because the former method will no longer be able to compete with what has now become the cheaper method. It is true, however, that it is scarcely possible adequately to explain this, if one thinks only of the direct effect of a change in the money rate of interest on cost of production, and does not proceed to consider the changes in relative prices which ultimately govern the profitability of the various methods of production. It is only via these price changes that we can explain why a method of production which was profitable when the rate of int rest was 5 per cent should become unprofitable when it falls to 3 per cent. Similarly, it is only in terms of price changes that we can adequately explain why a change in the rate of interest will make methods of production profitable which were previously unprofitable.

The most important conclusion, then, which emerges from this discussion is that the method of production that will be adopted, or the proportional amount of capital that it will be profitable to use, will depend not on the rate of interest at which money can be borrowed but on the relations between different prices and the shape of the profit schedule (or investment demand schedule) as determined by these price differences. And these relative prices will in turn depend on the relative scarcity of the various kinds of resources compared with the direction of demand. The rate of interest will, in the main, determine only to what point on the schedule investment will be carried, that is, it will determine only the marginal rate of profit, and, through the latter, it will exercise a minor influence on the volume of *output* that it is profitable to produce with a given demand. The volume of investment, however, will depend as much if not more on how much investment it will be profitable to undertake in order to obtain a certain output. And with a high " rate of profit " any given marginal rate of profit will be reached with relatively little investment per unit of output, because with a high rate of profit the investmend demand schedule will be steep, while with a low " rate of profit " the same marginal rate of profit will only be reached with much more investment per unit of output, because the investment demand schedule will be flat.[1]

[1] For a discussion of the significance of these effects for the explanation of industrial fluctuations and particularly their relation to the so-called " acceleration principle of derived demand ", see Hayek, **1939**. In particular it is shown there that the " rate of profit " determines the " multiplier " with which the " acceleration principle " operates (or Mr. Harrod's " Relation "), and that changes in this multiplier are likely to have a greater effect on the volume of investment than the second of the two factors which determine the acceleration effect (the " multiplicand "), namely final demand.

We must now return to the problem of the effect of
all these changes on the money rate of interest (and the
marginal rate of profit) which, in the discussion of these
The determination of changes, we have so far treated as given.
the money rate of The effect will clearly depend on what
interest and the mar-
ginal rate of profit happens (a) to the shape of the investment
demand schedule in monetary terms, and (b) to the supply
of money. So far as the latter is concerned, we shall here
continue to assume that the supply of basic money is
fixed, so that all we need to concern ourselves with is the
increase in the supply of investible funds at increasing
rates of interest due to the release of money from idle
balances. (This can, of course, be interpreted to include
any increase in the credit superstructure erected on the
given cash basis.) The supply side may therefore be
represented by a curve like the one used before in Fig. 27
(Chapter XXVI, p. 363 above), and our main problem
will be what will happen to the monetary investment
demand schedule. This we can deduce from what happens
to this demand schedule described in real terms. All we
need to do is to show the effect of the price changes we
have already discussed on the demand for investible
funds, or to redraw this demand schedule, in terms of the
new prices, instead of using the pre-existing price (which
is what expressing it in " real terms " essentially means
in this connection).

We have seen that, when expressed in real terms, the
demand schedule will be tilted by a rise in the price of
the final product, that is, that it will be raised on the
Changes in the mone- left and lowered on the right. But as the
tary investment de- various kinds of input that will now be in
mand schedule
greater demand will also rise in price in
different degrees, less real investment will be associated
with the investment of any given amount of money, *i.e.*
the monetary investment demand curve, besides being
tilted, will also be shifted to the right. Any given amount
of real investment, *i.e.* any amount of investment corre-

sponding to a given marginal rate of profit and leading
to a given amount of product, will require more money
and will therefore cause the rate of interest to rise to an
extent which will depend on the shape of our liquidity
preference schedule. If the supply of investible funds
were completely inelastic, and the amount invested could
not be increased at all, this would clearly mean a considerable rise in the rate of interest and a decrease in the
amount of real investment. The tilting of the demand
schedule would in this case have the effect of making it
profitable to employ less input of the kind which rises in
price and more input of the kind which falls in price.
(This, incidentally, also illustrates how misleading it is to
concentrate on the existence of unemployed resources or
" full employment " as the case may be, and to argue in
terms of changes in the general price level, the movements
of which are supposed to depend on whether full employment exists or not. What is relevant is not whether full
employment exists, but whether the particular kinds of
resources needed exist in the proportions corresponding
to the state of demand.)

If, however, the supply of investible funds is not
altogether inelastic, and the increase of demand for investible funds brings forth an increased supply, the rate of
interest will not rise to the full extent of the
rise in the demand curve, and real invest- *Effect on interest rates when supply of money is elastic*
ment will not be curtailed so much or may
not be curtailed at all, and may even rise further. But as
this means a further increase in money incomes, it will
lead to a new increase in the monetary demand for consumers' goods, a further rise in their prices, and consequently a further tilting of the real investment demand
schedule and a tilting and shifting of the monetary investment demand schedule. The elasticity of the supply of
money, which in the short run tends to keep the rate of
interest low, has thus the effect — at least for some time —
of simultaneously raising the rate of return on the invest-

ment of any given amount of money and lowering the amount of real investment that will correspond to it. And since every further increase in money incomes will strengthen this tendency, this process must go on till the combined effect of the tilting of the investment demand curve and of the rise in the rate of interest finally outbalances the effect of the further rise in demand, and thus prevents a further increase in the amount of money invested. Either of these two factors alone may bring about this effect. Elsewhere [1] we have tried to show that, even if the supply of money were perfectly elastic and the rate of interest therefore kept constant, the " tilting " effect by itself would in the end bring further expansion to a stop. And we have seen before that, if the supply of money were perfectly inelastic, the rise in the rate of interest would prevent the expansion before the tilting effect could occur. In real life, however, the two factors, the tilting of the investment demand curve and the rise in the rate of interest, will as a rule work conjointly. In such circumstances the process of expansion will come to an end only when the rate of interest and the marginal rate of profit have been kept low by monetary expansion for a long enough time to allow the repercussions, through changes in relative prices and price margins, to have so changed the slope of the investment demand curve as both greatly to reduce the amount of real investment which is profitable at a given rate of interest, and greatly to increase the amount of money which is required for that amount of investment, thus raising the rate of interest corresponding to any given supply of money.

We cannot at this stage attempt any more exhaustive treatment of this complex mechanism. For it would comprise a discussion of the whole subject of industrial fluctuations and we should require a separate book to deal with it adequately. Some further considerations which are

[1] See Hayek, **1939,** pp. 24 *et seq.*

relevant in this connection will be added in the final chapter of this book. We will conclude the present treatment by once more stressing the fact that, though in the short run monetary influences may delay The basic importance the tendencies inherent in the real factors of the real factors from working themselves out, and temporarily may even reverse these tendencies, it will in the end be the scarcity of real resources relative to demand which will decide what kind of investment, and how much, is profitable. The fundamental fact which guides production, and in which the scarcity of capital expresses itself, is the price of input in terms of output, and this in turn depends on the proportion of income spent on consumers' goods compared with the proportion of income earned from the current production of consumers' goods. These proportions cannot be altered at will by adjustments in the money stream, since they depend on the one hand on the real quantities of the various types of goods in existence, and on the other hand on the way in which people will distribute their income between expenditure on consumers' goods and saving. Neither of these factors can be deliberately altered by monetary policy. As we have seen, any delay by monetary means of the adjustments made necessary by real changes can only have the effect of further accentuating these real changes, and any purely monetary change which in the first instance deflects interest rates in one direction is bound to set up forces which will ultimately change them in the opposite direction.

Ultimately, therefore, it is the rate of saving which sets the limits to the amount of investment that can be successfully carried through. But the effects of the rate of saving do not operate directly on the The significance of the rate of interest or on the supply of in- rate of saving vestible funds, which will always be influenced largely by monetary factors. Its main influence is on the *demand* for investible funds, and here it operates in a direction opposite to that which is assumed by all the under-consumptionist theories. It will be via investment demand that a change in the rate of saving will affect the volume of investment. Similarly, it will be via investment demand that, if monetary influences should have caused investment to get out of step with saving, the balance will be restored. If throughout this discussion we have had little occasion to make explicit mention of the rate of saving, this is due to the fact that the effects considered will take place whatever the rate of saving, so long as this is a given magnitude and does not spontaneously change so as to restore the disrupted equilibrium. All that is required to make our analysis applicable is that, when incomes are increased by investment, the share of the additional income spent on consumers' goods during any period of time should be larger than the proportion by which the new investment adds to the output of consumers' goods during the same period of time. And there is of course no reason to expect that more than a fraction of the new income, and certainly not as much as has been newly invested, will be saved, because this would mean that practically all the income earned from the new investment would have to be saved.[1]

[1] The rate at which a given amount of new investment will contribute during any given interval of time to the output of consumers'-goods stands of course in a very simple relation to the proportion between any new demand and the amount of investment to which it gives rise : the latter is simply the reciprocal value of the former. For a fuller discussion of this relationship between this " quotient " and the " multiplier " with which the " acceleration principle of derived demand " operates I must again refer to Hayek, 1939, pp. 48-52.

It cannot be objected to this argument that, since investment automatically creates an identical amount of saving, the situation contemplated here cannot arise. The irrelevant tautology, that *during any interval of time* the amount of income which has not been received from the sale of consumers' goods, and which therefore has been saved (namely, by those who spent that income), must have been spent on something other than consumers' goods (and therefore *ex definitione* must have been invested), is of little significance for this or for any other economic problem. What is relevant here is not the relation between one classification of money expenditure and another, but the

The relative prices of the various types of goods and services, and therefore the rate of profit to be earned in their production, will always be determined by the impact of the monetary demand for the various kinds of goods and the supplies of these goods. And unless we study the factors limiting the supplies of these various types of goods, and particularly if we assume, as Mr. Keynes does, that they are all freely reproducible in practically unlimited quantities

The supply of capital and the rate of profit and interest in disequilibrium

relation of two streams of money expenditure to the streams of goods which they meet. We are interested in the amount of investment because it determines in what proportions (in terms of their relative costs) different kinds of goods will come into existence. And we are interested to know how these proportions between quantities of different kinds of goods are related to the proportions in which money expenditure will be distributed between the two kinds of goods, because it depends on the relation between these two proportions whether the production of either kind of good will become more or less profitable. It does not matter whether we put this question in the form of asking whether the distribution of income between expenditure on consumers' goods and saving corresponds to the proportion between the relative (replacement) *costs* of the total supply of consumers' goods and new investment goods, or whether the available resources are now distributed in the same proportion between the production of consumers' goods and the production of investment goods as those in which income earned from this production *will* be distributed between the two kinds of goods. Whichever of the two aspects of the question we prefer to stress, the essential thing, if we want to ask a meaningful question, is that we must always compare the result of investment embodied in concrete goods with the money expenditure on these goods. It is never the investment which is going on at the same time as the saving, but the result of *past* investment, that determines the supply of capital goods to which the monetary demand may or may not correspond. Playing about with the relationships between various classifications of total money expenditure during any given period will lead only to meaningless questions, and never to any result of the slightest relevance to any real problem.

I do not wish to suggest that the recent discussions of the various meanings of these concepts have been useless. They have helped us to make clear the conditions under which it is meaningful to talk about relations between saving and investment. But now that the obscurities and confusions connected with these concepts have been cleared up, the meaningless tautological use of these concepts ought clearly to disappear from scientific discussion. On the whole question, and the recent discussions about it, compare now the excellent exposition in the new chapter eight of the second edition of Professor Haberler's *Prosperity and Depression* (Geneva, 1939).

and without any appreciable lapse of time, we must remain in complete ignorance of the factors guiding production. In long-run equilibrium, the rate of profit and interest will depend on how much of their resources people want to use to satisfy their current needs, and how much they are willing to save and invest. But in the comparatively short run the quantities and kinds of consumers' goods and capital goods in existence must be regarded as fixed, and the rate of profit will depend not so much on the absolute quantity of real capital (however measured) in existence, or on the absolute height of the rate of saving, as on the relation between the proportion of the incomes spent on consumers' goods and the proportion of the resources available in the form of consumers' goods. For this reason it is quite possible that, after a period of great accumulation of capital and a high rate of saving, the rate of profit and the rate of interest may be higher than they were before — if the rate of saving is insufficient compared with the amount of capital which entrepreneurs have attempted to form, or if the demand for consumers' goods is too high compared with the supply. And for the same reason the rate of interest and profit may be higher in a rich community with much capital and a high rate of saving than in an otherwise similar community with little capital and a low rate of saving.[1]

[1] For some further discussion of this point see Hayek, **1937**.

CHAPTER XXVIII

DIFFERENCES BETWEEN INTEREST RATES :
CONCLUSIONS AND OUTLOOK

THERE is one more complex of problems which, in a work so largely concerned with the question of the rate of interest, must be briefly considered, although its systematic study falls outside the scope of this book. I refer to the problem of the relationship between the various rates of interest and profit, and the causes of the differences in their height. We have of course already seen that in so far as rates of interest earned over periods of different lengths are concerned, there is, even apart from monetary influences, no reason why they should be the same in a non-stationary economic system. But we have so far had little to say about the way in which we should expect these various rates to differ. The main reason for this is that this problem, unlike that of the existence, and the long-run movements of the rate of profit, is very definitely a problem which belongs more to the field of monetary theory or economic dynamics generally than to the field of general equilibrium analysis to which this book has been mainly confined. We can here do little to contribute to its solution, and what attention we can give to it in this final chapter will be concerned mainly with showing what is the proper field of application of that " liquidity preference analysis " which we could not place among the primary factors that determine the height or the movement of the rate of profit or (except in the very short run) the rate of interest.

Differences between Interest rates (and rates of profit) a monetary problem —

Even in the last two chapters, when we were already considering the significance of monetary influences, we disregarded the possibility that there might be a difference between the various interest rates or between the rates of interest and the marginal rates of profit on various types of investment. This procedure was justified, because we had in effect assumed that there were only two sharply divided types of assets, money on the one hand and real capital goods on the other.

—connected with differences of liquidity attaching to various income-bearing assets which were so far disregarded

Money was implicitly assumed to be one homogeneous group of assets which possessed the attribute of liquidity to so much greater an extent than anything else that the holding of money could be regarded as practically the sole means of satisfying the desire for liquidity or for providing against uncertainty. All investments proper, on the other hand, whether they took the form of the lending of money or of the purchase of commodities or services to be employed for gain, were regarded as equally illiquid and risky, so that the returns expected from those various investments would tend towards equality (subject to the qualifications necessary if this statement is to apply to a non-stationary equilibrium : see p. 167 above). Although the return on the use of any particular kind of resource in terms of itself might be different for different kinds of resources, the returns on the investment of different resources over any given period would have to be the same if all were measured in terms of any one given unit.

We have found that, under these circumstances, liquidity preference possessed little significance beyond providing an explanation as to why some assets would earn no interest (or perhaps a lower rate of interest than others), but that it certainly did not explain either the level of the rates of interest (except under most unlikely conditions) or the direction in which they would move. It appeared at most to describe one of the cost factors (*i.e.* of the " alternative uses " of funds) which had to be taken into account in determining the rate of return on investment. In other words, it provided an explanation of why people withheld some funds that might be invested (or invested at a higher rate of return). But it clearly did not explain even the size of the total *supply* of funds which at any moment would be available for investment (which depends also on the rate of saving), and it had therefore to be regarded as altogether insufficient to explain why there was a positive return on investment at all, or what its actual height would be.

We have also found that even in the short run during which liquidity preference, and changes in liquidity preference, may have a predominant influence in determining the rate of interest (and the marginal rate of profit), the latter will be related only in an indirect manner to those price differences (the " rate of profit ") which express the true scarcity of capital and regulate the proportional amount of capital that will be used in production. And the indirect influence which the monetary forces, acting on the rate of interest, will have in that way will be directly opposite to that commonly supposed. A reduction of the rate of interest in consequence of changes in liquidity preference will tend to bring about an increase in price differences and the rate of profit (not the marginal rate of profit), and will thus lead to a reduction in the proportional amount of investment, and *vice versa*.

We shall now see that if we consider the effects of changes in liquidity preference further, and if we take account of the fact that, because of differences in the liquidity of different types of assets, the marginal rate of profit and the rate of interest not only need not be identical but may actually move in opposite directions, the connection between the money rate of interest and the profitability of investment becomes even looser than we have so far assumed. It is clear that in real life there is no such sharp division between one single kind of money on the one hand, and a mass of income-bearing assets, all equally illiquid, on the other. In the first place

Changes in liquidity preference may cause divergent movements of rate of interest and marginal rate of profit there are of course further alternatives to investment in real assets which we have not yet considered, in the shape of all the various " securities " (claims to money), some at least of which must be regarded as so highly liquid as to form very close substitutes for money, while others will be more nearly akin to the less liquid types of real assets. And the real assets will also differ greatly with respect to the possibility of disposing of them rapidly and without great loss, if this should become unexpectedly necessary. There is in fact a long and practically continuous range over which the various types of assets can be grouped according to the degrees of liquidity which they possess and the risk attaching to them.

It is not possible here to enter into any more detailed analysis of the meaning of liquidity and the problem of the relation of this concept to that of risk. This is most definitely a subject belonging to economic dynamics, and little could be gained by scratching on the surface of this problem when no really systematic inquiry can be undertaken. Much work on these problems has been done in recent years and a great deal more remains to be done for the theory of the subject to be deemed satisfactory.[1] All that we shall mention here is that neither risk nor liquidity can be adequately expressed as simple, one-dimensional magnitudes, since they are both of the nature of probabilities which can be sufficiently described only in terms of the properties of a frequency distribution. This means that, strictly speaking, it is not possible to arrange the various assets in a simple linear order according to the liquidity or the risk attaching to them, and that some multi-dimensional arrangement would have to be used instead.

For our purposes, however, we must be satisfied with

The meaning of liquidity and its relation to risk

---

[1] In addition to the work of Mr. Keynes, various articles by Professor Hicks and Dr. Hawtrey, and, at an earlier date, F. Lavington, are of special importance in this connection.

some more rough and common-sense concept of liquidity, without making an attempt at exact classification. If in this rough sense we classify the various assets according to their liquidity, we shall have, at one end of the scale, investments which promise a very high rate of return, but which require that funds be irrevocably committed to a particular use for a long time, so that in the meantime there will be no possibility of diverting them to other purposes which in consequence of a change in conditions may then appear more attractive. At the other end of the scale we shall have pure money, which, while yielding no direct return, because of its universal acceptability puts the holder in the position of being immediately able to take advantage of any newly appearing opportunities for investment. And between these two extremes we shall have to range the great majority of assets, capital goods and securities, so that the decreasing magnitude of the return will be balanced in each case by a correspondingly greater capacity of the assets for being " liquidated " at short notice, *i.e.* a greater or smaller chance that, in case of an unforeseen change, it will be possible to preserve at least a high proportion of their present value by turning these assets to other uses.[1]

For our purposes all this means that, for assets possessing different degrees of liquidity, we shall at any moment have not one uniform rate of return but a long series of different rates of return, ranging Effects of changes in from some positive figure down to zero relative liquidity of and perhaps even negative figures (in cases different types of assets — where a payment is made for the safe-keeping of money,

---

[1] The difference between the risk attaching to holding a particular asset and its liquidity is mainly that risk may refer merely to a loss that may be incurred although the date when the asset in question will have to be sold (or otherwise used) is definitely known beforehand, while liquidity stresses the extra loss (or rather absence of danger of this particular kind of loss) which may be incurred because the asset may have to be disposed of at a date which cannot be foreseen, and at very short notice.

etc.). This would not make very much difference to our whole argument up to this point, if we could assume that the grouping of various types of assets according to their liquidity, and therefore the relations between the rates of return from the different types of assets, were constant. But this is of course very far from being so. In changing conditions the views people will hold about the relative liquidity of different types of assets will also change ; and this will cause modifications in the working of the prices mechanism very similar to those which we have seen will occur in consequence of changes in the rate of money expenditure. In fact we shall see that the effects of changes in liquidity preference in the narrower sense in which we have so far used the term, that is, as referring solely to changes in the preference for holding money on the one hand and any other kinds of asset on the other, is only one special case of a much wider category ; and that where there is no sharp separation between one perfectly liquid asset, money, and the mass of all the other equally illiquid assets, it becomes impossible either to draw any sharp distinction between monetary changes (changes in the quantity of money or its " velocity of circulation ") and changes in the relative liquidity attached to any group of assets, or to make a clear distinction between changes in the quantity of money and changes in its velocity of circulation.

If assets which are expected to bring a lower return are held, because of their greater liquidity, in preference to others which promise a higher rate of return, a reduction in this liquidity preference will have effects very similar to a rise in the investment demand schedule. This is so for several reasons. Firstly, because the amounts that will be invested at any given rate of interest will increase. Secondly, since, in general, investments for longer periods are likely to be less liquid than investments for shorter periods, the former will be increased relatively more than

— similar to effects of changes in quantity of money

the latter. Thirdly, because any increase in the liquidity of a particular asset will make it capable of acting to some extent as a substitute for money or at least for some other more liquid asset. Thus it will decrease the demand for these more liquid assets, and this effect, via the fall in the price of, or the rise in the rate of return on, these more liquid assets, will gradually work upwards in the scale of liquidity till it reaches the most perfectly liquid kind of asset, money. In this way, every increase in the liquidity attached to any sort of asset will tend to bring about an increase in the supply of investible money funds ; and similarly any decrease in the liquidity attached to any particular type of asset is likely to increase the demand for money and to decrease the supply of investible money funds.

How this operates can be aptly illustrated if we consider a more particular case. Incidentally, this case will also show how, under conditions where we have to deal with an almost continuous range of assets which possess various degrees of liquidity almost imperceptibly shading into each other, it becomes impossible to draw any sharp distinction between the effects of changes in the quantity of money and changes in its velocity of circulation, or, what is the same thing, in the proportional size of the liquidity reserve people will want to hold compared to their transactions. The case we shall consider is that of some form of readily transferable short-term debt, *e.g.* treasury bills, which we suppose suddenly to acquire the reputation of being more liquid than it was previously. It is irrelevant for our purpose what the particular circumstances are, whether an increase in the credit of the debtor, the issue of a new particularly convenient type of security, increased confidence in the stability of interest rates, or any other factor which makes a security more widely acceptable, and thus provides an income-yielding asset which is confidently expected to be readily convertible into money at any time and at a practically unchanged price. It is clear that the availability of this new alternative for holding reserves in a highly liquid form will lead to the substitution of some of the assets concerned for other more liquid assets, and particularly for money. This means that some of the money which before was held as a liquidity reserve will now be invested and that, with the increase in the supply of, and the fall in the return on, the more liquid types of assets, there will be a general shift of investments in the direction of less liquid assets.

If we assume this kind of change to occur, not with respect to some security but (in a country where the use of cheques is still somewhat limited) with respect to bank deposits, it is at once evident that it would be equally legitimate to describe what happens either as an increase in the quantity of money or as an increase in the velocity of circulation of the unchanged quantity of money. We can either say that bank deposits have now become money (or at least money substitutes having in all respects the same significance as money), or we can say that the availability of close substitutes for money makes it possible to economise money and to hold less real money in proportion to any given volume of transactions, that is, to increase the velocity of circulation of money. Indeed, K. Wicksell, as is well known, preferred to treat increases in bank credit, not as increases of the quantity of money but as increases of what he called the " virtual velocity of circulation " of the basic money.[1]

The same reasons which make it impossible in this particular case to distinguish clearly between what are changes in the quantity of money and changes in its velocity of circulation apply, however, equally well to all other cases where the relative liquidity of various types of assets is changed ; and they make it exceedingly difficult, if not impossible, to distinguish between the

It is often difficult to decide whether a particular change is better treated as a change in the liquidity of an asset or as a change in the quantity of money

---

[1] *Lectures on Political Economy*, vol. ii, pp. 67 *et seq.*

effects of what may properly be regarded as monetary changes in the narrower sense of the term, and the exactly similar effects of changes in the relative liquidity of various real assets which have nothing to do with any change in anything which can properly be called money. Resources may be withdrawn from investment, or from more profitable investments, not because people desire to use them in the current production of consumers' goods, but because they want to hold assets of a more liquid character, which need not be money or securities, but may, according to the circumstances, be anything from raw materials or certain storable foodstuffs to postage stamps or jewellery or works of art. And, similarly, fewer consumers' goods may be produced, not because people want to make definite provision for an increased output of consumers' goods in the more distant future, but because they desire for the time being to convert part of their resources into what they regard as the safest and most adaptable forms.[1]

Any such change in the relative preferences for assets possessing different degrees of liquidity will involve a change in the rate of return earned on these types of assets. We must therefore recognise that the various rates of interest and profit, which we find in a developed capital market, will be subject to all sorts of autonomous changes which will have no connection with changes in the profitability of investment or changes in the rate of saving. In consequence, the movement of interest rates in the narrower sense may sometimes take a direction opposite to that of the marginal rates of profit on real investment, and thus a given change in interest rates may be accompanied by a change in real investment which is the reverse of what we usually associate with a

---

[1] The reason why the effect of such a change is similar to that of monetary changes proper is, of course, that in these cases too we have to deal with a sort of indirect exchange, only the medium which is kept as a store of value is not money but may be anything which in the circumstances seems to be specially suitable for the purpose.

rise or fall of interest rates. If, for instance, a spontaneous change in liquidity preference leads to a shifting of funds from real investment to the holding of gilt-edged securities, the fall in interest rates proper will be accompanied by a rise in marginal rates of profit and will indicate that real investment is being curtailed. Similarly, a rise in money rates of interest may be accompanied by a fall in marginal rates of profit and may be merely a symptom of the fact that real investment is now regarded as relatively more attractive, with the result not only that no real investment which was formerly profitable will become unprofitable on account of the rise in the rate of interest, but that some new real investments will now be undertaken which were not undertaken at the lower rate of interest.

We cannot here further follow up the causes which make the connection between the money rate of interest and the factors which directly govern the profitability of investment even more loose and distant than we have already seen to be the case under the more favourable assumptions of the last chapter. We must be satisfied with having shown not only that the movement of money rates will be determined to a large extent by factors other than those which determine the profitability of investment, but also that the influences which changes in the money rates of interest do exert on the profitability of investment will often be the opposite from what we are led to expect if we identify these money rates with the "rate of interest" of pure theory. To give a brief summary of the main results, we may say that changes in money rates will have the effects commonly assumed only if and in so far as they correspond to real changes and serve merely to bring about changes made necessary by the real situation. If, however, interest rates are affected either by spontaneous monetary changes (changes in liquidity preference or changes in the supply of resources of different degrees of liquidity) or induced monetary changes (changes in the relative demand for assets of various liquidities due to changes in their returns, the liquidity preferences for, as well as the supplies of, these assets being given), these monetary influences on the rates of interest will set up forces which will work in a direction opposite to their immediate effect through interest rates. Thus in the short run money may prevent real changes from showing their effect, and may even cause real changes for which there is no justification in the underlying real position. In the long run, however, it will always merely accentuate the change it has at first prevented, or will bring about changes which are the opposite of the impact effects. We have already referred before to this self-reversing character of monetary changes. In the real world, of course, all changes must work through this monetary mechanism, which frequently delays adaptation and will often be the source of spontaneous disturbances. Money is of course never " neutral " in the sense of being merely an instrument or servant : it always exercises some positive influence on the course of events. It would not be difficult to show how this rôle of money is bound to lead to constant fluctuations of economic activity, even if we had never heard of the existence of such fluctuations. And the theory of fluctuations largely consists, of course, of a study of the interaction between the monetary and the real factors.

This, however, is outside our present task. That task has been to bring out the importance of the real factors, which in contemporary discussion are increasingly disregarded. But even without further continuing the discussion of the rôle money plays in this connection, we are certainly entitled to conclude from what we have already shown that the extent to which we can hope to shape events at will by controlling money are much more limited, that the scope of monetary policy is much more restricted, than is to-day widely believed. We cannot, as some writers seem to think, do more or less what we please with the economic system by playing on the monetary instrument. In every situation there will in fact always be only one monetary policy which will not have a disequilibrating effect and therefore eventually reverse its short-term influence. That it will always be exceedingly difficult, if not impossible, to know exactly what this policy is does not alter the fact that we cannot hope even to approach this ideal policy unless we understand not only the monetary but also, what are even more important, the real factors that are at work. There is little ground for believing that a system with the modern complex credit structure will ever work smoothly without some deliberate control of the monetary mechanism, since money by its very nature constitutes a kind of loose joint in the self-equilibrating apparatus of the price mechanism which is bound to impede its working — the more so the greater is the play in the loose joint. But the existence of such a loose joint is no justification for concentrating attention on that loose joint and disregarding the rest of the mechanism, and still less for making the greatest possible use of the short-lived freedom from economic necessity which the existence of this loose joint permits. On the contrary, the aim of any successful monetary policy must be to reduce as far as possible this slack in the self-correcting forces of the price mechanism, and to make adaptation more prompt so as to reduce the necessity for a later, more violent, reaction. For this, however, an understanding of the underlying real forces is even more important than an understanding of the monetary surface, just because this surface does not merely hide but often also disrupts the underlying mechanism in the most unexpected fashion. All this is not to deny that in the very short run the scope of monetary policy is very wide indeed. But the problem is not so much what we *can* do, but what we *ought* to do in the short run, and on this point a most harmful doctrine has gained ground in the last few years which can only be explained by a complete neglect — or complete lack

of understanding — of the real forces at work. A policy
has been advocated which at any moment aims at the
maximum short-run effect of monetary policy, completely disregarding the fact that what is best in the
short run may be extremely detrimental in the long run,
because the indirect and slower effects of the short-run
policy of the present shape the conditions, and limit the
freedom, of the short-run policy of to-morrow and the
day after.

I cannot help regarding the increasing concentration
on short-run effects — which in this context amounts to
the same thing as a concentration on purely monetary
factors — not only as a serious and dangerous intellectual
error, but as a betrayal of the main duty of the economist
and a grave menace to our civilisation. To the understanding of the forces which determine the day-to-day
changes of business, the economist has probably little to
contribute that the man of affairs does not know better.
It used, however, to be regarded as the duty and the
privilege of the economist to study and to stress the long
effects which are apt to be hidden to the untrained eye,
and to leave the concern about the more immediate effects
to the practical man, who in any event would see only the
latter and nothing else. The aim and effect of two
hundred years of continuous development of economic
thought have essentially been to lead us away from, and
" behind ", the more superficial monetary mechanism and
to bring out the real forces which guide long-run development. I do not wish to deny that the preoccupation
with the " real " as distinguished from the monetary
aspects of the problems may sometimes have gone too
far. But this can be no excuse for the present tendencies
which have already gone far towards taking us back to
the pre-scientific stage of economics, when the whole
working of the price mechanism was not yet understood,
and only the problems of the impact of a varying money
stream on a supply of goods and services with given prices

aroused interest. It is not surprising that Mr. Keynes finds his views anticipated by the mercantilist writers and gifted amateurs : concern with the surface phenomena has always marked the first stage of the scientific approach to our subject. But it is alarming to see that after we have once gone through the process of developing a systematic account of those forces which in the long run determine prices and production, we are now called upon to scrap it, in order to replace it by the short-sighted philosophy of the business man raised to the dignity of a science. Are we not even told that, " since in the long run we are all dead ", policy should be guided entirely by short-run considerations ? I fear that these believers in the principle of *après nous le déluge* may get what they have bargained for sooner than they wish.

APPENDICES

APPENDIX I

TIME PREFERENCE AND PRODUCTIVITY

THE treatment in Chapters XVII and XVIII of the rôle of psychic elements in the determination of the rate of interest differs from the classical discussion of the same questions as we find it in the writings of Böhm-Bawerk and his School in three main points. *Firstly*, it stresses from the outset that there is not one single significant rate of " time preference " (at least for any given person), but that this rate of time preference itself varies with the changes in the relative size of the present and future income for which provision is made. If the concept of the single rate of time preference is to have any meaning, it must therefore be confined to that rate which would prevail if provision for incomes of equal magnitude were made for present and future. *Secondly*, time preference involves no " perspective under-valuation ", no " psychic discount " of the " true " future value, but is simply a description of the relative values that will be attached to present and future commodities under different conditions. And, *thirdly*, time preference is a subordinate factor compared with the productivity of investment in determining the rate of interest, since it operates only by way of determining the rate of saving and the rate of capital accumulation, and hence the productivity of investment. In the short run, it merely adapts itself to the given marginal productivity of investment.

On the first point there is now fairly general agreement among economists, and at any rate nothing has been said here which is not already contained in the most modern exposition of the views of the Time Preference School, Professor Irving Fisher's *Theory of Interest*. On the second point also the difference between the preceding exposition and that given in the work just mentioned is probably but largely verbal. Since, however, the terms employed by Professor Irving Fisher, particularly the term "impatience", still carry with them some of the flavour of the earlier less defensible views, it

413

is perhaps necessary to supplement what has already been said by a more explicit refutation of the confusions contained in the earlier theories. On the third point, finally, the views expressed definitely diverge from those still commonly (though not universally) held, and although all that is really essential is already contained in Chapters XVII and XVIII, a few further remarks on the general nature of the problem involved may not be out of place. The two sections which follow will accordingly be devoted to a more explicit discussion of the views defended here on the two latter points in comparison with other widely held views on these problems.

(1) The way in which Böhm-Bawerk formulated the problem of interest has gained considerable support. Particularly in the form in which Professor Schumpeter [1] has quite consistently developed the Böhm-Bawerkian approach, it has led to the assertion that the existence of interest is incompatible with stationary conditions, a view which is now widely held. The whole approach, therefore, needs more explicit examination than was possible to give in Chapters XVII and XVIII. We shall try to demonstrate here that in the form in which Böhm-Bawerk put the central question it is meaningless and is merely one of those pseudo-problems which arose out of the idea of utility as an absolute magnitude.

The starting point of the Böhm-Bawerkian analysis was the question why people did not avail themselves of the opportunity of increasing by investment the product obtainable from given resources to such a point that the utility of the future product would fall to a level corresponding to that of the alternative current product which might have been obtained from the same resources. This is what one would expect from the general rule that all resources will be distributed among their different uses in such a way that the marginal utility of a product of a unit of resources will be everywhere the same, and hence also equal to the (derived) marginal utility of the factors used. If one started from the idea that, unless tastes change, the marginal utility in an absolute sense of equal quantities of commodities should be the same at different dates, the only possible explanation why people did not in fact act in accordance with this rule seemed

---

[1] In particular his *Theory of Economic Development*, chap. i.

to be that they did not attach this true utility to future products but attached a lower valuation to them which decreased in proportion with their time-distance from consumption. This would mean that people would stop investing for the future before the true future utility of the (greater) future product had fallen to the level of that of the (smaller) alternative present product. This would account for the existence of the "gap" between the utility of the factors and the utility of the product, which, according to Böhm-Bawerk, is the true source of interest.

If, however, one denied, along with Professor Schumpeter, the existence of any such psychical discount, the same assumptions would necessarily lead to the conclusion that saving must continue so long as additional investments brought a greater produce than could be obtained from the use of the same resources for the current satisfaction of wants and that, in consequence, a stationary state could be reached only after interest had disappeared. At any one moment, it is true, the amount which it would be advantageous to invest would be limited by the fact that the marginal utility of given additions to the output at any future moment would fall, and that, in consequence, even if the future product obtainable from further doses of investment was greater in quantity than the alternative present output, it might have a smaller utility than the latter. But this would only limit the rate of saving, it would not alter the fact that some saving would continue so long as the physical return from any factor could be increased by investing it for a longer period. Only the complete exhaustion of all opportunities for increasing output from any factor in this way could put a stop to further saving. And since a stationary state implies the absence of new saving, such a state could exist only if the productivity of capital, and therefore interest, had disappeared.

It will be seen that this proposition is nothing more than the logical outcome of the assumptions originally made by Böhm-Bawerk, provided the initial assumption about the identical shape of the utility curves at successive moments is not subsequently modified by the introduction of psychical discount.

This argument, as has already been pointed out, depends for its validity entirely on the older, absolute, concept of utility. It is therefore necessary to state more explicitly the difference between this older view and the modern view, and to indicate the special relevance of this difference to intertemporal comparisons.

With the utility of a commodity conceived as an absolute magnitude, it was natural to define constant tastes as implying that at all successive moments the marginal utility of equal quantities of a commodity available at successive dates must be the same. It makes little difference for our purpose whether this assumption is stated in the simpler and even more objectionable form $u_x = f(x)$, implying that the marginal utility of x depends on the quantity available of that commodity only, or whether it is stated in the slightly more meaningful form $u_x = f(x, y, z, \ldots)$, implying that the marginal utility of x depends on the quantities of all the commodities available. Whichever of these alternatives we adopt, the essential point remains the same. In either case it is assumed that the marginal utility of any commodity at a particular moment depends only on the quantities of commodities available at *that* moment, that it is independent of the quantities provided for other moments, and that this statement about the absolute utilities at different moments allows us to make deductions about the relative utility of quantities available at different moments. It does not matter whether the assumption made is that the supply of all other commodities is constant, or whether this is treated as being irrelevant. The result is in either case that the utility of different quantities is regarded as adequately represented by independent utility curves which, if tastes are assumed to be constant, must be of identical shape.[1]

It is no longer questionable that absolute utility functions have a definite meaning only in so far as they can be translated into a statement as to what quantities of the commodities in question will have the same utility under the given conditions, or be perfect substitutes for each other. The utility curve for any commodity would thus express the decreasing quantity of some other commodity (the total supply

---

[1] In an attempt which I made a number of years ago to clear some of the difficulties connected with this approach, I myself used this approach without being aware of the illegitimate assumptions which it involves. (Cf. Hayek, **1927**, pp. 517-532, especially p. 523.)

of which was assumed to be constant) which under otherwise
unchanged conditions would just be equal to the utility of
successive marginal additions to the supply of the first commodity. The meaning of the assumption that the two utility
curves for the same commodity at two different moments will
be identical, is slightly more complicated. It can, however,
also be expressed in the form of a statement about the relative
quantities of the commodities available at the two moments
which will give the same utility. As a little reflection shows,
this assumption must mean that if the total quantities of the
commodity available at each of the two dates are the same,
equal quantities will have the same value, and that if the total
quantities available at the two moments are different. a small
addition to the smaller total will be as useful as a larger addition
to the larger total.

This, however, would be merely a statement about the
attitude of the person concerned at the earlier of the two
dates in question. since it is only at this date that he could
actually choose between two such quantities. It would not
state whether his attitude was the same at the two dates
or different. In order to be able to make this latter kind of
statement, we should have to know how he would decide if he
were in a similar position at the second date. Of course, if the
assumption of constant utility curves refers not merely to the
two dates considered. but to all other possible dates as well,
this implies that his decision would be the same at the second
date. But it becomes at once obvious that this might just as
well be the case if the utility curves for the different moments
were not the same in an absolute sense. In order that my
choice between to-day and to-morrow may be the same as to-
morrow's choice between then and the day after, it is by no
means necessary that on each occasion the quantities of to-
day's goods and to-morrow's goods respectively. which I regard
as equally useful. should be identical quantities. All that is
necessary is that the proportion between the quantity of
to-day's goods and the quantity of to-morrow's goods, which
I regard as equally useful. should be the same on both occasions.

The fact is that the assumption of identical utility curves
at all successive moments does not merely state the general
postulate that the choice between present and future will be
made in the *same* way at different moments. It implies in

addition that the choice will be made in a *particular way*. Instead of being merely a formal assumption that the attitude of a person will be the same at successive points of time, it is a very definite assumption about the particular attitude he will take at each moment. We have seen to what extent this particular assumption has any merit which would justify us in regarding it as a particularly significant case, or as representing in any sense the normal case. At this point we are interested only in showing why it seemed to follow directly from the assumption of constant tastes necessary for static analysis, so long as utility was conceived as an absolute magnitude which could be described as a function of one variable, the quantity of the commodity in question.

But while the modern " substitution " or " indifference " approach makes it easy to see that any attitude as between present and future is compatible with the assumption of constant tastes, it is also not difficult to understand why the older approach led Böhm-Bawerk and his followers to introduce the idea of a " perspective undervaluation of future wants ". The special case which they regarded as *the* case of constant tastes would indeed require that people should save and invest until the value of the present factors had become equal to the future utility of their product, *i.e.* until interest had disappeared. In fact, however, by adopting this procedure, they did no more than overcome a difficulty of their own making. It was only because they had assumed that constant tastes implied that equal quantities of a commodity at two dates ought to have the same marginal utility to a person at a particular moment that they had to introduce a special explanation as to why this was in fact not the case. In the particular form in which they gave it, their explanation has little meaning. It implies a comparison between the present (absolute) utility of a future commodity and its future (absolute) utility which is regarded as its true utility. Such a comparison does not arise in any act of choice, since by the nature of things it is impossible to contemplate anything at one and the same time both from the standpoint of the present and from the standpoint of the future. All comparisons of relative utilities are necessarily made at one moment of time, so that all that they express are relations between present utilities of present goods and present utilities of future goods. The utilities attached to goods at different moments can only be compared by contrasting the relative utilities of one pair of commodities at the one moment with the relative utilities of a corresponding pair of physically similar commodities at the other moment.

The answer to Böhm-Bawerk's question as to why there is a difference between the value of the present factors and the value of their present product is that there is no such difference. If there is a rate of interest of 5 per cent, this means simply that 100 to-day *is equal* in value to 105 available a year hence. The contrary answer which Böhm-Bawerk gave was based on the assumption that if the present money value equivalent of the factors invested was 100 and the future value equivalent in money of the product was 105, this proved that there was a difference between the value of the product and the value of the factors. But this would follow only if he could maintain that 100 units of money to-day were equal in value to 100 units of money next year, which would be contrary to his own assumptions. The statement that there is a difference in value between the factors and their product, or (in an exchange economy) between the present goods and the quantity of future goods for which they are exchanged, is simply meaningless.

It would hardly have been justifiable to give so much space to the refutation of views which are now clearly obsolete if they had not left traces at least in the terms which are still commonly employed in this context. In particular there can be little doubt that, in the analysis of Professor Irving Fisher, although it is formally free from the confusion here discussed, the use of the term " impatience " still preserves something of the old idea of a " perspective undervaluation " of future needs. A person is " impatient " according to his terminology if, being assured of equal present and future incomes, he prefers some addition to his present income, even if only a very large one, to any permanent addition to his future income, even if only to a very small one.[1] That means that the term " impatience " actually implies what it conveys in popular language, *i.e.* that a person is *anxious to anticipate* his future income in order to increase his present income beyond the level at which it can be permanently kept. This, however, is by no means

[1] See I. Fisher, *The Theory of Interest*, pp. 61 *et seq.*

a necessary condition for the existence of interest in any society except a stationary one. All that is required in a progressive society for the existence of interest is that its members should feel some *reluctance to postpone* consumption of present income in order to increase future income beyond the present level at more than a limited rate.[1] But to say that people do not save more than they actually do because they are impatient is not only a rather peculiar way of putting it; it is definitely misleading if it suggests, as it undoubtedly does to some people, that there is one definite rate of impatience which determines the rate of interest.

(2) On the second question to be discussed here — the relative importance of time valuation and productivity in determining the rate of interest — there probably exists more disagreement among economists than on most other points connected with the theory of interest. The position taken here is as follows : Of the two branches of the Böhm-Bawerkian school, that which stressed the productivity element almost to the exclusion of time preference, the branch whose chief representative is K. Wicksell, was essentially right, as against the branch represented by Professors F. A. Fetter and I. Fisher, who stressed time preference as the exclusive factor and an at least equally important factor respectively. The weakness of Wicksell's case was that he never attempted expressly to justify his neglect of the time preference element. Professor Fisher, on the other hand, although he may claim to have furnished us with a formal apparatus which enables us to describe the interaction of all the relevant factors, even if he had attached no more than their equal importance to the two factors involved — and he certainly has been *understood* to regard the psychical element as the dominant one — would have given the psychical factor more than its due share. The most widely held view is probably that, as in Marshall's two blades of the scissors, the two factors are so inseparably bound up with each other, that it is impossible to say which has the greater and which the lesser influence.

Our problem here is indeed no more than a special case of

---

[1] The same distinction apparently underlies the distinction made by Professor F. X. Weiss between underestimation of future needs and the non-underestimation of present needs. See Weiss, **1928**, p. 1148, footnote.

the problem to which Marshall applied that famous simile, the problem of the relative influence of utility and cost on value. The time valuation in our case corresponds of course to his utility, while the technical rate of transformation is an expression of the relative costs of the commodities (or quantities of income at the two moments of time). But Marshall himself has pointed out there are cases where it is legitimate to distinguish between the magnitude of the two influences.[1] The statement of our problem in terms of relative costs and relative utilities, which is more in conformity with the modern theory of value than Marshall's formulation, will indeed enable us to show that even in the more general case there may yet be more sense in the question of the relative importance of the two factors than Marshall was willing to admit. The applications of the conclusions derived from the consideration of the more general case to our particular case will probably be obvious.

We have first to define what we mean when we say that in a particular case either utility or cost determines value. We shall say that utility alone determines the relative values of two commodities, and that it is unaffected by relative costs, if it can be shown that a change in the cost conditions will not affect these relative values. And we shall say that value depends solely on cost and not on utility if it can be shown that changes in the relative utilities (as expressed by the indifference curves) will not affect values.

If these definitions are accepted it can easily be shown that in certain extreme cases either utility alone or costs alone will determine the relative values of two commodities, while in other cases which come near to one of the extremes it would be legitimate to say that the influence of one of the two factors is so predominant as to make the influence of the other negligible.

To begin with the case where the relative values of the two commodities depend on costs alone, we shall assume that the quantity produced of each commodity can be changed at

---

[1] *Principles*, 8th ed., p. 349 : " a person . . . may be excused for speaking [in cases of constant cost] of price as governed by cost of production — provided only he does not claim scientific accuracy for the wording of his doctrine, and explains the influence of demand in its right place ".

the expense of the quantity of the other at a constant cost, in terms of that other commodity. In diagrammatic terms this means that the displacement curve which shows the rate at which the one commodity can be produced in place of the other, is a straight line. It is then immediately evident that, whatever the shape of the indifference curves representing the relative utilities of the two commodities, their relative values will be uniquely determined by their relative costs. In Fig. 30 the two different utility relations are shown by the alternative

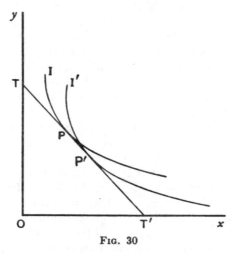

Fig. 30

indifference curves *I* and *I'* and the constant cost by the displacement (or transformation) curve *TT'*. The equilibrium value of the commodity, expressed by the slope of the curves at the points of contact *P* and *P'*, is of course the same in both cases.

The opposite case, where the relative utilities are entirely independent of the relative quantities of the two commodities, is more difficult to conceive.[1] But we get practically the same result if we assume that the curvature of the indifference curve (representing the elasticity of substitution) is so small as to approach, at least over the relevant range, a straight line. If at the same time the displacement curve has a con-

---

[1] It would mean that the two commodities were perfect substitutes yet still different commodities because produced in a different way so that their costs might change differently.

siderable curvature it is clear that the relative values of the two commodities will be practically unaffected by changes in relative costs (as represented by changes in the shape of the displacement curve) and that they will depend almost exclusively on the relative utilities. In Fig. 31 the two different

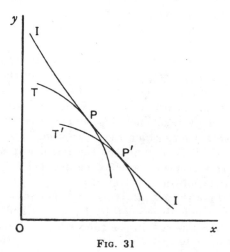

Fɪɢ. 31

cost conditions are represented by the displacement curves T and T', and the relative utilities by the indifference curve I. It will be seen that the value expressed by the slope at the points of contact is very nearly the same at P as at P'.

We need only substitute present and future income for the two different commodities in order to obtain the general results discussed in Chapter XVII.

APPENDIX II

THE " CONVERSION OF CIRCULATING CAPITAL INTO FIXED CAPITAL "

THE idea of a " conversion of circulating into fixed capital " has played a considerable rôle in the discussions of the dynamics of capital formation and of industrial fluctuations in particular from the times of Ricardo down to Knut Wicksell. A certain confusion about its exact meaning, and in particular between two different situations which the concept might describe, has, however, deprived it of much of the fertility it might have had. A short note may therefore be devoted to the task of clearing up the confusions involved.

The idea, if not the actual terms, appears to have been introduced into economic discussion by Ricardo, when in the new chapter " On machinery " in the third edition of his *Principles* he admitted in reply to Barton that the *sudden* discovery and extensive use of improved machinery may have the effect of "diverting capital from its actual employment " as circulating capital in order to increase the amount of fixed capital[1] and in consequence decrease the gross produce and consequently the fund for the employment of labour. As J. S. Mill put it later, the capital " has been converted from circulating into fixed capital, and has ceased to have any influence on wages or profits ".[2]

It was not, however, in connection with the doctrine of the effect of technical progress on wages and profits that this idea became most influential. The expressions used here seemed to provide a perfect description for the phenomena which were observed during the major booms, when a period of extensive construction of fixed capital was followed by an intense scarcity of capital, and the idea was consequently turned into

[1] *Works* (ed. McCulloch), p. 241.

[2] *Principles of Political Economy* (ed. Ashley), p. 734. A more systematic treatment of the subject, in fact the most complete to be found anywhere in the classical literature, is given earlier in Book I, chap. vi, of the same work.

an explanation of commercial crises which for a long period was very widely held. One of the first authors to explain the crises by a scarcity of circulating capital caused by an excessive conversion of circulating capital into fixed capital appears to have been the American Condy Raguet.[1] But it was largely through the considerable elaboration which this idea received in James Wilson's *Capital, Currency and Banking* (1847) that it became widely accepted and for the next thirty years remained almost the dominating explanation of crises. J. S. Loyd, T. H. Williams, O. Michaelis, R. Torrens, J. G. Courcelle-Seneuil, V. Bonnet, J. Garnier, W. S. Jevons, J. Mills, H. v. Mangoldt, Leone Levi, Bonamy Price, and Yves Guyot, to mention only the more important represent-atives in chronological order,[2] all made use to greater or less extent of this idea in their theories of crises.

In all these different versions of the theory the crucial point is that, towards the end of a boom a scarcity of circula-ting capital and a consequent rise in the rates of interest make it impossible either to complete the large projects for invest-ment in fixed capital or profitably to use the additional plant so created. It would lead us too far afield to discuss here the rela-tions which are supposed by the different writers to exist be-tween these phenomena and credit expansion. Nor is it possible

---

[1] *A Treatise on Currency and Banking* (London, 1839), pp. 62 *et seq.*

[2] Cf. Lord Overstone (J. S. Loyd), evidence given in 1848, *Tracts on Metallic and Paper Currency* (1857), pp. 489, 590 ; T. H. Williams, *Observations on Money, Credit and Panics* (1857) ; O. Michaelis, *Die Handelskrisis von 1857*, reprinted in *Volkswirtschaftliche Schriften* (1873), vol. i ; R. Torrens, *Principles and Practical Operations of Peel's Act* (3rd ed., 1858), p. 95 ; J. G. Courcelle-Seneuil, *Traité d'éco-nomie politique* (1858-9), vol. i, pp. 361-363 ; V. Bonnet, *Questions économiques et financières à propos des crises* (1859), pp. 1-11 ; J. Garnier, art. " Crises commerciales " in the *Dictionnaire universel théorique et pratique du commerce*, vol. i, p. 925 ; W. S. Jevons, *A Serious Fall in the Value of Gold* (1863), p. 10 (reprinted in *Investigations upon Currency and Finance*, p. 28) ; J. Mills, " On Credit Cycles and the Origin of Commercial Panics ", *Transactions of the Manchester Statistical Society* (Session 1867-68), 1868, pp. 9-40 ; H. v. Mangoldt, *Grundriss der Volks-wirthschaftslehre* (1863), p. 68 ; Leone Levi, *Banker's Magazine* (New York, 1878), vol. xxxiii, pp. 40-45, 118-126 ; Bonamy Price, *Chapters on Practical Political Economy* (1878), pp. 110-124 ; Yves Guyot, *La Science économique* (1881). On these authors see E. v. Bergmann, *Geschichte der Nationalökonomischen Krisentheorieen* (1895), and T. S. Ashton, *Economic and Social Investigations in Manchester* (1934).

here to trace the important influence which these views have had on the theory of crises of Karl Marx, through him on M. v. Tougan-Baranowski, and through the latter on such contemporary authors as G. Cassel, A. Spiethoff, and D. H. Robertson. K. Wicksell, on the other hand, who repeatedly makes use of these concepts, is probably more directly indebted to the earlier writers.[1]

In this note, however, we are not so much concerned with these elaborations of the theory. We want merely to disentangle the different meanings attached to the concept of the conversion of circulating capital into fixed capital. It will be shown that the original Ricardian contention about the effect of such a conversion on the size of the "gross produce" rested on a confusion between the stock of circulating capital proper and the stream of output available for current consumption — a confusion which also is responsible for the cruder forms of the wage fund analysis ; but that in the way in which the proposition was used by later writers as an explanation of crises, that is as referring to a temporary phenomenon during periods of transition, it described a real phenomenon, and that the "reduction of the fund destined for the support of labour" describes the same phenomenon which later became generally known under the name of forced saving.

Our discussion may be conveniently divided into three parts. We shall first try to show that the proposition which the classical economists used has really little to do with the particular distinction between circulating and fixed capital as defined by them, but is connected with changes in the time dimension of capital in general (or the substitution of a growth of capital in height for a growth in width) irrespective of whether this is in connection with a relative increase of fixed capital or not. Secondly, we shall show that so long as we compare alternative positions of equilibrium, one with relatively more and the other with relatively less fixed capital,

---

[1] Cf. *Lectures*, vol. i, p. 164 : " That the transformation of circulating capital into fixed capital, *i.e.* the change from short-term to long-term capital investment, may frequently injure labour, is beyond doubt ". *Ibid.* p. 185 : ". . . during booms, when large quantities of circulating capital are converted into fixed capital and it is not possible to replace the former quickly enough. In the subsequent depression the conditions are usually reversed ; there is plenty of circulating capital, but it is no longer *profitable* to convert it into fixed capital."

this difference cannot affect the size of the gross produce in the sense of the classical writers, and that consequently their argument about the effect of such a conversion on wages was mistaken. And thirdly, we shall try to explain how, under dynamic conditions and during periods of transition from one equilibrium position to another, the effect in question may actually lead to a temporary reduction of gross produce, and thus, if savings are not increased sufficiently, give rise to that scarcity of consumers' goods which is the real equivalent of the phenomenon described by the classical writers as a scarcity of capital.

(1) The argument rests in the first instance on the simple idea that while with a given amount of capital, if it assumes such a form that the whole of it is turned over once a year, say in the form of a stock of raw materials, the product derived from it in the course of a year will be equal to the total value of this capital, yet if the same amount of capital is invested in such forms that only one-tenth of it will be turned over in the course of one year, the annual product due to it will be only one-tenth of its former value. From this it follows that if " circulating capital " (in the sense of goods in process) is converted into " fixed capital " (in the sense of durable goods), the annual product due to that amount of capital will be decreased. But it will be seen without difficulty that this is quite independent of whether the lengthening of the investment periods involved is due to a substitution of durable goods for goods in process or not, and that exactly the same consequences will follow if a given amount of circulating capital is used to finance a process of longer duration instead of one of shorter duration. If a manufacturer who cannot increase the amount of capital at his disposal changes from one kind of process of production where the " period of production " in the narrower sense of the term is shorter to one where that period is longer, he will clearly now be able to employ only fewer men than before, and his annual output also (at least measured in factor terms) will be smaller than before (although presumably his profits will be larger). On the other hand, it is at least conceivable that a change which involves a substitution of durable goods for goods in process may not have that effect, because the periods for which the input remains invested in the durable good may be actually shorter than the investment

periods involved in some very time-consuming process, such as some kinds of tanning.

We must therefore conclude that the proposition that a conversion of circulating capital into fixed capital will bring about a reduction in the rate of output due to that capital is not strictly correct if we define fixed capital as durable goods and circulating capital as goods in process, but becomes true if we define the two kinds of capital, as has been suggested above (Chapter XXIV), according to their final distance from consumption. If, for in-

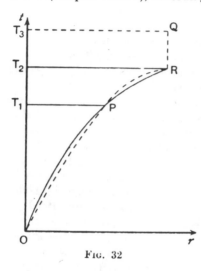

Fig. 32

stance, we decide to define all parts of the existing stock of capital which will be transformed into consumables within a year as circulating capital (including in this therefore those parts of durable goods which can be used up during the next year) and all other capital as fixed capital, it is clear that any change in the composition of a given quantity of capital so that less of it is now circulating capital in this sense and more of it is fixed, must mean that the rate of final output from that capital must decrease.

(2) This proposition applies, however, only to the output which is due to a particular quantity of capital, and it is a mistake to generalise this argument so as to apply to the output of society in general. This can be most conveniently demonstrated by adapting one of our earlier diagrams representing input function in its simplest form. In Fig. 32 the fully drawn curve *OR* represents the input curve in its inverted form, and the area enclosed by this curve and the two co-ordinates measures the quantity of capital (this, since we are using the input function and are disregarding interest, is measured in factor terms). If we decide to call circulating capital that part of the total capital stock which will mature

within a period of the length $T_1 T_2$, the stock of circulating capital will be represented by the area $T_1 T_2 RP$, while the area of the remaining part of the curvilinear triangle, $OT_1 P$, would represent the stock of fixed capital.

The dotted curve OR represents an alternative input function, that is, an alternative method of production which requires the same total amount of capital but is composed of a greater amount of fixed capital and a smaller amount of circulating capital. The amount of circulating capital in this case is represented by the area of $T_1 T_2 RP$ and is by an amount represented by the area enclosed between the fully drawn and the dotted curves RP smaller than the amount of circulating capital used in the first case, while the amount of fixed capital is correspondingly larger. The classical economists deduced from this that the amount that will be available for the payment of wages (and other incomes) during the unit period will be correspondingly reduced. But this is clearly wrong and due to a confusion between the stock of circulating capital and the flow of income derived from it, as can easily be shown. The rate at which income matures under stationary conditions is measured in our diagram by the line $T_2 R$, and the amount of income maturing during the unit period of time will, under stationary conditions, always be represented by the area of the rectangle $T_2 T_3 QR$, whatever the composition of the capital. The amount of income, if we measure it in terms of its own, will of course vary with changes in the methods of production, but measured in factor terms, as done for our present purposes and as the classical economists did, income (or output) will under stationary conditions always be equal to current input. We have seen before that changes in the structure of production due to technological changes may be injurious to labour by changing its marginal productivity. But although this may be accompanied by a conversion of circulating into fixed capital, it is not a direct or necessary consequence of it, as the classical economists believed.[1]

---

[1] Cf. Wicksell, *Lectures*, vol. i, p. 164: "That the transformation of circulating into fixed capital, *i.e.* the change from short-term to long-term capital investment, may frequently injure labour, is beyond doubt. But Ricardo was mistaken in his belief that this consequence was due to the fact that the gross product is simultaneously reduced. This, as may easily be proved, is theoretically inconceivable. The

(3) The situation is, however, different when, instead of considering two alternative positions of stationary equilibrium, we ask what happens during the period of transition from the one state to the other, particularly when the relative increase of circulating capital is merely a prelude to a change which required an increase in the aggregate quantity of capital. In the case where, in spite of the increase in the relative amount of fixed capital, the total amount of capital remained constant, this result was obtained because the lengthening of the investment periods of part of the input was compensated for by a shortening of the investment periods of other parts of the input. (In Fig. 32 this was shown by the new input curve in its left part lying below, and in its right part lying above the old one.) By this double change it was made possible for output to continue to mature throughout at a constant rate in spite of the change in individual investment periods. But it is of course conceivable that fixed capital may be increased at the expense of circulating capital by lengthening the investment periods of some input without a compensating shortening of others. And at first, and for a period corresponding to the original period of investment of the input which is now invested for a longer period than before, this will be possible merely at the expense of circulating capital, that is, without increasing the total quantity of capital. But after a while the effect of such a net lengthening of investment periods must be that for a time the current output will be reduced below the product of current input. And if the new investment structure is to be completed, it will be necessary that for a time people consume less, and by their saving make it possible to create the additional capital which the new structure requires. In this case the increase of fixed capital, which at first took place at the expense of circulating capital, will require a later net increase of capital by corresponding additions of capital in the lower stages, and of circulating capital in particular. In this case the conversion of circulating capital into fixed capital has created an *incomplete capital structure* which needs completing by further net additions to capital and corresponding saving.

gross product under free competition (where such is at all possible) always tends in the main towards the maximum which it is physically possible to obtain with the existing means of production."

This case may again be illustrated by a simple diagram. In Fig. 33 the fully drawn input curve *OR* represents again the old process before the conversion of the circulating capital into fixed, and the dotted curve *OQS* the situation after some of the existing circulating capital has been converted into fixed. In this case, however, the second curve represents not a complete structure but merely the position at a point during the process of transition when the new processes have

been started but not yet concluded. The complete new process would be described by the dotted curve *OQR*, and in order that it can be completed it will be necessary to add during the period T_1T_2 to the stock of capital an additional amount corresponding to *QRS* which can only be provided if during that period people reduce their consumption from T_2R to T_2S. If we could assume that at this stage people voluntarily and spontaneously will reduce their consumption to

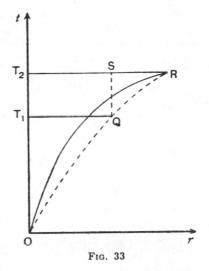

Fig. 33

this required extent, no problem arises. But if they do not and continue to spend on consumption goods as much as before, the amount of capital required for the completion of the process will not be forthcoming ; that is, there will arise that " scarcity of capital " discussed in classical theory, which of course means a scarcity of consumers' goods and a rise in their price and in profit margins generally, which will make investment in long processes of this kind unprofitable.

It hardly needs pointing out that to discuss this whole phenomenon in terms of changes between " circulating " and " fixed " capital is somewhat misleading. Quite apart from the fact that we have found it necessary, in order to make the argument consistent, to substitute a definition of what we mean by fixed and circulating capital other than the usual one, it is clear that even on our definition the argument does not apply only to shifts between the two parts of capital which we have arbitrarily divided on the basis of some standard period, but equally to any other change in investment periods, as for instance to an increase of what we would have to call relatively more fixed at the expense of relatively less fixed capital. It appears that here as elsewhere any attempt at a sharp division of capital into two groups, although sometimes illustrative, is dangerous and misleading, and has to give place, in more precise analysis, to a treatment which takes account of the essential continuity of the range of periods for which input is invested.

APPENDIX III

" DEMAND FOR COMMODITIES IS NOT DEMAND FOR LABOUR " *VERSUS* THE DOCTRINE OF " DERIVED DEMAND "

JOHN STUART MILL's celebrated proposition that " demand for commodities is not demand for labour " [1] is to the present day one of the most disputed theories of economics. It was the fourth [2] of his fundamental propositions respecting capital and is closely connected with the first of these propositions that " industry is limited by capital ". The idea underlying both these statements goes back at least as far as Adam Smith, who expressed it by saying that " the general industry of society never can exceed what the capital of society can employ ".[3] In the writing of Bentham the formula that " industry is limited by capital " became almost the *leitmotiv*, and it was of course familiar to all the members of the classical school of economists. When finally J. S. Mill explicitly stated his fourth proposition, which is more particularly the subject of this appendix, it was little more than a corollary of the first, which he had taken over from his predecessors, and of course closely connected with the wage fund theory. But like the

[1] J. S. Mill, *Principles of Political Economy* (ed. Ashley), Book I, chap. v/9, p. 79.

[2] The " second fundamental theorem regarding capital " is that capital is the result of saving, and the third, in its more complete formulation, that " capital is kept in existence from age to age not by preservation, but by perpetual reproduction : every part of it is used and destroyed generally very soon after it is produced, but those who consume it are employed meanwhile in producing more " (*ibid.* p. 74). It will be noticed that we are prepared to defend all four propositions and object only to what appears to us the erroneous conclusion drawn from the third that, when people " turn their income into capital, they do not thereby annihilate their power of consumption, they do but transfer it from themselves to the labourers to whom they give employment." (See above, p. 273.)

[3] *Wealth of Nations* (ed. Cannan), Book IV, chap. ii, vol. i, p. 419.

latter it was almost immediately assailed,[1] and has ever since been the butt of attack and even ridicule by a long list of eminent economists from Jevons [2] to E. Cannan [3] and J. M. Keynes.[4] It has, however, always had its defenders, including Marshall [5] and particularly Wicksell,[6] and Leslie Stephen even described it, as Mr. Keynes has recently reminded us, as " the doctrine so rarely understood, that its complete apprehension is, perhaps, the best test of an economist ".[7]

That in more modern times the doctrine has suffered a marked eclipse is mainly due to the fact that the modern subjective theory of value was erroneously thought to have provided an effective refutation. This modern view of value taught, of course, and nobody can seriously quarrel with this general proposition, that the value of the factors of production is based on the utility of their products and that in this sense it can be said to be "derived" from the value of their products. In so far as this idea was used to explain why the value of particular factors of production changed relatively to that of others, it provided indeed an extremely important key to the solution of problems which had puzzled many earlier generations of economists. And in general it may be said that in so far as the theory of the *kapitallose Wirtschaft* is concerned the principle is valid without restrictions.

It was thought, however, that the application to an economy using extensive capital equipment not only did not diminish

---

[1] The fullest adverse criticism of the four propositions known to the present author is to be found in A. Musgrave, *Studies in Political Economy* (London, 1875), pp. 55-102, and S. Newcomb, *Principles of Political Economy*, New York, 1886.

[2] See particularly Jevons' *Principles of Economics* (1905), pp. 120-133.

[3] *Theories of Production and Distribution*, p. 381.

[4] J. M. Keynes, **1936**, p. 359.   [5] *Principles*, p. 828.

[6] K. Wicksell, *Wert, Kapital und Rente* (1893), p. 67 : " Es bestätigt sich hier der bekannte Satz von J. S. Mill (dem er freilich selbst eine ganz ungehörige Ausdehnung gab), dass die Nachfrage nach Gütern *nicht* mit Nachfrage nach Arbeit identisch ist " ; and *Lectures*, vol. i, p. 191 : " Broadly speaking, even if not in detail, we must recognise the truth of Mill's well-known principle that demand for commodities is not the same as demand for labour — unless it results in the accumulation of capital."

[7] *History of English Thought in the Eighteenth Century*, p. 297.

the significance of the principle but even increased it. The simple " principle of derived demand " became the basis of the so-called " acceleration principle of derived demand ", based on the idea that in a system using highly capitalistic methods of production any increase in final demand would give rise, not only to an equal increase in the demand for factors but to a much greater increase in the latter, since in order to satisfy the increased final demand it would be necessary to build up, within a short period, all the additional capital equipment required to produce the additional output.

In so far as this argument is applied to the demand for a particular product and its effect on the demand for the factors from which it is produced, there is still little to object to. The meaning and validity of the argument become, however, much more questionable as soon as it is applied, as it immediately was when used in the theory of the trade cycle, to the relation between the demand for consumers' goods in general and the demand for factors of production in general. In its original form, based on the modern utility analysis of value, the argument is clearly not capable of this extension. In fact it is difficult to see what meaning we could attach to the statement that an increase in the value of consumers' goods in general would lead to a similar increase in the value of the factors of production in general, since this would imply that the aggregate value of all goods taken together has increased — a statement which in terms of the modern utility analysis would clearly have no meaning.

Before we proceed further, however, it will be advisable to re-state Mill's proposition in a form which leaves no doubt about its exact meaning. In the first instance it is probably clear from that use to which the doctrine has been generally put that we are entitled, as we have already done, to substitute consumers' goods for " commodities " and that the " demand for commodities " will have to be described, not as a simple quantity, but as a demand schedule or curve describing the quantities of consumers' goods that will be bought at different prices. Secondly, the test of whether demand for consumers' goods " is " demand for labour (or, we may say, demand for pure input) must clearly be whether a rise in the demand curve for consumers' goods raises the demand curve for pure input (and whether a lowering of the former lowers the latter), or whether a change in the demand for consumers' goods causes no change in the same direction or perhaps even a change in the opposite direction to the demand for pure input.

It remains to decide in terms of what we are going to measure the two kinds of demand. And it will presently be seen that this decision is indeed crucial for the solution of our problem. If we decide to measure demand in terms of money, the problem will clearly be indeterminate unless we make further assumptions with regard to the effect of a change in final demand on expectations of future prices and on the supply of money. Circumstances are clearly conceivable in which an increase in final demand will bring about an increase in the demand for labour (in terms of money) many times its size. This indeed is the case which is treated as the normal one by the " acceleration principle of derived demand". If, on the other hand, we decide to measure demand in real terms, as we clearly ought to do so long as we treat the proposition as one of pure theory, it will quickly be seen that the opposite proposition becomes almost a pure tautology. An increase in the demand for consumers' goods in real terms can only mean an increase in terms of things other than consumers' goods ; either more capital goods or more pure input or both must be offered in exchange for consumers' goods, and their price must consequently rise in terms of these other things ; and similarly a change in the demand for labour (*i.e.* pure input) in real terms must mean a change of demand either in terms of consumers' goods or in terms of capital goods or both, and the price of labour expressed in these terms will rise. But since it is probably clear without further explanation that if the demand for capital goods in terms of consumers' goods falls, the demand for labour in terms of consumers' goods must also fall (and *vice versa*), and that if the demand for labour in terms of capital goods rises (or falls) it must also rise (or fall) in terms of consumers' goods, we can leave out the capital goods for our purpose and conclude that an increase in the real demand for consumers' goods can only mean a fall in the price of labour in terms of consumers' goods, or that, since an increase in the demand for consumers' goods in real terms must be an increase in terms of labour, it just means a decrease in the demand for labour in terms of consumers' goods.

We see, therefore, that if we treat the problem in real terms and in its simplest forms, an increase in the demand for consumers' goods not only does not increase but actually decreases the demand for labour. And we obtain of course the same result if we approach the problem more specifically from the point of view of the theory of capital. From this point of view the real demand for labour will depend on its marginal productivity, which in turn will increase and decrease with the " supply of capital ", that is with that part of the total available resources which people in general do *not* want to consume currently but devote to production for the future. Any increase in the share of the resources at their command which they devote to current consumption, any increase in the demand for consumers' goods, therefore means a decrease in the supply of capital and consequently a decrease in the productivity of labour and the amount of labour that will be demanded at any given real wage.

The doctrine still retains its validity, in so far as the effect on the real demand for labour is concerned, if we merely introduce money into the picture but assume an equilibrium position in which the supply of all factors equals demand (*i.e.* in which there are no unemployed resources). The mechanism by which in such a system an increase in final demand will decrease the demand for labour is somewhat more complicated, but still fundamentally the same. It is easiest to show if we assume that the increase in the demand for consumers' goods occurs in a system which before has been in stationary equilibrium — although the argument applies also when this condition is not satisfied. We shall assume that the initial increase in demand is brought about by a net increase in total money expenditure (involving either dishoarding or an increase in the quantity of money), since otherwise the increase in expenditure on consumers' goods would simply mean a simultaneous decrease in the outlay on factors of production (mixed input). Such an increase in the monetary demand for consumers' goods will in the first instance bring about a rise in the prices of consumers' goods which undoubtedly will to some extent be transmitted to the demand for pure input. But for obvious reasons, discussed fully above in Chapter XXVII, the money price of pure input and of labour in particular can (under the conditions of full

employment assumed) never rise in full proportion to the rise
in final demand, since some part of the available output will
have to be used to satisfy the additional new demand and the
real remuneration of the pure input will have to be reduced
by the amount of this new demand, that is, real wages will
fall. It has been shown in the chapter just referred to how
in turn this fall in " real wages " will lead to such a reorganisation of production as to reduce the marginal productivity of
labour (and pure input generally) all round (by using it in
combination with proportionately less capital) so that with
the lower real wages a new equilibrium will be reached. This
lower real wage will now be the only wage rate at which, with
the reduced supply of capital (or, what amounts to the same
thing, the increased urgency in the demand for consumers'
goods), the whole supply of labour will be employed. If in
these conditions labour should insist on unchanged real wages
and succeed in raising its money wage accordingly, the result
can only be that less labour than formerly will be employed.

The situation will, of course, be different if at the pre-
existing level of wages and prices supply exceeded demand,
and an increase in final demand makes it possible immediately
and proportionately to increase output by employing formerly
unemployed resources of all the kinds required. In this case,
and in this case only, an increase in final demand will lead to
a proportionate increase of employment, and this effect will of
course be limited to the period during which such unemployed
reserves are available. There will of course be intermediate
cases where, although there may not be unemployed resources
of all kinds available, there will be sufficient reserves in existence of a number of the more important kinds of input to
make it possible to increase output, although not in proportion to the increase in final demand, yet to some extent.
In this case a very slight reduction of real wages may be
accompanied by a very considerable increase in employment.
In both these cases the " principle of derived demand " will
approximately apply if money wages can be assumed to be
given and constant, because the effect of an increase in final
demand will here not dissipate itself in an increase in the
prices of output and — to a lesser extent — input, but can
bring about an increase in employment at more or less
unchanged prices.

That under conditions of under-employment the general principle does not directly apply was of course well known to "orthodox" economists, and to J. S. Mill in particular. In his exposition the statement that "industry is limited by capital", on which, as we have seen, the proposition under discussion is based, is immediately followed by the further statement that it "does not always come up to that limit ".[1] And few competent economists can ever have doubted that, in positions of disequilibrium where unused reserves of resources of all kinds existed, the operation of this principle is temporarily suspended, although they may not always have said so.[2] But while this neglect to state an important qualification is regrettable and may mislead some people, it involves surely less intellectual confusion than the present fashion of flatly denying the truth of the basic doctrine which after all is an essential and necessary part of that theory of equilibrium (or general theory of prices) which every economist uses if he tries to explain anything. The result of this fashion is that economists are becoming less and less aware of the special conditions on which their arguments are based, and that many now seem entirely unable to see what will happen when these conditions cease to exist, as sooner or later they inevitably must. More than ever it seems to me to be true that the complete apprehension of the doctrine that "demand of commodities is not demand for labour" — and of its limitations — is "the best test of an economist".

[1] *Principles*, Book I, chap. v/2 and table of contents (ed. Ashley), pp. 65 and xxxiv. Mill is mainly concerned with the case where there is not as much labour available as might be employed with the existing capital, but although this case looks very different from those with which we are now concerned, it is not really so different from the case of artificial scarcity caused by labour refusing to work for less than a certain wage.

[2] As was clearly done, to mention only the leading representative of a school that is often accused of overlooking this, by Professor L. v. Mises. See his *Geldwertstabilisierung und Konjunkturpolitik* (1928) p. 49.

BIBLIOGRAPHY

The following abbreviations are used :

A.E.R. = *American Economic Review*
A.S. = *Archiv für Sozialwissenschaft und Sozialpolitik*
E.J. = *Economic Journal*
G.E. = *Giornale degli Economisti*
J.N.S. = *Jahrbücher für Nationalökonomie und Statistik*
J.P.E. = *Journal of Political Economy*
Q.J.E. = *Quarterly Journal of Economics*
R.E.S. = *Review of Economic Studies*
W.A. = *Weltwirtschaftliches Archiv*
Z.N. = *Zeitschrift für Nationalökonomie*

The two figures following immediately after the title of a
journal (*e.g.* 48/4) give the number of the volume and the
issue respectively.

G. ÅKERMAN, 1923/4, *Realkapital und Kapitalzins*, Heft 1 & 2,
Stockholm.
1931, *Om den industrielle rationaliseringen och dess verkningar*,
Stockholm.
W. E. ARMSTRONG, 1936, *Saving and Investment. The Theory of
Capital in a Developing Community*, London.
A. BARTH, 1934, *Der Kapitalverzehr als Wirtschaftsprozess*, Frei-
burg i. Br.
A. BILIMOVIC, 1937, Zins und Unternehmergewinn im Gleichungs-
system der stationären Wirtschaft, *Z.N.* 8/3.
A. BOÉR, jun., 1938, Kapitaltheorie und Kapitalbildung, *J.N.S.*
147/1.
K. E. BOULDING, 1934, The Application of the Pure Theory of
Population to the Theory of Capital, *Q.J.E.* 48/4.
1935, The Theory of a Single Investment, *Q.J.E.* 49/3.
1936a, Professor Knight's Capital Theory, *Q.J.E.* 50/3.
1936b, Time and Investment, *Economica*, N.S. 3/10.
1936c, Time and Investment, A Reply, *Economica*, N.S. 3/12.
C. BRESCIANI-TURRONI, 1932, Kapitalmangel und Währungs-
stabilisierung, *Die Wirtschaftstheorie der Gegenwart*, Vol. II,
Vienna.
1936, The Theory of Saving, *Economica*, N.S. 3/9 & 10.
F. BROCK, 1938, Kapital, Kapitalzins, und Investitionsspanne,
W.A. 47/3.
H. BROMMELS, 1928, *Die eigentliche Abschreibung in der dynami-
schen Bilanz*, Helsingfors.

441

442 Bibliography

W. BRYLEWSKI, 1932, *Die verschiedenen Vorstellungsinhalte des Begriffes Kapital*, Stuttgart.

F. BURCHARDT, 1931/2, Die Schemata des stationären Kreislaufes bei Böhm-Bawerk und Marx, *W.A.* 34/2, 35/1.

E. CARELL, 1933, Kann der Zins ein Preis für "Warten" sein ?, *Z.N.* 3/5.

S. CARLSON, 1935, On the Notion of Equilibrium in Interest Theory, *Economic Studies* (Cracow), no. 1.

F. DIVISIA, 1928, *L'Épargne et la richesse collective*, Paris.

P. H. DOUGLAS, 1934, *The Theory of Wages*, New York.

V. EDELBERG, 1933, The Ricardian Theory of Profits, *Economica*, no. 39.

1936a, An Econometric Model of Production and Distribution, *Econometrica*, 4/3.

1936b, A Note on Capital Theory, *Economica*, N.S. 3/11.

E. EGNER, 1928, Zur Lehre vom Zwangssparen, *Zeitschrift für die gesamte Staatswissenschaft*, 84/3.

H. S. ELLIS, 1935, Die Bedeutung der Produktionsperiode für die Krisentheorie, *Z.N.* 6/2.

O. ENGLAENDER, 1930, *Theorie der Volkswirtschaft. II. Geld und Kapital*, Vienna.

W. EUCKEN, 1934, *Kapitaltheoretische Untersuchungen*, Jena.

1937, Vom Hauptproblem der Kapitaltheorie, *J.N.S.* 145/5.

S. FABRICANT, 1938, *Capital Consumption and Adjustment*, New York.

A. G. B. FISHER, 1933, Capital and the Growth of Knowledge, *E.J.* 43/171.

J. M. FLEMING, 1935, The Period of Production and Derived Concepts, *R.E.S.* 3/1.

1938, The Determination of the Rate of Interest, *Economica*, 5/19.

B. FOÀ, 1932a, *Il capitale nell' equilibrio economico*, Messina.

1932b, Risparmio, Investimento e Interesse, *G.E.*

R. F. FOWLER, 1934, *The Depreciation of Capital Analytically Considered*, London.

C. A. J. GADOLIN, 1934, Om gynnsammaste livslängden på de varaktiga kapitalföremalen, *Ekonomiska Samfundets Tidskrift*, Helsingfors, N.S. 2.

1936a, Kapitalet och Produktionsomvägarna, *Ekonomiska Samfundets Tidskrift*, Helsingfors, N.S. 36.

1936b, *Produktionsomvägsbegreppet i kapitalanalysen*, Helsingfors.

1937, Bemerkungen zur Diskussion über die Zeitkonzeption des Kapitals, *Z.N.* 8/1.

1939, Einige Bemerkungen über die zeitbezogene Kapitalstheorie mit besonderer Rücksicht auf die Stellung der Kapitalsgüter, *W.A.* 49/3.

H. T. N. GAITSKELL, 1936–8, Notes on the Period of Production, *Z.N.* 7/5 and 9/2.

A. GAMBINO, 1936, Risparmio abortivo, *G.E.*
1938, Risparmio e consumo, *G.E.*

C. H. P. GIFFORD, 1933, The Concept of the Length of the Period of Production, *E.J.* 43/172.

B. GLOERFELT-TARP, 1933, Produktivitet og Kapitalbegrep, *Nationalökonomisk Tidsskrift*, 71, Tillaegshefte.

R. GOCHT, 1939, Der zeitliche Aufbau der Produktion und das Gesetz von der Mehrergiebigkeit der Produktionsumwege, *J.N.S.* 149/4.

G. HABERLER, 1931, Irving Fisher's "Theory of Interest", *Q.J.E.* 45/3.

G. HALM, 1926, Das Zinsproblem am Geld- und Kapitalmarkt, *J.N.S.* 125/2.
1931, " Warten " und " Kapitaldisposition ", *J.N.S.* 135/6.

B. HARMS, editor, 1931, *Kapital und Kapitalismus*, 2 vols., Berlin.

A. G. HART, 1937, Anticipations, Business Planning, and the Cycle, *Q.J.E.* 51/2.

R. G. HAWTREY, 1937, *Capital and Employment*, London.
1938, *A Century of Bankrate*, London.

F. A. VON HAYEK, 1927, Zur Problemstellung der Zinstheorie, *A.S.* 58/3.
1928, Das intertemporale Gleichgewichtssystem der Preise und die Bewegungen des " Geldwertes ", *W.A.* 27/1.
1931, *Prices and Production*, London (2nd ed., 1935).
1932a, Money and Capital, *E.J.* 42/2.
1932b, Kapitalaufzehrung, *W.A.* 36/1.
1934a, Capital and Industrial Fluctuations, *Econometrica*, 2/2 (reprinted in *Prices and Production*, 2nd ed., 1935).
1934b, On the Relationship between Investment and Output, *E.J.* 44/174.
1934c,* Saving, *Encyclopaedia of the Social Sciences*, Vol. XIII.
1935a,* Preiserwartungen, monetäre Störungen und Fehlinvestitionen, *Nationalökonomisk Tidsskrift*, Copenhagen, 73/3 : also in a French translation in *Revue des sciences économiques*, Liége, October 1935, and in an English translation in 1939 below.
1935b,* The Maintenance of Capital, *Economica*, N.S. 2/7.
1936a, The Mythology of Capital, *Q.J.E.* 50/2.
1936b, Utility Analysis and Interest, *E.J.* 46/181.
1936c, Technischer Fortschritt und Überkapazität, *Oesterreichische Zeitschrift für Bankwesen*, 1/1.
1937,* Investment that Raises the Demand for Capital, *Review of Economic Statistics*, 19/4.

444   *Bibliography*

1939,* *Profits, Interest, and Investment,* London.
(* This last item contains reprints of the earlier articles marked with an asterisk.)

G. Heinze, 1928, *Statische oder dynamische Zinstheorie,* Leipzig.

A. Heydel, 1936, Economic Activity and Interest, *Economic Studies* (Cracow), no. 2.

J. R. Hicks, 1932, *The Theory of Wages,* London.
1935, Wages and Interest: the Dynamic Problem, *E.J.* 45/179.
1937, Mr. Keynes and the Classics ; a Suggested Interpretation, *Econometrica,* 5/2.
1939, *Value and Capital,* London.

R. M. Hidajat, 1938, De Kapitaalinteresttheoriën van E. von Böhm-Bawerk en Alfred Marshall, *De Economist,* 87/1.

M. Hill, 1933, The Period of Production and Industrial Fluctuations, *E.J.* 43/172.

H. C. Hillman, 1938, Depreciation Policy, *Manchester School,* 9/1.

A. Hoffmann, 1932, *Wirtschaftslehre der kaufmännischen Unternehmung,* Leipzig.

F. Homan, 1927, *Das Sparen als ein Grundproblem der Theorie der kapitalistischen Wirtschaft,* Jena.

H. Hotelling, 1925, General Mathematical Theory of Depreciation, *Journal of the American Statistical Association.*
1931, The Economics of Exhaustible Resources, *J.P.E.* 39/2.

C. Iversen, 1936, Die Probleme des festen Realkapitals, *Z.N.* 7/2.

P. Joseph and K. Bode, 1935, Bemerkungen zur Kapital- und Zinstheorie, *Z.N.* 6/2.

A. Kaehler, 1933, *Theorie der Arbeiterfreisetzung durch die Maschine,* Leipzig.

N. Kaldor, 1937, The recent Controversy on the Theory of Capital, *Econometrica,* 5/3.
1939, Capital Intensity and the Trade Cycle, *Economica,* N.S. 6/21.

J. M. Keynes, 1936, *The General Theory of Employment, Interest, and Money,* London.

H. Kirchmann, 1930, *Studien zur Grenzproduktivitätstheorie des Kapitalzinses,* Greifswald.

F. H. Knight, 1916, Neglected Factors in the Problem of Normal Interest, *Q.J.E.* 30/2.
1932a, Professor Fisher's Interest Theory. A Case in Point, *J.P.E.* 39/2.
1932b, Interest, *Encyclopaedia of the Social Sciences,* Vol. III, reprinted in *The Ethics of Competition and other Essays,* London, 1935.
1933, Capitalistic Production, Time, and the Rate of Interest, *Economic Essays in Honour of Gustav Cassel,* London.

1934, Capital, Time, and the Interest Rate, *Economica*, N.S.
    1 3.
1935a, Professor Hayek and the Theory of Investment, *E.J.*
    4.7 177.
1935b, The Ricardian Theory of Production and Distribution,
    The Canadian Journal of Economics and Political Science,
    1/1 & 2.
1935c, The Theory of Investment once more; Mr. Boulding and
    the Austrians, *Q.J.E.* 50 1.
1935d, Comment (on Professor Machlup's article), *J.P.E.* 43/5.
1935e, The Period of Production, A Final Word, *J.P.E.* 43/6.
1936, The Quantity of Capital and the Rate of Interest, *J.P.E.*
    44/4.
1937, Note on Dr. Lange's Interest Theory, *R.E.S.* 4/3.
O. KRAUSE, 1936, *Zins und Produktion*, Munich.
E. B. KURTZ, 1930, *Life Expectancy of Physical Property*, New York.
L. M. LACHMANN, 1938, Investment and Cost of Production,
    A.E.R. 28 3.
A. LAMPE, 1926, *Zur Theorie des Sparprozesses und der Kredit-
    schöpfung*, Jena.
O. LANGE, 1936, The Place of Interest in the Theory of Pro-
    duction, *R.E.S.* 3 3.
1937, Professor Knight's Note on Interest Theory, *R.E.S.* 4/3.
1938, The Rate of Interest and the Optimum Propensity to
    Consume, *Economica*, N.S. 5 17.
W. LEONTIEFF, 1934, Interest on Capital and Distribution,
    Q.J.E. 49 1.
A. P. LERNER, 1937, Capital, Investment, and Interest, *Man-
    chester Statistical Society, Group Meetings 1936-7*.
E. LINDAHL, 1925, Review of G. Åkerman, *Realkapital und
    Kapitalzins*, in *Staatsvetenskaplig Tidskrift*, 1923, pp. 349
    ff., and 1925, pp. 80 ff.
1929, Prisbildningsproblemets Uppläggning från kapital-
    teoretisk synpunkt, *Ekonomisk Tidskrift*; English trans-
    lation in the following volume :
1939, *Studies in the Theory of Money and Capital*, London.
J. LINDBERG, 1905, Boehm - Bawerks Kapitalrentetheorie,
    Nationalökonomisk Tidsskrift, 43/5. German Translation,
    Die Kapitalzinstheorie Boehm-Bawerks, *Z.N.* 4/4, 1933.
A. LOEWE, 1937, The Social Productivity of Technical Improve-
    ments, *Manchester School*, 8/2.
F. LUTZ, 1927, *Der Kampf um den Kapitalbegriff in neuester Zeit*,
    Jena.
F. R. MACAULEY, 1938, *The Movements of Interest Rates, Bond
    Yields and Bond Prices in the United States since 1856*,
    National Bureau of Economic Research, New York.

446   *Bibliography*

F. MACHLUP, 1931a, *Börsenkredit, Industriekredit und Kapital-bildung*, Vienna.

1931b, Begriffliches und Terminologisches zur Kapitalstheorie, *Z.N.* 2/4.

1932, The Liquidity of Short Term Capital, *Economica*, 37.

1935a, Interest as Cost and Capitalization Factor, *A.E.R.* 25/3.

1935b, Professor Knight and the "Period of Production", *J.P.E.* 43/5.

1935c, The Period of Production, A Further Word, *J.P.E.* 43/6.

1935d, The Consumption of Capital in Austria, *Review of Economic Statistics*, January.

1937, On the Meaning of the Marginal Product, *Explorations in Economics*, New York.

G. MACKENROTH, 1930, Period of Production, Durability, and the Rate of Interest, *J.P.E.* 38/6.

A. MAHR, 1929, *Untersuchungen zur Zinstheorie*, Jena.

1931, Abstinenztheorie und Lehre von der Minderschätzung, *Z.N.* 2/1.

1936, Das Zeitmoment in der Theorie des Produktivzinses, *Z.N.* 7/1.

K. MAINZ, 1933, Kann der Zins ein Preis für "Warten" sein?, *Z.N.* 4/5.

J. MARSCHAK, 1933, Volksvermögen und Kassenbedarf, *A.S.* 68/4.

1934, A Note on the Period of Production, *E.J.* 44/173.

J. MARSCHAK and W. LEDERER, 1936, *Kapitalbildung*, London.

H. MARZELL, 1927, *Das Kapitalzinsproblem im Lichte des Kreislaufes der Waren und des Geldes*, Jena.

H. MAYER, 1925, Produktion, *Handwörterbuch der Staatswissenschaften*, 4th ed. Vol. VI.

L. v. MISES, 1931, Das festangelegte Kapital, *Economische Opstellen aangeboden aan C. A. Verrijn Stuart*, Haarlem, reprinted in *Grundprobleme der Nationalökonomie*, Jena, 1933.

O. MORGENSTERN, 1935, Zur Theorie der Produktionsperiode, *Z.N.* 6/2.

J. NEUGEBAUER, 1937, Kapital und Zeitverlauf, *J.N.S.* 146/3.

A. M. NEUMAN, 1933, Osservazione sul concetto di "capitale inalterato" e sulla recente formulazione de prof. Pigou, *Rivista Internazionale di Science Sociale e Discipline Ausiliare*, Anno XLI, Serie III, 4/5.

R. NURKSE, 1935, The Schematic Representation of the Structure of Production, *R.E.S.* 2/3.

E. PELTZER, *Der reale Kapitalzins und der Darlehenszins*, Jena.

H. PETER, 1935a, Zu dem Versuche einer naturalökonomischen Begründung der Kapitalzinstheorie, *J.N.S.* 142/6.

1935b, Studien zur Kapitalzins- oder Profittheorie, *J.N.S.* 142/6.

A. C. Pigou, 1935, Net Income and Capital Depletion, *E.J.* 45/178.

N. J. Polak, 1926, *Grundzüge der Finanzierung mit Rücksicht auf die Kreditdauer*, Berlin.

G. A. D. Preinreich, 1938, Annual Survey of Economic Theory : The Theory of Depreciation, *Econometrica*, 6/3.

1939, The Practice of Depreciation, *Econometrica*, 7/3.

E. Preiser, 1933, *Grundzüge der Konjunkturtheorie*, Tübingen.

E. P. Ramsay, 1928, A Mathematical Theory of Saving, *E.J.* 38/152.

C. v. Reichenau, 1931, Der Einfluss des Zinsfusses auf dem Sparer, *Schmollers Jahrbuch für Gesetzgebung, etc.*, 55/1.

U. Ricci, 1926, L' offerta del risparmio, *G.E.*

1927, Ancora sull' offerta del risparmio, *G.E.*

1932, Die Kurve des Grenznutzens und die Theorie des Sparens, *Z.N.* 3/3.

C. Rist, 1921, Théorie de l'Épargne, *Revue de métaphysique et de morale*, reprinted in *Essais sur quelques problèmes économiques et monétaires*, Paris, 1933.

D. H. Robertson, 1933, Saving and Hoarding, *E.J.* 43/171.

1934, Industrial Fluctuation and the Natural Rate of Interest, *E.J.* 44/176.

W. Roepke, 1929, *Theorie der Kapitalbildung*, Tübingen.

E. Rolph, 1939, The Discounted Marginal Productivity Doctrine, *J.P.E.* 47/4.

P. A. Samuelson, 1937, Some Aspects of the Pure Theory of Capital, *Q.J.E.* 51/3.

T. Schaefer, 1931, Kapitalbildung und Zinshöhe, *A.S.* 45/3.

E. Schiff, 1933, *Kapitalbildung und Kapitalaufzehrung im Konjunkturverlauf*, Vienna.

W. Schmidt, 1938, *Kapital und Kapitalzins in der Planwirtschaft*, Düsseldorf.

E. Schneider, 1935–6, Das Zeitmoment in der Theorie der Produktion, *J.N.S.* 112/3, 113/1, and 114/2.

1938, Bemerkungen zum Hauptproblem der Kapitaltheorie, *J.N.S.* 147/2.

H. Schneider, 1934, " Warten " und " Kapital ", *J.N.S.* 140/2.

H. Seidel, 1939, Zur Theorie der Kapitalbildung, *J.N.S.* 149/4 & 5.

L. H. Seltzer, 1932, The Mobility of Capital, *Q.J.E.* 50/1.

G. Silverstolpe, 1919, *Kapitalbildning*, Stockholm.

E. v. Sivers, 1924, *Die Zinstheorie Eugen von Böhm-Bawerks im Lichte der deutschen Kritik*, Jena.

A. Smithies, 1935, The Austrian Theory of Capital with Relation to Partial Equilibrium Theory, *Q.J.E.* 50/1.

C. Snyder, 1936, Capital Supply and National Wellbeing, *A.E.R.* 7/2.

448   *Bibliography*

E. Sommarin, 1927, Laurits V. Birck contra Böhm-Bawerk och Knut Wicksell, *Staatsvetenskaplige Tidskrift*, N.F. 9.

P. Sraffa, 1932, Dr. Hayek on Money and Capital, *E.J.* 42/166.

H. v. Stackelberg, 1938, Beitrag zur Theorie des individuellen Sparens, *Z.N.* 9/2.

J. Steindl, 1937, Der historische Regress in der Theorie der Produktionsumwege, *J.N.S.* 145/2.

K. H. Stephans, 1935, Zur neueren Kapitalstheorie, *W.A.* 41/1.
1936, Zur Problematik der Zinstheorie, *Z.N.* 7/3.

R. v. Strigl, 1934a, *Kapital und Produktion*, Vienna.
1934b, Lohnfonds und Geldkapital, *Z.N.* 5/1.
1935, Zeit und Produktion, *Z.N.* 6/2.

I. Svennilson, 1936, Den tidskävande Produktionsprocessen, *Nordisk Tidskrift for Teknisk Oekonomi*.
1938, *Ekonomisk Planering*, Uppsala.

Y. Takata, 1936, Introductory Discourse on the Theory of Interest, *Kyoto University Economic Review*, 10/6.

E. Theiss, 1932, Time and Capitalistic Production, *J.P.E.* 40/4.
1933, A Quantitative Theory of Industrial Fluctuations caused by the Capitalistic Technique of Production, *J.P.E.* 41/3.

G. F. Thirlby, 1939, The Rate of Interest, *South African Journal of Economics*, 7/1.

J. M. Thompson, 1936, Mathematical Theory of Production Stages in Economics, *Econometrica*, 6/1.

C. E. Troxel, 1936, Economic Influence of Obsolescence, *A.E.R.* 7/2.

E. C. Van Dorp, 1931, Agio oder Lohnfonds ? *A.S.* 46/2.
1933, Löhne und Kapitalzins, *Z.N.* 4/2.
1937, *A Simple Theory of Capital, Wages, and Profit or Loss*, London.

R. Van Genechten, 1929, De Waarde van den Kapitaaldiens, het Agio van tegenwoordige op toekomstige Goederen en de Rente, *De Economist*, 75/10.
1930, Ueber das Verhältnis zwischen der Produktivität des Kapitals, den Löhnen und Zinsen, *Z.N.* 2/2.
1932, Kritische Anmerkungen zur Zinstheorie, *Z.N.* 3/3.
1934, Zur Lohn und Zinstheorie, *Z.N.* 5/2.
1935, Verdediging eener synthetischen Loon- en Rentetheorie, *De Economist*, 84/3.

F. Vito, 1933, La nozione di lunghezza media del processo produttivo, *Rivista Internazionale di Science Sociali e Discipline Ausiliare*, Anno XLI, Serie III, 4/5.

J. R. Walsh, 1935, The Capital Concept Applied to Man, *Q.J.E.* 49/2.

G. Warmdahl, 1934, Grundforholdet mellem Realkapital, Kapitaldisposition og Kredit, *Nationalekonomisk Tidsskrift*.

F. X. WEISS, 1921, Produktionsumwege und Kapitalzins, *Zeitschrift für Volkswirtschaft und Sozialpolitik*, N.F. 1/4.

1928, Zins, *Handwörterbuch der Staatswissenschaften*, 4th ed. Vol. VIII.

K. WICKSELL, 1923, Realkapital och Kapitalränta, *Ekonomisk Tidskrift*, 25/5-6, English translation as appendix to Vol. I of his *Lectures on Political Economy*, London, 1934.

1928, Zur Zinstheorie (Böhm-Bawerks Dritter Grund), *Die Wirtschaftstheorie der Gegenwart*, Vol. III, Vienna.

F. WIEN-CLAUDI, 1936, *Austrian Theories of Capital, Interest, and the Trade Cycle*, London.

C. A. WRIGHT, 1936, A Note on "Time and Investment", *Economica*, N.S. 3/12.

A. A. YOUNG, 1928, Increasing Returns and Economic Progress, *E.J.* 38/4.

1929, article "Capital" in *Encyclopaedia Britannica*, 14th ed. Vol. IV.

30

INDEX OF DEFINITIONS OF SOME
TECHNICAL TERMS

INDEX OF AUTHORS CITED

453

THE END